"The old world is dying, and the new world struggles to be born: now is the time of monsters."

— Antonio Gramsci (as translated by Slavoj Žižek)

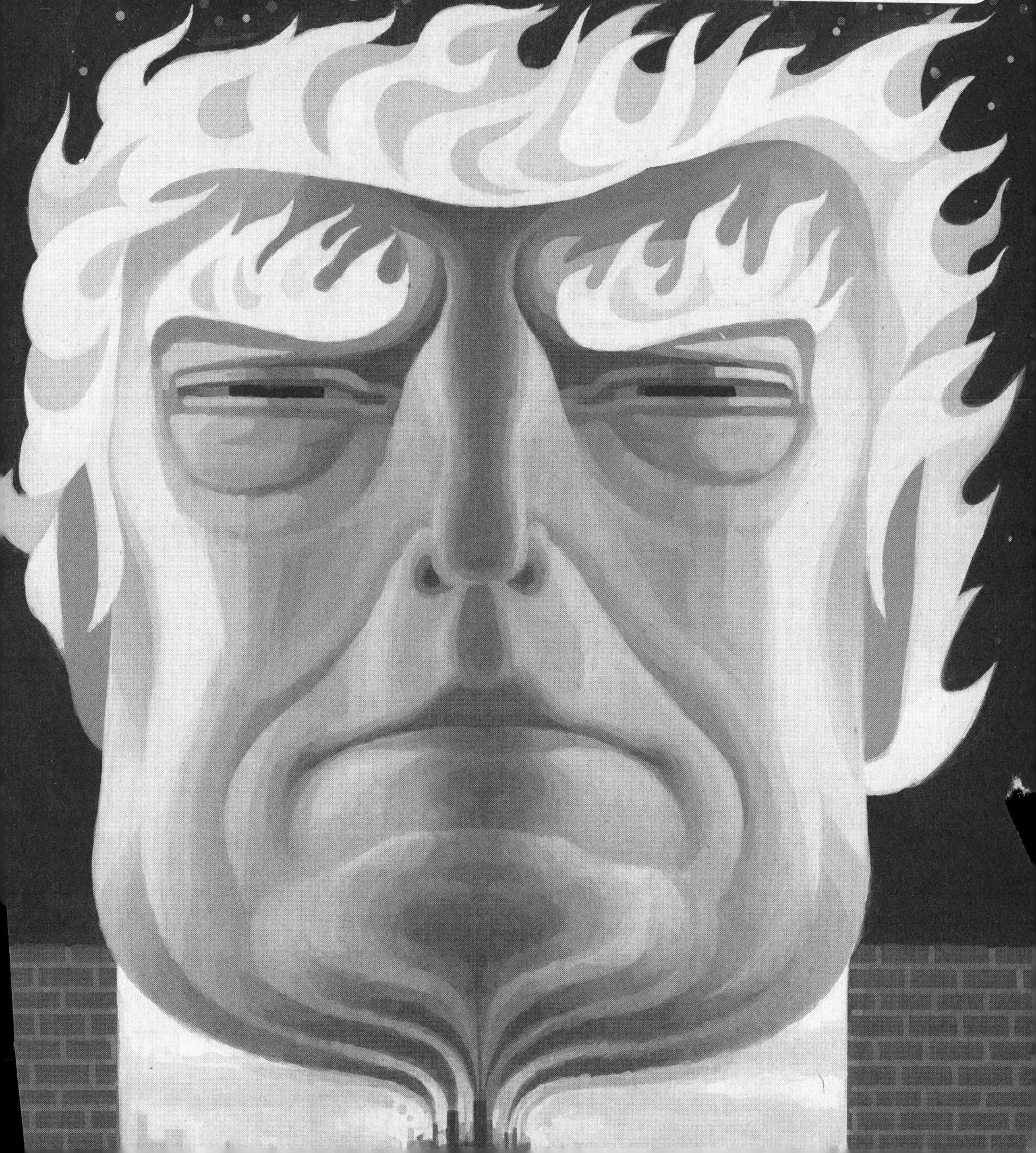

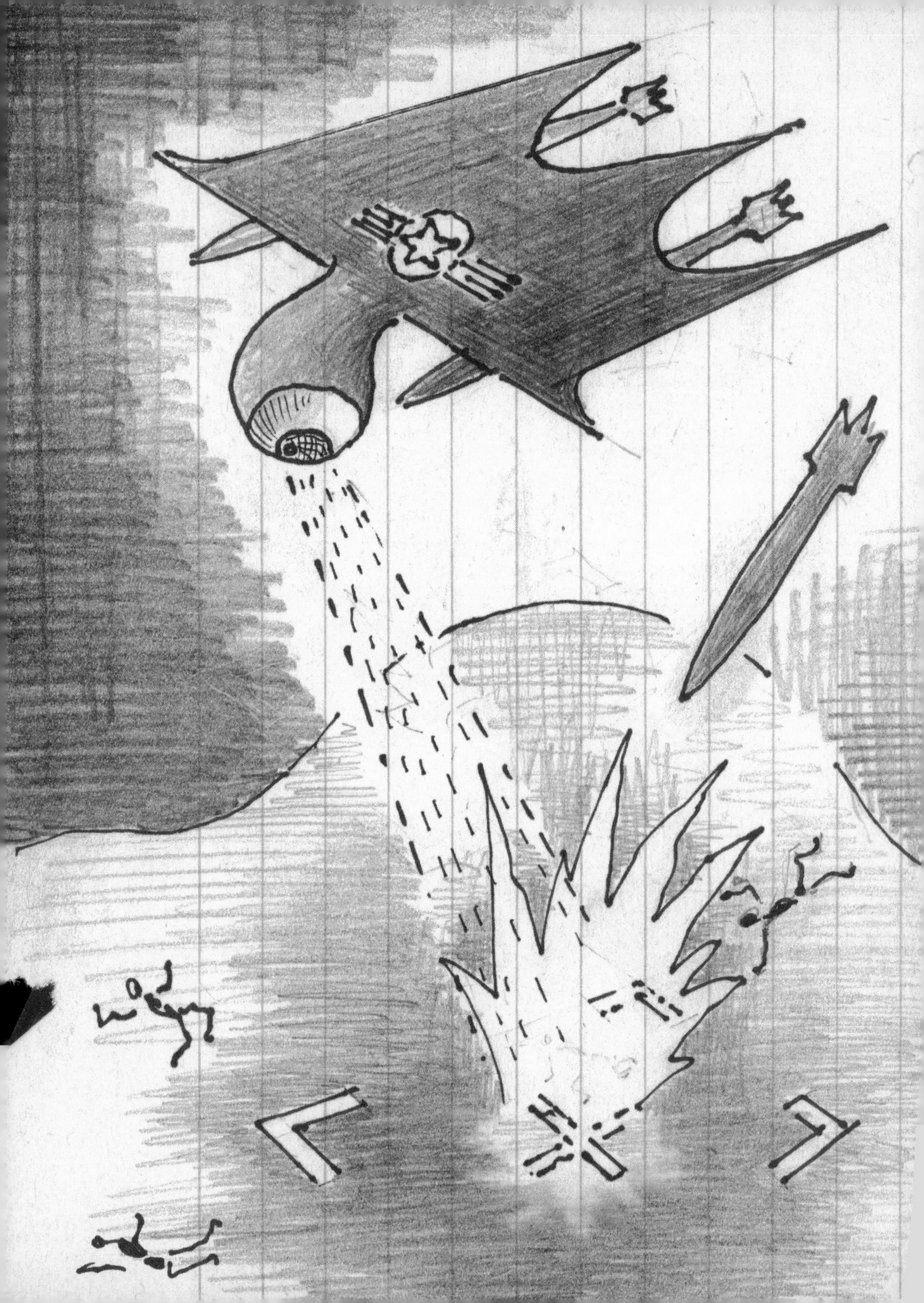

WORLD WAR *3 ILLUSTRATED* #49

NOW IS THE TIME OF MONSTERS

A graphic discourse on predatory Capitalism

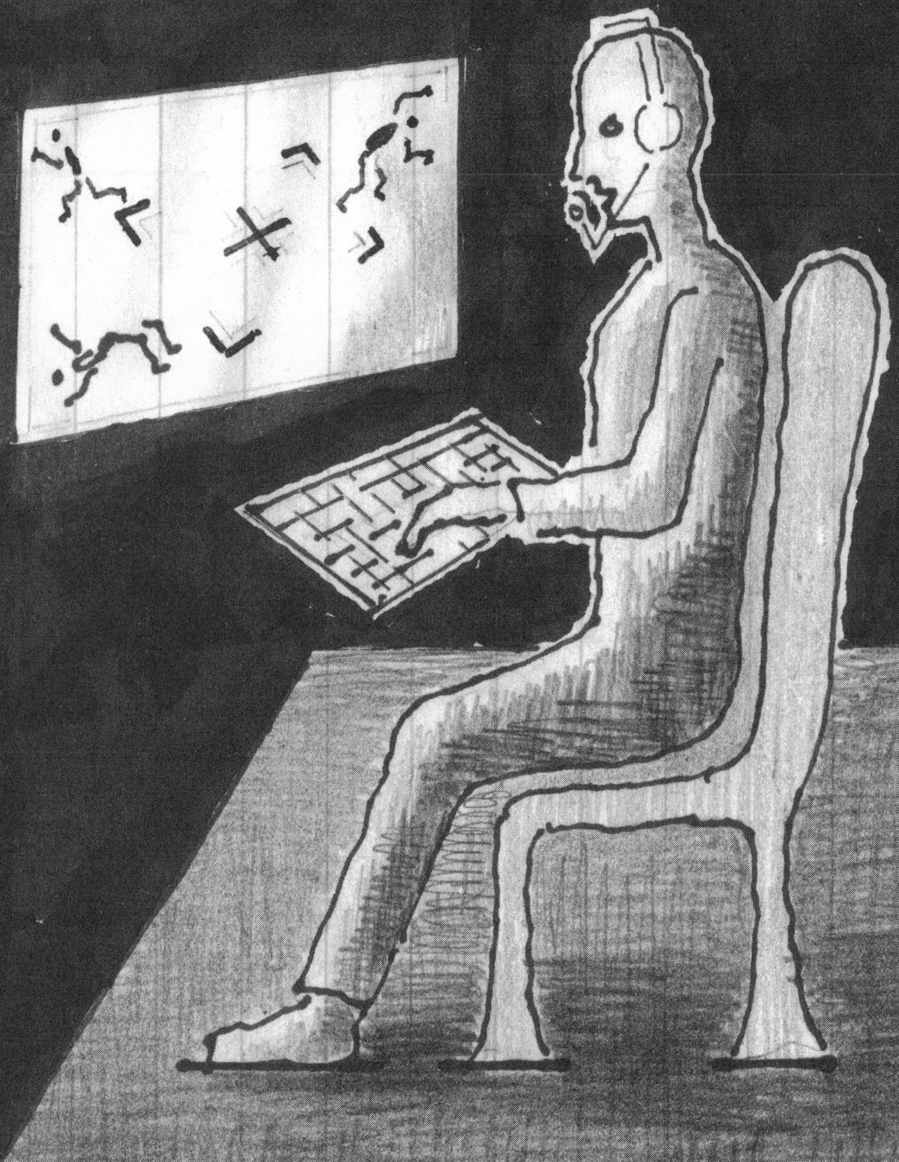

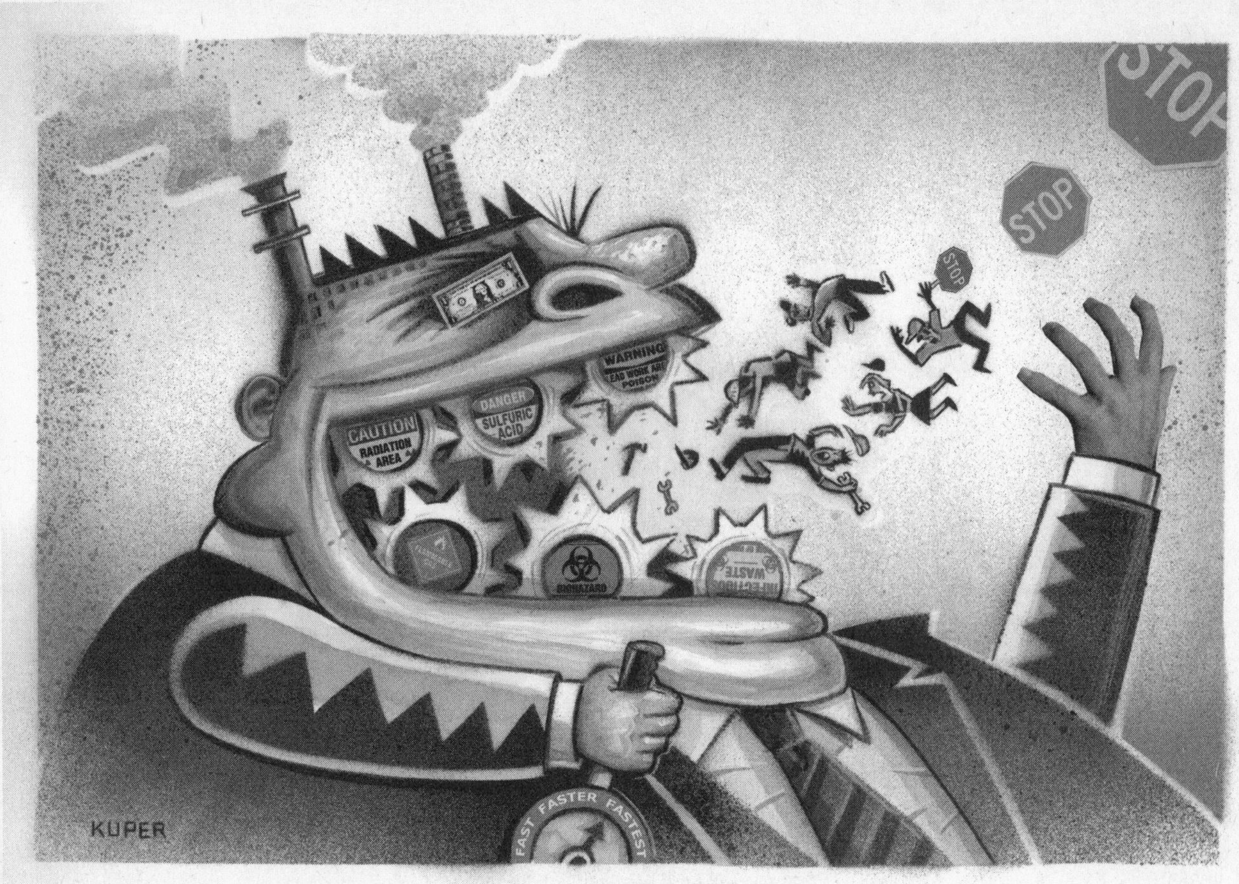
STOP
STOP
STOP
WARNING
CAUTION
RADIATION AREA
DANGER
SULFURIC ACID
BIOHAZARD
FAST FASTER FASTEST
KUPER

The **TWIN MONSTERS** of xenophobia and predatory capitalism have been fully released. In a country as rich as the United States, scarcity is an artificial condition necessary for the continued production of profit for a few. Whether conscious of it or not, we all feel this reality and search for solutions. This is when the twin brothers (of course they are male) tag team us. As the joke goes: A billionaire, a worker and an immigrant are sitting at a table with a thousand cookies. The billionaire takes nine hundred and ninety-nine and says to the worker, "*Watch out, the immigrant is going to take your cookie.*" But then the predatory logic kicks in. The worker is overworked, eventually injured, can't afford health care and is sold addictive opiates instead. The immigrant is thrown in privately run, for-profit detention, where he works for a dollar a day doing a job his detention is supposed to prevent him from stealing. Predatory logic is the logic of the monster. And the monster is capitalism.

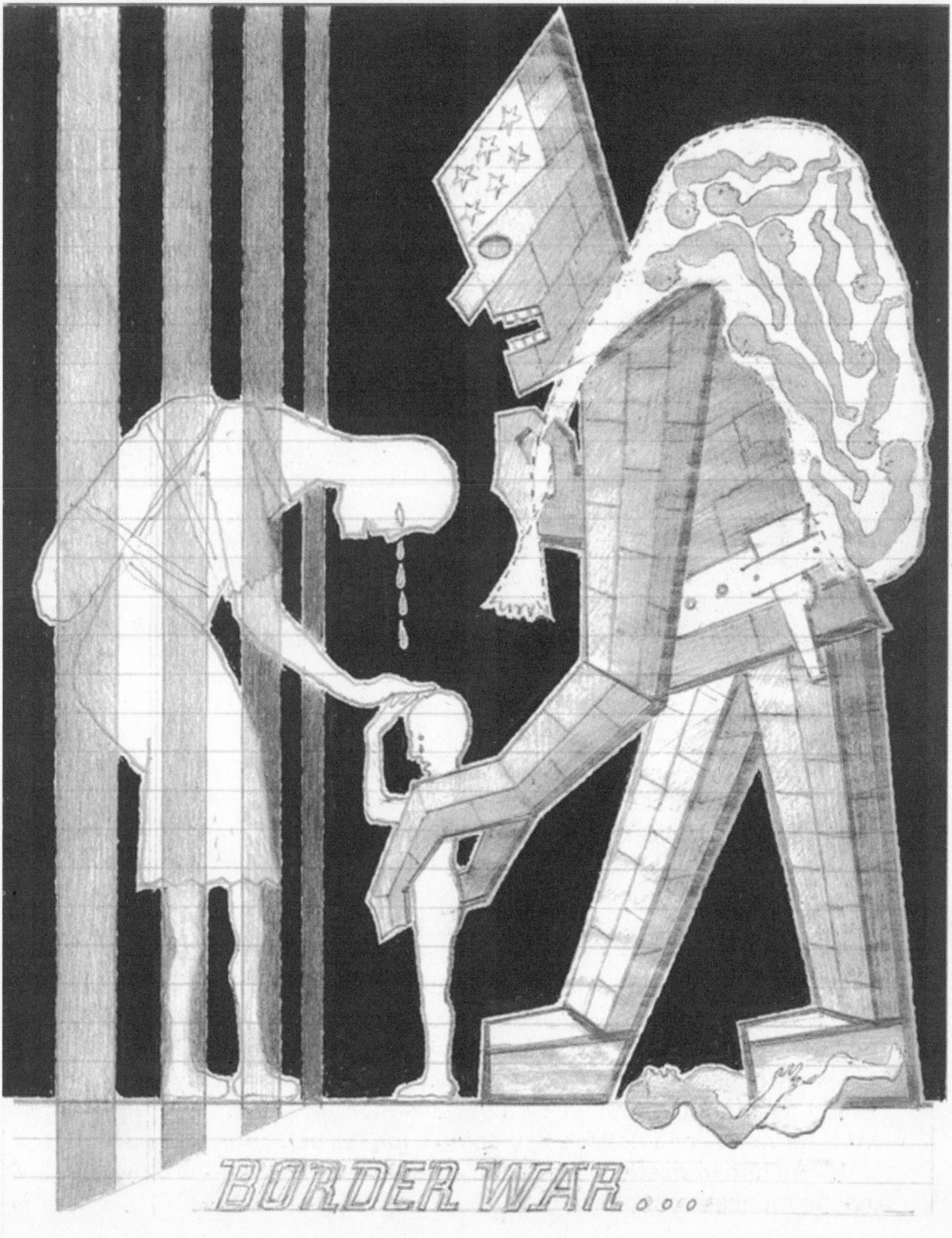
BORDER WAR...

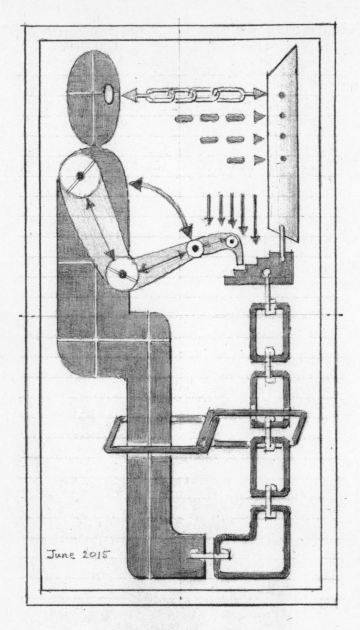

June 2015

CONTENTS:

front cover:
Anthony Freda

inside front:
Jordan Worley

inside back:
Chris Cardinale

back cover:
David Sandlin

half title/quote page:
James Williamson

frontispiece/title:
Anton van Dalen

editorial art:
Peter Kuper
Anton van Dalen

table of contents art:
Anton van Dalen
Tom Keough

Editors this issue:
Susan Simensky Bietila
Rebecca Migdal
Kevin Pyle
Seth Tobocman
Jordan Worley

Graphic design:
Jordan Worley

Website: ww3.nyc

Order copies from: akpress.org

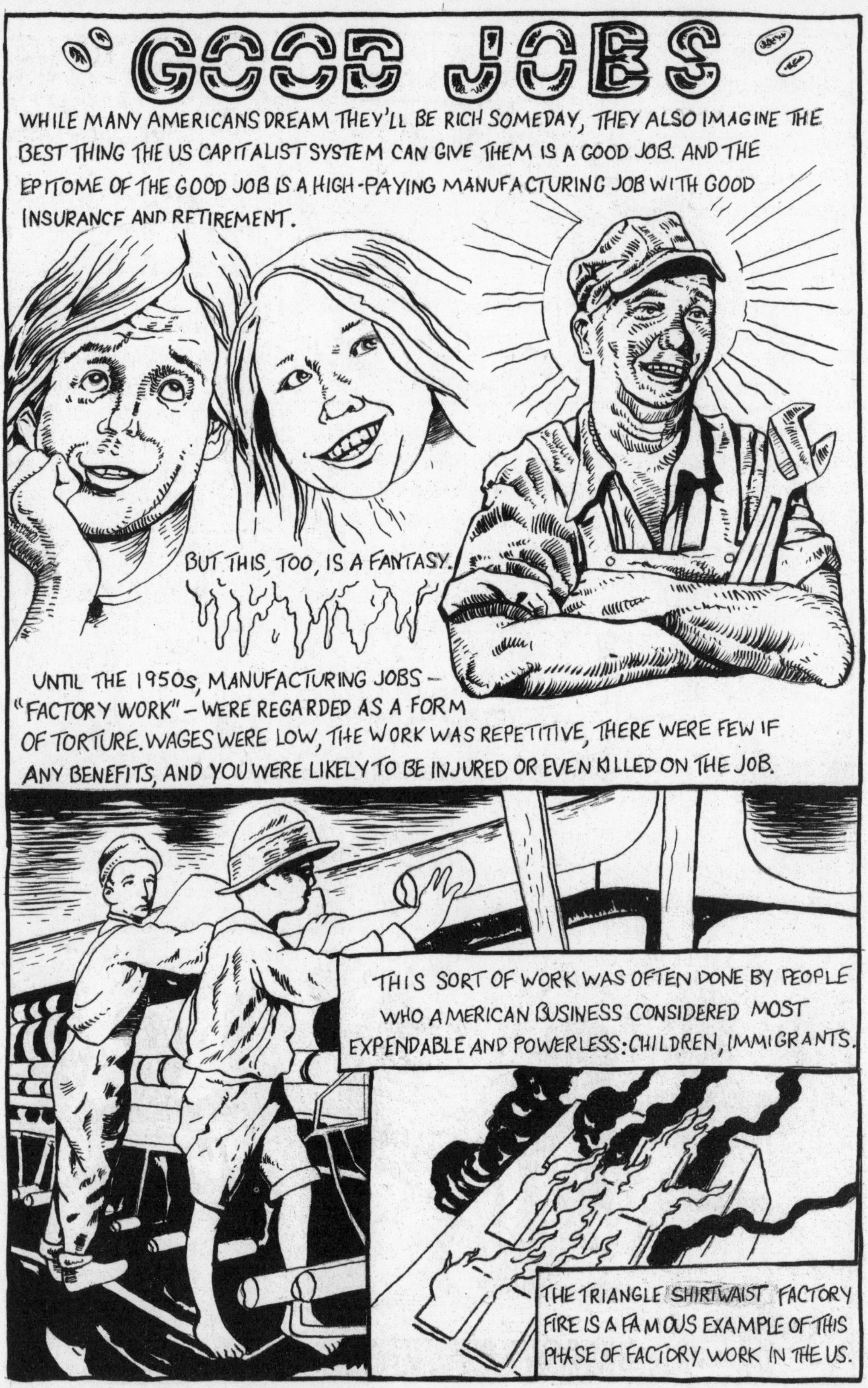
GOOD JOBS
WHILE MANY AMERICANS DREAM THEY'LL BE RICH SOMEDAY, THEY ALSO IMAGINE THE BEST THING THE US CAPITALIST SYSTEM CAN GIVE THEM IS A GOOD JOB. AND THE EPITOME OF THE GOOD JOB IS A HIGH-PAYING MANUFACTURING JOB WITH GOOD INSURANCE AND RETIREMENT.
BUT THIS, TOO, IS A FANTASY.
UNTIL THE 1950s, MANUFACTURING JOBS – "FACTORY WORK" – WERE REGARDED AS A FORM OF TORTURE. WAGES WERE LOW, THE WORK WAS REPETITIVE, THERE WERE FEW IF ANY BENEFITS, AND YOU WERE LIKELY TO BE INJURED OR EVEN KILLED ON THE JOB.
THIS SORT OF WORK WAS OFTEN DONE BY PEOPLE WHO AMERICAN BUSINESS CONSIDERED MOST EXPENDABLE AND POWERLESS: CHILDREN, IMMIGRANTS.
THE TRIANGLE SHIRTWAIST FACTORY FIRE IS A FAMOUS EXAMPLE OF THIS PHASE OF FACTORY WORK IN THE US.

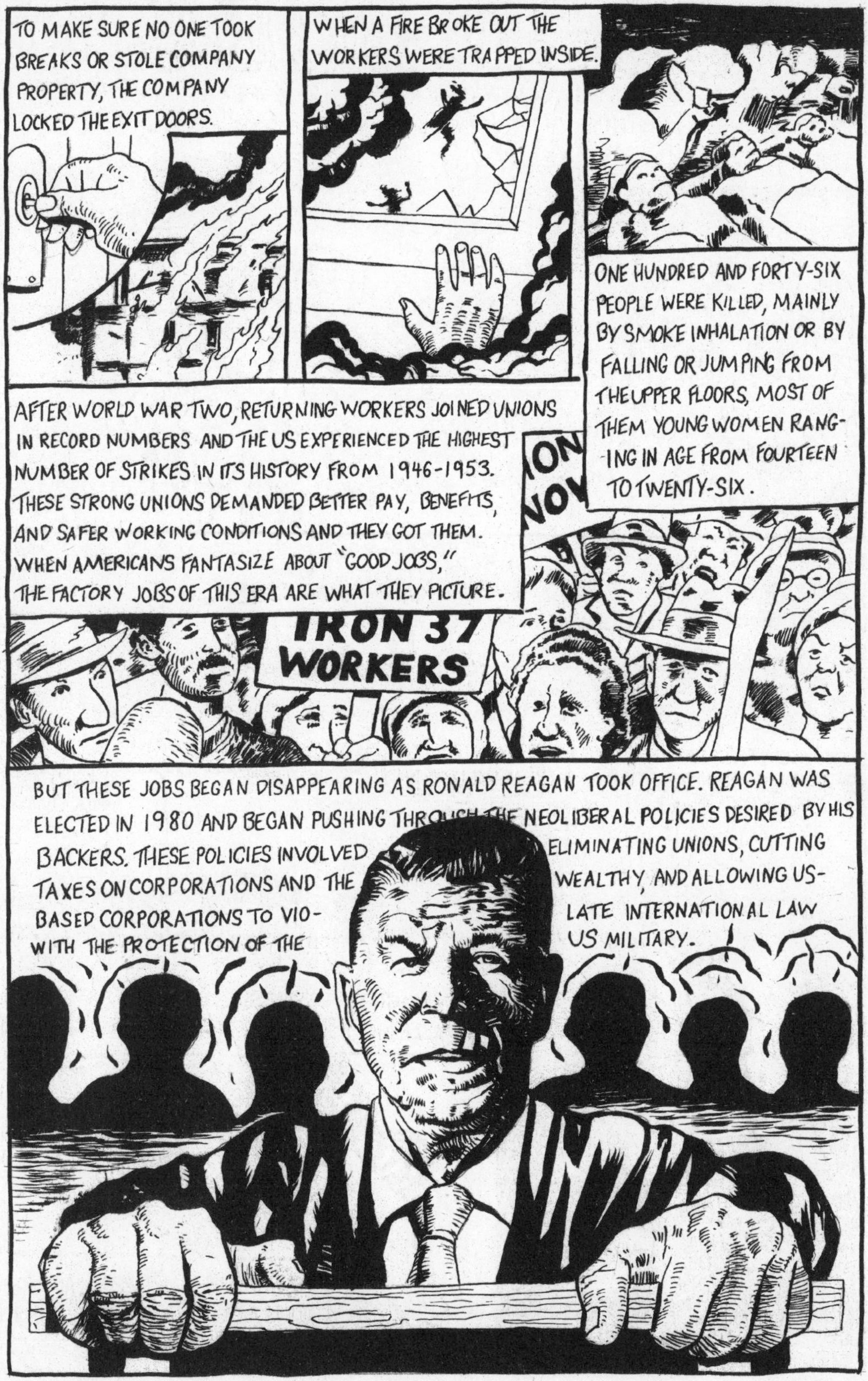
TO MAKE SURE NO ONE TOOK BREAKS OR STOLE COMPANY PROPERTY, THE COMPANY LOCKED THE EXIT DOORS.
WHEN A FIRE BROKE OUT THE WORKERS WERE TRAPPED INSIDE.
ONE HUNDRED AND FORTY-SIX PEOPLE WERE KILLED, MAINLY BY SMOKE INHALATION OR BY FALLING OR JUMPING FROM THE UPPER FLOORS, MOST OF THEM YOUNG WOMEN RANGING IN AGE FROM FOURTEEN TO TWENTY-SIX.
AFTER WORLD WAR TWO, RETURNING WORKERS JOINED UNIONS IN RECORD NUMBERS AND THE US EXPERIENCED THE HIGHEST NUMBER OF STRIKES IN ITS HISTORY FROM 1946-1953. THESE STRONG UNIONS DEMANDED BETTER PAY, BENEFITS, AND SAFER WORKING CONDITIONS AND THEY GOT THEM. WHEN AMERICANS FANTASIZE ABOUT "GOOD JOBS," THE FACTORY JOBS OF THIS ERA ARE WHAT THEY PICTURE.
IRON 37 WORKERS
BUT THESE JOBS BEGAN DISAPPEARING AS RONALD REAGAN TOOK OFFICE. REAGAN WAS ELECTED IN 1980 AND BEGAN PUSHING THROUGH THE NEOLIBERAL POLICIES DESIRED BY HIS BACKERS. THESE POLICIES INVOLVED ELIMINATING UNIONS, CUTTING TAXES ON CORPORATIONS AND THE WEALTHY, AND ALLOWING US-BASED CORPORATIONS TO VIOLATE INTERNATIONAL LAW WITH THE PROTECTION OF THE US MILITARY.

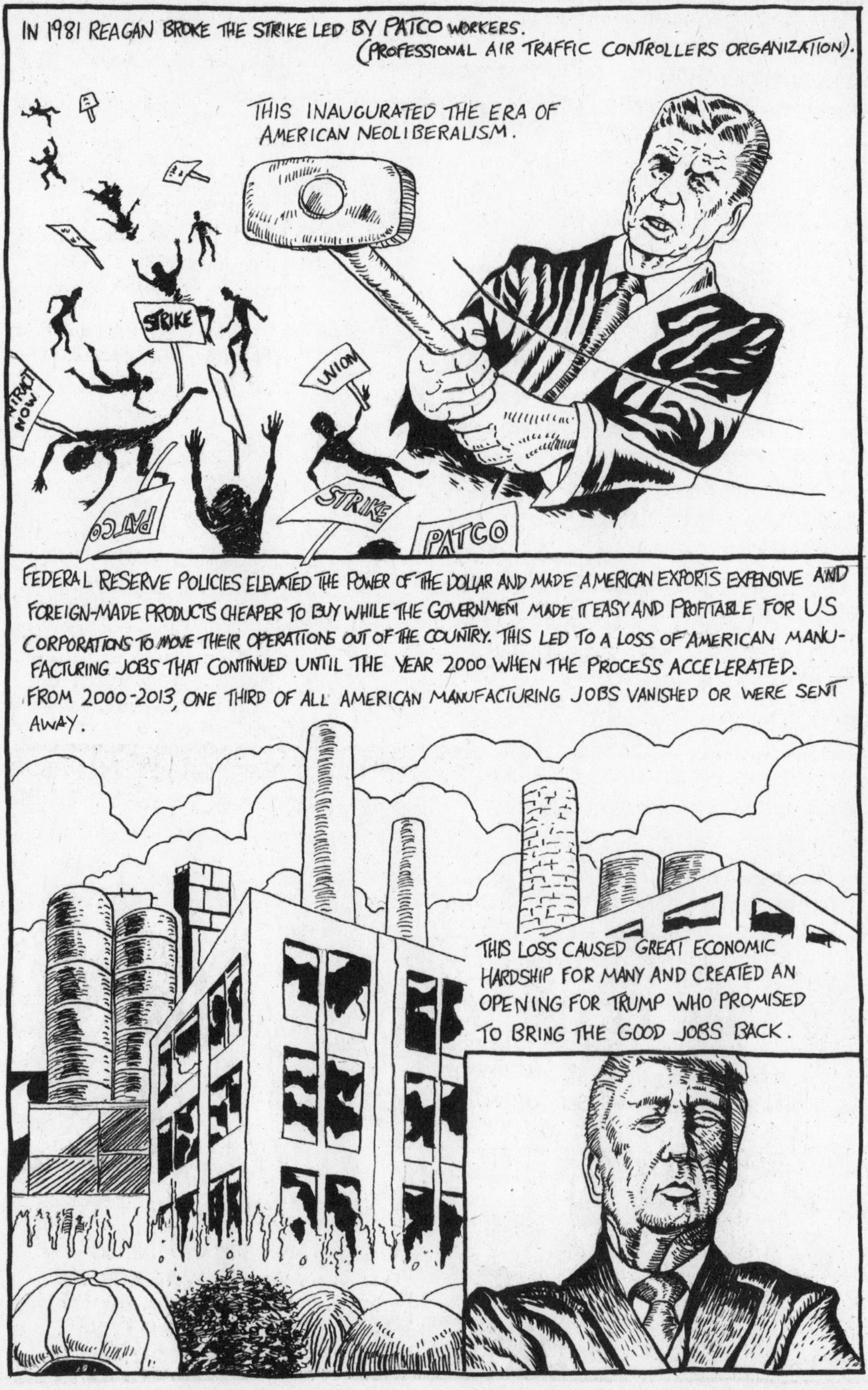
IN 1981 REAGAN BROKE THE STRIKE LED BY PATCO WORKERS.
(PROFESSIONAL AIR TRAFFIC CONTROLLERS ORGANIZATION).
THIS INAUGURATED THE ERA OF AMERICAN NEOLIBERALISM.
STRIKE
UNION
PATCO
STRIKE
PATCO
FEDERAL RESERVE POLICIES ELEVATED THE POWER OF THE DOLLAR AND MADE AMERICAN EXPORTS EXPENSIVE AND FOREIGN-MADE PRODUCTS CHEAPER TO BUY WHILE THE GOVERNMENT MADE IT EASY AND PROFITABLE FOR US CORPORATIONS TO MOVE THEIR OPERATIONS OUT OF THE COUNTRY. THIS LED TO A LOSS OF AMERICAN MANUFACTURING JOBS THAT CONTINUED UNTIL THE YEAR 2000 WHEN THE PROCESS ACCELERATED.
FROM 2000-2013, ONE THIRD OF ALL AMERICAN MANUFACTURING JOBS VANISHED OR WERE SENT AWAY.
THIS LOSS CAUSED GREAT ECONOMIC HARDSHIP FOR MANY AND CREATED AN OPENING FOR TRUMP WHO PROMISED TO BRING THE GOOD JOBS BACK.

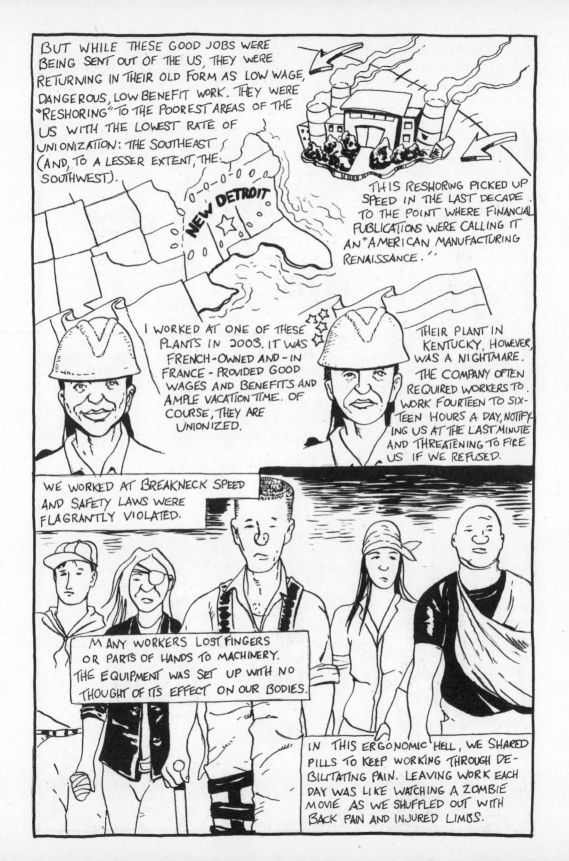

BUT WHILE THESE GOOD JOBS WERE BEING SENT OUT OF THE US, THEY WERE RETURNING IN THEIR OLD FORM AS LOW WAGE, DANGEROUS, LOW BENEFIT WORK. THEY WERE "RESHORING" TO THE POOREST AREAS OF THE US WITH THE LOWEST RATE OF UNIONIZATION: THE SOUTHEAST (AND, TO A LESSER EXTENT, THE SOUTHWEST).

NEW DETROIT

THIS RESHORING PICKED UP SPEED IN THE LAST DECADE. TO THE POINT WHERE FINANCIAL PUBLICATIONS WERE CALLING IT AN "AMERICAN MANUFACTURING RENAISSANCE."

I WORKED AT ONE OF THESE PLANTS IN 2003. IT WAS FRENCH-OWNED AND — IN FRANCE — PROVIDED GOOD WAGES AND BENEFITS AND AMPLE VACATION TIME. OF COURSE, THEY ARE UNIONIZED.

THEIR PLANT IN KENTUCKY, HOWEVER, WAS A NIGHTMARE. THE COMPANY OFTEN REQUIRED WORKERS TO WORK FOURTEEN TO SIXTEEN HOURS A DAY, NOTIFYING US AT THE LAST MINUTE AND THREATENING TO FIRE US IF WE REFUSED.

WE WORKED AT BREAKNECK SPEED AND SAFETY LAWS WERE FLAGRANTLY VIOLATED.

MANY WORKERS LOST FINGERS OR PARTS OF HANDS TO MACHINERY. THE EQUIPMENT WAS SET UP WITH NO THOUGHT OF ITS EFFECT ON OUR BODIES.

IN THIS ERGONOMIC HELL, WE SHARED PILLS TO KEEP WORKING THROUGH DEBILITATING PAIN. LEAVING WORK EACH DAY WAS LIKE WATCHING A ZOMBIE MOVIE AS WE SHUFFLED OUT WITH BACK PAIN AND INJURED LIMBS.

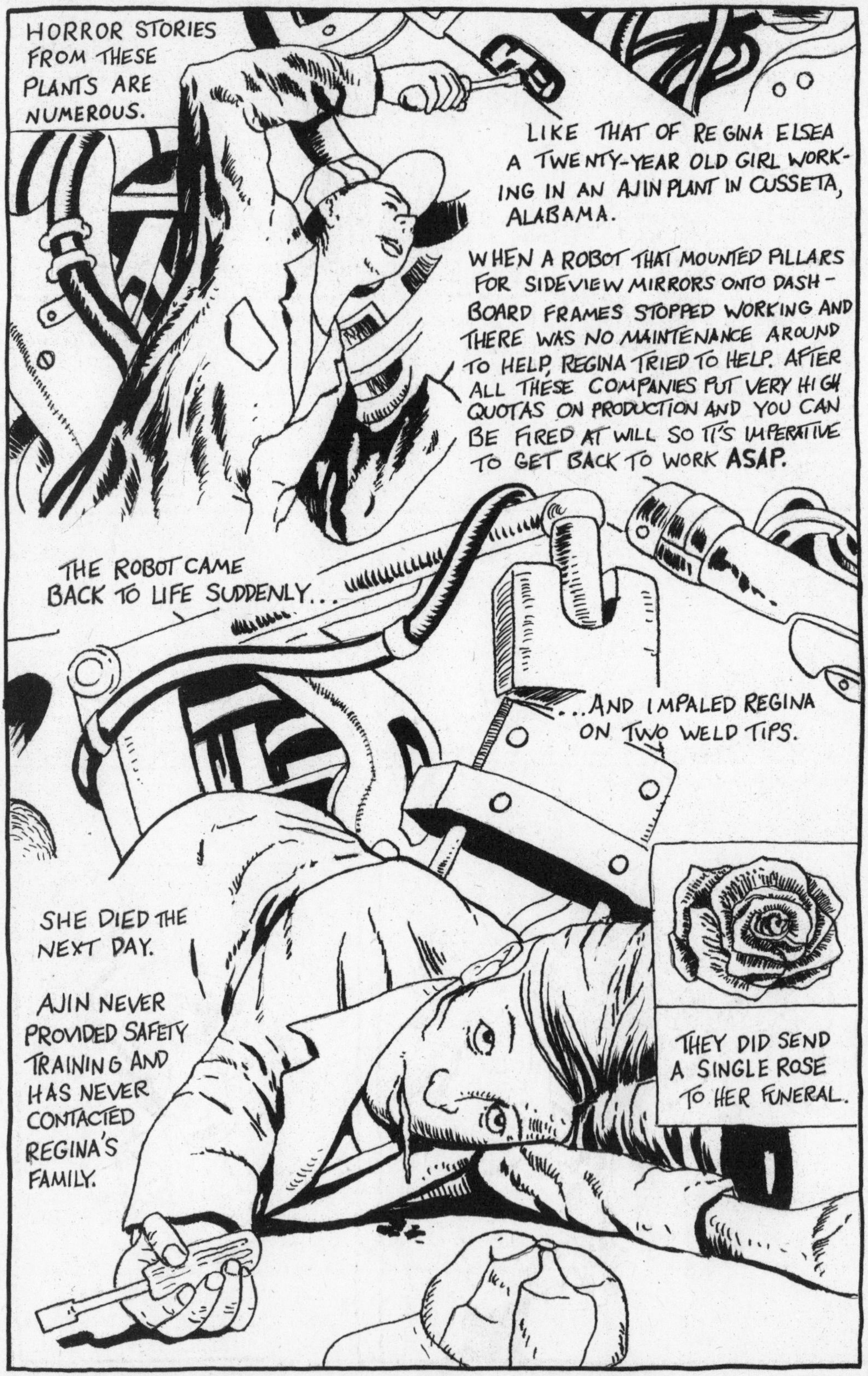
HORROR STORIES FROM THESE PLANTS ARE NUMEROUS.
LIKE THAT OF REGINA ELSEA A TWENTY-YEAR OLD GIRL WORKING IN AN AJIN PLANT IN CUSSETA, ALABAMA.
WHEN A ROBOT THAT MOUNTED PILLARS FOR SIDEVIEW MIRRORS ONTO DASH-BOARD FRAMES STOPPED WORKING AND THERE WAS NO MAINTENANCE AROUND TO HELP, REGINA TRIED TO HELP. AFTER ALL THESE COMPANIES PUT VERY HIGH QUOTAS ON PRODUCTION AND YOU CAN BE FIRED AT WILL SO TI'S IMPERATIVE TO GET BACK TO WORK ASAP.
THE ROBOT CAME BACK TO LIFE SUDDENLY...
...AND IMPALED REGINA ON TWO WELD TIPS.
SHE DIED THE NEXT DAY.
AJIN NEVER PROVIDED SAFETY TRAINING AND HAS NEVER CONTACTED REGINA'S FAMILY.
THEY DID SEND A SINGLE ROSE TO HER FUNERAL.

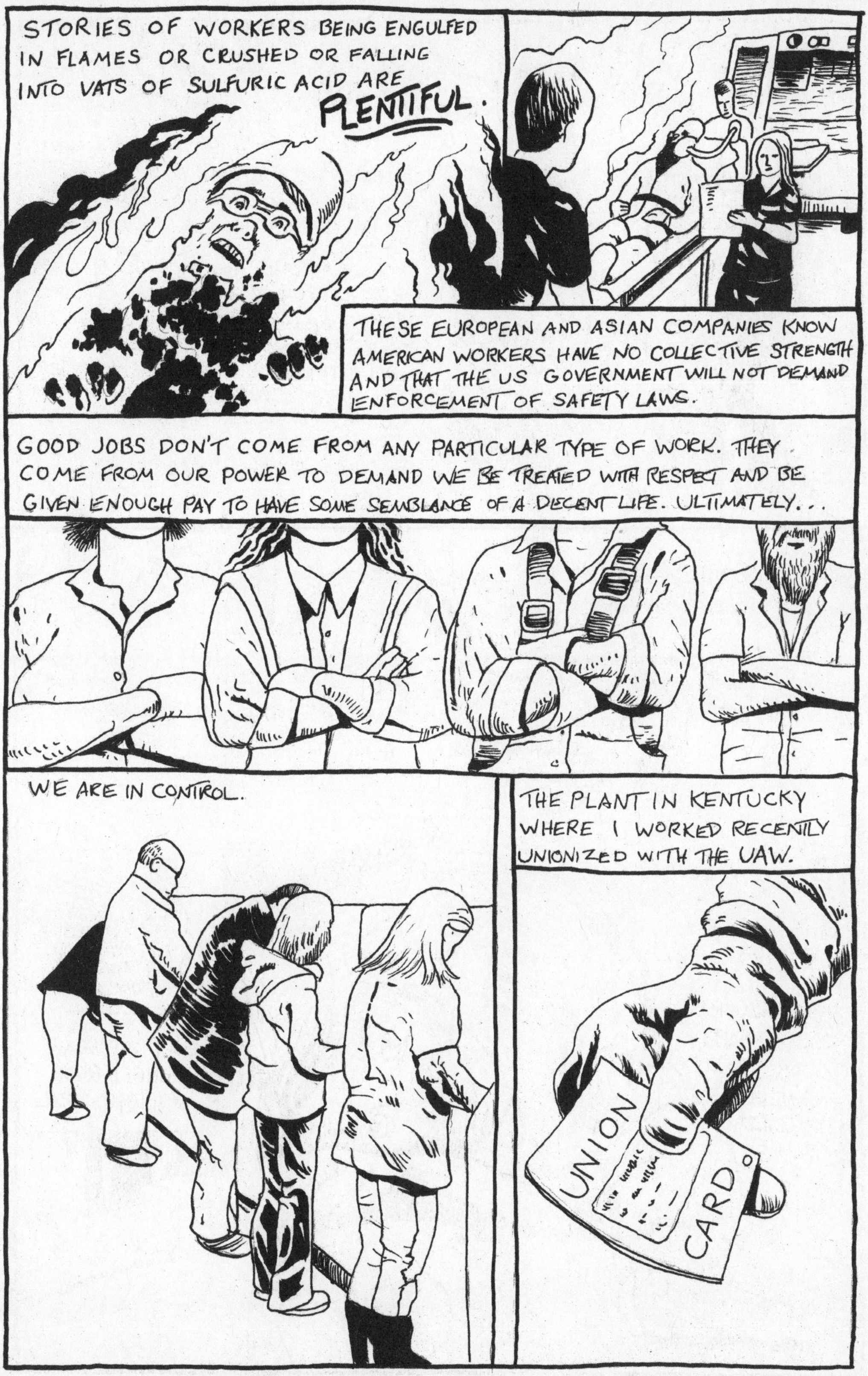
STORIES OF WORKERS BEING ENGULFED IN FLAMES OR CRUSHED OR FALLING INTO VATS OF SULFURIC ACID ARE PLENTIFUL.
THESE EUROPEAN AND ASIAN COMPANIES KNOW AMERICAN WORKERS HAVE NO COLLECTIVE STRENGTH AND THAT THE US GOVERNMENT WILL NOT DEMAND ENFORCEMENT OF SAFETY LAWS.
GOOD JOBS DON'T COME FROM ANY PARTICULAR TYPE OF WORK. THEY COME FROM OUR POWER TO DEMAND WE BE TREATED WITH RESPECT AND BE GIVEN ENOUGH PAY TO HAVE SOME SEMBLANCE OF A DECENT LIFE. ULTIMATELY...
WE ARE IN CONTROL.
THE PLANT IN KENTUCKY WHERE I WORKED RECENTLY UNIONIZED WITH THE UAW.
UNION CARD

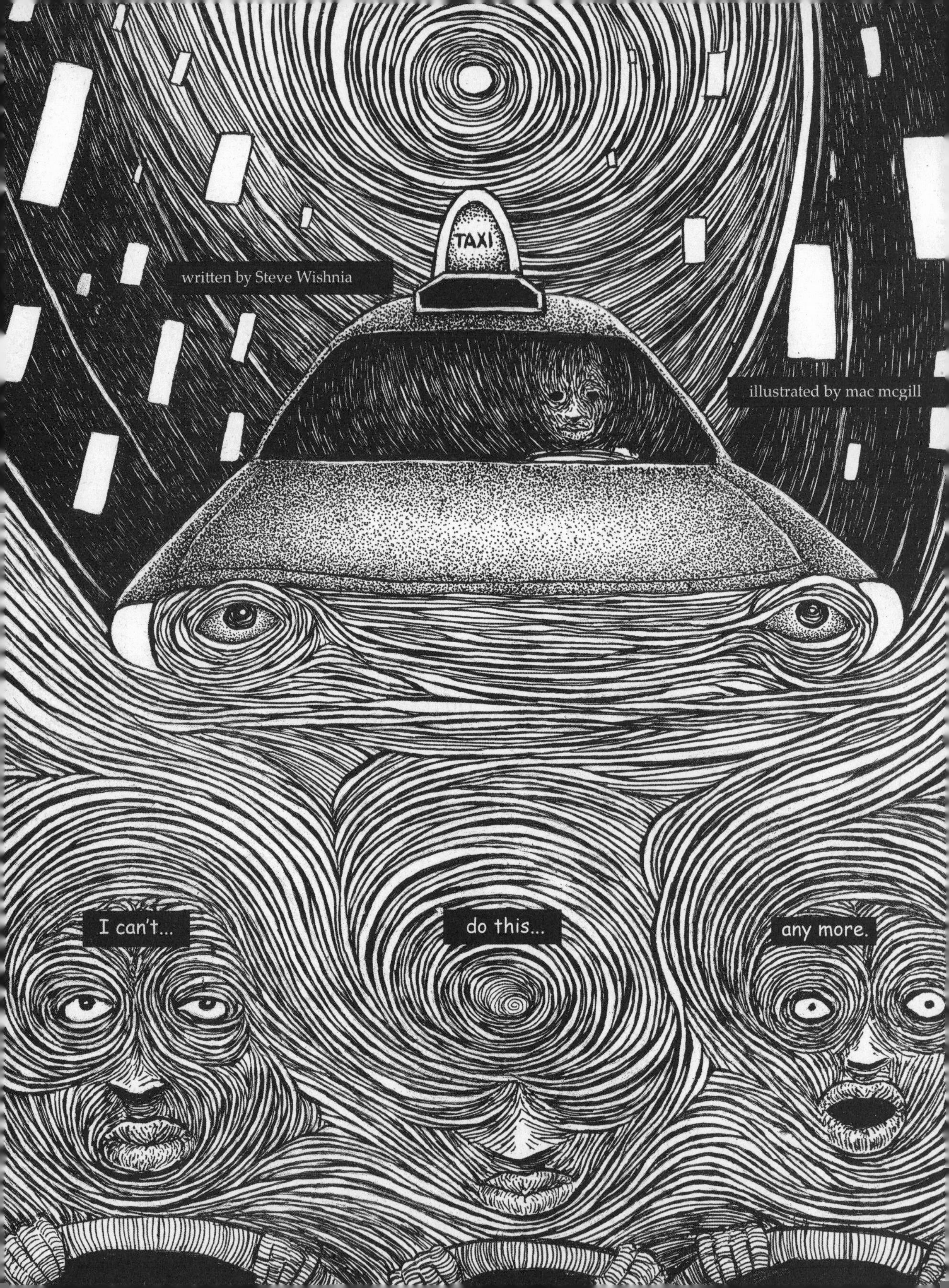
TAXI
written by Steve Wishnia
illustrated by mac mcgill
I can't...
do this...
any more.

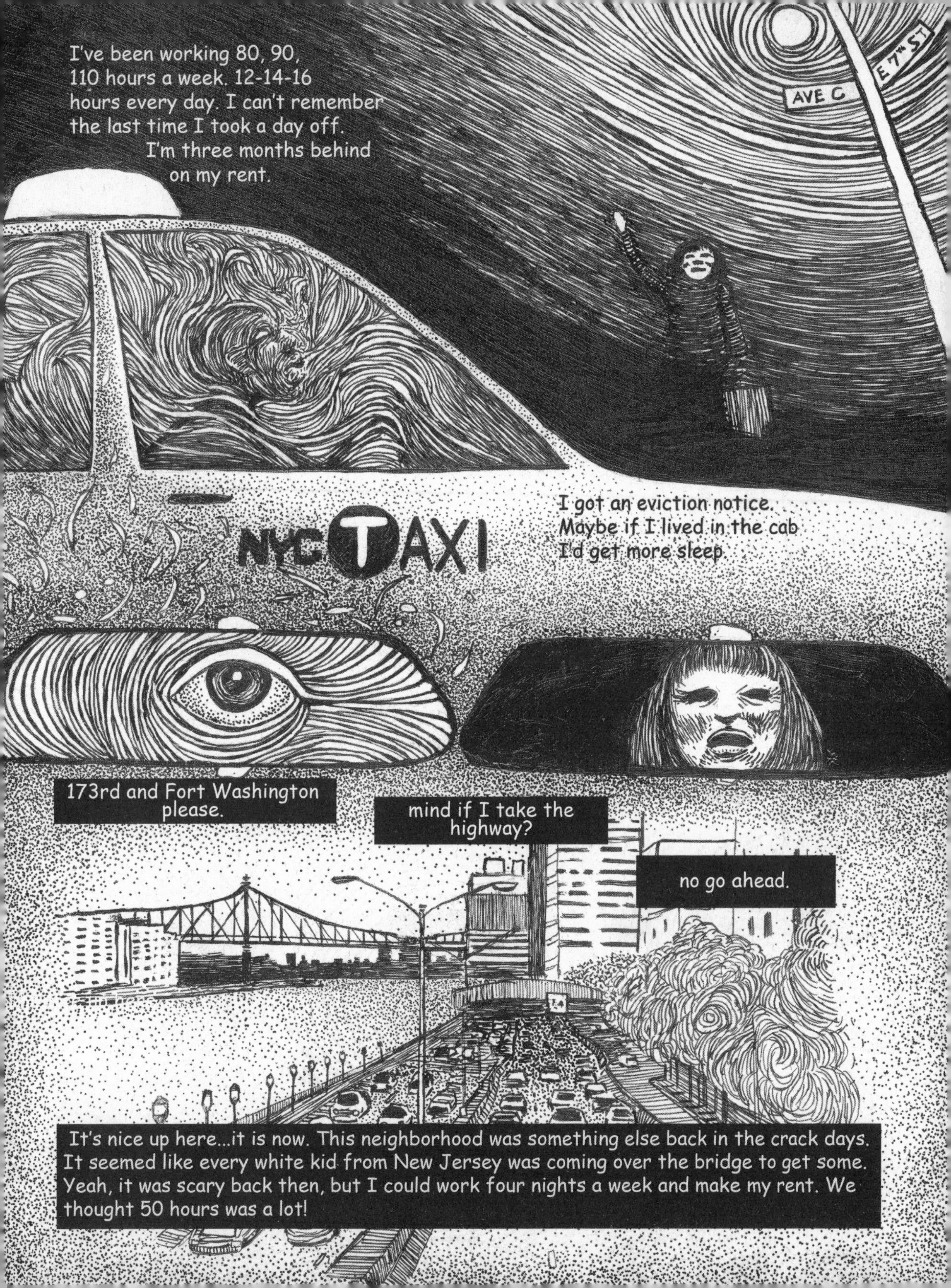

I've been working 80, 90, 110 hours a week. 12-14-16 hours every day. I can't remember the last time I took a day off.
I'm three months behind on my rent.
AVE C
E 7th ST
NYC TAXI
I got an eviction notice. Maybe if I lived in the cab I'd get more sleep.
173rd and Fort Washington please.
mind if I take the highway?
no go ahead.
It's nice up here...it is now. This neighborhood was something else back in the crack days. It seemed like every white kid from New Jersey was coming over the bridge to get some. Yeah, it was scary back then, but I could work four nights a week and make my rent. We thought 50 hours was a lot!

Look at this traffic. There's like 100,000 cabs on the street now. It's like trying to feed 15 people on one pizza. It's ruined the industry. Uber doesn't care if anyone makes money. They don't have to pay for the car or gas. They just get a piece of everything. The politicians let them do it. They're all bought off or dazzled with their we-are-the-future bullshit.

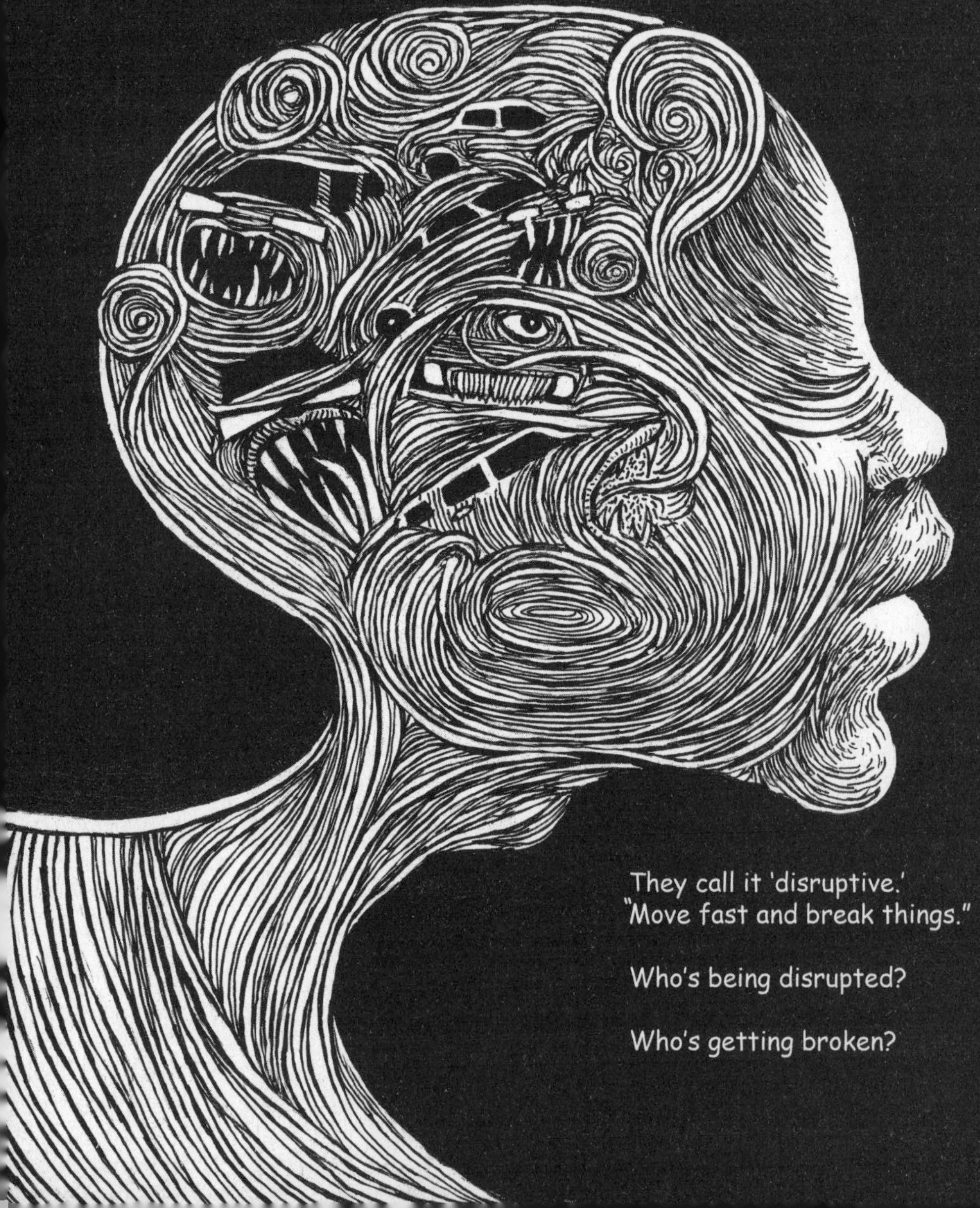

They call it 'disruptive.'
"Move fast and break things."

Who's being disrupted?

Who's getting broken?

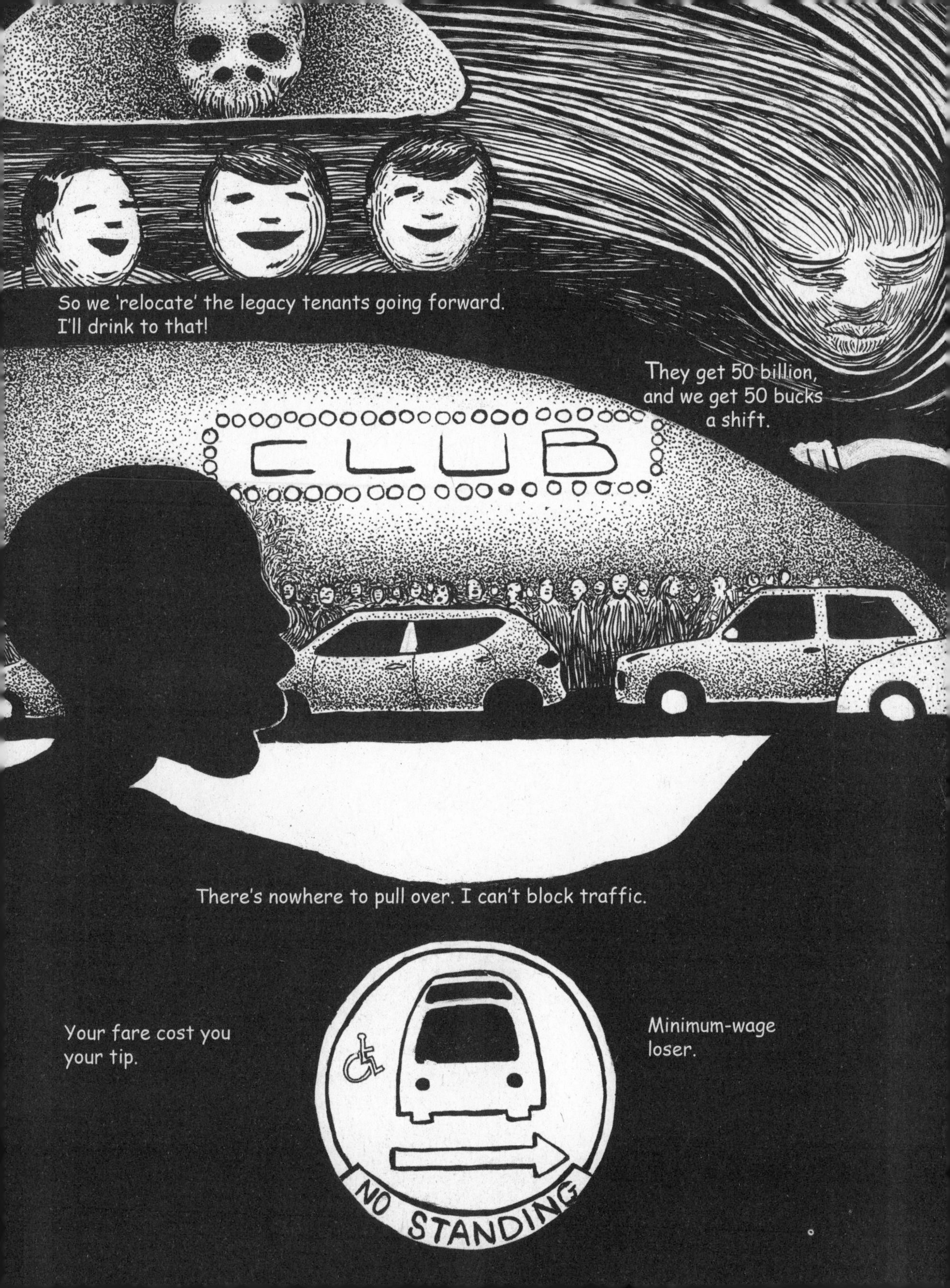
So we 'relocate' the legacy tenants going forward.
I'll drink to that!
They get 50 billion, and we get 50 bucks a shift.
CLUB
There's nowhere to pull over. I can't block traffic.
Your fare cost you your tip.
Minimum-wage loser.
NO STANDING

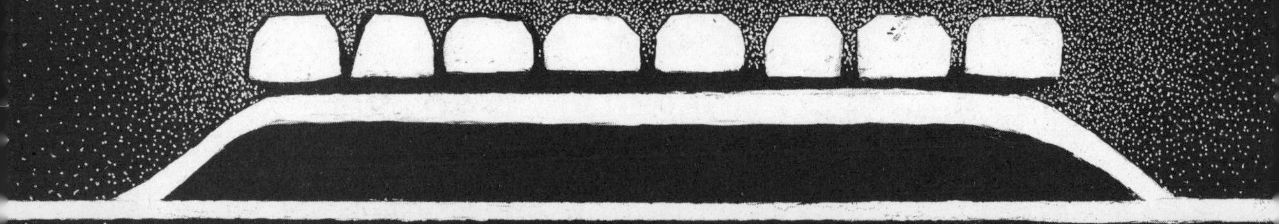

Ah, shit.

A hundred fifteen bucks. There goes my whole fuckin' night. $150 for the lease, now this. I'm gonna lose money.

I can't do this anymore. I can't make it. But what else can I do? Move to Bumfuck, Pennsylvania and be like "Hi, I'm Michael. Welcome to Walmart" for seven-fuckin'-twenty-five an hour?

We need a revolution. Seriously. But I don't have enough time left to wait around for it. I'm passing the torch to a new generation.

I see no point in going on.

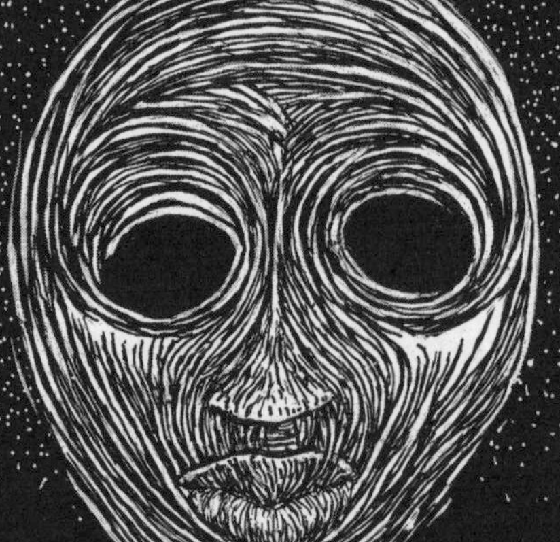

Six New York City cab drivers committed suicide between December 2017 and July 2018.

36TH CHAMBER OF COMMERCE

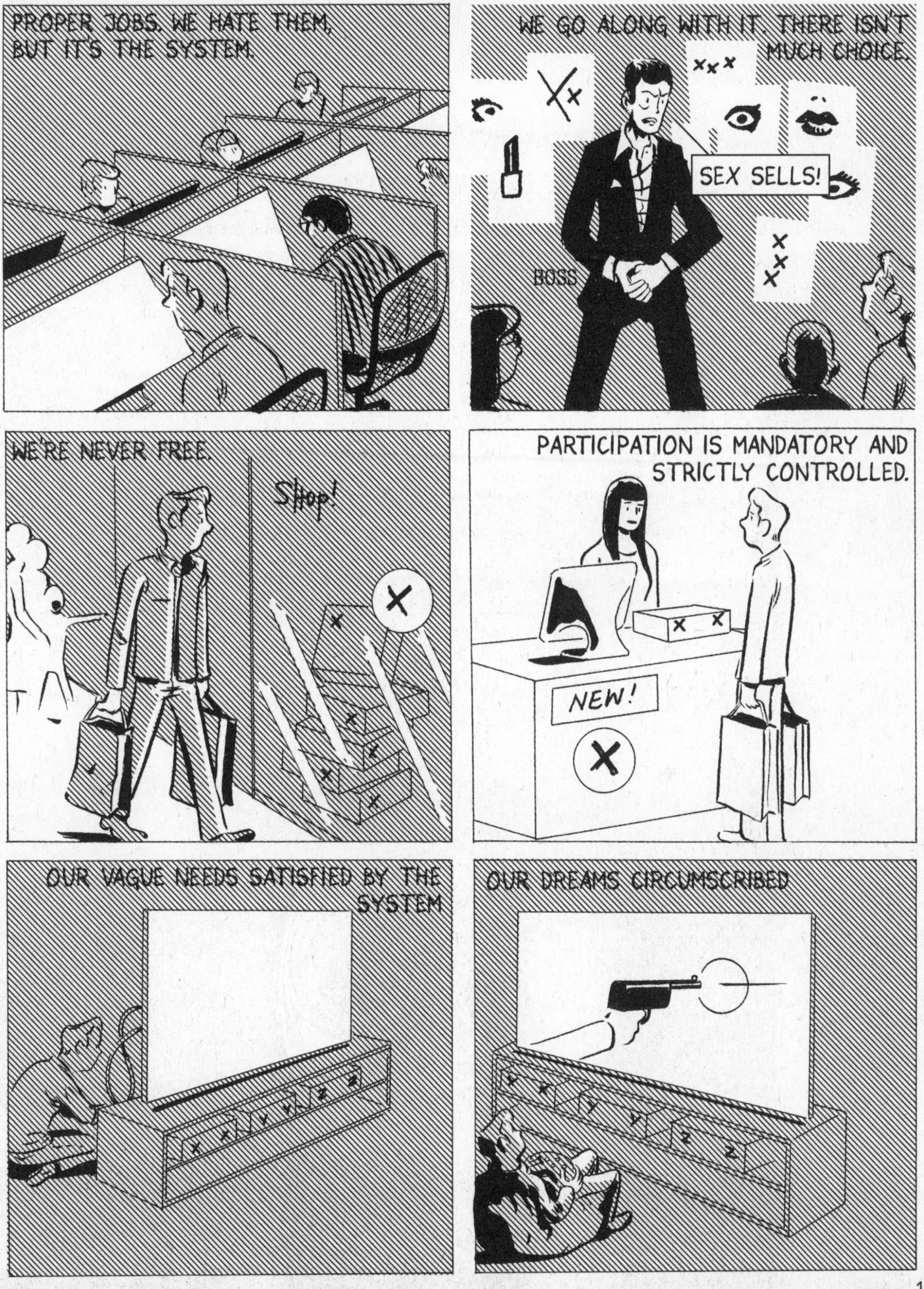
PROPER JOBS. WE HATE THEM, BUT IT'S THE SYSTEM.
WE GO ALONG WITH IT. THERE ISN'T MUCH CHOICE.
BOSS
SEX SELLS!
WE'RE NEVER FREE.
Shop!
PARTICIPATION IS MANDATORY AND STRICTLY CONTROLLED.
NEW!
OUR VAGUE NEEDS SATISFIED BY THE SYSTEM
OUR DREAMS CIRCUMSCRIBED

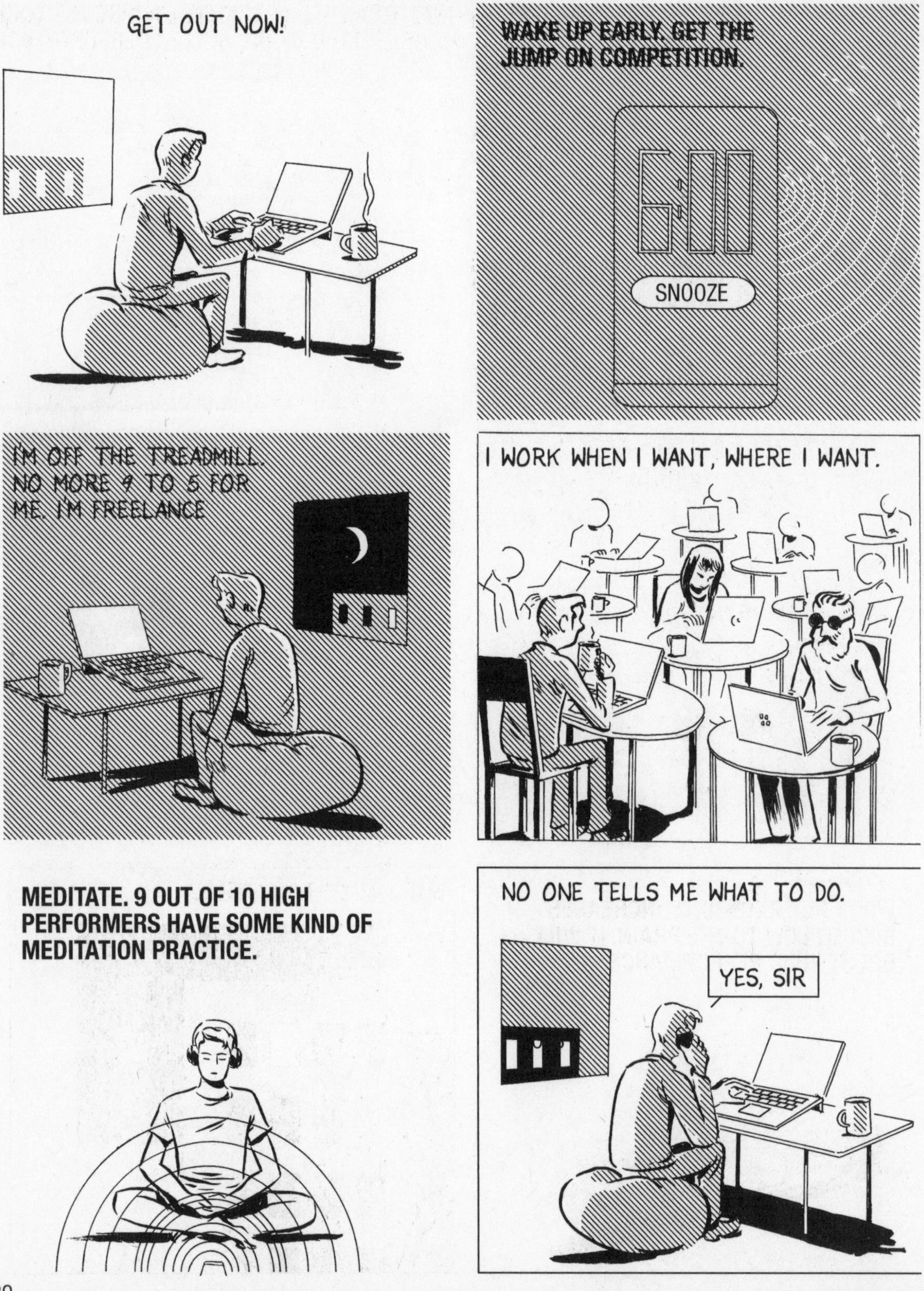
GET OUT NOW!
WAKE UP EARLY. GET THE JUMP ON COMPETITION.
6:00
SNOOZE
I'M OFF THE TREADMILL. NO MORE 9 TO 5 FOR ME. I'M FREELANCE
I WORK WHEN I WANT, WHERE I WANT.
MEDITATE. 9 OUT OF 10 HIGH PERFORMERS HAVE SOME KIND OF MEDITATION PRACTICE.
NO ONE TELLS ME WHAT TO DO.
YES, SIR

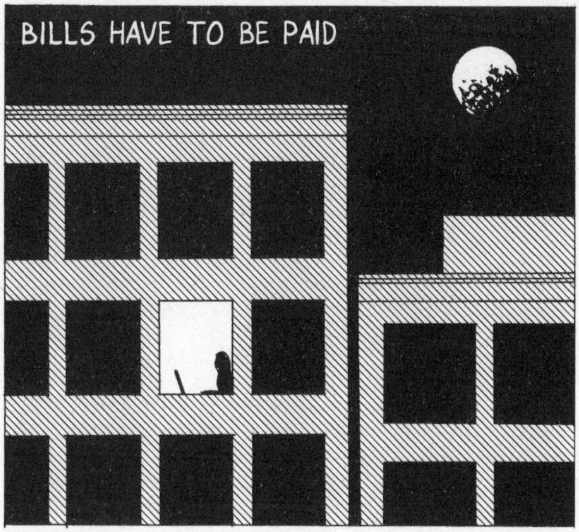
BILLS HAVE TO BE PAID

GRATITUDE. BEING GRATEFUL IMPROVES YOUR MOOD. BETTER MOOD, BETTER PERFORMANCE.

1. I'm grateful this project is done

... I think?

2. ..

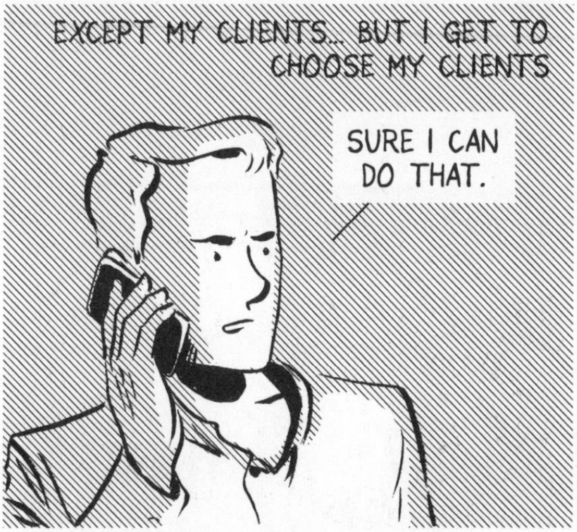
EXCEPT MY CLIENTS... BUT I GET TO CHOOSE MY CLIENTS
SURE I CAN DO THAT.

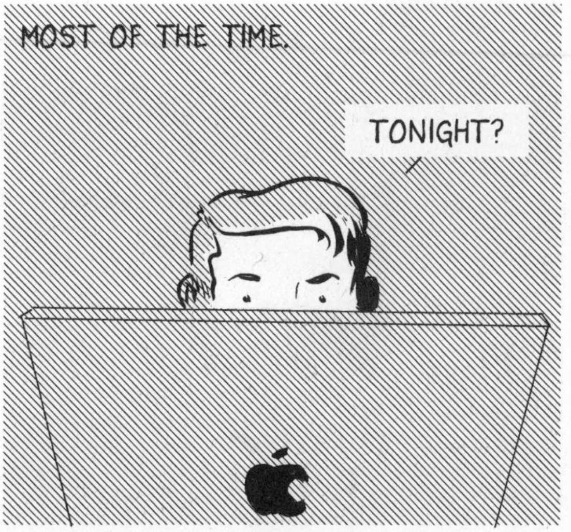
MOST OF THE TIME.
TONIGHT?

WORK OUT. EXCERCISE INCREASES BLOOD FLOW TO THE BRAIN. IT WILL BOOST YOUR PERFORMANCE.

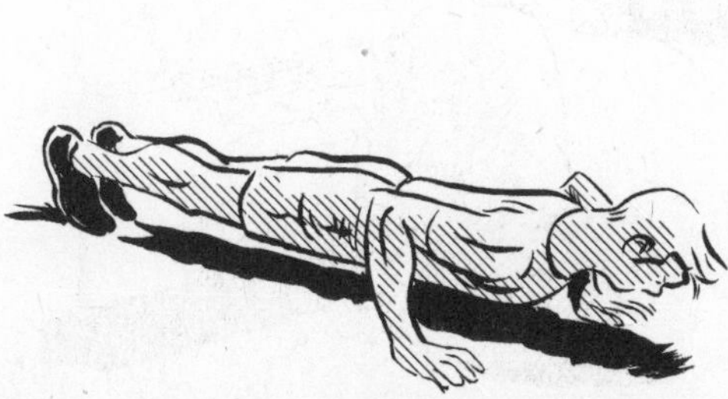

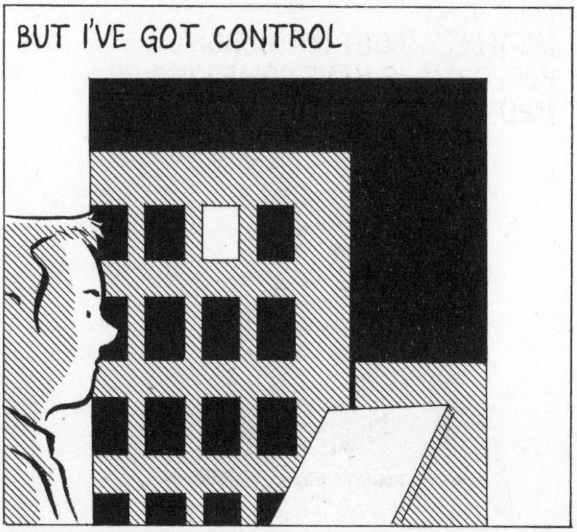
BUT I'VE GOT CONTROL

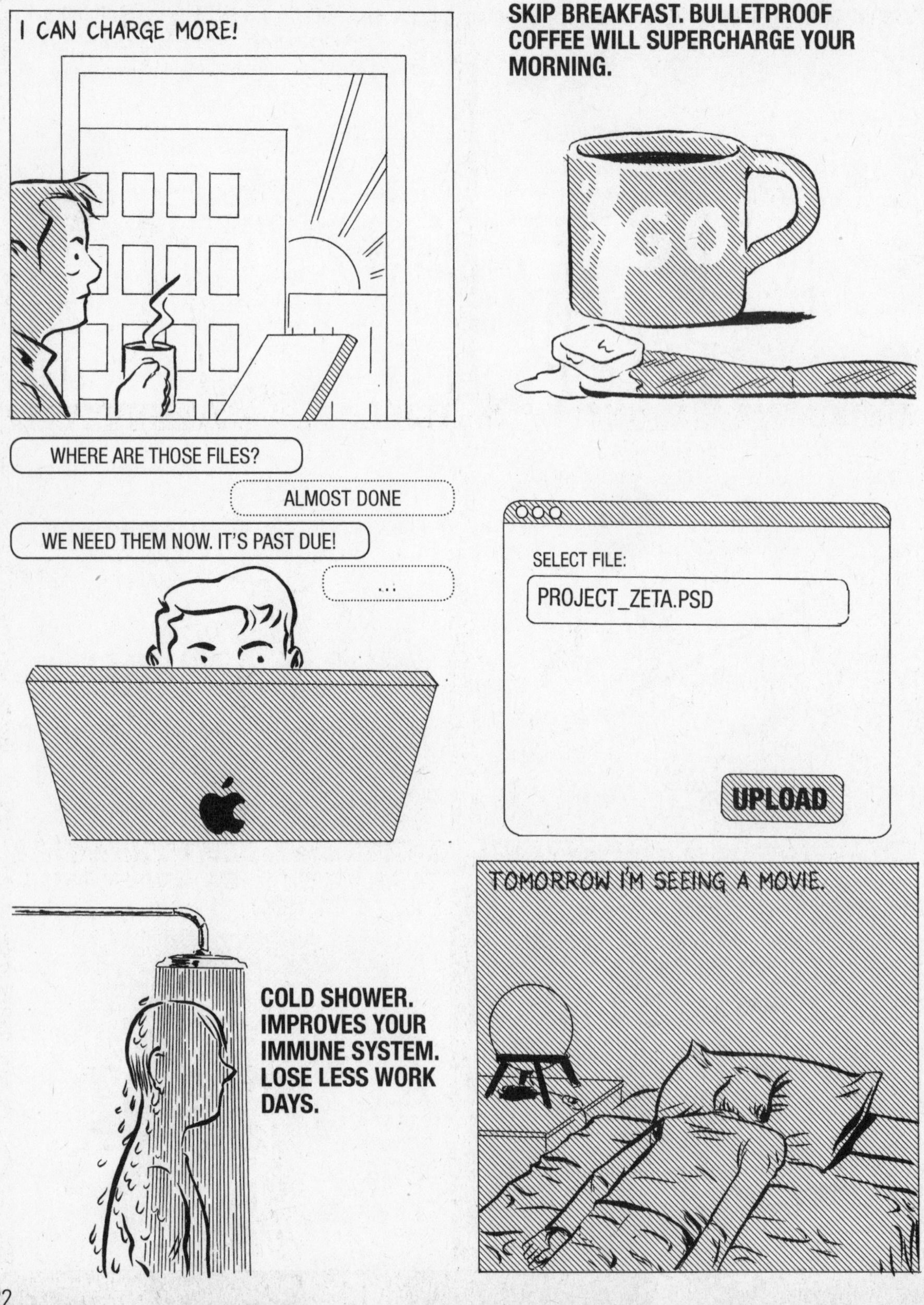
I CAN CHARGE MORE!
SKIP BREAKFAST. BULLETPROOF COFFEE WILL SUPERCHARGE YOUR MORNING.
WHERE ARE THOSE FILES?
ALMOST DONE
WE NEED THEM NOW. IT'S PAST DUE!
...
SELECT FILE:
PROJECT_ZETA.PSD
UPLOAD
COLD SHOWER. IMPROVES YOUR IMMUNE SYSTEM. LOSE LESS WORK DAYS.
TOMORROW I'M SEEING A MOVIE.

36TH CHAMBER OF SHAOLIN IS MORE THAN A MOVIE.

LIU—A NOBODY—THROUGH TRAINING AND AMBITION MASTERS ALL 35 DISCIPLINES OF SHAOLIN KUNG-FU.

LIKE A KUNG-FU ELON MUSK, HE INNOVATES NEW STYLES AND FOUNDS...

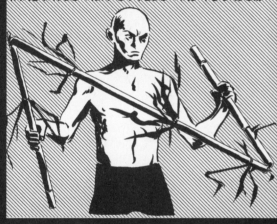

THE 36TH CHAMBER

A GAME CHANGER... HE SHARES HIS MASTERY WITH OTHERS

TO HELP THEM DEFEND AGAINST THE EVIL GOVERNMENT.

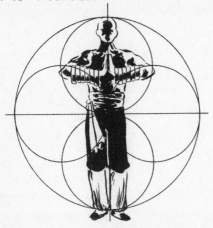

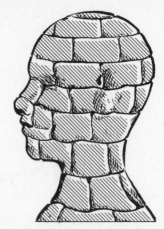

RITUAL, ROUTINE AND DISCIPLINE. THE BODY IS A TEMPLE.
LIU BECOMES A ONE-MAN-TEMPLE OF SHAOLIN.
RITUAL, ROUTINE AND DISCIPLINE. THE MODERN BODY IS A CORPORATION.
BUT WE DON'T HAVE TO FIGHT THE EVIL EMPIRE ANYMORE.
THE CHAMBERS ARE DIFFERENT TODAY.
PM
HR
COO
QA
CEO
CD
CPA
MD
DM
ONE-MAN CORPORATION: MARKET ORIENTED, FLEXIBLE, FAST, INVINCIBLE.
POINTER
BOSS
STIM
MOBILE
CLOUD
IDEATION

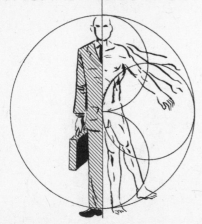

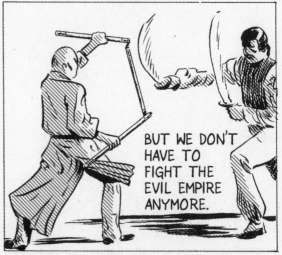

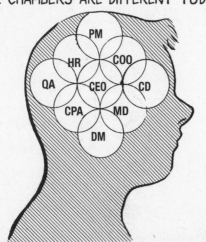

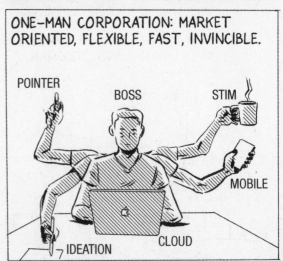

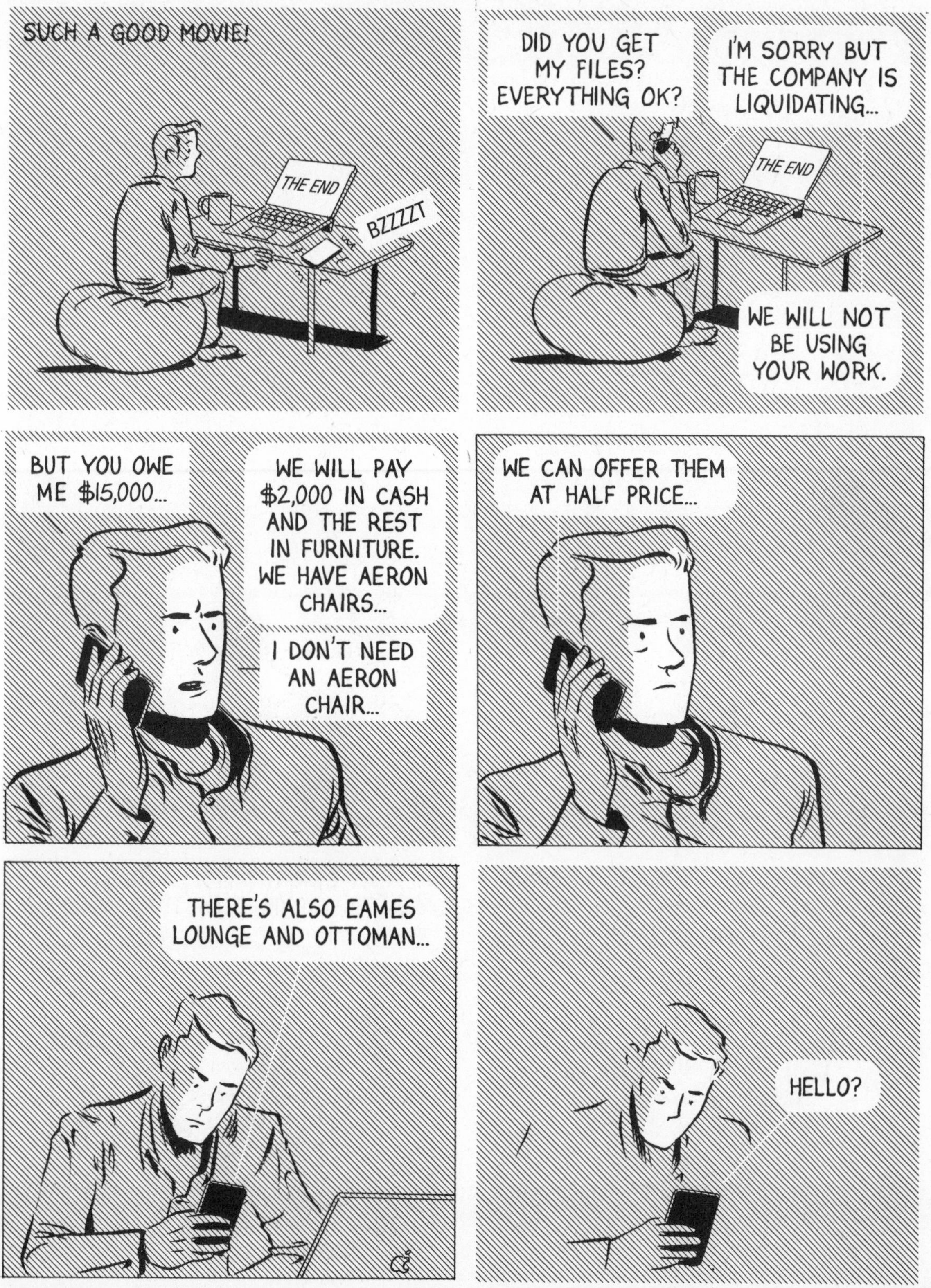
SUCH A GOOD MOVIE!
THE END
BZZZZT
DID YOU GET MY FILES? EVERYTHING OK?
I'M SORRY BUT THE COMPANY IS LIQUIDATING...
THE END
WE WILL NOT BE USING YOUR WORK.
BUT YOU OWE ME $15,000...
WE WILL PAY $2,000 IN CASH AND THE REST IN FURNITURE. WE HAVE AERON CHAIRS...
I DON'T NEED AN AERON CHAIR...
WE CAN OFFER THEM AT HALF PRICE...
THERE'S ALSO EAMES LOUNGE AND OTTOMAN...
HELLO?

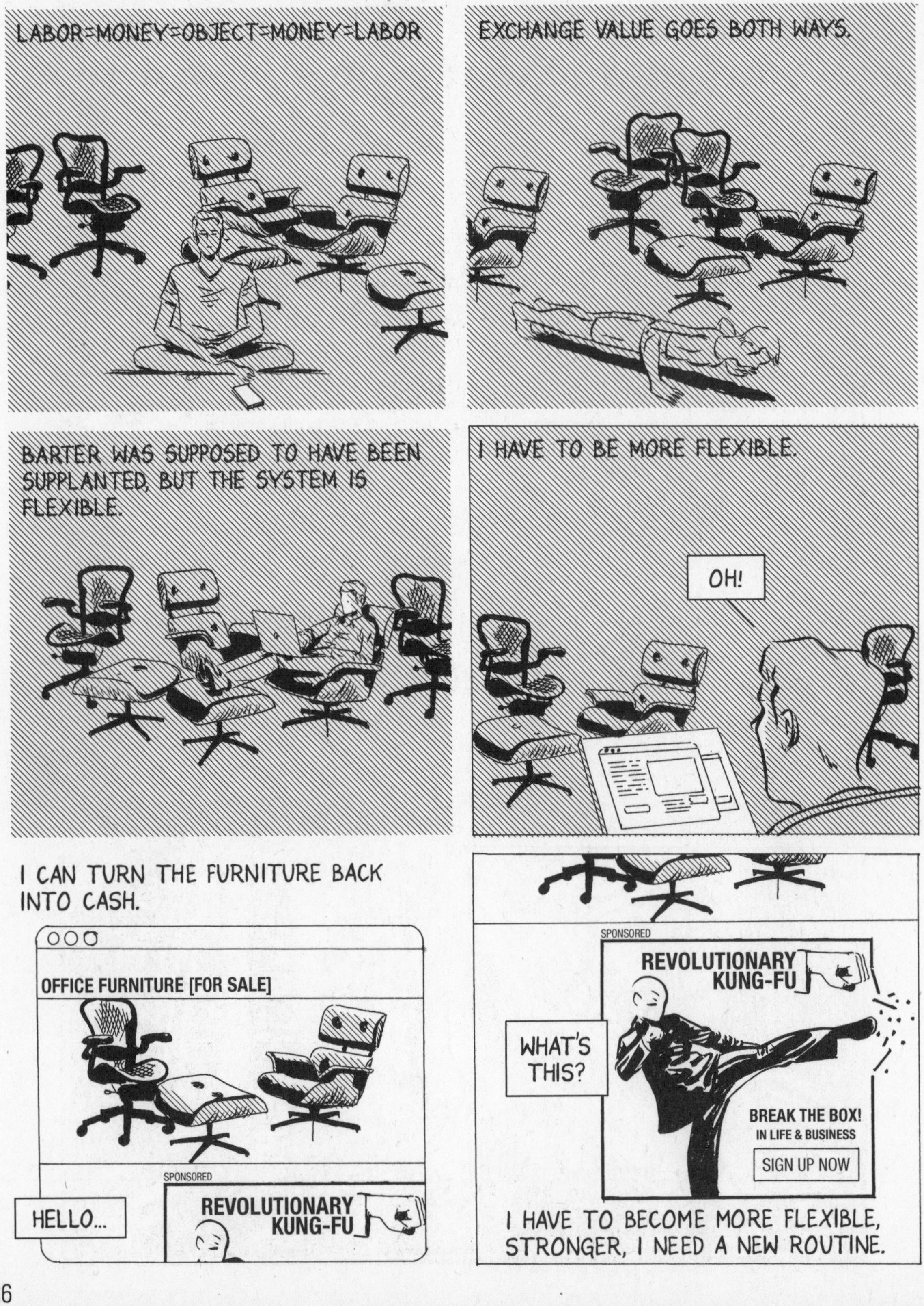

LABOR=MONEY=OBJECT=MONEY=LABOR
EXCHANGE VALUE GOES BOTH WAYS.
BARTER WAS SUPPOSED TO HAVE BEEN SUPPLANTED, BUT THE SYSTEM IS FLEXIBLE.
I HAVE TO BE MORE FLEXIBLE.
OH!
I CAN TURN THE FURNITURE BACK INTO CASH.
OFFICE FURNITURE [FOR SALE]
SPONSORED
REVOLUTIONARY KUNG-FU
HELLO...
SPONSORED
REVOLUTIONARY KUNG-FU
WHAT'S THIS?
BREAK THE BOX!
IN LIFE & BUSINESS
SIGN UP NOW
I HAVE TO BECOME MORE FLEXIBLE, STRONGER, I NEED A NEW ROUTINE.

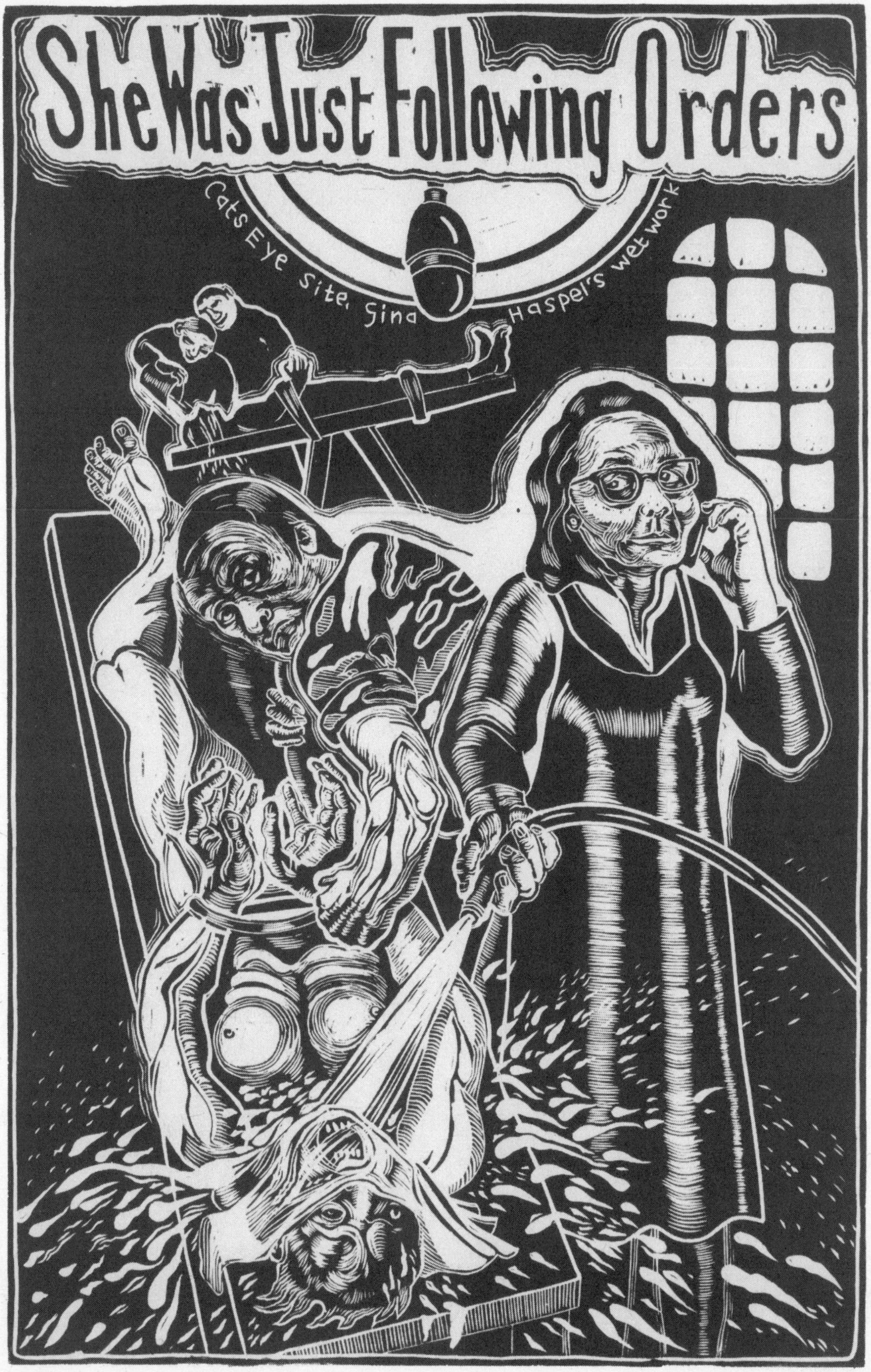
She Was Just Following Orders
Cats Eye Site, Gina Haspel's wet work

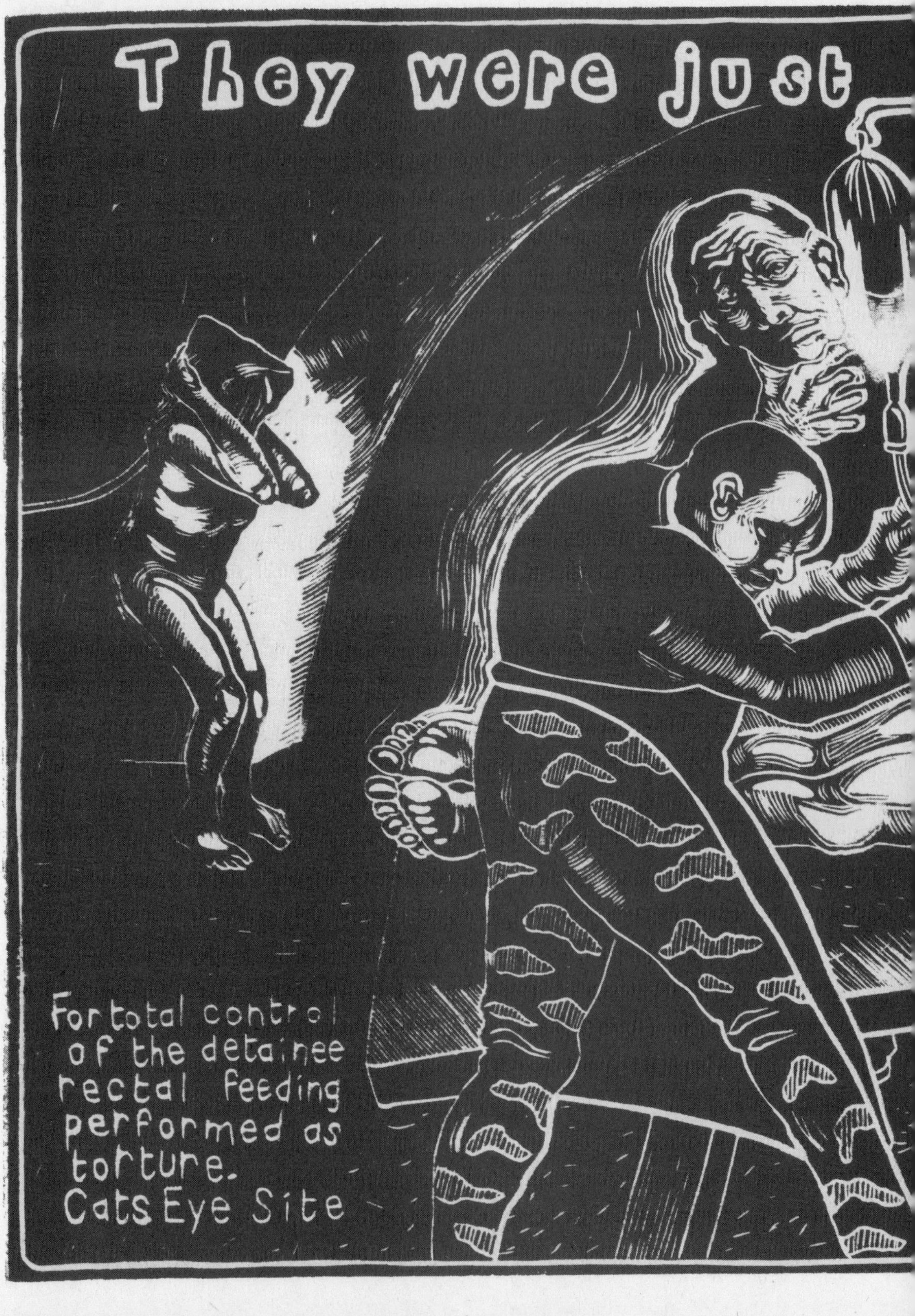
They were just
For total control of the detainee rectal feeding performed as torture.
Cats Eye Site

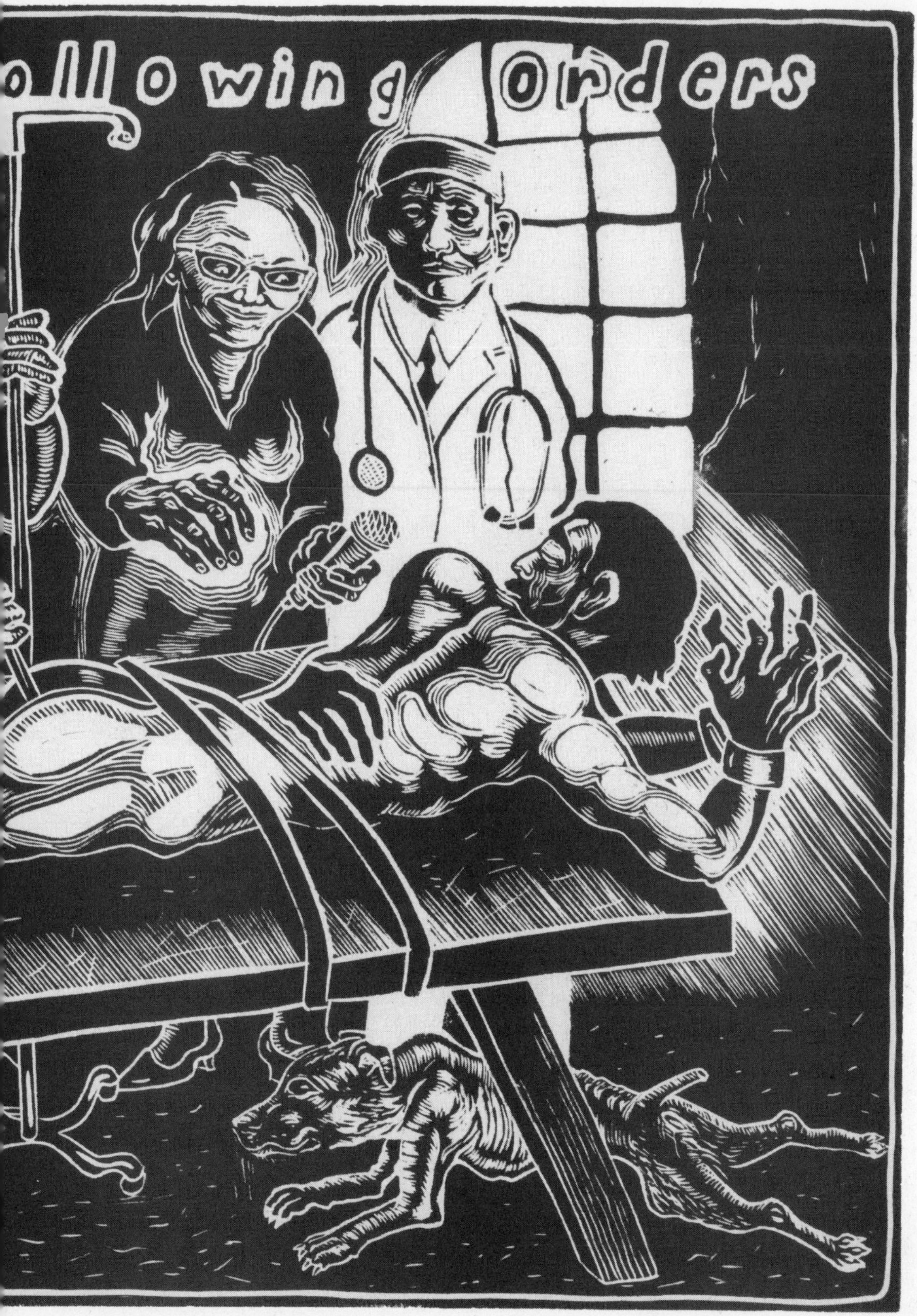
ollowing Orders

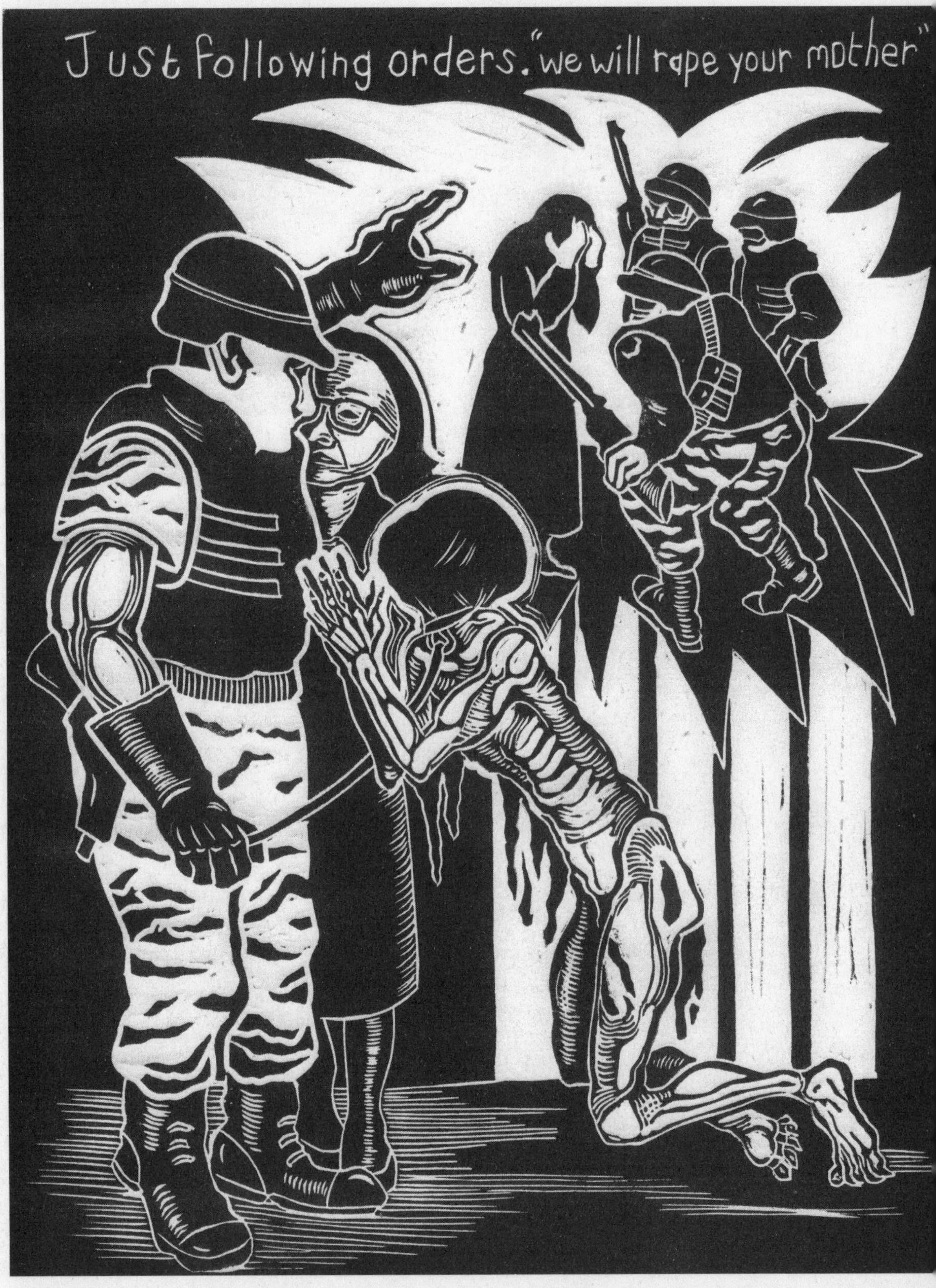
Just following orders. "we will rape your mother"

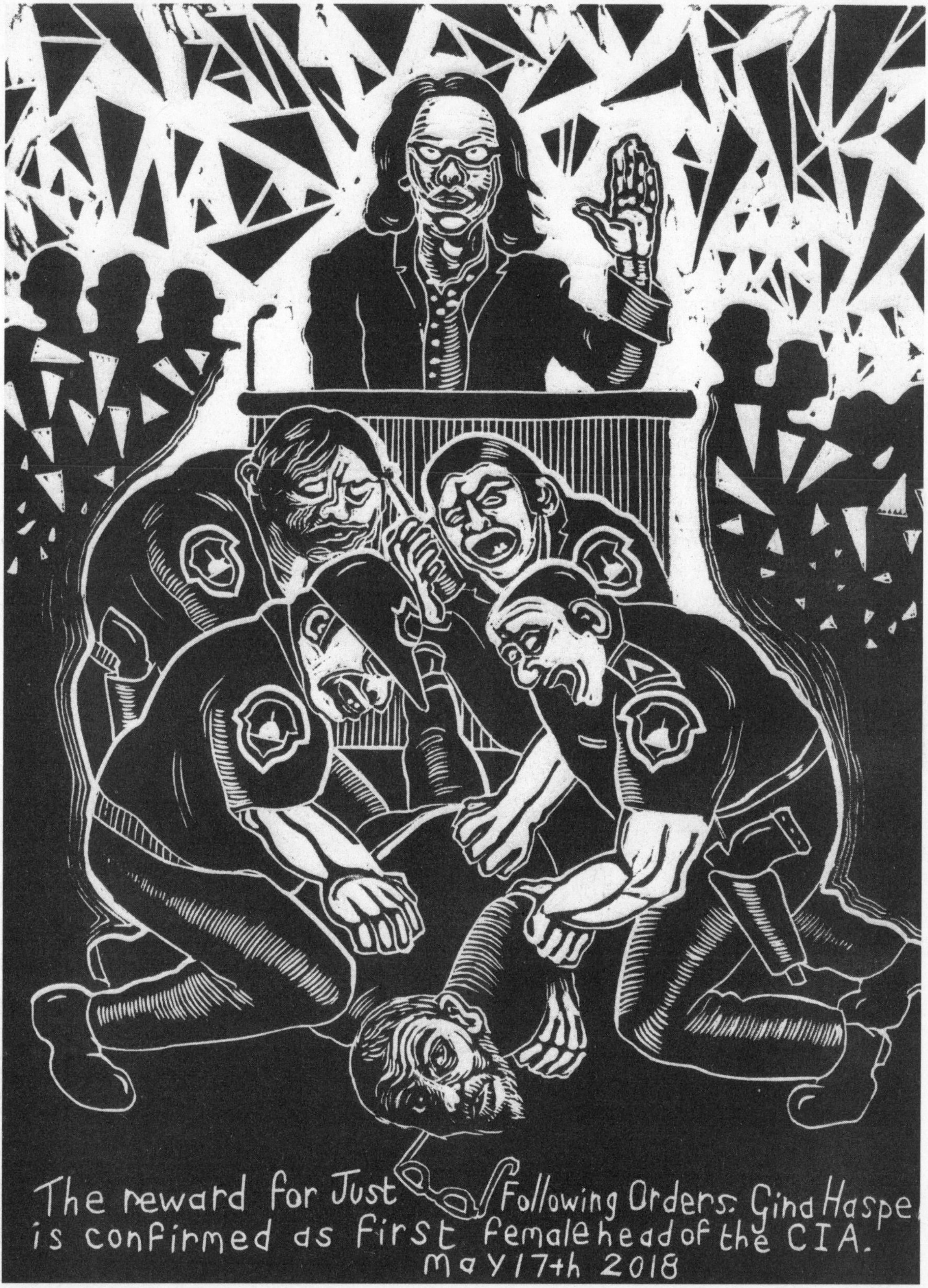
The reward for Just Following Orders: Gina Haspel
is confirmed as first female head of the CIA.
May 17th 2018

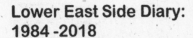

Lower East Side Diary:
1984 -2018

1984 AUTUMN: He came up north with his bandmates and not much else. Somebody told him that Jessie, from 3 Teens Kill 4, had disappeared and left his apartment vacant. Mr.Cooper, the building's owner, said " you look like a nice boy … you can take the apartment now"

Mr. Cooper's building was a typical six floor rent stabilized LES tenement - each apartment had two rooms, a bathroom down the hall, bathtub in the kitchen and a tiny gas heater with pilot light. Except for the big KATZ'S sign the street had no illumination at night. Rats. Junkies. Burnt out buildings. Seems like a cliche now, but the neighborhood was not prime real estate.

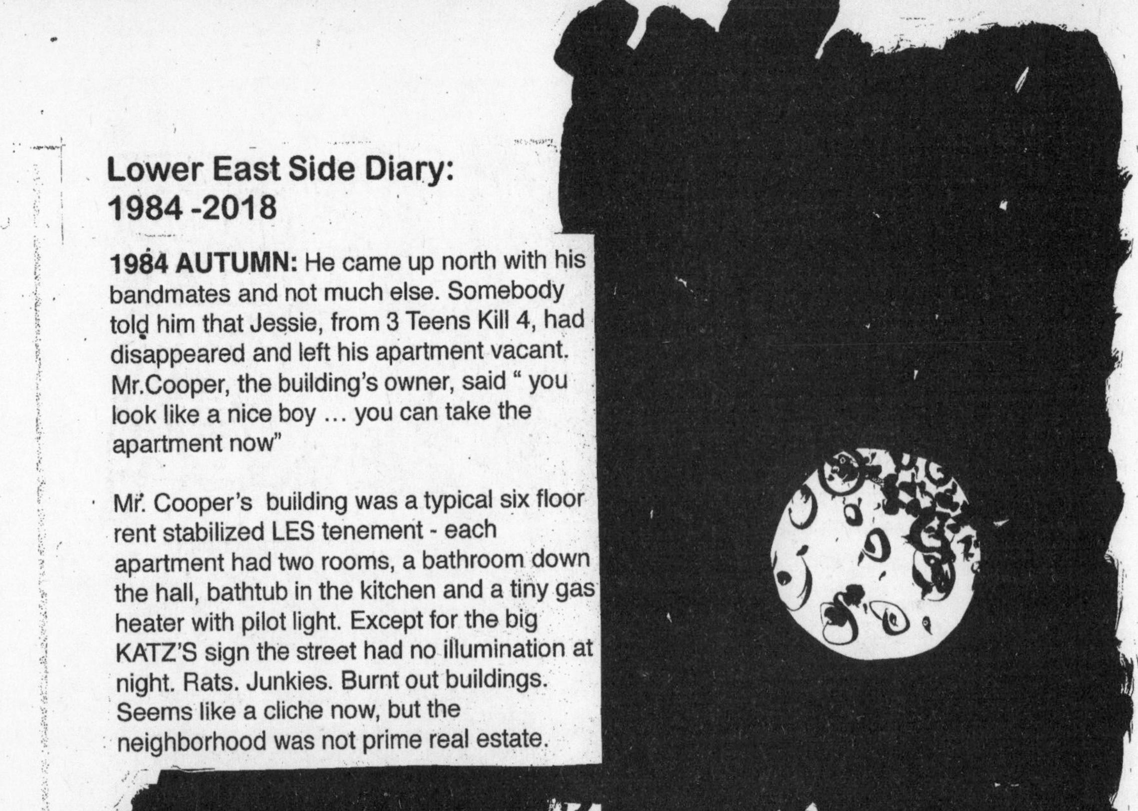

His apartment was barren and cold.
But it was his. It was grand. He'd never had a place of his own before.
Soon he had a job at a good bookstore, and space for his books and music.
He crossed paths with the interesting and infamous circle of writers and musicians and filmmakers that hung out and worked on the east side downtown. He was 22 yrs old.

1995 WINTER: Mr. Cooper sold the building.
His new landlord was Mark Weiss.
He paid rent in cash to a woman downstairs.
The neighborhood started to liven up.Bars and bodegas opened up.
More people came around and settled in. The streetlights come on at night.

1999 JANUARY: He found out from the newspaper who his landlord really was.
"LANDLORD FROM HELL IS GUILTY IN TENANT SLAY BID" NY POST 1990
Mark Glass AKA Alvin Weiss AKA Mark Weiss owned his building and 20 others on the lower east side.
He had been arrested for attempting to murder two of his rent controlled tenants.
He confessed and was sentenced to 7 years.

After that the building got real real quiet.
Tenants kept paying rent to various LLC's INC's ASSO.s and finally Arwen Properties LLC, owned by Luthien Investment Group.

The building started to fall apart and repairs were not done.
His kitchen ceiling fell down in chunks. He put up plastic.
The outlets in the kitchen shorted out. He ran extension cords from other sockets.
The tub filled with mysterious black water. He hired a plumber. He used the sink.
If it rained hard he knew the bed would be wet and covered in grit when he got home from work.
The walls had plumes of carbon monoxide from the gas heater.
He told Con Ed to turn off the gas.
Once he had an electrician in to rewire stuff. They unscrewed and old bulb and a black river of slime poured out. The electrician said "You know what that is? Those are cockroach eggs"
The mailboxes got ripped out - repaired and ripped out again.
His kitchen window casement rotted away leaving gaps between the glass and the wall.
His neighbors paid to have things fixed but some couldn't afford it or didn't know how.

You are supposed to complain - of course you complain but that didn't mean you get help.
Mostly he held things together with duct tape and plastic.

2014 JANUARY: Winter was cold enough to freeze the pipes in his apartment and they burst, flooding the tenants downstairs. The LLC sent workers to board up his window and turn off his water. They refused to get him a new window and threatened to evict him for causing a flood.

2015 SPRING:
A camera appears in the hall right above his apartment door.
There is only one other tenant on his floor.
Whenever a tenant moved out - the apartment stayed vacant.
Some of his neighbors got phone calls offering buyouts.

2016 JUNE: Eviction papers are served claiming he doesn't live in his apartment.
He has to appear in court to prove he lives in his unlivable home.
He is terrified but determined to fight back.
He retains a tenant lawyer who says the case could take several years.

"These people don't care if you are swinging naked from a lightbulb - they just want to wear you out - and get you out." "I know their lawyers - real creeps, they'll churn this case as long as they can…" etc etc

Months crawl by - the court dates get postponed - nothing is resolved.
He continues paying rent as he had for 30 years. His rent checks are deposited.

34

2017 JUNE: The building is sold to a mega developer - Slate Property Group

From their website: slatepg.com
"Slate's vertically integrated platform enables it to maintain a streamlined decision-making process, to then quickly analyze investment opportunities, quantify risks and commit the resources necessary to immediately capitalize on every opportunity."

See for example : Rivington House Nursing Home condo conversion debacle

His eviction remains in place. The building is now managed by Mgt Property Management. Notices appear in the hall from Mgt Mgt"

Rent is to be sent to an address in N.J. His rent checks are returned. His lawyer says to keep paying by certified document. Each month his rent is returned.
He has never ever not paid his rent.

2017 JULY: Now all remaining tenants under siege.
They meet collectively with GOLES lawyers and form association to monitor construction.

Empty units will be converted into high end 35k+ rentals. Ongoing construction will start immediately. Front door and inner door locks will be changed. All tenants must report to mgt mgt office in mid-town with ID and proof of occupancy lease.

Demolition begins. The workers are careless. They punch holes in his ceiling and in his neighbors ceiling. One tenant is clobbered by a falling crowbar. His toilet down the hall vanishes -then is replaced unlocked and soon becomes worker's toilet.
Ceilings fall down in several apartments.
His bathtub fills with rubble.
Fiber filled dust clouds the air and covers everything.
Every violation documented and 311 called.

His lawyer and GOLES lawyers, Urban Justice lawyers all fight to maintain legal rights of tenants.
Every day begins with a battle. Tenants share nightmares of workers coming into their apartments

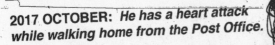

2017 OCTOBER: *He has a heart attack while walking home from the Post Office.*

Ambulance takes him to hospital where he gets a stent put in.

Doctors ask "Risk Questions"

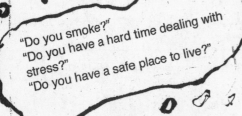

"Do you smoke?"
"Do you have a hard time dealing with stress?"
"Do you have a safe place to live?"

He gets his meds from Bellevue clinic and continues to fight.

And fight and fight ..
Until one day he can't go on.

He can't go up the six flights of stairs and unzip the plastic taped outside his door and sit in the dark surrounded by his "things" - his beautiful library - books and music and art. covered in dust and rubble. He is very tired.

He decides to walk away with whatever days he has left.
Since there is no place to put his belongings he leaves everything behind.
Leaves it to "them" to put down in the street.

Looking back, sometimes he thought somehow it was all his fault.
Maybe he took a wrong turn somewhere.
Or maybe his part of the city, his home - had already walked away.

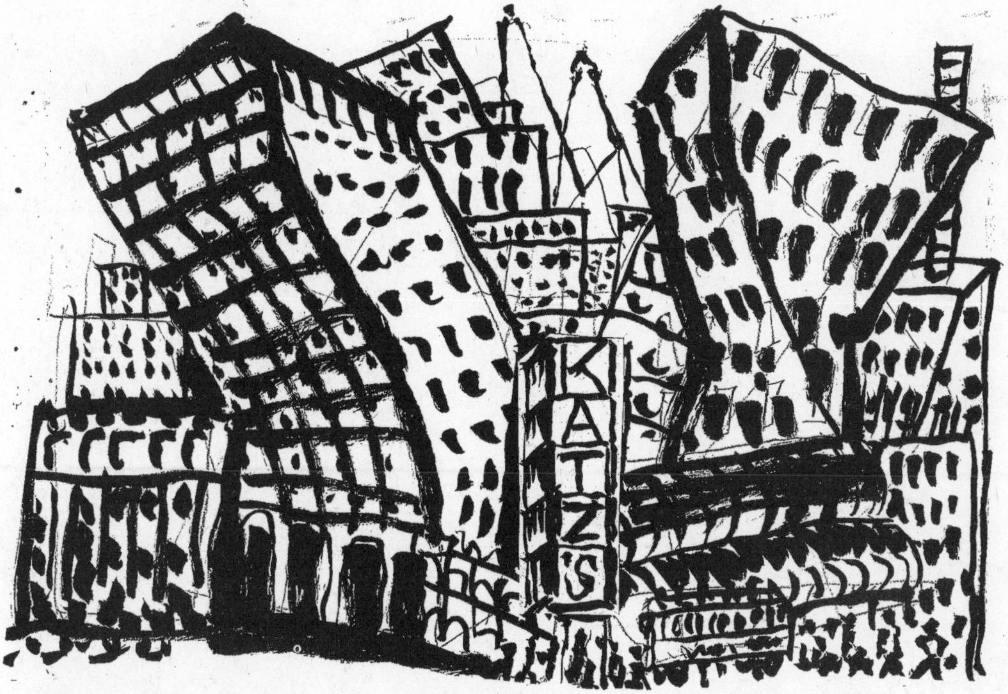
KATZ'S

Between 2013 and 2015 alone - 450,000 eviction notices were filed in NYC (ny.curbed.com)

Rent Stabilization in NYC:
Rent Stabilization, which applies in buildings built before 1974 that have six or more units, as well as in those that receive certain tax breaks, means that your rent can be increased only by the percentage set each year by the city's Rent Guidelines Board. This year, it's 1.25 percent for one-year leases and 2 percent for two years.

When someone moves out of a rent-stabilized apartment, the landlord can raise the rent by up to 20 percent, plus a portion of the cost of any improvements made — one-fortieth or one-sixtieth, depending on the size of the building.

To breach the rent stabilized threshold of $2733.75 * and thus deregulate a stabilized apartment, mega-landlords tend to follow the same playbook: After buying a building they will try to get tenants in rent regulated apartments to leave, often offering buyouts or harassing them with poor services or eviction suits. Once an apartment is empty they can tack on allowed vacancy increases and perform renovations enabling them to raise the rent even higher.

* https://www1.nyc.gov/site/rentguidelinesboard/resources/rent-control.page

If you live in LES and are served eviction papers:
Contact GOLES Good Old Lower East Side
https://goles.org/
And Urban Justice Center
https://www.urbanjustice.org/

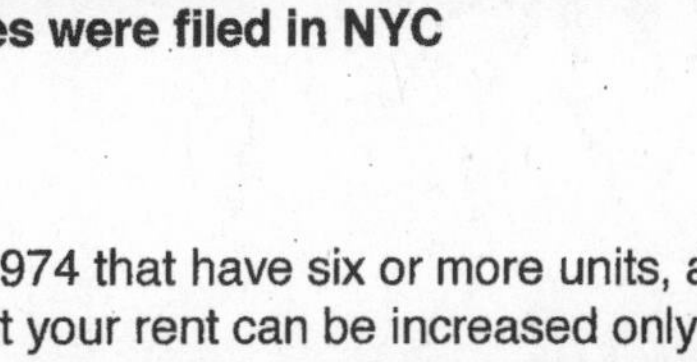
R.I.P.
Ray Johnson
1928-1995

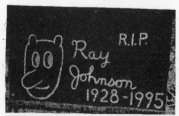

Outside the door on Ludlow, mural for Ray Johnson by Ed Higgins, his pal. Mural is gone now - Ed's still there - one of the tenants who is still left.

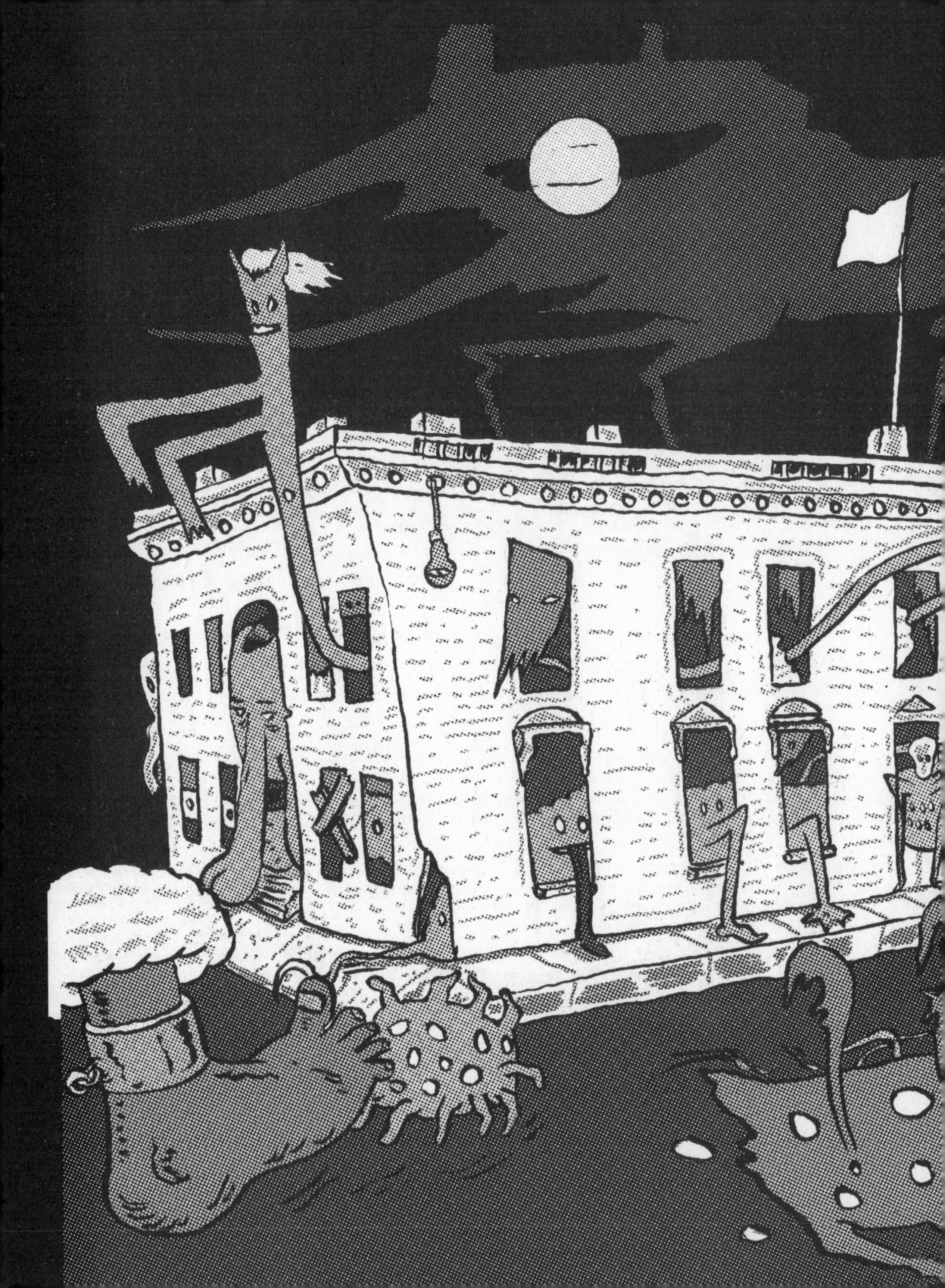

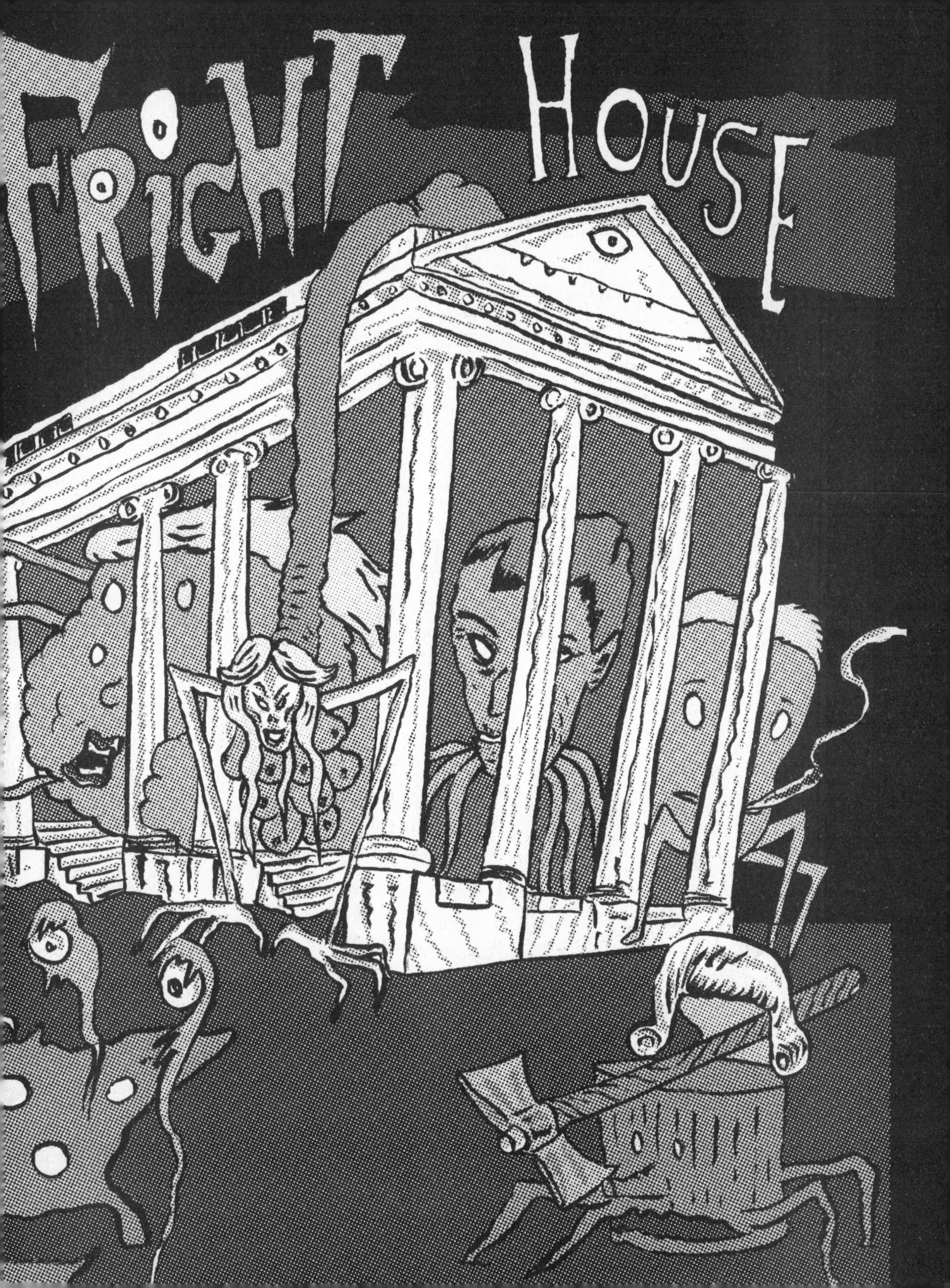
FRIGHT HOUSE

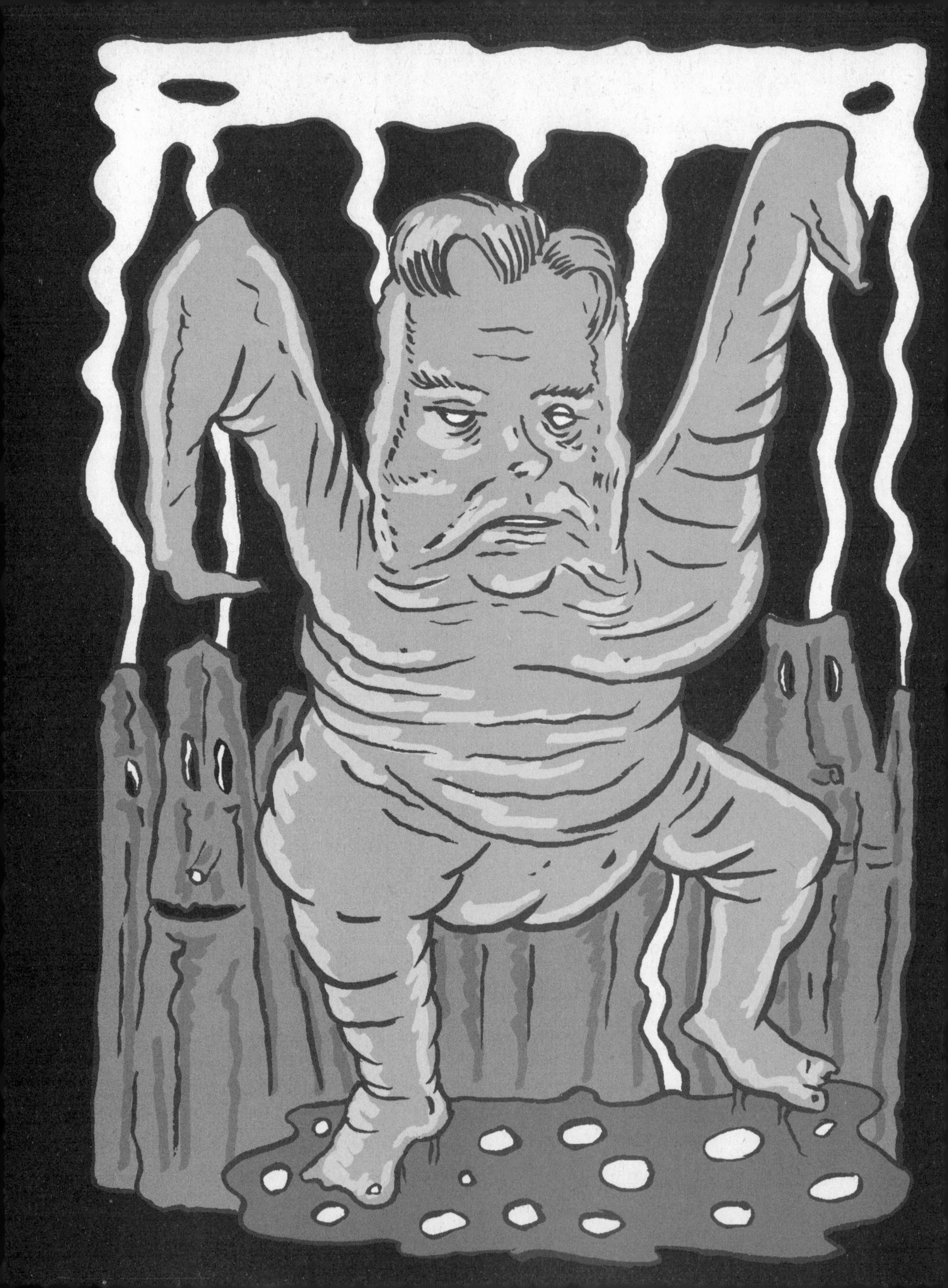

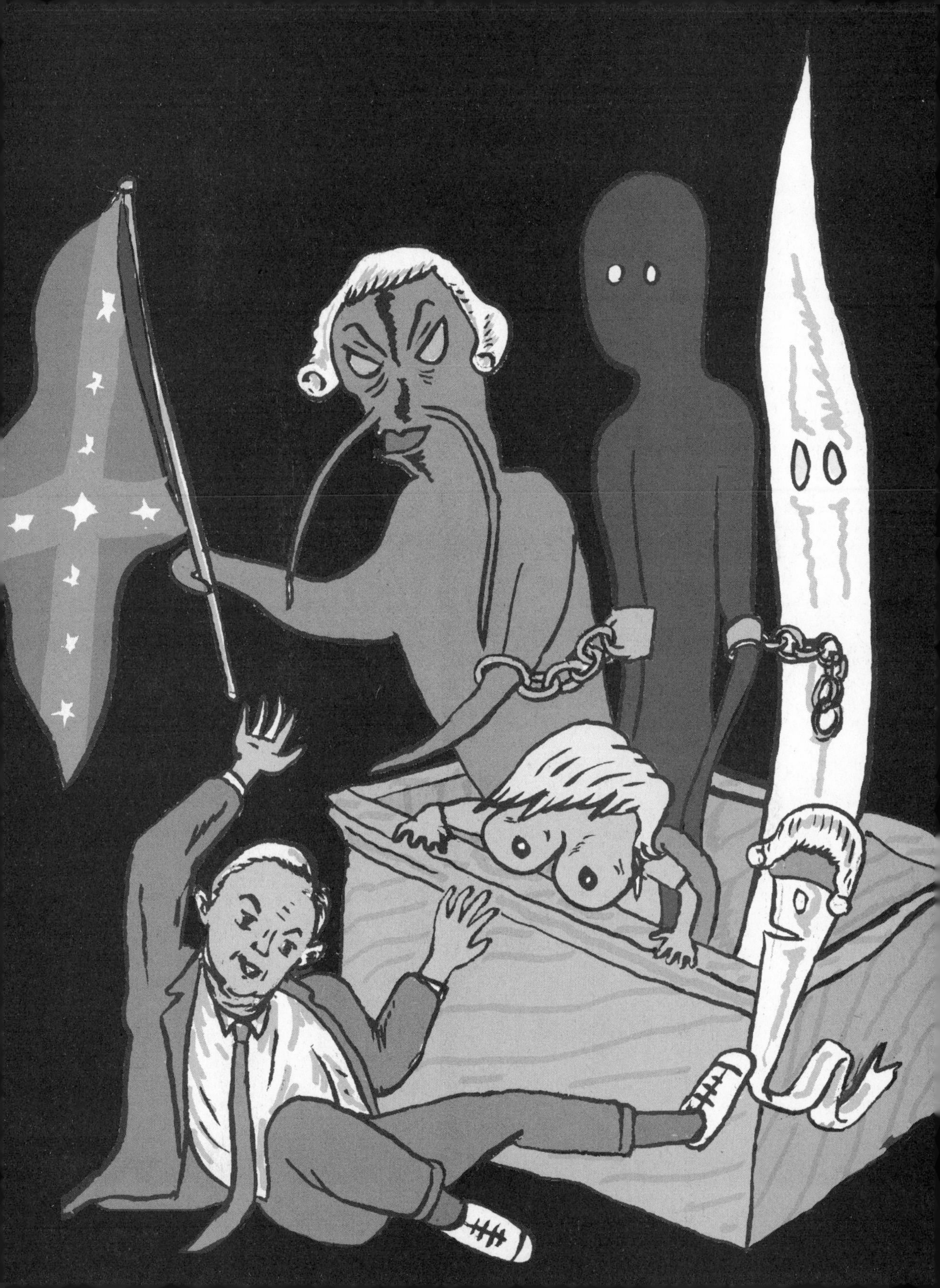

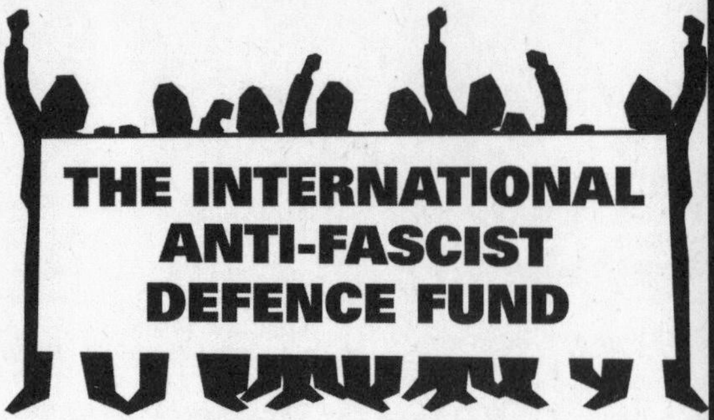
THE INTERNATIONAL
ANTI-FASCIST
DEFENCE FUND

Defending & Supporting Antifa Since 2015

SOLIDARITY IS OUR WEAPON!

Donate today!

The International Anti-Fascist Defence Fund provides direct, immediate support to anti-fascists and anti-racists anywhere in the world, whenever they find themselves in a difficult situation as a result of their stand against hate.

Whether it's replacing damaged or stolen property, paying medical bills, helping them find a safe place to stay, funding legal defence, helping their families, or doing antifa prisoner support, the Fund seeks to alleviate harm that results from doing the right thing.

In its first year alone, the International Anti-Fascist Defence Fund donated thousands of dollars to more than three dozen anti-fascists and anti-racists in ten countries.

Anyone can make a proposal to support an anti-fascist/anti-racist by emailing us at:

antifaintl@gmail.com

We depend on donations to do our work and can accept monthly recurring donations or one-time donations via Patreon, PayPal or credit card. Any group or individual that donates more than $20US/€20/£15 will be invited to help make decisions on proposals the Fund receives.

To donate:

https://intlantifadefence.wordpress.com/donate/

The International Anti-Fascist Defence Fund is a way to show real solidarity with anti-fascists and anti-racists worldwide when they need our support the most!

Find out more:

intlantifadefence.wordpress.com

FIGHTING HATE IS NOT A CRIME!
ANTI-FASCISM = SELF-DEFENCE!

sane energy project

BUILD Community-led Renewable

STOP Fracking Infrastructure

What we do: Win campaigns
Share our skills • Build community
Work with joy

Come to our bi-monthly meetings in the East Village.
contact@saneenergyproject.org

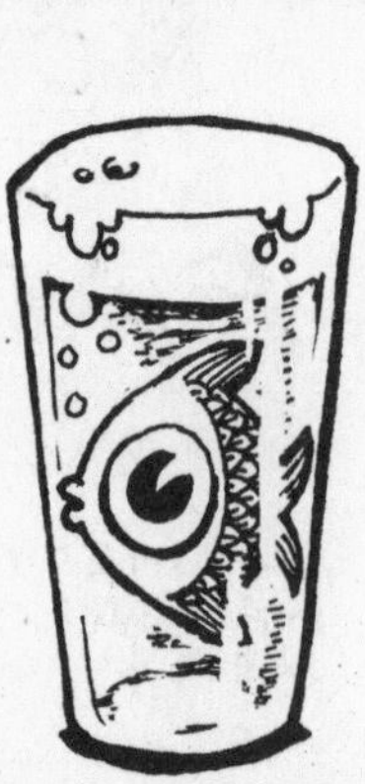

FIVE: 30 PM - FOUR AM

120 Orchard

MAX FISH

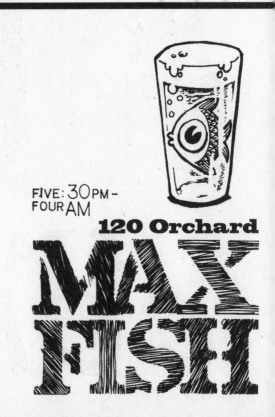

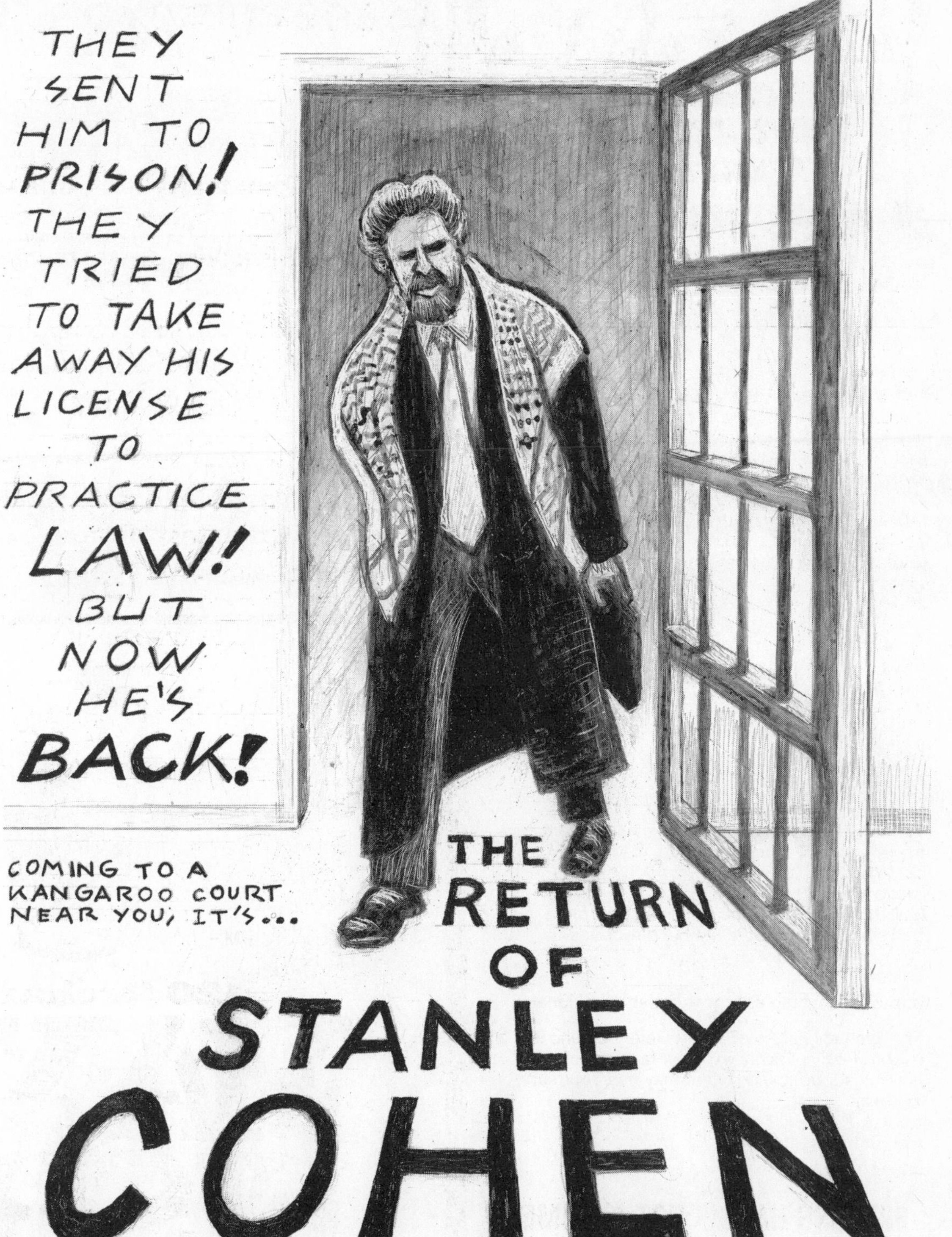
THEY SENT HIM TO PRISON! THEY TRIED TO TAKE AWAY HIS LICENSE TO PRACTICE LAW! BUT NOW HE'S BACK!
COMING TO A KANGAROO COURT NEAR YOU, IT'S...
THE RETURN OF STANLEY COHEN

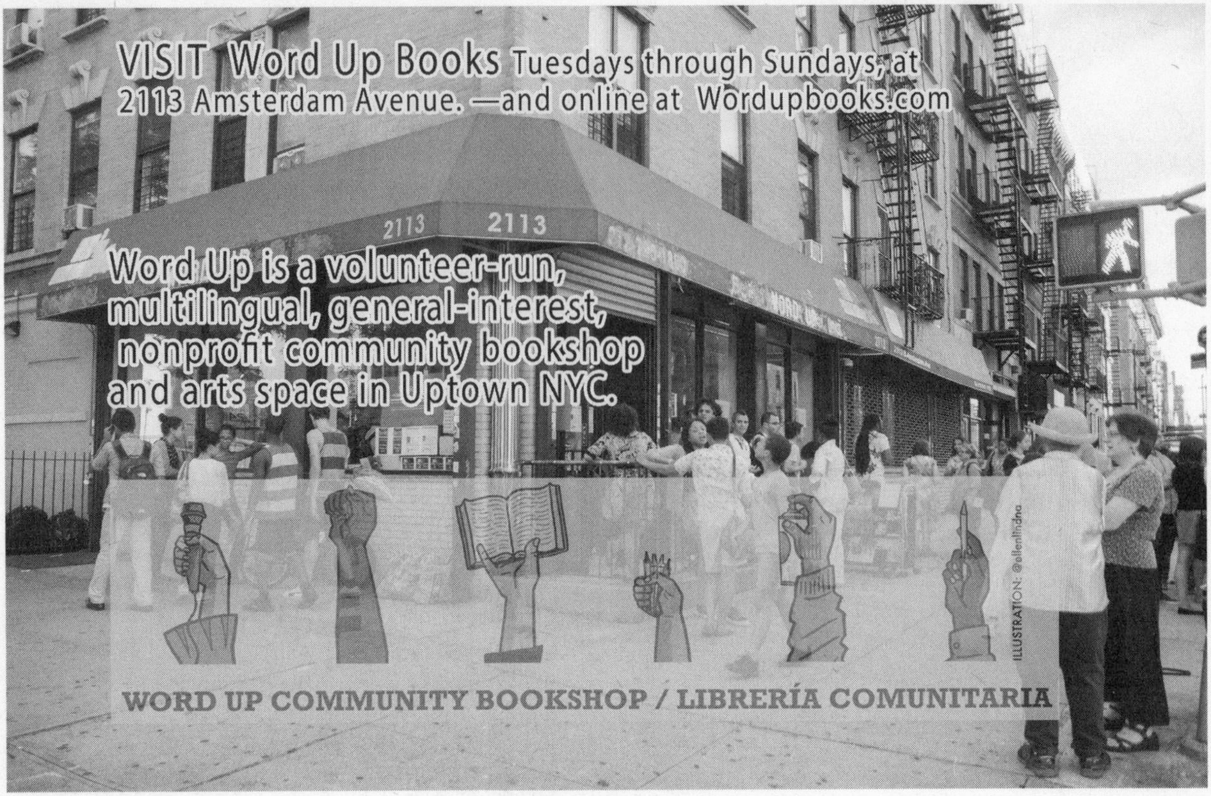
VISIT Word Up Books Tuesdays through Sundays, at
2113 Amsterdam Avenue. —and online at Wordupbooks.com
2113
2113
Word Up is a volunteer-run,
multilingual, general-interest,
nonprofit community bookshop
and arts space in Uptown NYC.
WORD UP COMMUNITY BOOKSHOP / LIBRERÍA COMUNITARIA

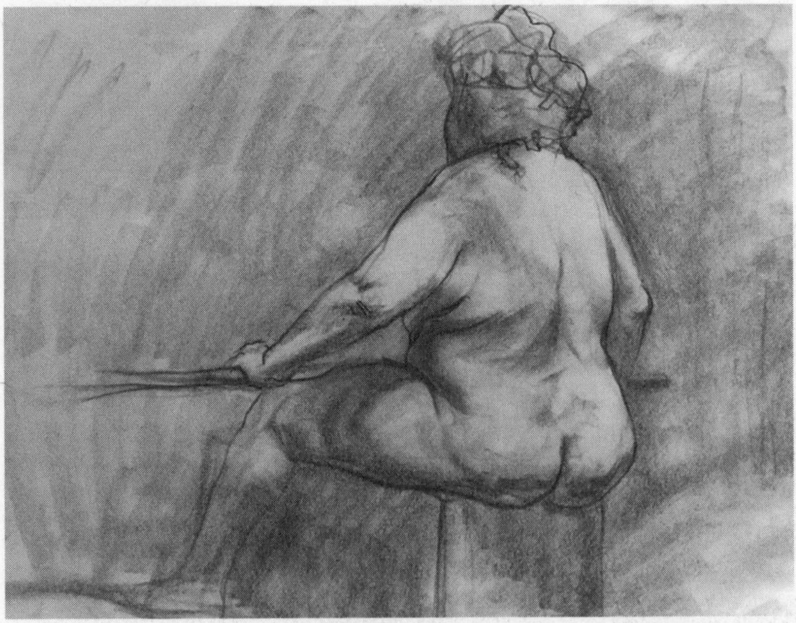

boatfire.tumblr.com

PREDATORY CAPITALISM IS KILLING US

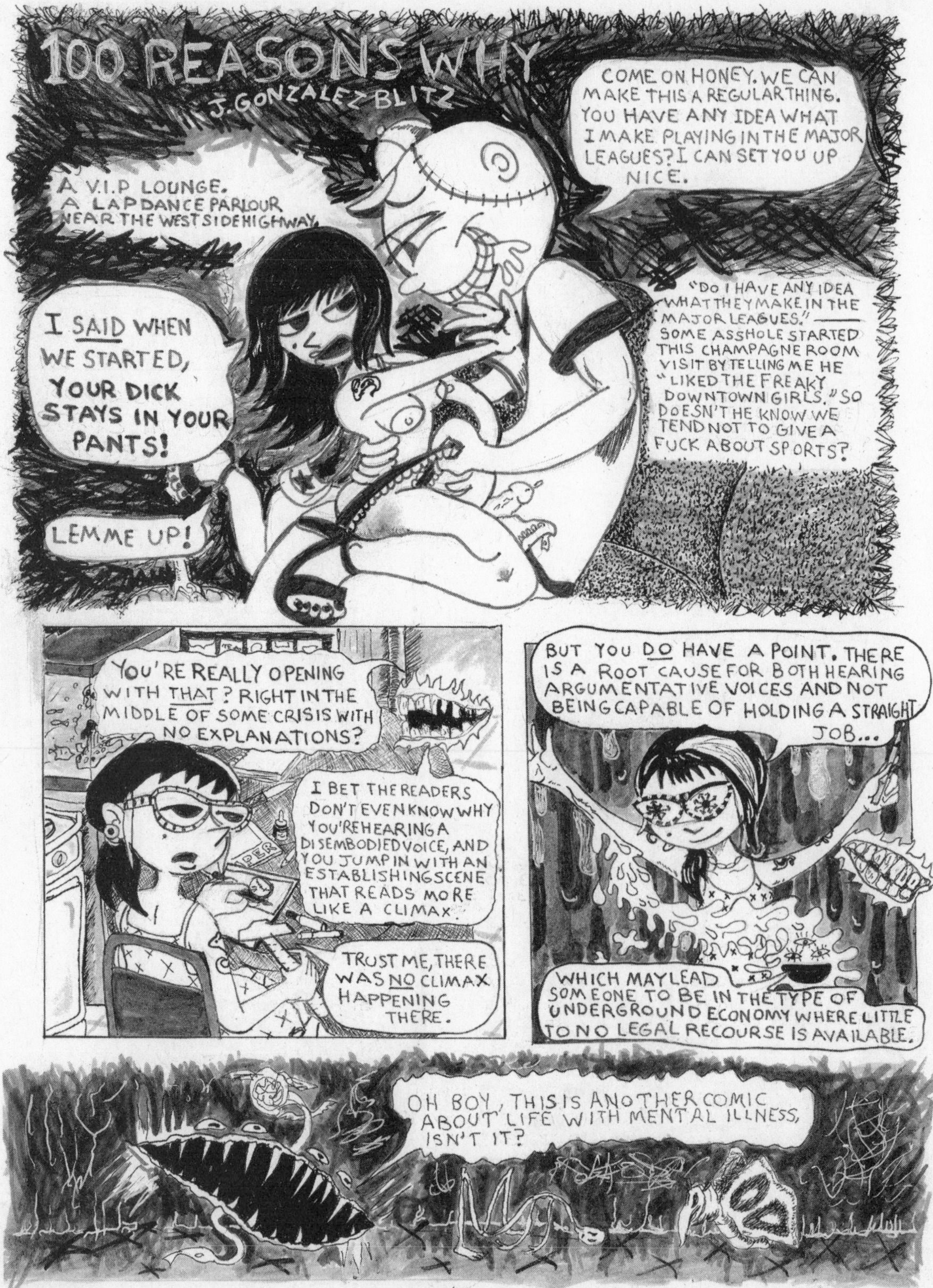
100 REASONS WHY
J. GONZALEZ BLITZ
A V.I.P LOUNGE. A LAPDANCE PARLOUR NEAR THE WEST SIDE HIGHWAY.
COME ON HONEY. WE CAN MAKE THIS A REGULAR THING. YOU HAVE ANY IDEA WHAT I MAKE PLAYING IN THE MAJOR LEAGUES? I CAN SET YOU UP NICE.
I SAID WHEN WE STARTED, YOUR DICK STAYS IN YOUR PANTS!
"DO I HAVE ANY IDEA WHAT THEY MAKE IN THE MAJOR LEAGUES." — SOME ASSHOLE STARTED THIS CHAMPAGNE ROOM VISIT BY TELLING ME HE "LIKED THE FREAKY DOWNTOWN GIRLS." SO DOESN'T HE KNOW WE TEND NOT TO GIVE A FUCK ABOUT SPORTS?
LEMME UP!
YOU'RE REALLY OPENING WITH THAT? RIGHT IN THE MIDDLE OF SOME CRISIS WITH NO EXPLANATIONS?
I BET THE READERS DON'T EVEN KNOW WHY YOU'RE HEARING A DISEMBODIED VOICE, AND YOU JUMP IN WITH AN ESTABLISHING SCENE THAT READS MORE LIKE A CLIMAX.
TRUST ME, THERE WAS NO CLIMAX HAPPENING THERE.
BUT YOU DO HAVE A POINT. THERE IS A ROOT CAUSE FOR BOTH HEARING ARGUMENTATIVE VOICES AND NOT BEING CAPABLE OF HOLDING A STRAIGHT JOB...
WHICH MAY LEAD SOMEONE TO BE IN THE TYPE OF UNDERGROUND ECONOMY WHERE LITTLE TO NO LEGAL RECOURSE IS AVAILABLE.
OH BOY, THIS IS ANOTHER COMIC ABOUT LIFE WITH MENTAL ILLNESS, ISN'T IT?

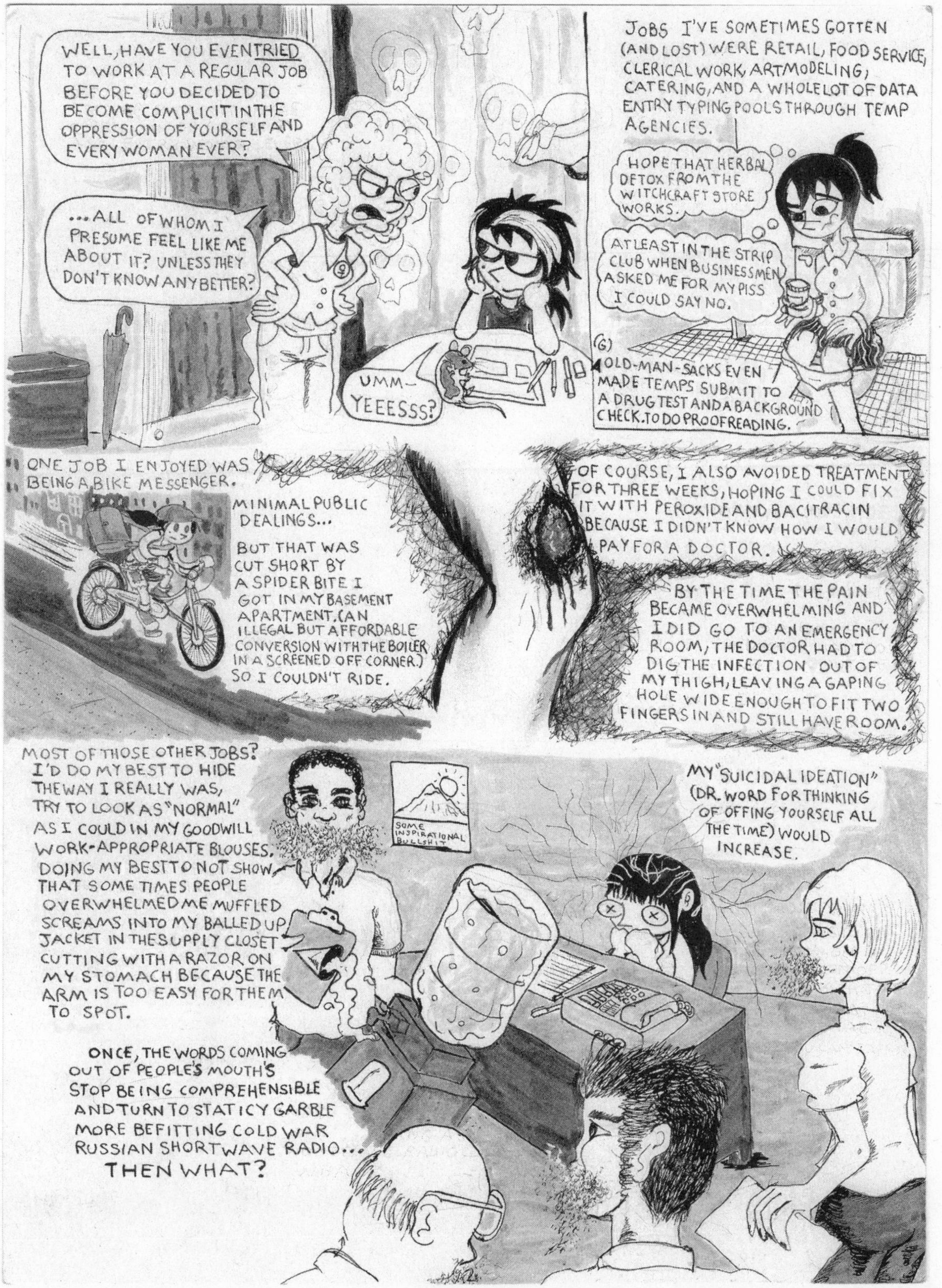
WELL, HAVE YOU EVEN TRIED TO WORK AT A REGULAR JOB BEFORE YOU DECIDED TO BECOME COMPLICIT IN THE OPPRESSION OF YOURSELF AND EVERY WOMAN EVER?
...ALL OF WHOM I PRESUME FEEL LIKE ME ABOUT IT? UNLESS THEY DON'T KNOW ANY BETTER?
UMM- YEEESSS?
JOBS I'VE SOMETIMES GOTTEN (AND LOST) WERE RETAIL, FOOD SERVICE, CLERICAL WORK, ART MODELING, CATERING, AND A WHOLE LOT OF DATA ENTRY TYPING POOLS THROUGH TEMP AGENCIES.
HOPE THAT HERBAL DETOX FROM THE WITCHCRAFT STORE WORKS.
AT LEAST IN THE STRIP CLUB WHEN BUSINESSMEN ASKED ME FOR MY PISS I COULD SAY NO.
(G) OLD-MAN-SACKS EVEN MADE TEMPS SUBMIT TO A DRUG TEST AND A BACKGROUND CHECK. TO DO PROOFREADING.
ONE JOB I ENJOYED WAS BEING A BIKE MESSENGER.
MINIMAL PUBLIC DEALINGS...
BUT THAT WAS CUT SHORT BY A SPIDER BITE I GOT IN MY BASEMENT APARTMENT. (AN ILLEGAL BUT AFFORDABLE CONVERSION WITH THE BOILER IN A SCREENED OFF CORNER.) SO I COULDN'T RIDE.
OF COURSE, I ALSO AVOIDED TREATMENT FOR THREE WEEKS, HOPING I COULD FIX IT WITH PEROXIDE AND BACITRACIN BECAUSE I DIDN'T KNOW HOW I WOULD PAY FOR A DOCTOR.
BY THE TIME THE PAIN BECAME OVERWHELMING AND I DID GO TO AN EMERGENCY ROOM, THE DOCTOR HAD TO DIG THE INFECTION OUT OF MY THIGH, LEAVING A GAPING HOLE WIDE ENOUGH TO FIT TWO FINGERS IN AND STILL HAVE ROOM.
MOST OF THOSE OTHER JOBS? I'D DO MY BEST TO HIDE THE WAY I REALLY WAS, TRY TO LOOK AS "NORMAL" AS I COULD IN MY GOODWILL WORK-APPROPRIATE BLOUSES, DOING MY BEST TO NOT SHOW THAT SOME TIMES PEOPLE OVERWHELMED ME MUFFLED SCREAMS INTO MY BALLED UP JACKET IN THE SUPPLY CLOSET CUTTING WITH A RAZOR ON MY STOMACH BECAUSE THE ARM IS TOO EASY FOR THEM TO SPOT.
SOME INSPIRATIONAL BULLSHIT
MY "SUICIDAL IDEATION" (DR. WORD FOR THINKING OF OFFING YOURSELF ALL THE TIME) WOULD INCREASE.
ONCE, THE WORDS COMING OUT OF PEOPLE'S MOUTH'S STOP BEING COMPREHENSIBLE AND TURN TO STATICY GARBLE MORE BEFITTING COLD WAR RUSSIAN SHORTWAVE RADIO... THEN WHAT?

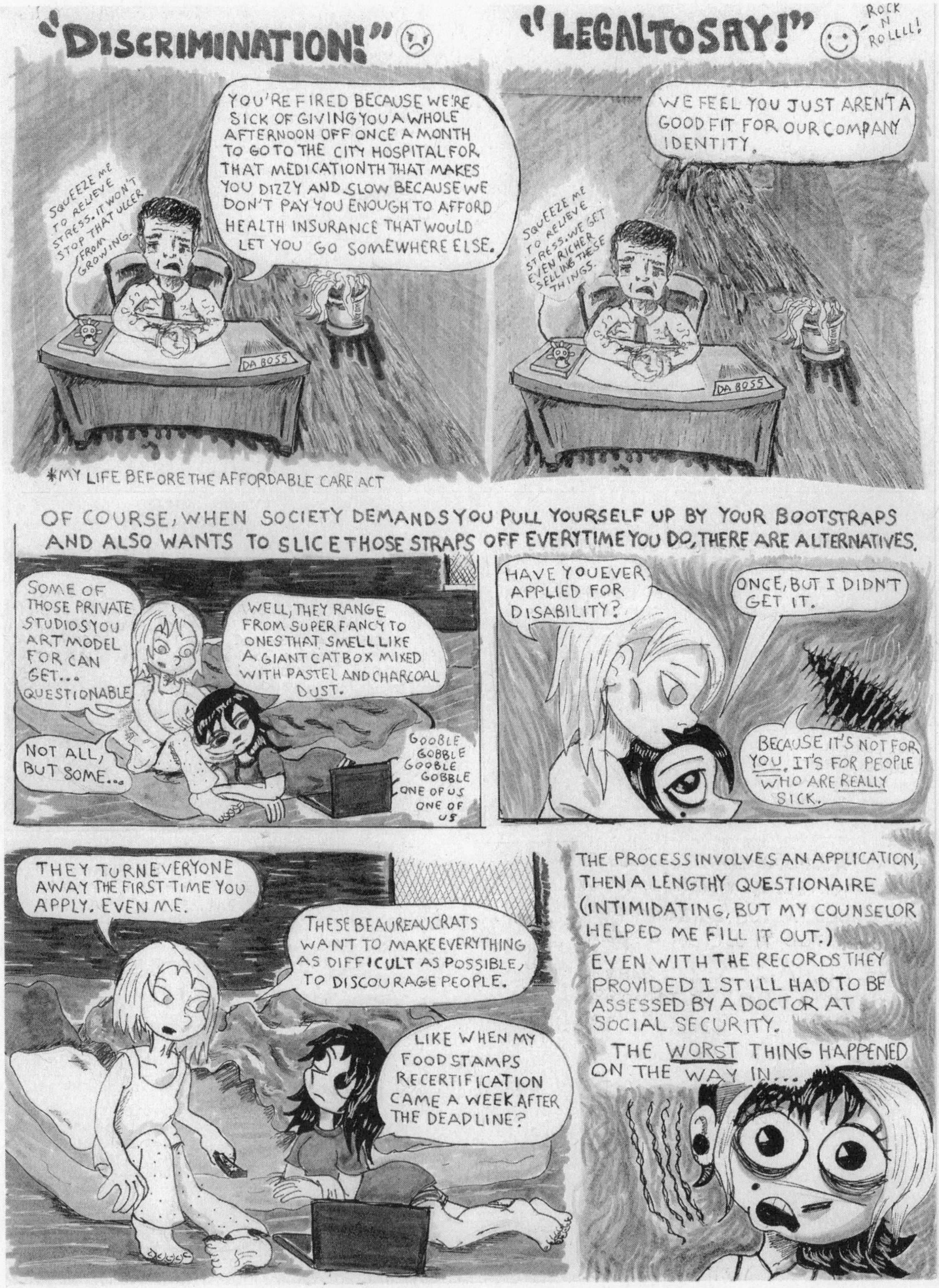
"DISCRIMINATION!"
YOU'RE FIRED BECAUSE WE'RE SICK OF GIVING YOU A WHOLE AFTERNOON OFF ONCE A MONTH TO GO TO THE CITY HOSPITAL FOR THAT MEDICATIONTH THAT MAKES YOU DIZZY AND SLOW BECAUSE WE DON'T PAY YOU ENOUGH TO AFFORD HEALTH INSURANCE THAT WOULD LET YOU GO SOMEWHERE ELSE.
SQUEEZE ME TO RELIEVE STRESS. IT WON'T STOP THAT ULCER FROM GROWING.
DA BOSS
"LEGALTOSAY!"
ROCK N ROLLLL!
WE FEEL YOU JUST AREN'T A GOOD FIT FOR OUR COMPANY IDENTITY.
SQUEEZE ME TO RELIEVE STRESS. WE GET EVEN RICHER SELLING THESE THINGS.
DA BOSS
*MY LIFE BEFORE THE AFFORDABLE CARE ACT
OF COURSE, WHEN SOCIETY DEMANDS YOU PULL YOURSELF UP BY YOUR BOOTSTRAPS AND ALSO WANTS TO SLICE THOSE STRAPS OFF EVERYTIME YOU DO, THERE ARE ALTERNATIVES.
SOME OF THOSE PRIVATE STUDIOS YOU ART MODEL FOR CAN GET... QUESTIONABLE.
WELL, THEY RANGE FROM SUPER FANCY TO ONES THAT SMELL LIKE A GIANT CATBOX MIXED WITH PASTEL AND CHARCOAL DUST.
NOT ALL, BUT SOME...
GOOBLE GOBBLE GOOBLE GOBBLE ONE OF US ONE OF US
HAVE YOU EVER APPLIED FOR DISABILITY?
ONCE, BUT I DIDN'T GET IT.
BECAUSE IT'S NOT FOR YOU. IT'S FOR PEOPLE WHO ARE REALLY SICK.
THEY TURN EVERYONE AWAY THE FIRST TIME YOU APPLY. EVEN ME.
THESE BEAUREAUCRATS WANT TO MAKE EVERYTHING AS DIFFICULT AS POSSIBLE, TO DISCOURAGE PEOPLE.
LIKE WHEN MY FOOD STAMPS RECERTIFICATION CAME A WEEK AFTER THE DEADLINE?
THE PROCESS INVOLVES AN APPLICATION, THEN A LENGTHY QUESTIONAIRE (INTIMIDATING, BUT MY COUNSELOR HELPED ME FILL IT OUT.) EVEN WITH THE RECORDS THEY PROVIDED I STILL HAD TO BE ASSESSED BY A DOCTOR AT SOCIAL SECURITY.
THE WORST THING HAPPENED ON THE WAY IN...

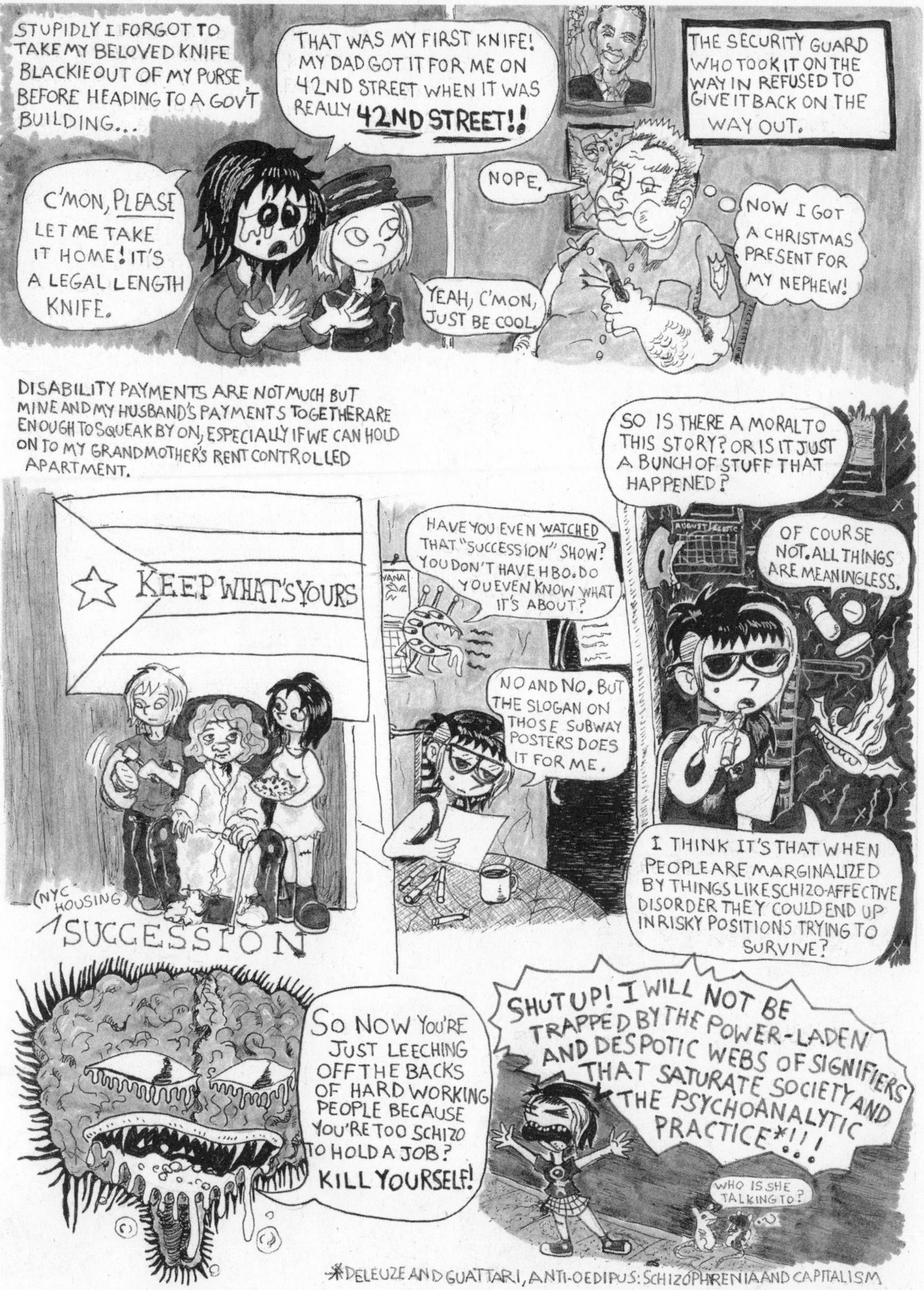

STUPIDLY I FORGOT TO TAKE MY BELOVED KNIFE BLACKIE OUT OF MY PURSE BEFORE HEADING TO A GOV'T BUILDING...
THAT WAS MY FIRST KNIFE! MY DAD GOT IT FOR ME ON 42ND STREET WHEN IT WAS REALLY 42ND STREET!!
THE SECURITY GUARD WHO TOOK IT ON THE WAY IN REFUSED TO GIVE IT BACK ON THE WAY OUT.
C'MON, PLEASE LET ME TAKE IT HOME! IT'S A LEGAL LENGTH KNIFE.
NOPE.
NOW I GOT A CHRISTMAS PRESENT FOR MY NEPHEW!
YEAH, C'MON, JUST BE COOL.
DISABILITY PAYMENTS ARE NOT MUCH BUT MINE AND MY HUSBAND'S PAYMENTS TOGETHER ARE ENOUGH TO SQUEAK BY ON, ESPECIALLY IF WE CAN HOLD ON TO MY GRANDMOTHER'S RENT CONTROLLED APARTMENT.
KEEP WHAT'S YOURS
(NYC HOUSING)
SUCCESSION
HAVE YOU EVEN WATCHED THAT "SUCCESSION" SHOW? YOU DON'T HAVE HBO. DO YOU EVEN KNOW WHAT IT'S ABOUT?
NO AND NO. BUT THE SLOGAN ON THOSE SUBWAY POSTERS DOES IT FOR ME.
SO IS THERE A MORAL TO THIS STORY? OR IS IT JUST A BUNCH OF STUFF THAT HAPPENED?
OF COURSE NOT. ALL THINGS ARE MEANINGLESS.
I THINK IT'S THAT WHEN PEOPLE ARE MARGINALIZED BY THINGS LIKE SCHIZO-AFFECTIVE DISORDER THEY COULD END UP IN RISKY POSITIONS TRYING TO SURVIVE?
SO NOW YOU'RE JUST LEECHING OFF THE BACKS OF HARD WORKING PEOPLE BECAUSE YOU'RE TOO SCHIZO TO HOLD A JOB? KILL YOURSELF!
SHUT UP! I WILL NOT BE TRAPPED BY THE POWER-LADEN AND DESPOTIC WEBS OF SIGNIFIERS THAT SATURATE SOCIETY AND THE PSYCHOANALYTIC PRACTICE*!!!
WHO IS SHE TALKING TO?

*DELEUZE AND GUATTARI, ANTI-OEDIPUS: SCHIZOPHRENIA AND CAPITALISM

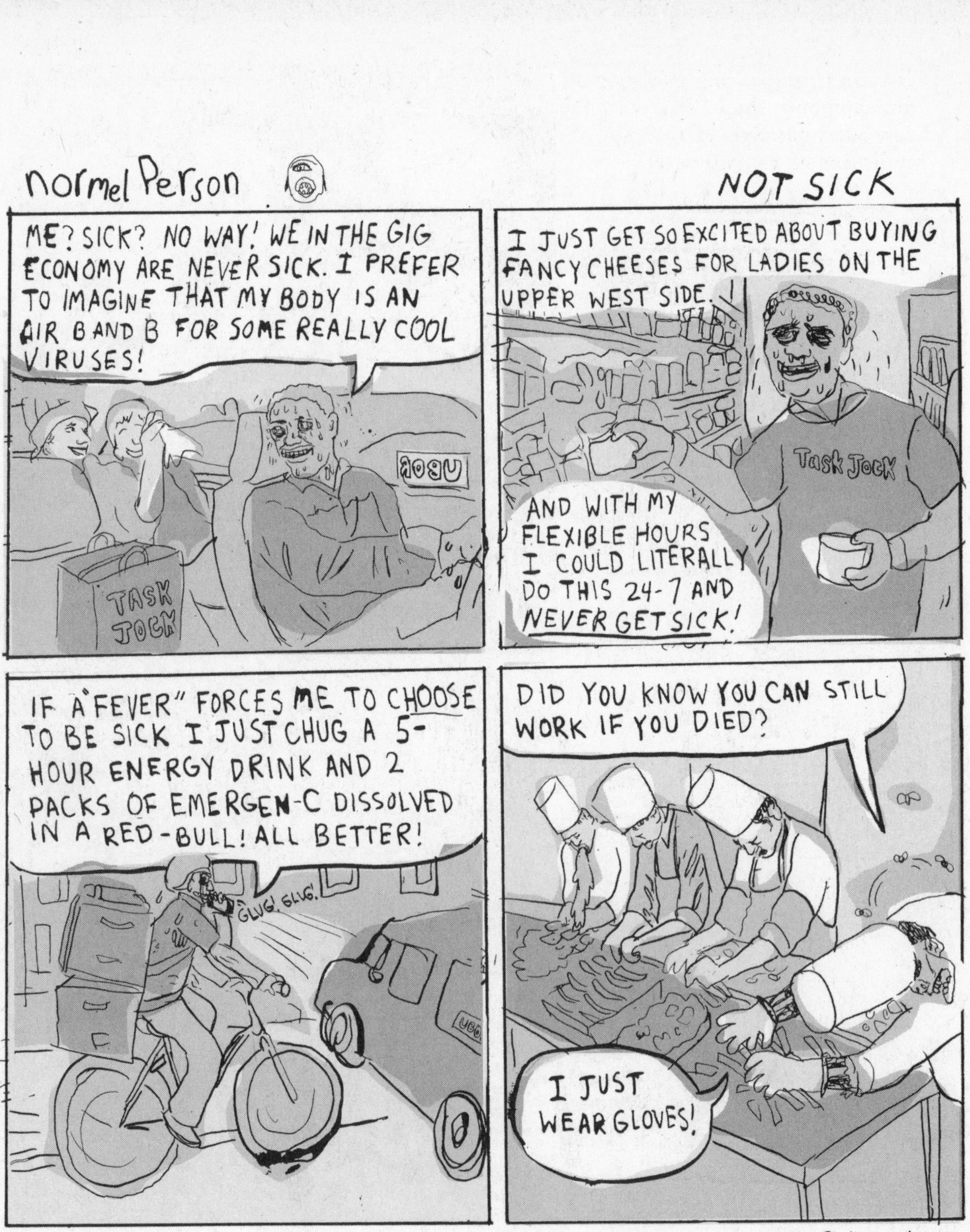
normel Person
NOT SICK
ME? SICK? NO WAY! WE IN THE GIG ECONOMY ARE NEVER SICK. I PREFER TO IMAGINE THAT MY BODY IS AN AIR B AND B FOR SOME REALLY COOL VIRUSES!
TASK JOCK
I JUST GET SO EXCITED ABOUT BUYING FANCY CHEESES FOR LADIES ON THE UPPER WEST SIDE.
Task Jock
AND WITH MY FLEXIBLE HOURS I COULD LITERALLY DO THIS 24-7 AND NEVER GET SICK!
IF A "FEVER" FORCES ME TO CHOOSE TO BE SICK I JUST CHUG A 5-HOUR ENERGY DRINK AND 2 PACKS OF EMERGEN-C DISSOLVED IN A RED-BULL! ALL BETTER!
GLUG! GLUG!
DID YOU KNOW YOU CAN STILL WORK IF YOU DIED?
I JUST WEAR GLOVES!
♡ Lauren R. Weinstein

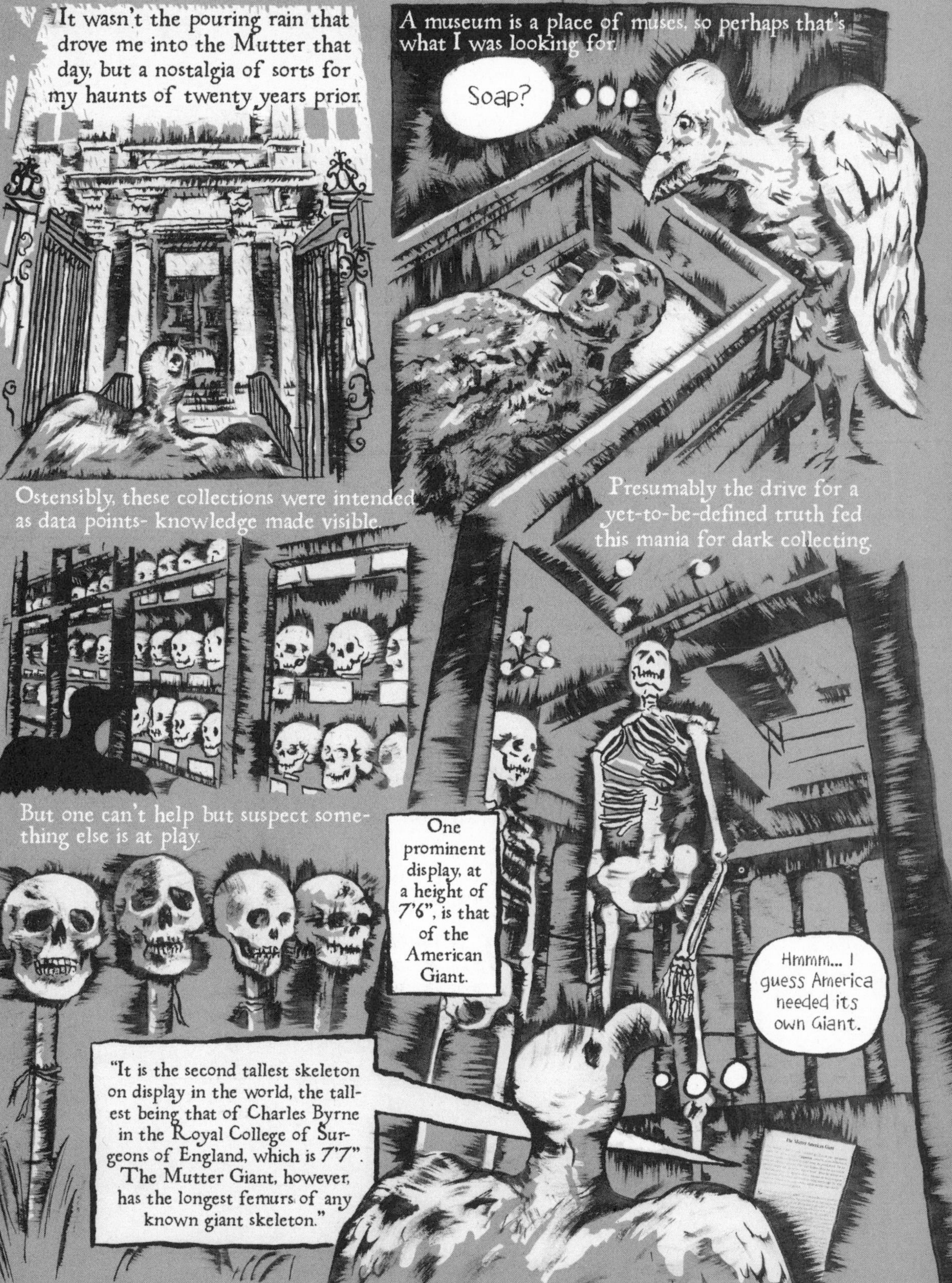
It wasn't the pouring rain that drove me into the Mutter that day, but a nostalgia of sorts for my haunts of twenty years prior.
A museum is a place of muses, so perhaps that's what I was looking for.
Soap?
Ostensibly, these collections were intended as data points- knowledge made visible.
Presumably the drive for a yet-to-be-defined truth fed this mania for dark collecting.
But one can't help but suspect something else is at play.
One prominent display, at a height of 7'6", is that of the American Giant.
Hmmm... I guess America needed its own Giant.
"It is the second tallest skeleton on display in the world, the tallest being that of Charles Byrne in the Royal College of Surgeons of England, which is 7'7". The Mutter Giant, however, has the longest femurs of any known giant skeleton."

The Giant and THE HUNTER

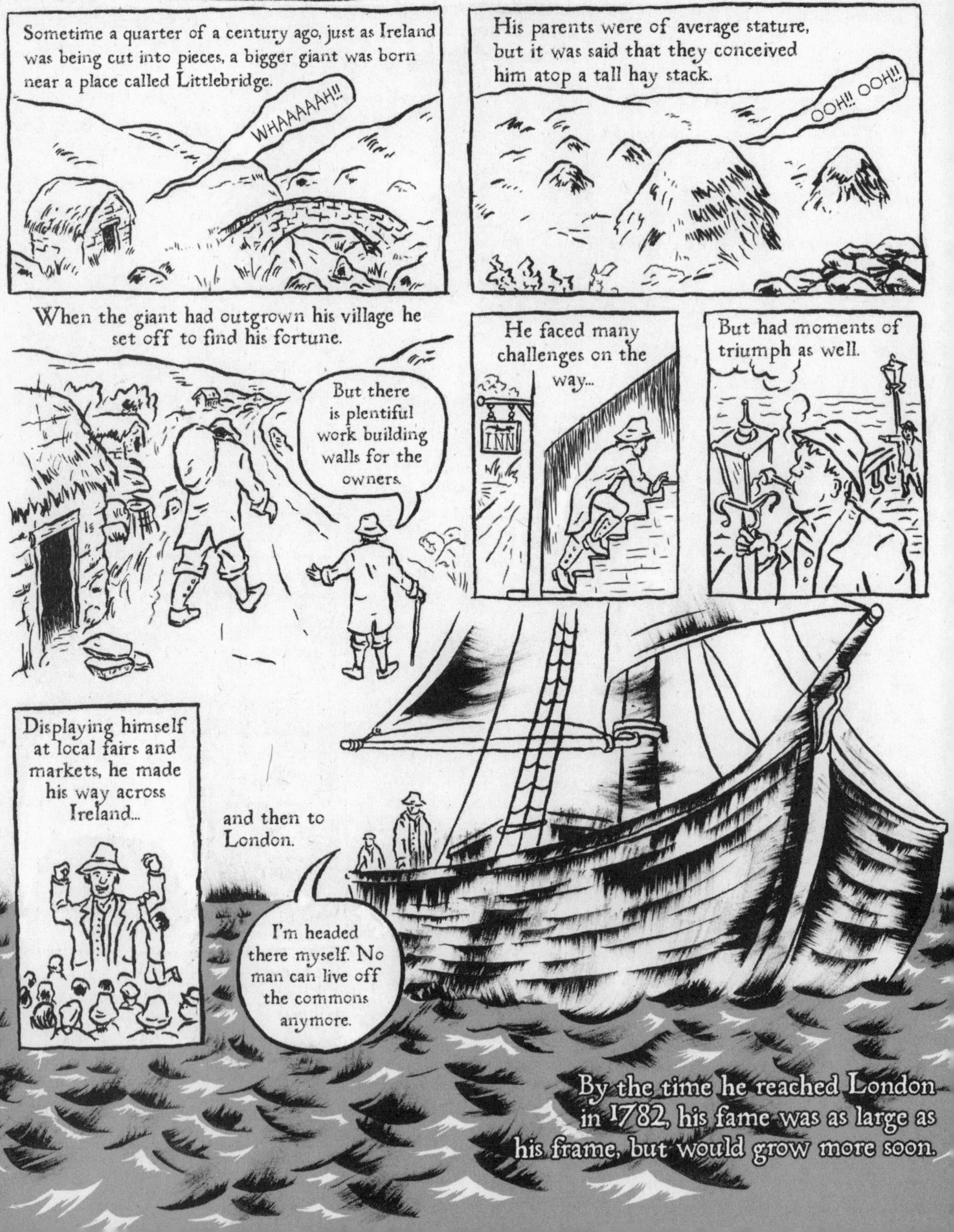
Sometime a quarter of a century ago, just as Ireland was being cut into pieces, a bigger giant was born near a place called Littlebridge.
WHAAAAAH!!
His parents were of average stature, but it was said that they conceived him atop a tall hay stack.
OOH!! OOH!!
When the giant had outgrown his village he set off to find his fortune.
But there is plentiful work building walls for the owners.
He faced many challenges on the way...
INN
But had moments of triumph as well.
Displaying himself at local fairs and markets, he made his way across Ireland...
and then to London.
I'm headed there myself. No man can live off the commons anymore.
By the time he reached London in 1782, his fame was as large as his frame, but would grow more soon.

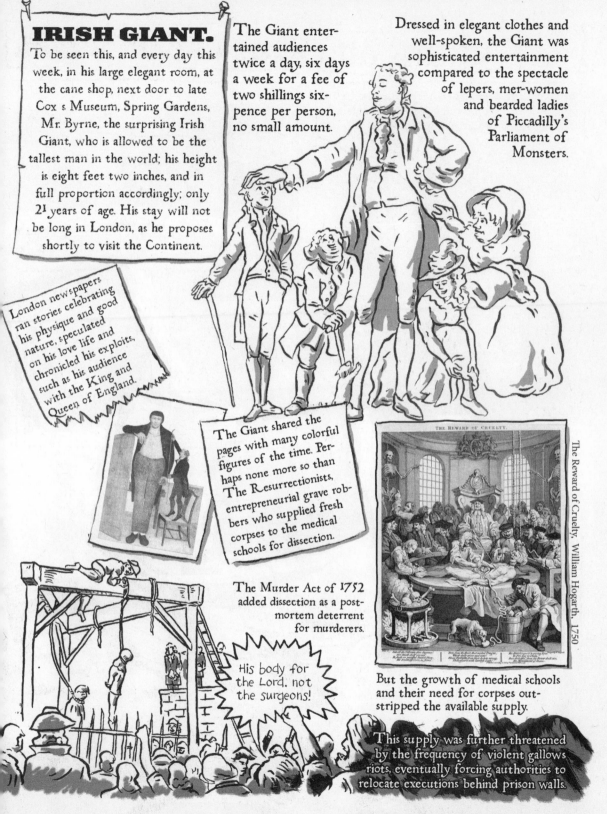

IRISH GIANT.

To be seen this, and every day this week, in his large elegant room, at the cane shop, next door to late Cox's Museum, Spring Gardens, Mr. Byrne, the surprising Irish Giant, who is allowed to be the tallest man in the world; his height is eight feet two inches, and in full proportion accordingly; only 21 years of age. His stay will not be long in London, as he proposes shortly to visit the Continent.

The Giant entertained audiences twice a day, six days a week for a fee of two shillings sixpence per person, no small amount.

Dressed in elegant clothes and well-spoken, the Giant was sophisticated entertainment compared to the spectacle of lepers, mer-women and bearded ladies of Piccadilly's Parliament of Monsters.

London newspapers ran stories celebrating his physique and good nature, speculated on his love life and chronicled his exploits, such as his audience with the King and Queen of England.

The Giant shared the pages with many colorful figures of the time. Perhaps none more so than The Resurrectionists, entrepreneurial grave robbers who supplied fresh corpses to the medical schools for dissection.

The Murder Act of 1752 added dissection as a post-mortem deterrent for murderers.

His body for the Lord. not the surgeons!

THE REWARD OF CRUELTY.

The Reward of Cruelty, William Hogarth, 1750

But the growth of medical schools and their need for corpses outstripped the available supply.

This supply was further threatened by the frequency of violent gallows riots, eventually forcing authorities to relocate executions behind prison walls.

Working with wooden shovels to dampen the noise and light-limiting lanterns, these "Corporations of Corpse-Stealers" favored the graveyards of the poor, where mass graves were common and the coffins built of flimsy materials.

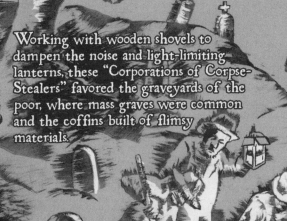

Though the wealthy were not spared. Soon security devices like the mortsafe, a protective cage, became available to those who could afford it.

Prices varied widely, but one average price quoted for a fresh body was eight guineas, compared to the one guinea a manservant to the wealthy could earn in a week.

One of the resurrectionists most reliable clients was John Hunter, who procured corpses for his older brother William's anatomy school.

Not above snatching a body or two himself, John Hunter came to excel at anatomical preparation and surgery, eventually serving as surgeon to King George III.

Hunter also amassed a huge collection of anatomical specimens, including "monstorous" births, the skeletons of murderers and physical freaks of nature.

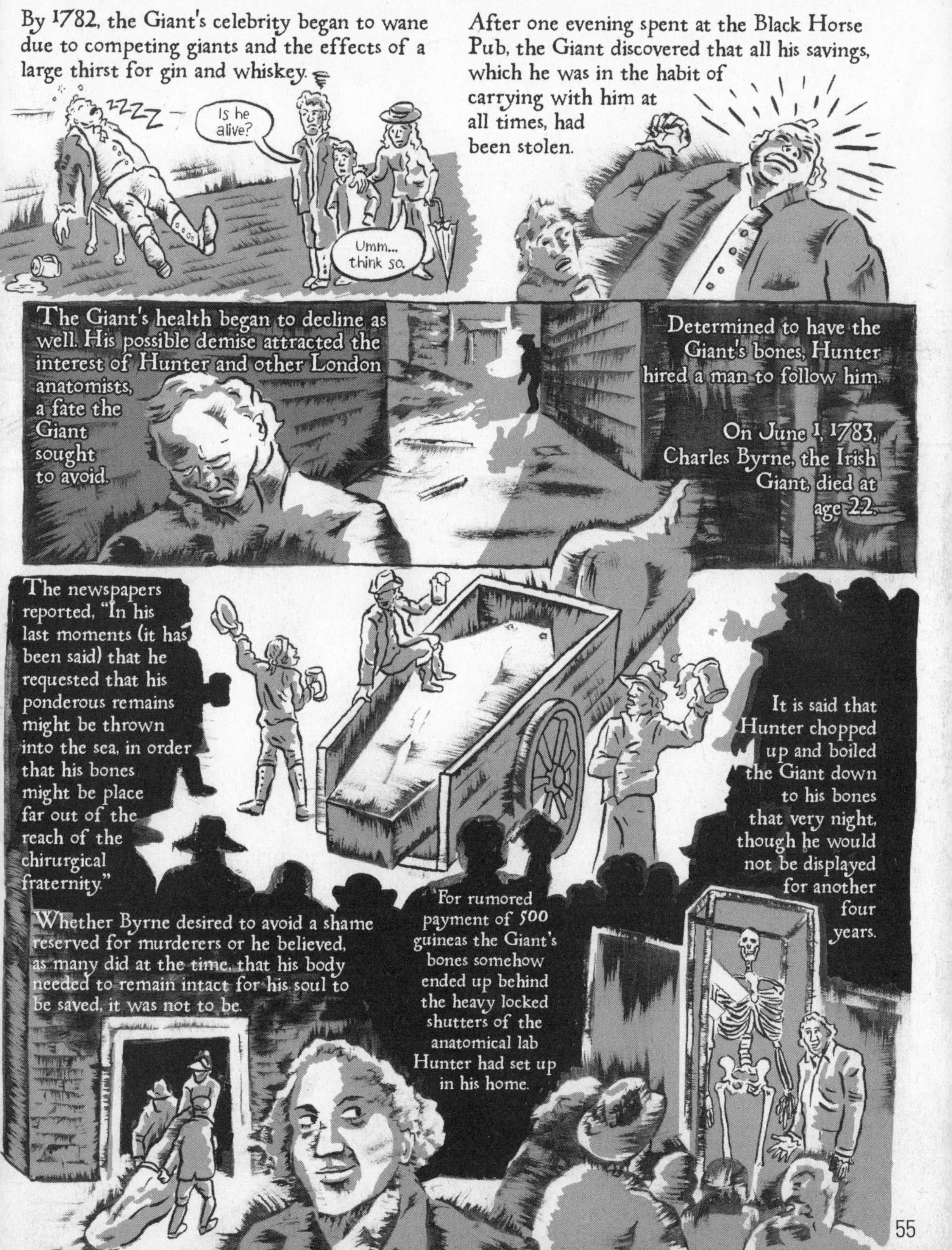
By 1782, the Giant's celebrity began to wane due to competing giants and the effects of a large thirst for gin and whiskey.
ZZZZ
Is he alive?
Umm... think so.
After one evening spent at the Black Horse Pub, the Giant discovered that all his savings, which he was in the habit of carrying with him at all times, had been stolen.
The Giant's health began to decline as well. His possible demise attracted the interest of Hunter and other London anatomists, a fate the Giant sought to avoid.
Determined to have the Giant's bones, Hunter hired a man to follow him.
On June 1, 1783, Charles Byrne, the Irish Giant, died at age 22.
The newspapers reported, "In his last moments (it has been said) that he requested that his ponderous remains might be thrown into the sea, in order that his bones might be place far out of the reach of the chirurgical fraternity."
It is said that Hunter chopped up and boiled the Giant down to his bones that very night, though he would not be displayed for another four years.
Whether Byrne desired to avoid a shame reserved for murderers or he believed, as many did at the time, that his body needed to remain intact for his soul to be saved, it was not to be.
For rumored payment of 500 guineas the Giant's bones somehow ended up behind the heavy locked shutters of the anatomical lab Hunter had set up in his home.

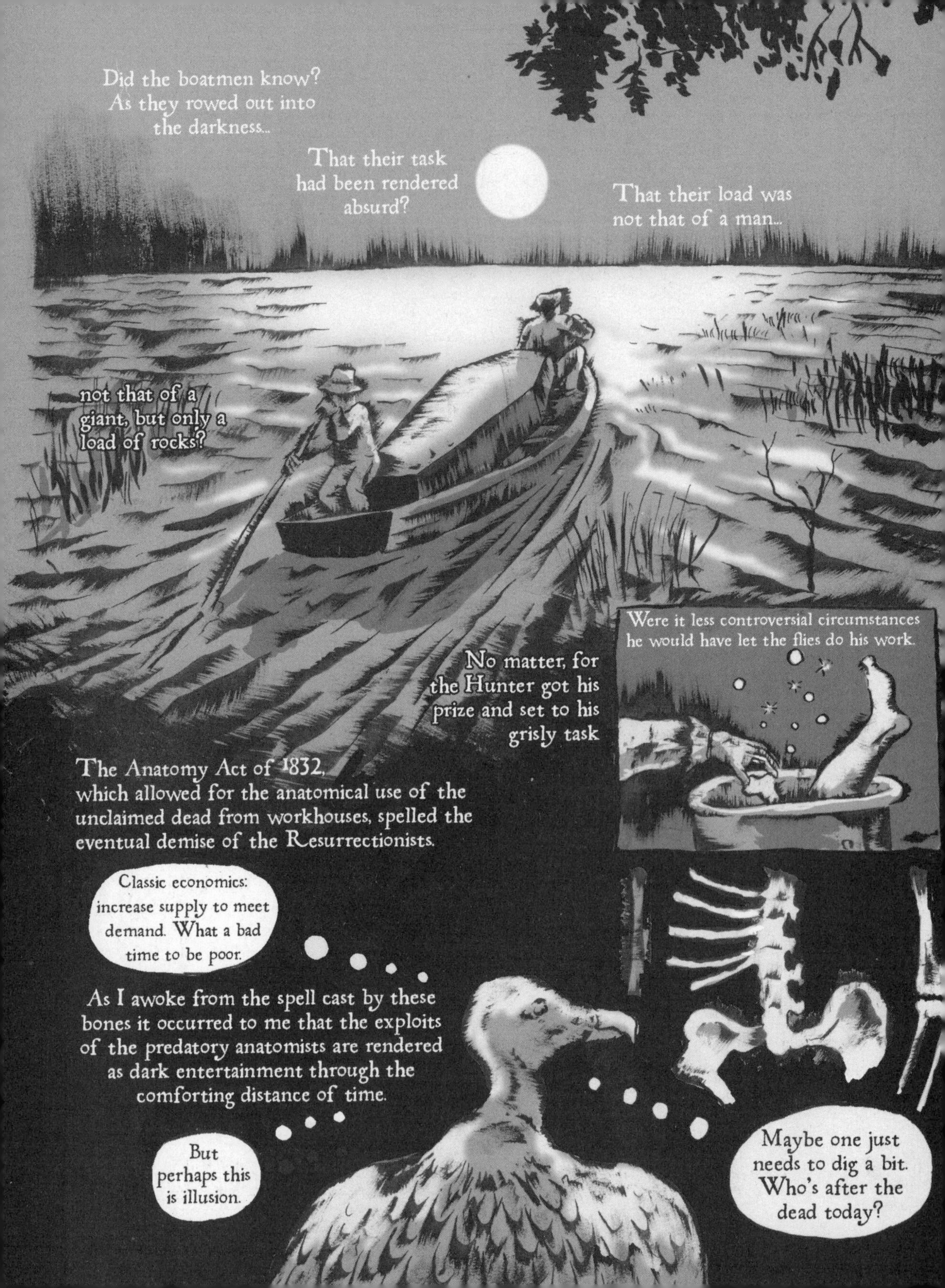
Did the boatmen know? As they rowed out into the darkness...
That their task had been rendered absurd?
That their load was not that of a man...
not that of a giant, but only a load of rocks?
No matter, for the Hunter got his prize and set to his grisly task
Were it less controversial circumstances he would have let the flies do his work.
The Anatomy Act of 1832, which allowed for the anatomical use of the unclaimed dead from workhouses, spelled the eventual demise of the Resurrectionists.
Classic economics: increase supply to meet demand. What a bad time to be poor.
As I awoke from the spell cast by these bones it occurred to me that the exploits of the predatory anatomists are rendered as dark entertainment through the comforting distance of time.
But perhaps this is illusion.
Maybe one just needs to dig a bit. Who's after the dead today?

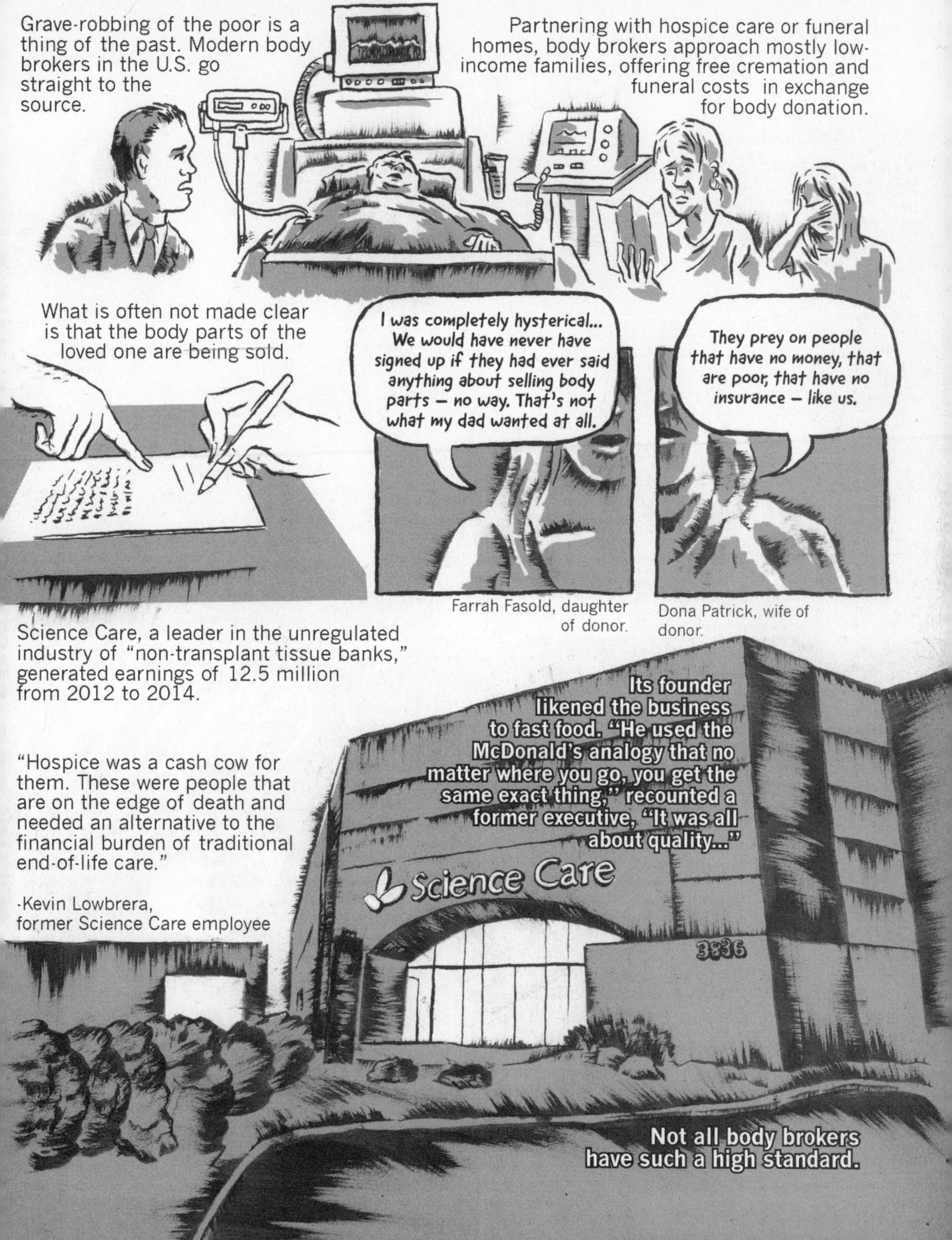
Grave-robbing of the poor is a thing of the past. Modern body brokers in the U.S. go straight to the source.
Partnering with hospice care or funeral homes, body brokers approach mostly low-income families, offering free cremation and funeral costs in exchange for body donation.
What is often not made clear is that the body parts of the loved one are being sold.
I was completely hysterical... We would have never have signed up if they had ever said anything about selling body parts – no way. That's not what my dad wanted at all.
They prey on people that have no money, that are poor, that have no insurance – like us.
Farrah Fasold, daughter of donor.
Dona Patrick, wife of donor.
Science Care, a leader in the unregulated industry of "non-transplant tissue banks," generated earnings of 12.5 million from 2012 to 2014.
"Hospice was a cash cow for them. These were people that are on the edge of death and needed an alternative to the financial burden of traditional end-of-life care."
-Kevin Lowbrera, former Science Care employee
Its founder likened the business to fast food. "He used the McDonald's analogy that no matter where you go, you get the same exact thing," recounted a former executive, "It was all about quality..."
Science Care
3836
Not all body brokers have such a high standard.

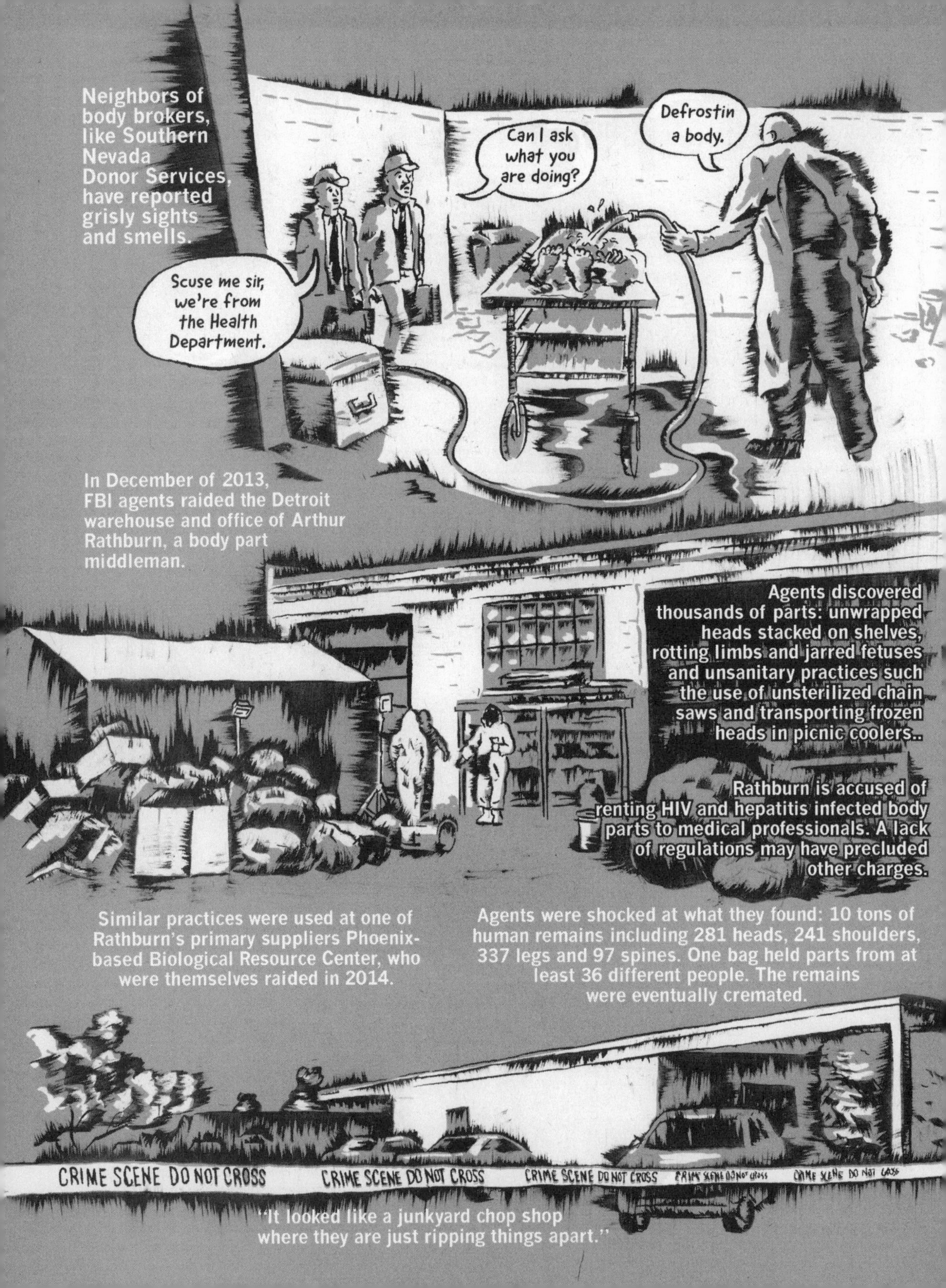
Neighbors of body brokers, like Southern Nevada Donor Services, have reported grisly sights and smells.
Scuse me sir, we're from the Health Department.
Can I ask what you are doing?
Defrostin a body.
In December of 2013, FBI agents raided the Detroit warehouse and office of Arthur Rathburn, a body part middleman.
Agents discovered thousands of parts: unwrapped heads stacked on shelves, rotting limbs and jarred fetuses and unsanitary practices such the use of unsterilized chain saws and transporting frozen heads in picnic coolers..
Rathburn is accused of renting HIV and hepatitis infected body parts to medical professionals. A lack of regulations may have precluded other charges.
Similar practices were used at one of Rathburn's primary suppliers Phoenix-based Biological Resource Center, who were themselves raided in 2014.
Agents were shocked at what they found: 10 tons of human remains including 281 heads, 241 shoulders, 337 legs and 97 spines. One bag held parts from at least 36 different people. The remains were eventually cremated.
CRIME SCENE DO NOT CROSS
CRIME SCENE DO NOT CROSS
CRIME SCENE DO NOT CROSS
"It looked like a junkyard chop shop where they are just ripping things apart."

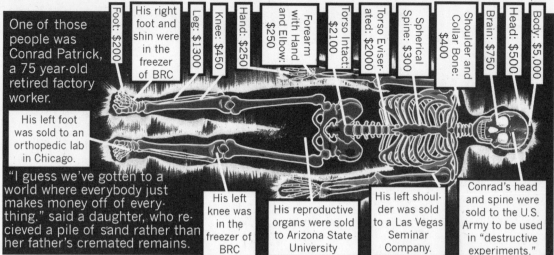

One of those people was Conrad Patrick, a 75 year-old retired factory worker.

His left foot was sold to an orthopedic lab in Chicago.

"I guess we've gotten to a world where everybody just makes money off of everything." said a daughter, who recieved a pile of sand rather than her father's cremated remains.

Labels around the skeleton:
- Foot: $200
- His right foot and shin were in the freezer of BRC
- Leg: $1300
- Knee: $450
- Hand: $250
- Forearm with Hand and Elbow: $250
- Torso Intact: $2100
- Torso Eviserated: $2000
- Spherical Spine: $300
- Shoulder and Collar Bone: $400
- Brain: $750
- Head: $500
- Body: $5,000

His left knee was in the freezer of BRC

His reproductive organs were sold to Arizona State University

His left shoulder was sold to a Las Vegas Seminar Company.

Conrad's head and spine were sold to the U.S. Army to be used in "destructive experiments."

Conrad's left shoulder may have ultimately ended up at medical convention in a top tier hotel such as a Hyatt, Hilton or Disney's Yacht and Beach Club.

Ohh-Disney on Ice!

No Entry Convention in progress

According to Reuters at least 90 "cadaver labs"· mobile surgical theaters· have taken place in dozens of hotels since 2012.

I think I went to a wedding here.

Often held in "regal and resplendent" ballrooms, plastic is placed on a portion of the floor, though sinks and running water are not often available.

Critics point out that these conditions and a lack of safety regulations and oversight is an accident waiting to happen.

SPLAT

In fact in 2011, a diseased head and neck from Rathburn's supply was used in a lab at a Hyatt hotel in Cambridge, MA. though no illness among the participants have been reported.

Incoming!

The Hyatt has hosted 10 similar events since then.

Some, like Dr. Charles Dinerstein, Senior Medical Fellow at the American Council on Science and Health, have additional concerns about what level of dignity should be afforded the dead.

This is a disgrace to our profession. Where is the sanctity of human life where you remove all the trappings of science and medicine and practice in a hotel ballroom?

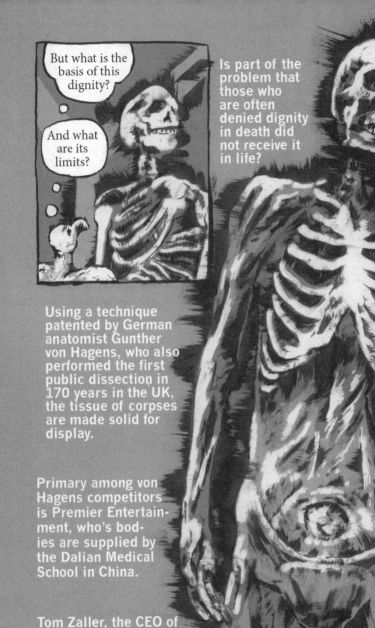

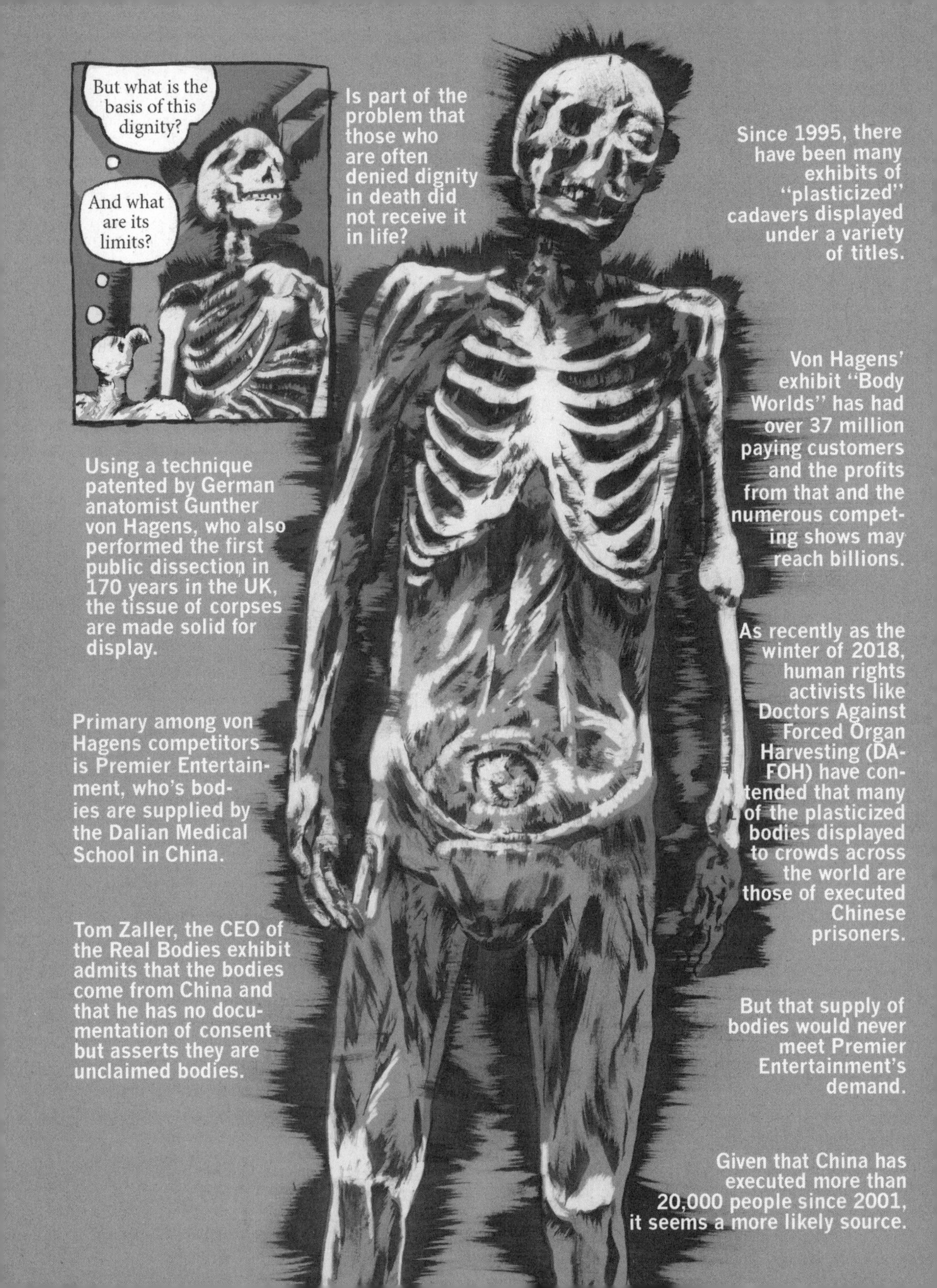

But what is the basis of this dignity?

And what are its limits?

Is part of the problem that those who are often denied dignity in death did not receive it in life?

Since 1995, there have been many exhibits of "plasticized" cadavers displayed under a variety of titles.

Von Hagens' exhibit "Body Worlds" has had over 37 million paying customers and the profits from that and the numerous competing shows may reach billions.

Using a technique patented by German anatomist Gunther von Hagens, who also performed the first public dissection in 170 years in the UK, the tissue of corpses are made solid for display.

Primary among von Hagens competitors is Premier Entertainment, who's bodies are supplied by the Dalian Medical School in China.

Tom Zaller, the CEO of the Real Bodies exhibit admits that the bodies come from China and that he has no documentation of consent but asserts they are unclaimed bodies.

As recently as the winter of 2018, human rights activists like Doctors Against Forced Organ Harvesting (DA-FOH) have contended that many of the plasticized bodies displayed to crowds across the world are those of executed Chinese prisoners.

But that supply of bodies would never meet Premier Entertainment's demand.

Given that China has executed more than 20,000 people since 2001, it seems a more likely source.

It is unlikely anyone will ever know the identities of those whimsically displayed bodies.

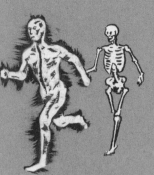

Just as it is with the American Giant at the Mutter museum. What is known is that his body was bought in 1877 in Kentucky. It could be that of a local giant, John M. Baker, buried 10 years prior. But there was one condition of the sale: no questions could be asked that might lead to the identification of the body.

But would it have mattered? We know the name of the Irish Giant and his final wishes are known as well.

Yet Charles Byrne is still on display today in the Hunterian museum, right under the bust of John Hunter.

Hunter had the power to extend his desires beyond the grave.

Queen Elizabeth, 1962

We would probably agree that Hunter would be harmed if his collection was disbanded, sold off and his life's work destroyed.

But what of the Giant who had only himself and his final wishes?

Should they not be honored?

Simply because someone who wanted his bones had enough money to buy them?

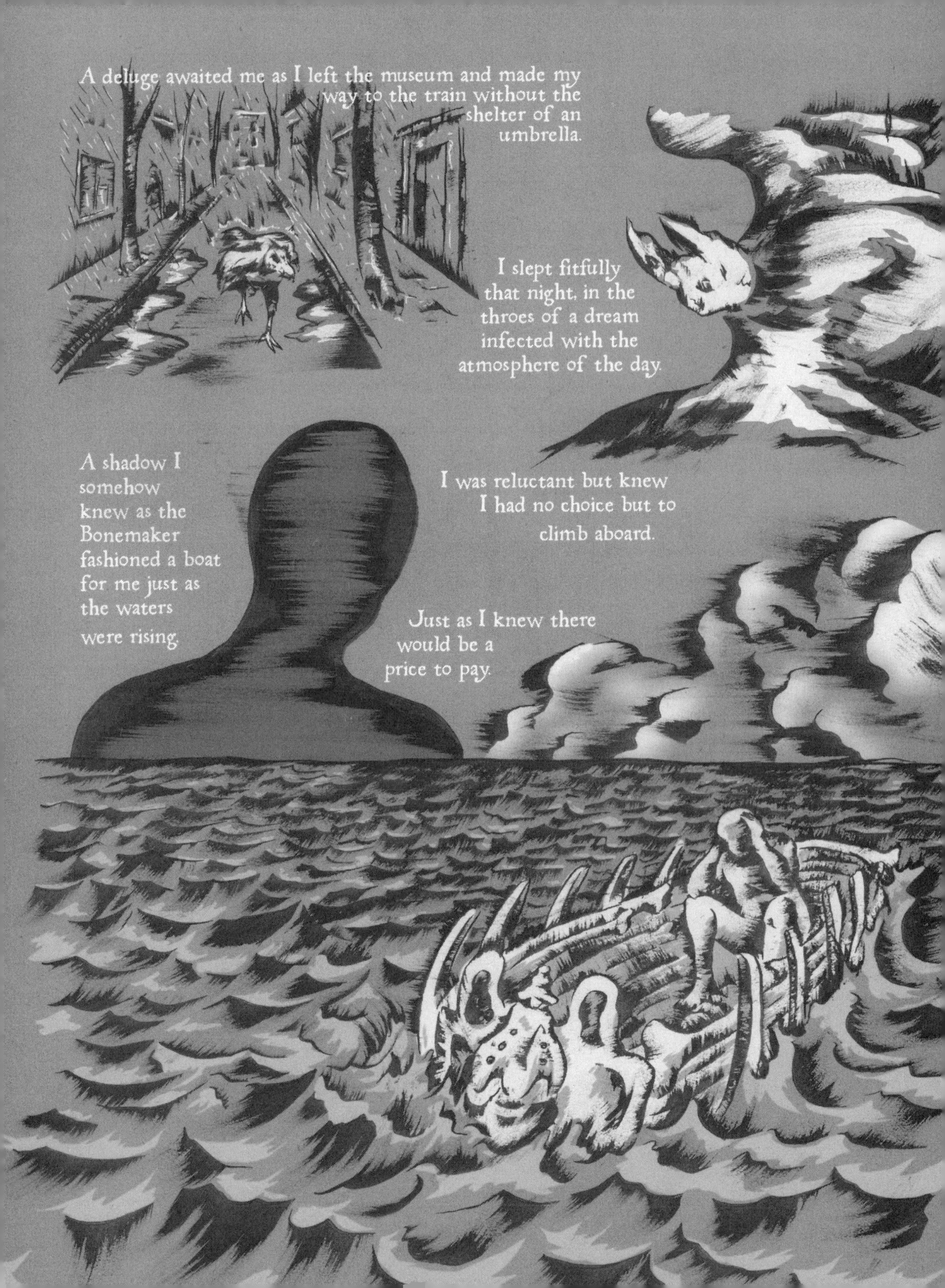
A deluge awaited me as I left the museum and made my way to the train without the shelter of an umbrella.
I slept fitfully that night, in the throes of a dream infected with the atmosphere of the day.
A shadow I somehow knew as the Bonemaker fashioned a boat for me just as the waters were rising.
I was reluctant but knew I had no choice but to climb aboard.
Just as I knew there would be a price to pay.

Who Killed Luke Mandrake?*

WHO KILLED LUKE MANDRAKE?
Vol. 1
FAMEBEAU
Book I of
The Goddammerung
by R. L. Migdal
With illustrations by the Author

Vol. 1: Famebeau

WHO KILLED LUKE MANDRAKE?
Vol. 2
REQUIEM FOR THE DAMNED
Book I of
The Goddammerung
by R. L. Migdal
With illustrations by the Author

Vol. 2: Requiem for the Damned

COCK ROBIN'S WEDDING
A HISTORY OF THE
TRIALS OF EROS
ACT I, PART 1
A GRAPHIC NOVEL BY
rebecca
migdal

Cock Robin's Wedding, Act I Part 1*

ANA AND THE CALABASH
HOW ONE SMALL GIRL
LED A VILLAGE TO VICTORY
by REBECCA MIGDAL

Ana and the Calabash
Color, handmade codex, 14 pp

KATE CHOPIN'S
THE AWAKENING
ILLUSTRATED BY
REBECCA MIGDAL

The Awakening by Kate Chopin, Adapted by Rebecca Migdal

ZOMBIE PUNK
ISSUE #1
by RLMIGDAL
FOR MATURE READERS
GIVE US THE CHILD!
THE CHILD– WE MUST SUCK OUT HER BRAINS!
UHHH!
GAAA
WHA?!

Zombie Punk No.1- The Curtain Falls*

The Lost
Treasure
of Nauru
by Rebecca Migdal

The Lost Treasure of Nauru
13x19" Hand bound, 10 pp

books by Rebecca Migdal available at bookandpuppet.com
*and through your local bookseller

Mythoprint publishing
2018 Catalog

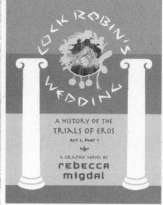

MAGDY EL-SHAFEE

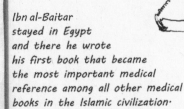

No one monopolizes Anise

Ibn al-Baitar stayed in Egypt and there he wrote his first book that became the most important medical reference among all other medical books in the Islamic civilization.

1400 herbs and medical substances were included in the book he named, "The Whole." His book was a tremendous success making Ibn al-Baitar the leader of herbal therapists.

The King [al Saleh] gave him a 10,000 dinar grant (worth 1 million dollars today) to continue his research.

Ibn al-Baitar travelled to Palestine and there ...

There was a scientist called "Ibn al-Baitar" He came from a very rich family. His family held the most prestigious jobs in all of Al-Andalus.

He decided to read all the previous medical books and try all herbal medicines himself. His journey took him from Al-Andalus to Morocco ..to Egypt.

There he became Egypt's chief doctor with the blessing of the Ayub King, Al-Saleh and the Ayyubids (Descendants of Saladin), who had a great deal of respect and passion for medicine.

He fell in love with a gorgeous young woman called "Mariam" and the Andalusi scientist and researcher dissolved in the sweet taste of love.

The Andalusi lover spent all his grant money to make each and every day a happy day.

Ibn al-Baitar learned Latin to be able to read in the original language of the Patriarchs of medicine like Hippocrates, Dioscorides, etc. He continued his medical research and investigation building on previous work by Ibn Sina and Al-Razi, brilliantly blending nomadic traditions with the remains left from the ancient Egyptian medicine practiced one generation after another.

From what he learned reading Hippocrates's work, Ibn al-Baitar passed to us the knowledge that Anise helps treating the signs of Influenza.

When the King returned, he asked to see Ibn al-Baitar who stalled and wanted to spend all day with his new lover. They spent all night singing, drinking and enjoying themselves until it was very late at night when Ibn al-Baitar took out a piece of weed. He crushed it, swallowed it and went to sleep saying he didn't want anyone to wake him up.

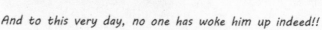

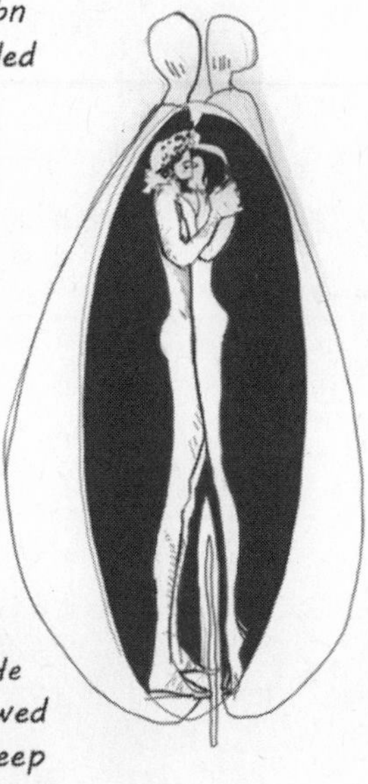

And to this very day, no one has woke him up indeed!!

When the King found out about how Ibn al-Baitar recklessly spent his grant money he said "I swear If I knew, I would have given him 10,000 Dinar so he could have enjoyed himself more and he could have entertained us even more!"

Penelope Ody, THE COMPLETE MEDICINAL HERBAL, Academia ed. p71

Ibrahim Bin Mourad review; DI SCORIDIS TRANSLATION ACCORDING TO THE MALAQI IBN AL-BAITAR, Elghrab Ellslami ed. p28-29

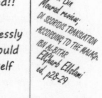

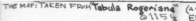

THE MAP: TAKEN FROM "Tabula Rogeriana" (A WORLD MAP BY THE ARAB GEOGRAPHER EL-IDRISI-MOHAMMED TO KING ROGER OF SICILY @1154

800 years later,

1800'S

The German Pharmacist Sertuner succeeded in extracting Morphine from the Opium Flower.

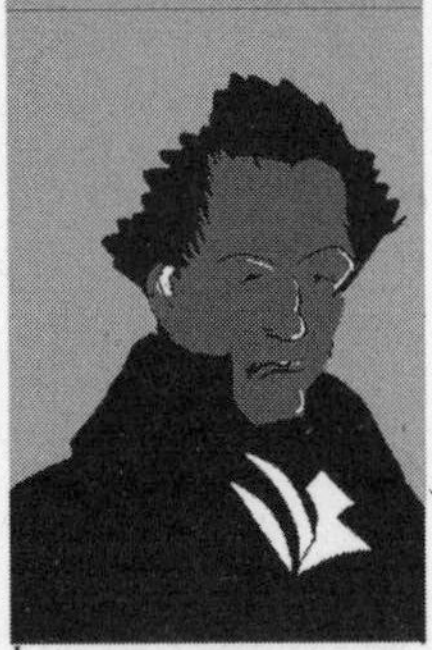

Morphine became a very important medicine.
The first medicine to be chemically extracted from it's source.

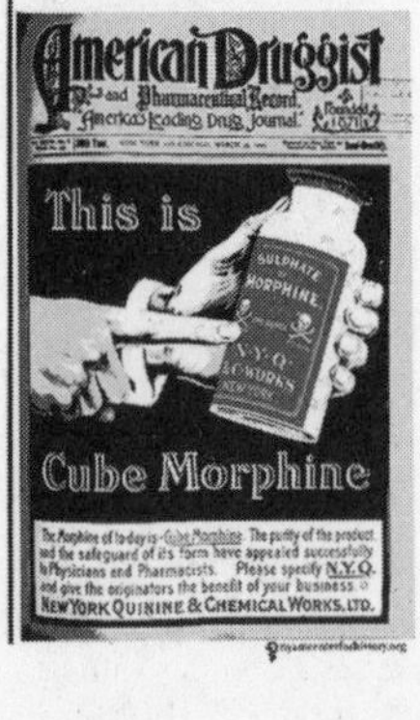

American Druggist
and Pharmaceutical Record.
"America's Leading Drug Journal."
This is
Sulphate
Morphine
N.Y.Q.
Cube Morphine
The Morphine of to-day is Cube Morphine. The purity of the product and the safeguard of it's form have appealed successfully to Physicians and Pharmacists. Please specify N.Y.Q. and give the originators the benefit of your business.
NEW YORK QUININE & CHEMICAL WORKS, LTD.

However, Opium, the main source of Morphine, which has been used for so many years since the days of the pharaohs to the days of the pioneers of medicine in the Muslim world, has been made illegal.

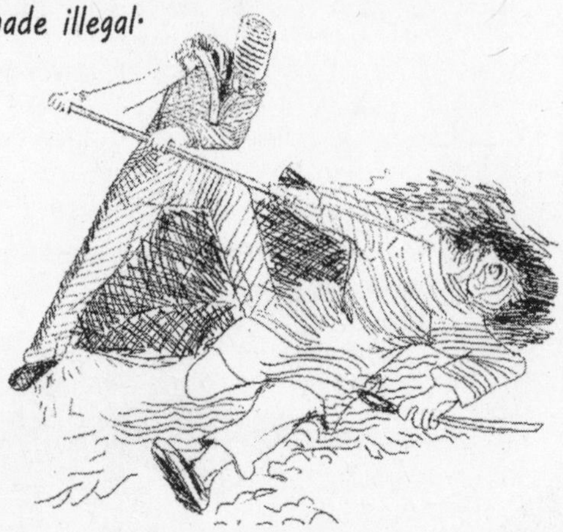

And from that day forward, "Chemistry" has declared war on natural medicine and gradually, chemistry has even stripped natural medicine of the title "medicine". With time, medicine started to become manufactured by companies, companies that could not monopolize natural medicine, but can monopolize chemistry.

And the companies accomplished a lot of great things but ..

Gradually, scientific discovery has moved from the laboratories of the great pioneers to fall into the laps of pharmaceutical companies and despite there being advanced technology, it's been 20 years since we last discovered new antibiotics.

bacteria that was so efficiently killed by Penicillin 70 years ago, can now be fatal to us, because The company's "profit" would not justify their "investment"." .That's what it is nowadays.

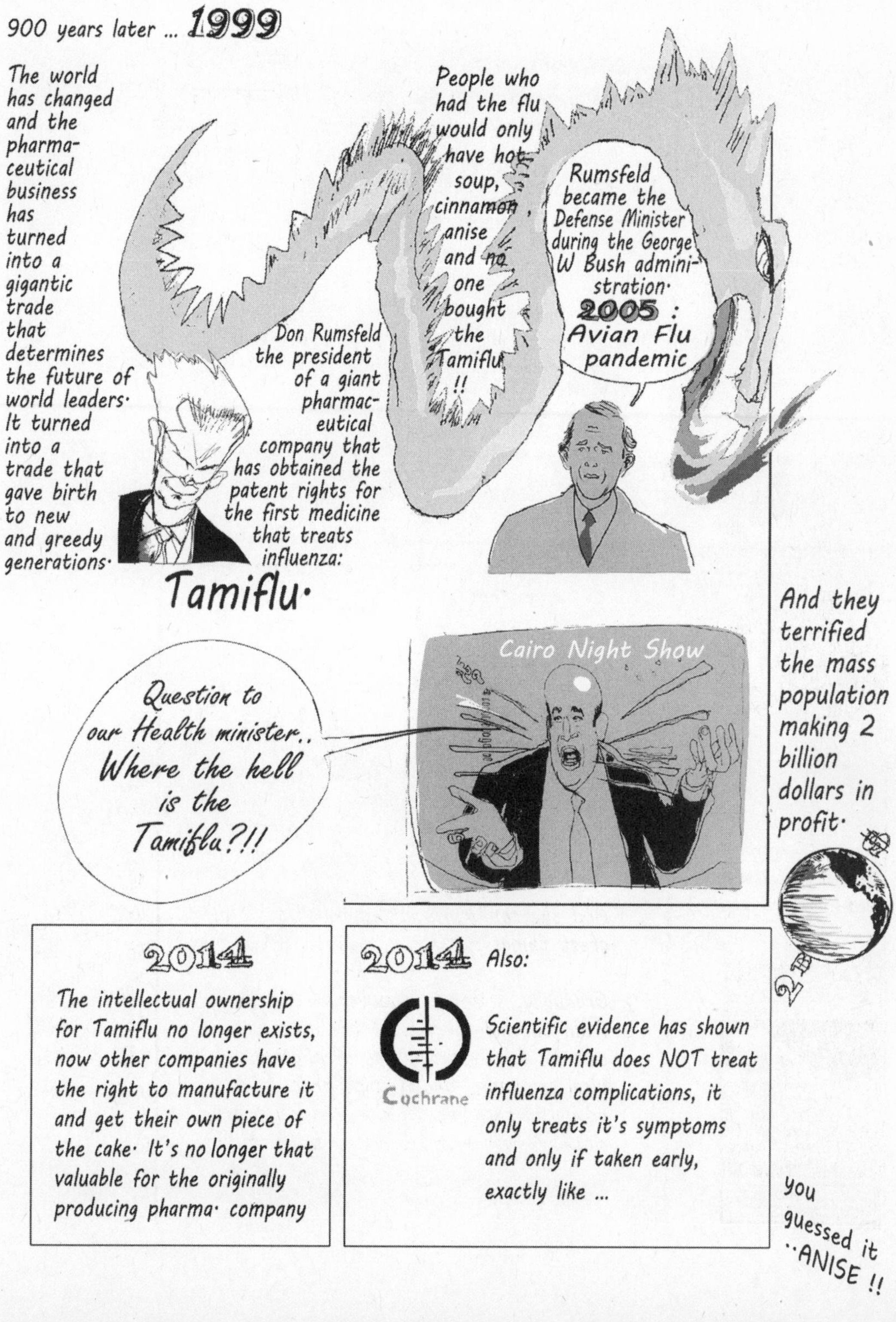
900 years later ... 1999
The world has changed and the pharma-ceutical business has turned into a gigantic trade that determines the future of world leaders. It turned into a trade that gave birth to new and greedy generations.
Don Rumsfeld the president of a giant pharmac-eutical company that has obtained the patent rights for the first medicine that treats influenza:
Tamiflu.
People who had the flu would only have hot soup, cinnamon, anise and no one bought the Tamiflu !!
Rumsfeld became the Defense Minister during the George W Bush admini-stration.
2005 : Avian Flu pandemic
And they terrified the mass population making 2 billion dollars in profit.
Cairo Night Show
Question to our Health minister.. Where the hell is the Tamiflu?!!
2014
The intellectual ownership for Tamiflu no longer exists, now other companies have the right to manufacture it and get their own piece of the cake. It's no longer that valuable for the originally producing pharma. company
2014 Also:
Cochrane
Scientific evidence has shown that Tamiflu does NOT treat influenza complications, it only treats it's symptoms and only if taken early, exactly like ...
you guessed it ..ANISE !!

It's better not to waste our energy in this vicious circle and start thinking about the kind of medicine that combines both traditional medical heritage with modern science, as they do in Germany.

◈ **Anise** ◈

anise, pimpinella anisum family: Apiaceae

International J. of Research in Ayurveda & Pharmacy 2017

Apiaceae is the family that anise, fennel and celery belong to.

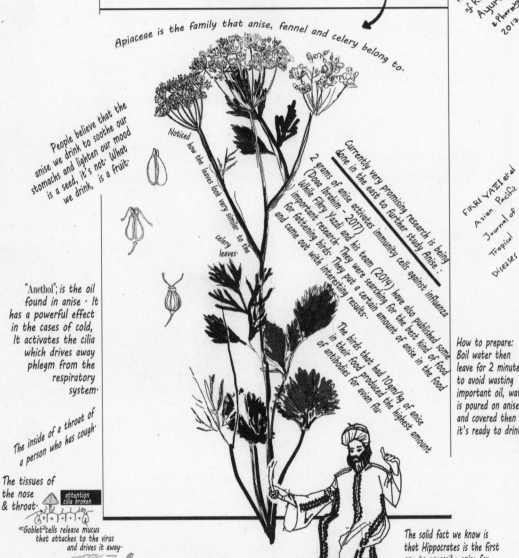

Noticed how the leaves look very similar to the celery leaves.

People believe that the anise we drink to soothe our stomachs and lighten our mood is a seed, it's not. What we drink, is a fruit.

Currently very promising research is being done in the east to further study Anise: 2 grams of anise activates immunity cells against influenza (Doaa Ibrahim - 2017) While Fikry Yazdi and his team (2014) have also published some important research. They were searching for the best kind of food for fattening birds. They put a certain amount of anise in the food and came out with interesting results.

The birds that had 10gm/kg of anise in their food produced the highest amount of antibodies for avian flu.

FIKRI YAZI et al Asian Pacific Journal of Tropical Diseases

"Anethol"; is the oil found in anise . It has a powerful effect in the cases of cold, It activates the cilia which drives away phlegm from the respiratory system.

How to prepare: Boil water then leave for 2 minutes, to avoid wasting important oil, water is poured on anise and covered then it's ready to drink.

The inside of a throat of a person who has cough.

The tissues of the nose & throat.

attention cilia broken

"Goblet" cells release mucus that attaches to the virus and drives it away.

The solid fact we know is that Hippocrates is the first one to prescribe anise for treatment of influenza.

. The Muslim doctors followed in the footsteps
of Hippocrates and applied the treatment principles
that he vowed to follow and they came up with their
own code which stated that the real treatment agent is:

The guardian of bodies and souls

Monopolists do not believe in morals
or values and the majority of Muslim
Salafi officials in the medical union
in Egypt believe that people
should not swear loyalty to
anything but Allah and so,
Hippocrates` oath is
HARAM .

All they care about is to
please those in power and
their respective companies.
They know nothing about
Hippocrates or Ibn al-Baitar
they don't believe in the people's
power or the power of love.

They don't know that something
as simple as anise can help
balance people's moods
and hormones. They
don't know that
this marvel of
nature carries both
feminine hormones
(estrogen) and hormones
to counter balance feminine
hormones.

And so,
the memory of the Andalusi lover lives
and the human heritage, in spite of all scientific advancements,
still lies in our hands.
Here and
Now

The European Medicines Agency (EMA) in it's 2013 report has officially declared
that anise can be used as a traditional medical herb to treat 1- Patients who
have gastric disorders including bloated stomach and gases. 2- Flu patients who
have phlegm. It's also used by women to alleviate pain during the monthly period.
It was advised in the report not to use anise a lot for those under 18.

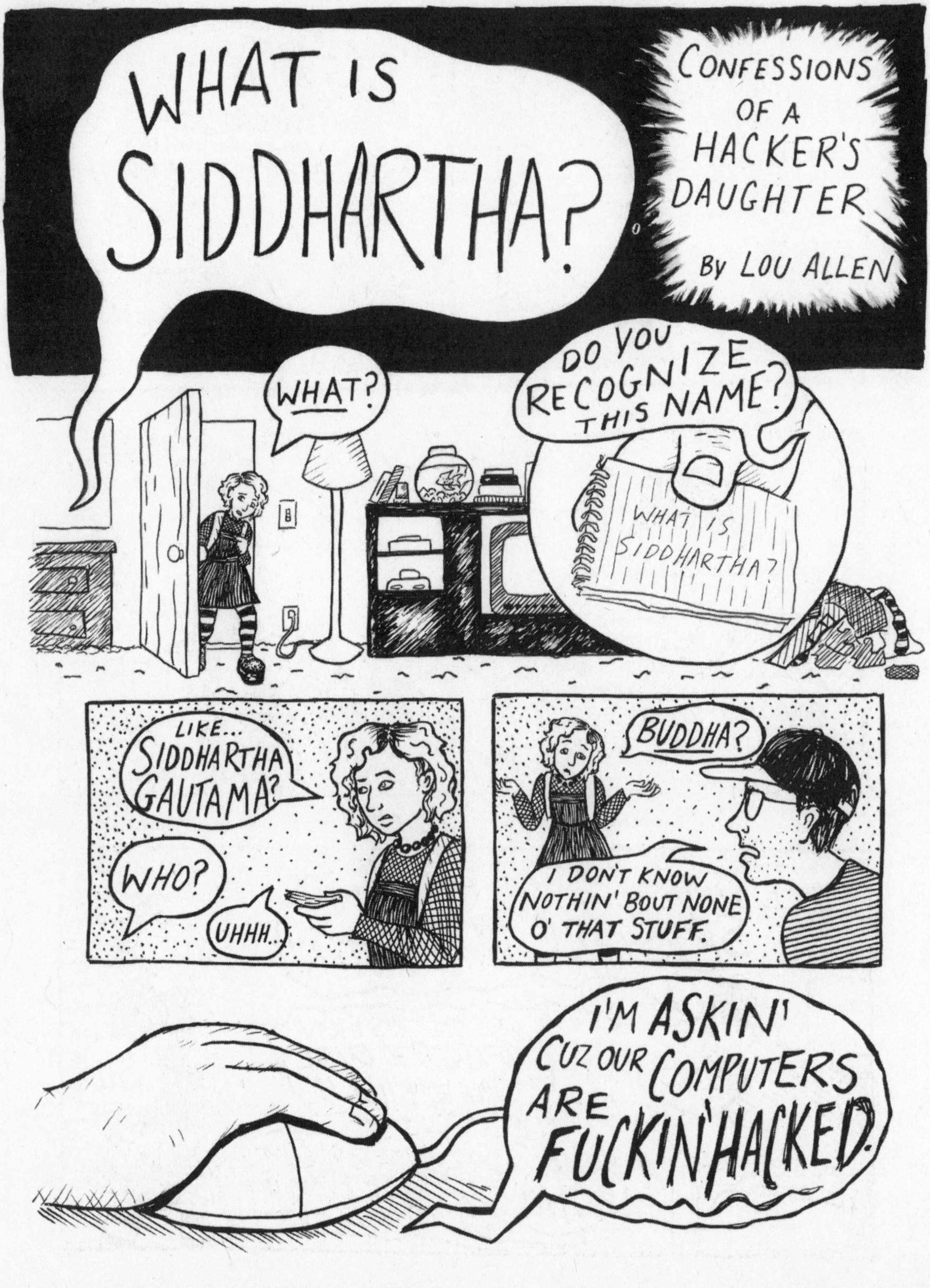

WHAT IS SIDDHARTHA?
CONFESSIONS OF A HACKER'S DAUGHTER
BY LOU ALLEN
WHAT?
DO YOU RECOGNIZE THIS NAME?
WHAT IS SIDDHARTHA?
LIKE... SIDDHARTHA GAUTAMA?
WHO?
UHHH...
BUDDHA?
I DON'T KNOW NOTHIN' BOUT NONE O' THAT STUFF.
I'M ASKIN' CUZ OUR COMPUTERS ARE FUCKIN' HACKED.

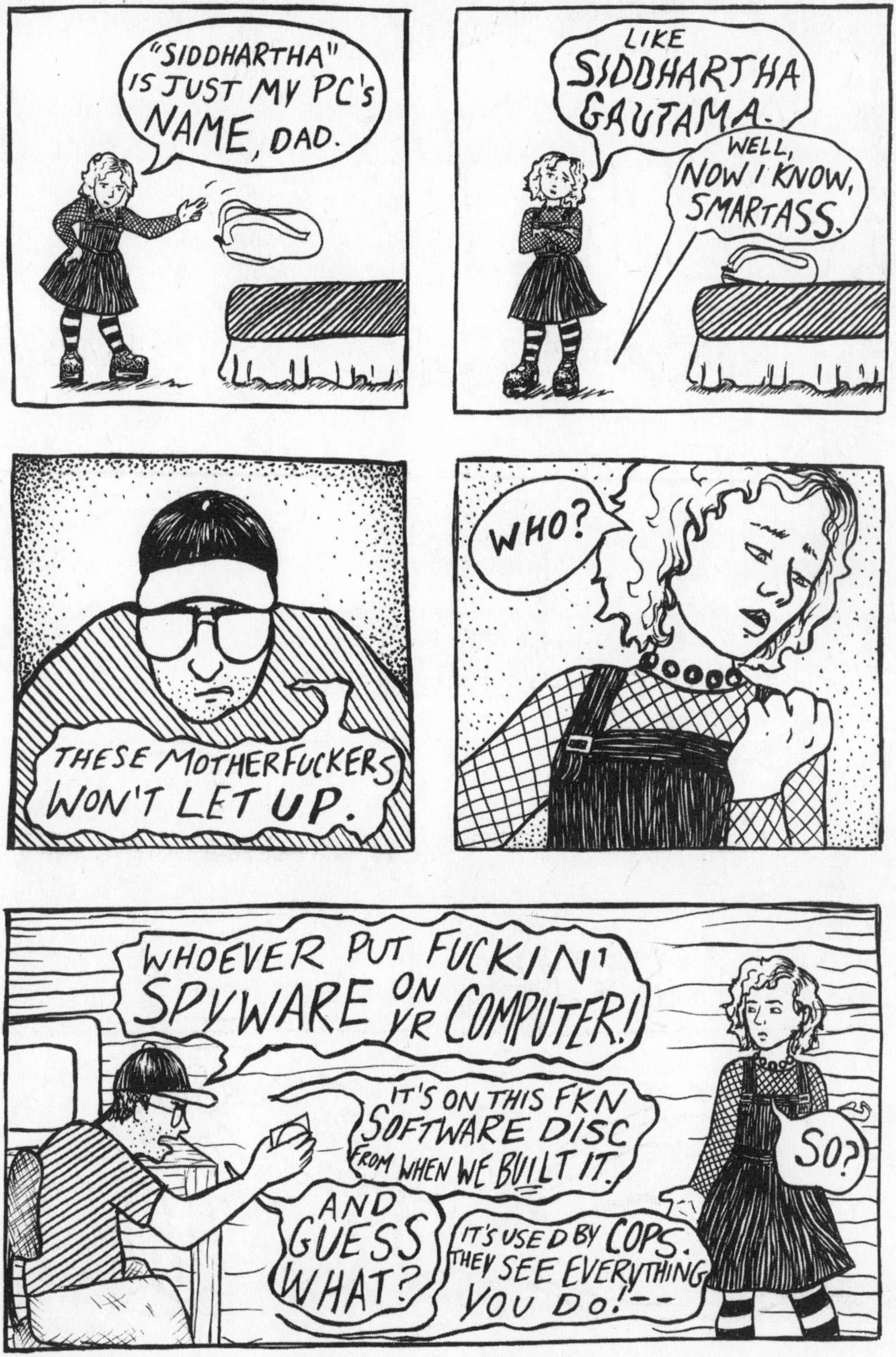
"SIDDHARTHA" IS JUST MY PC's NAME, DAD.
LIKE SIDDHARTHA GAUTAMA.
WELL, NOW I KNOW, SMARTASS.
THESE MOTHERFUCKERS WON'T LET UP.
WHO?
WHOEVER PUT FUCKIN' SPYWARE ON YR COMPUTER!
IT'S ON THIS FKN SOFTWARE DISC FROM WHEN WE BUILT IT.
AND GUESS WHAT?
IT'S USED BY COPS. THEY SEE EVERYTHING YOU DO!--
SO?

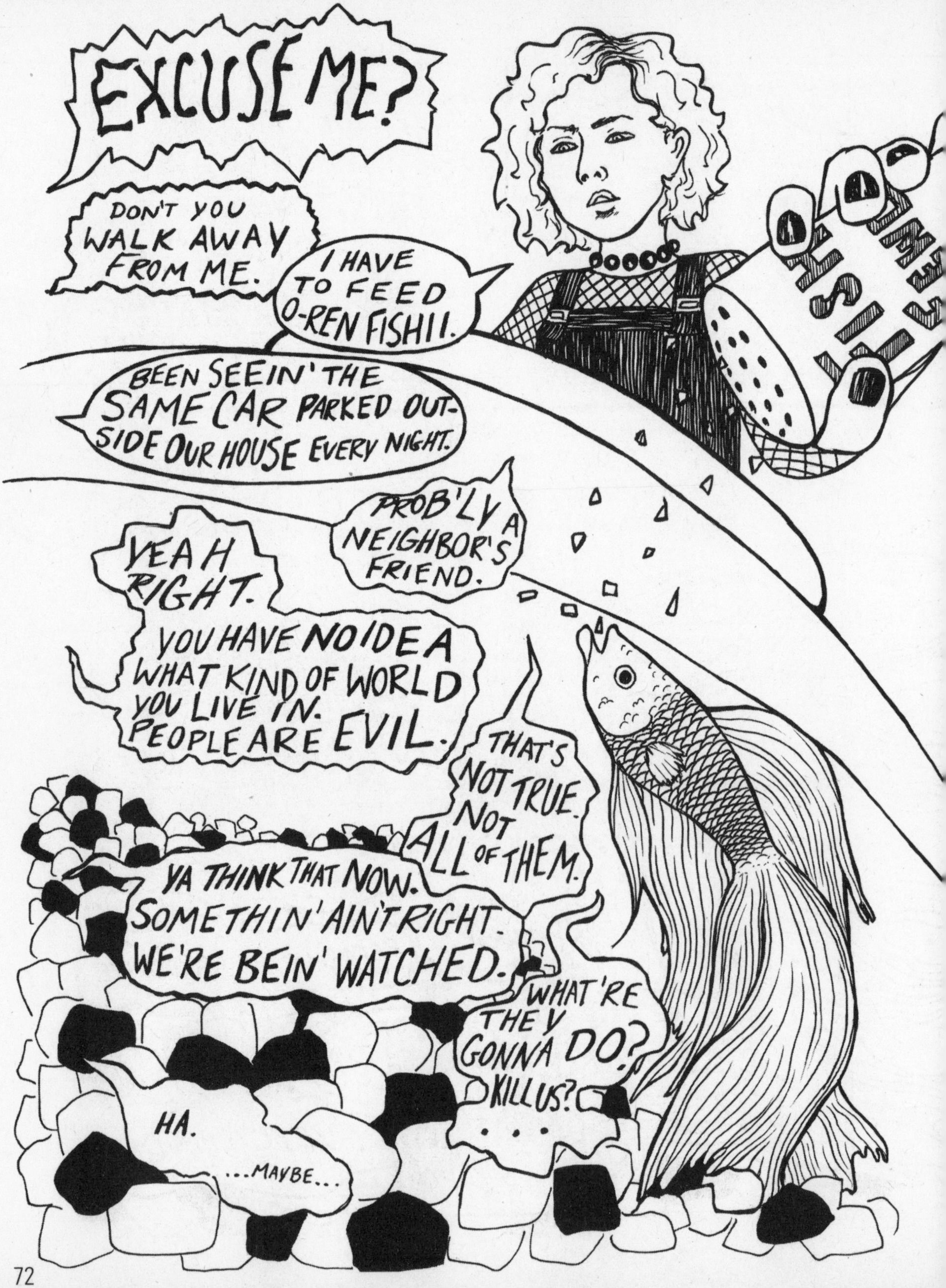
EXCUSE ME?
DON'T YOU WALK AWAY FROM ME.
I HAVE TO FEED O-REN FISH II.
BEEN SEEIN' THE SAME CAR PARKED OUT-SIDE OUR HOUSE EVERY NIGHT.
PROB'LY A NEIGHBOR'S FRIEND.
YEAH RIGHT.
YOU HAVE NO IDEA WHAT KIND OF WORLD YOU LIVE IN. PEOPLE ARE EVIL.
THAT'S NOT TRUE. NOT ALL OF THEM.
YA THINK THAT NOW. SOMETHIN' AIN'T RIGHT. WE'RE BEIN' WATCHED.
WHAT'RE THEY GONNA DO? KILL US?
HA.
...
...MAYBE...

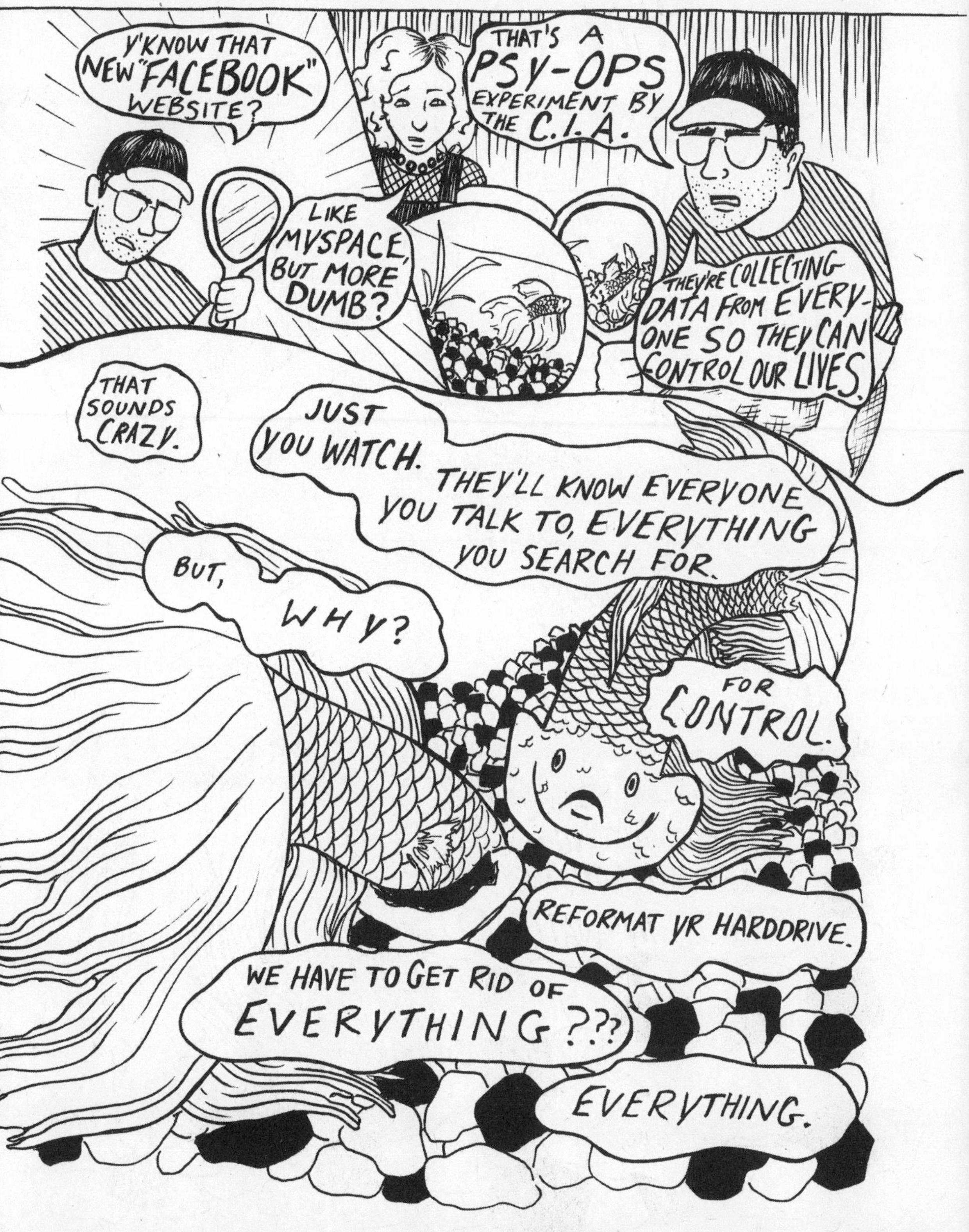
Y'KNOW THAT NEW "FACEBOOK" WEBSITE?
THAT'S A PSY-OPS EXPERIMENT BY THE C.I.A.
LIKE MYSPACE, BUT MORE DUMB?
THEY'RE COLLECTING DATA FROM EVERY-ONE SO THEY CAN CONTROL OUR LIVES.
THAT SOUNDS CRAZY.
JUST YOU WATCH.
THEY'LL KNOW EVERYONE YOU TALK TO, EVERYTHING YOU SEARCH FOR.
BUT, WHY?
FOR CONTROL.
REFORMAT YR HARDDRIVE.
WE HAVE TO GET RID OF EVERYTHING???
EVERYTHING.

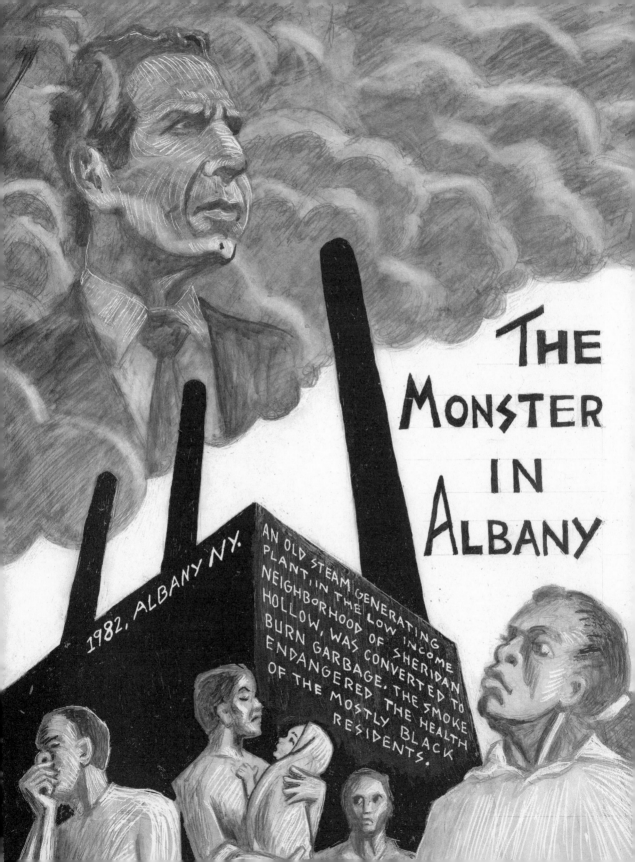

THE MONSTER IN ALBANY

1982, ALBANY N.Y.

AN OLD STEAM GENERATING PLANT IN THE LOW INCOME NEIGHBORHOOD OF SHERIDAN HOLLOW, WAS CONVERTED TO BURN GARBAGE. THE SMOKE ENDANGERED THE HEALTH OF THE MOSTLY BLACK RESIDENTS.

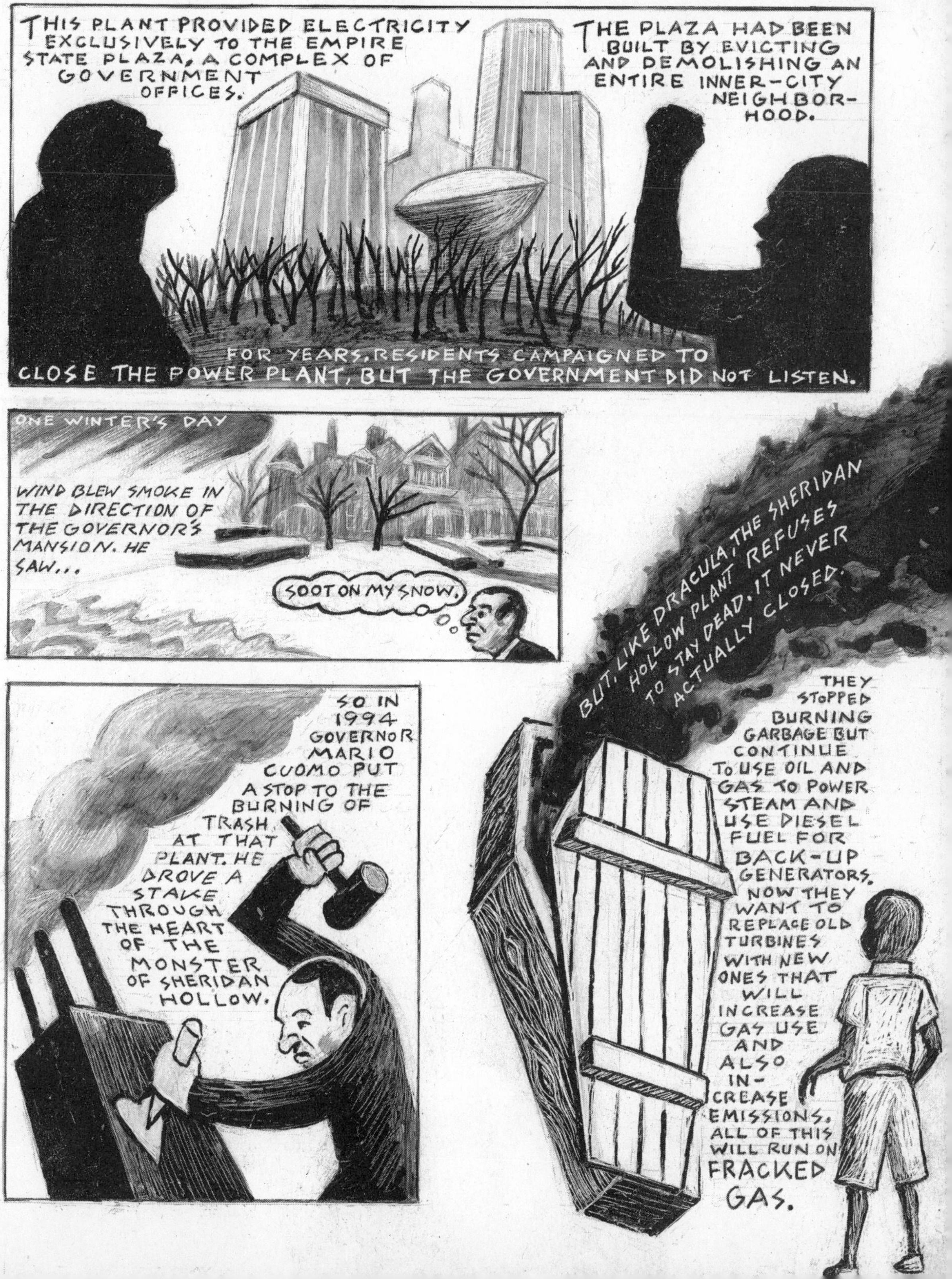
THIS PLANT PROVIDED ELECTRICITY EXCLUSIVELY TO THE EMPIRE STATE PLAZA, A COMPLEX OF GOVERNMENT OFFICES.
THE PLAZA HAD BEEN BUILT BY EVICTING AND DEMOLISHING AN ENTIRE INNER-CITY NEIGHBORHOOD.
FOR YEARS, RESIDENTS CAMPAIGNED TO CLOSE THE POWER PLANT, BUT THE GOVERNMENT DID NOT LISTEN.
ONE WINTER'S DAY
WIND BLEW SMOKE IN THE DIRECTION OF THE GOVERNOR'S MANSION. HE SAW...
SOOT ON MY SNOW.
SO IN 1994 GOVERNOR MARIO CUOMO PUT A STOP TO THE BURNING OF TRASH AT THAT PLANT. HE DROVE A STAKE THROUGH THE HEART OF THE MONSTER OF SHERIDAN HOLLOW.
BUT, LIKE DRACULA, THE SHERIDAN HOLLOW PLANT REFUSES TO STAY DEAD. IT NEVER ACTUALLY CLOSED.
THEY STOPPED BURNING GARBAGE BUT CONTINUE TO USE OIL AND GAS TO POWER STEAM AND USE DIESEL FUEL FOR BACK-UP GENERATORS. NOW THEY WANT TO REPLACE OLD TURBINES WITH NEW ONES THAT WILL INCREASE GAS USE AND ALSO INCREASE EMISSIONS. ALL OF THIS WILL RUN ON FRACKED GAS.

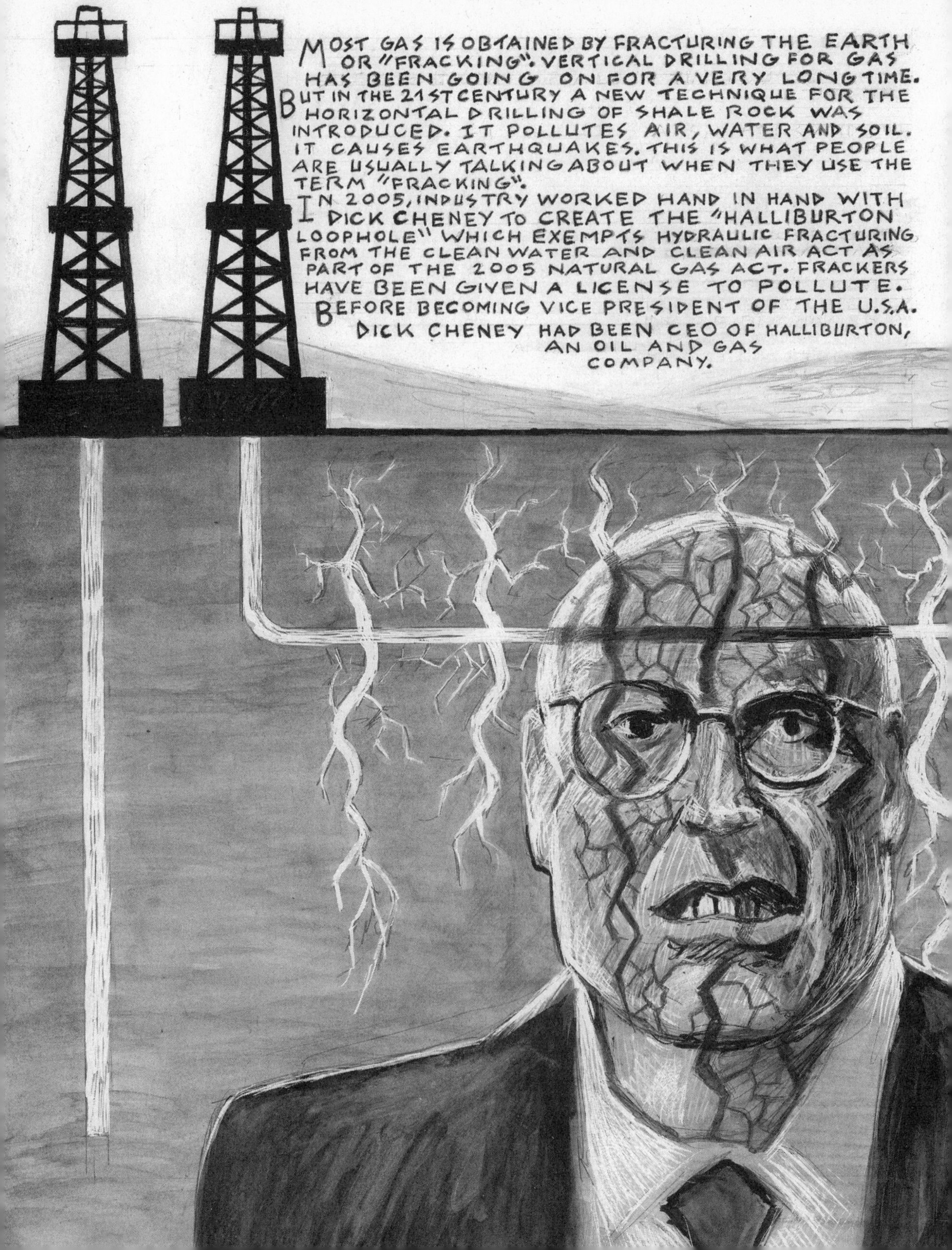
MOST GAS IS OBTAINED BY FRACTURING THE EARTH OR "FRACKING". VERTICAL DRILLING FOR GAS HAS BEEN GOING ON FOR A VERY LONG TIME.
BUT IN THE 21ST CENTURY A NEW TECHNIQUE FOR THE HORIZONTAL DRILLING OF SHALE ROCK WAS INTRODUCED. IT POLLUTES AIR, WATER AND SOIL. IT CAUSES EARTHQUAKES. THIS IS WHAT PEOPLE ARE USUALLY TALKING ABOUT WHEN THEY USE THE TERM "FRACKING".
IN 2005, INDUSTRY WORKED HAND IN HAND WITH DICK CHENEY TO CREATE THE "HALLIBURTON LOOPHOLE" WHICH EXEMPTS HYDRAULIC FRACTURING FROM THE CLEAN WATER AND CLEAN AIR ACT AS PART OF THE 2005 NATURAL GAS ACT. FRACKERS HAVE BEEN GIVEN A LICENSE TO POLLUTE.
BEFORE BECOMING VICE PRESIDENT OF THE U.S.A. DICK CHENEY HAD BEEN CEO OF HALLIBURTON, AN OIL AND GAS COMPANY.

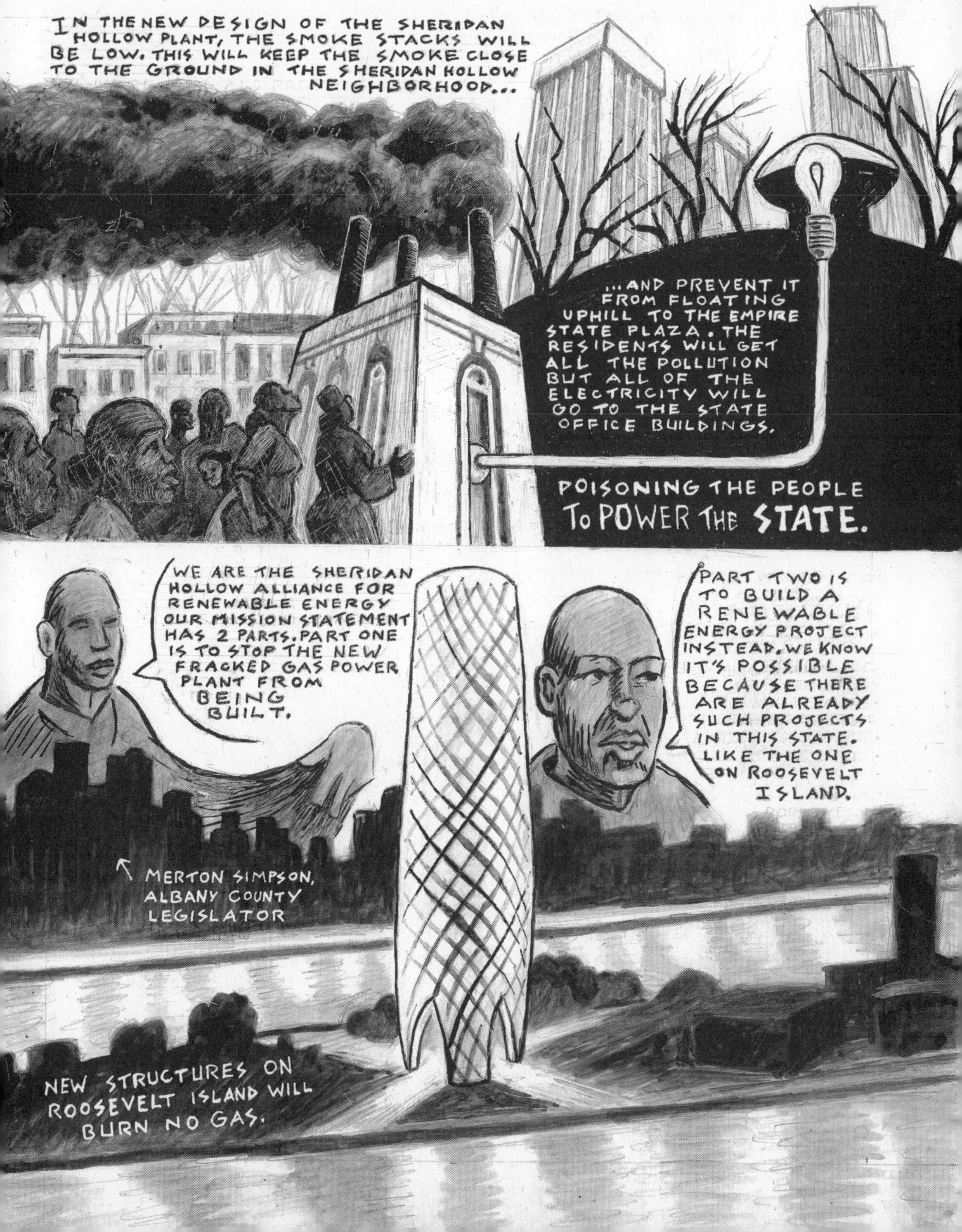
IN THE NEW DESIGN OF THE SHERIDAN HOLLOW PLANT, THE SMOKE STACKS WILL BE LOW. THIS WILL KEEP THE SMOKE CLOSE TO THE GROUND IN THE SHERIDAN HOLLOW NEIGHBORHOOD...
...AND PREVENT IT FROM FLOATING UPHILL TO THE EMPIRE STATE PLAZA. THE RESIDENTS WILL GET ALL THE POLLUTION BUT ALL OF THE ELECTRICITY WILL GO TO THE STATE OFFICE BUILDINGS.
POISONING THE PEOPLE TO POWER THE STATE.
WE ARE THE SHERIDAN HOLLOW ALLIANCE FOR RENEWABLE ENERGY OUR MISSION STATEMENT HAS 2 PARTS. PART ONE IS TO STOP THE NEW FRACKED GAS POWER PLANT FROM BEING BUILT.
MERTON SIMPSON, ALBANY COUNTY LEGISLATOR
PART TWO IS TO BUILD A RENEWABLE ENERGY PROJECT INSTEAD. WE KNOW IT'S POSSIBLE BECAUSE THERE ARE ALREADY SUCH PROJECTS IN THIS STATE. LIKE THE ONE ON ROOSEVELT ISLAND.
NEW STRUCTURES ON ROOSEVELT ISLAND WILL BURN NO GAS.

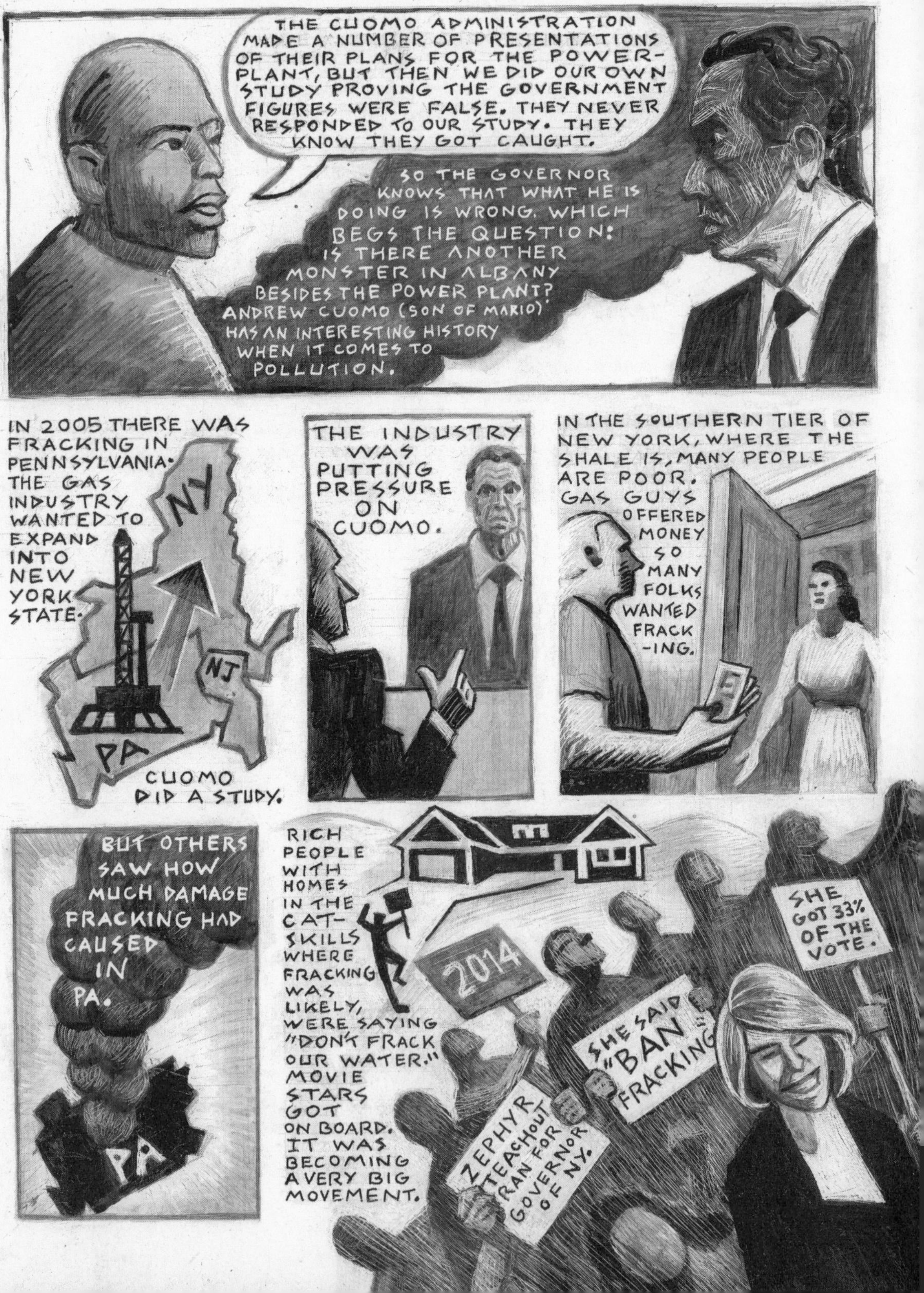

THE CUOMO ADMINISTRATION MADE A NUMBER OF PRESENTATIONS OF THEIR PLANS FOR THE POWER-PLANT, BUT THEN WE DID OUR OWN STUDY PROVING THE GOVERNMENT FIGURES WERE FALSE. THEY NEVER RESPONDED TO OUR STUDY. THEY KNOW THEY GOT CAUGHT.
SO THE GOVERNOR KNOWS THAT WHAT HE IS DOING IS WRONG. WHICH BEGS THE QUESTION: IS THERE ANOTHER MONSTER IN ALBANY BESIDES THE POWER PLANT?
ANDREW CUOMO (SON OF MARIO) HAS AN INTERESTING HISTORY WHEN IT COMES TO POLLUTION.
IN 2005 THERE WAS FRACKING IN PENNSYLVANIA. THE GAS INDUSTRY WANTED TO EXPAND INTO NEW YORK STATE.
NY
NJ
PA
CUOMO DID A STUDY.
THE INDUSTRY WAS PUTTING PRESSURE ON CUOMO.
IN THE SOUTHERN TIER OF NEW YORK, WHERE THE SHALE IS, MANY PEOPLE ARE POOR.
GAS GUYS OFFERED MONEY SO MANY FOLKS WANTED FRACK-ING.
BUT OTHERS SAW HOW MUCH DAMAGE FRACKING HAD CAUSED IN PA.
PA
RICH PEOPLE WITH HOMES IN THE CAT-SKILLS WHERE FRACKING WAS LIKELY, WERE SAYING "DON'T FRACK OUR WATER." MOVIE STARS GOT ON BOARD. IT WAS BECOMING A VERY BIG MOVEMENT.
2014
ZEPHYR TEACHOUT RAN FOR GOVERNOR OF NY.
SHE SAID "BAN FRACKING"
SHE GOT 33% OF THE VOTE.

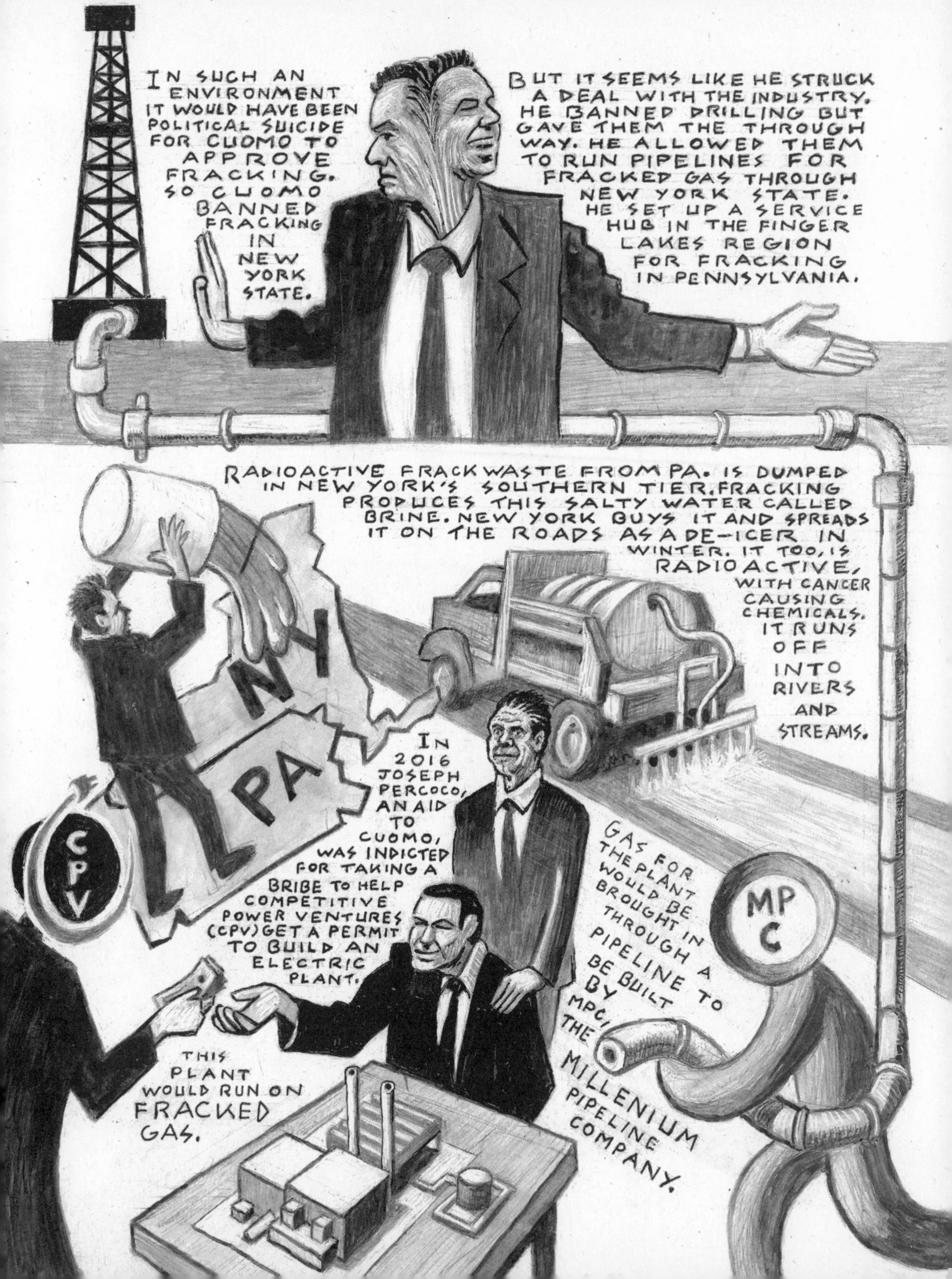

IN SUCH AN ENVIRONMENT IT WOULD HAVE BEEN POLITICAL SUICIDE FOR CUOMO TO APPROVE FRACKING. SO CUOMO BANNED FRACKING IN NEW YORK STATE.
BUT IT SEEMS LIKE HE STRUCK A DEAL WITH THE INDUSTRY. HE BANNED DRILLING BUT GAVE THEM THE THROUGH WAY. HE ALLOWED THEM TO RUN PIPELINES FOR FRACKED GAS THROUGH NEW YORK STATE. HE SET UP A SERVICE HUB IN THE FINGER LAKES REGION FOR FRACKING IN PENNSYLVANIA.
RADIOACTIVE FRACKWASTE FROM PA. IS DUMPED IN NEW YORK'S SOUTHERN TIER. FRACKING PRODUCES THIS SALTY WATER CALLED BRINE. NEW YORK BUYS IT AND SPREADS IT ON THE ROADS AS A DE-ICER IN WINTER. IT TOO, IS RADIOACTIVE, WITH CANCER CAUSING CHEMICALS. IT RUNS OFF INTO RIVERS AND STREAMS.
NY
PA
CPV
IN 2016 JOSEPH PERCOCO, AN AID TO CUOMO, WAS INDICTED FOR TAKING A BRIBE TO HELP COMPETITIVE POWER VENTURES (CPV) GET A PERMIT TO BUILD AN ELECTRIC PLANT.
GAS FOR THE PLANT WOULD BE BROUGHT IN THROUGH A PIPELINE TO BE BUILT BY MPC, THE MILLENIUM PIPELINE COMPANY.
MPC
THIS PLANT WOULD RUN ON FRACKED GAS.

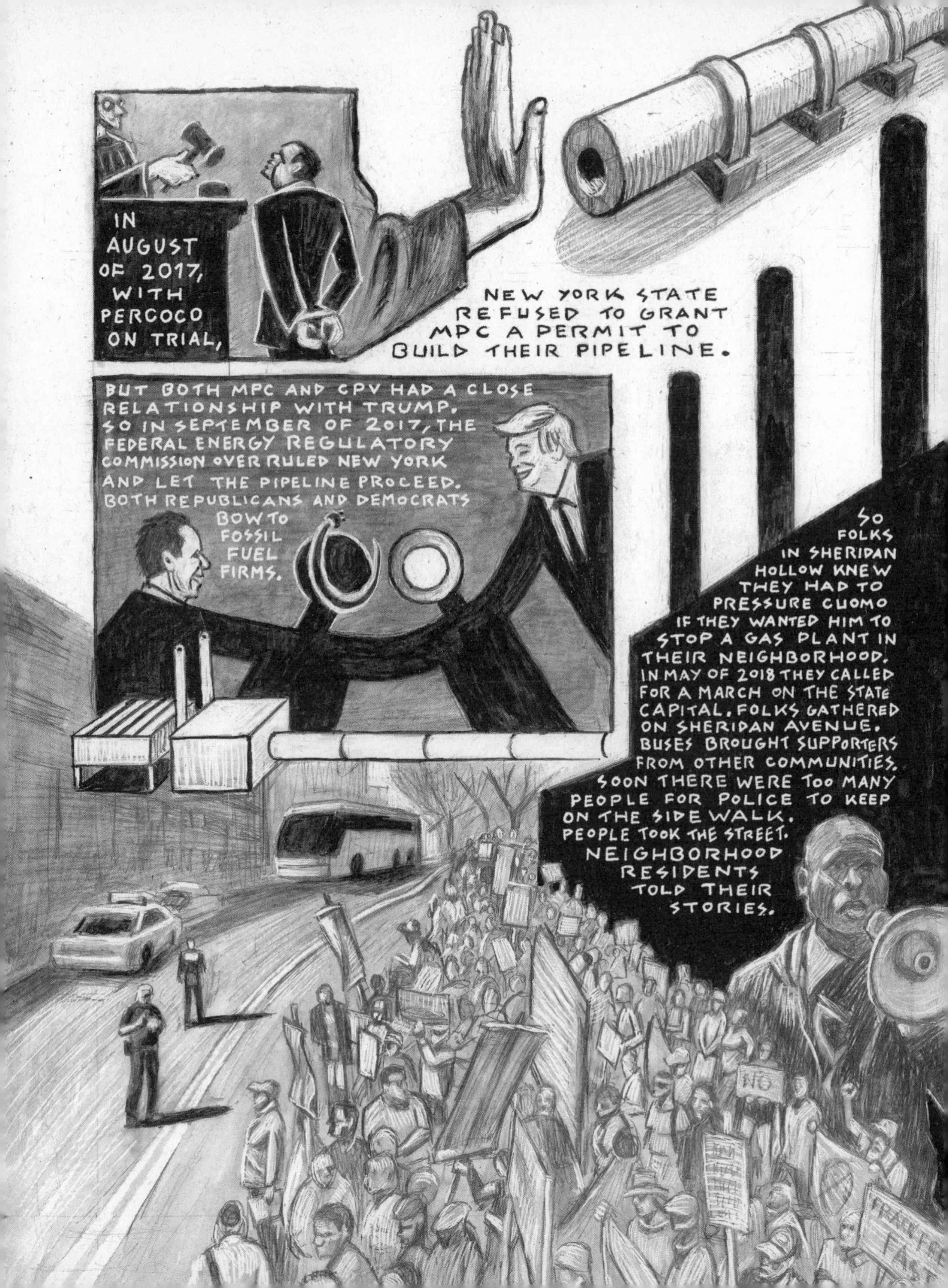
IN AUGUST OF 2017, WITH PERCOCO ON TRIAL,
NEW YORK STATE REFUSED TO GRANT MPC A PERMIT TO BUILD THEIR PIPELINE.
BUT BOTH MPC AND CPV HAD A CLOSE RELATIONSHIP WITH TRUMP. SO IN SEPTEMBER OF 2017, THE FEDERAL ENERGY REGULATORY COMMISSION OVERRULED NEW YORK AND LET THE PIPELINE PROCEED.
BOTH REPUBLICANS AND DEMOCRATS BOW TO FOSSIL FUEL FIRMS.
SO FOLKS IN SHERIDAN HOLLOW KNEW THEY HAD TO PRESSURE CUOMO IF THEY WANTED HIM TO STOP A GAS PLANT IN THEIR NEIGHBORHOOD. IN MAY OF 2018 THEY CALLED FOR A MARCH ON THE STATE CAPITAL. FOLKS GATHERED ON SHERIDAN AVENUE. BUSES BROUGHT SUPPORTERS FROM OTHER COMMUNITIES. SOON THERE WERE TOO MANY PEOPLE FOR POLICE TO KEEP ON THE SIDEWALK. PEOPLE TOOK THE STREET.
NEIGHBORHOOD RESIDENTS TOLD THEIR STORIES.
NO

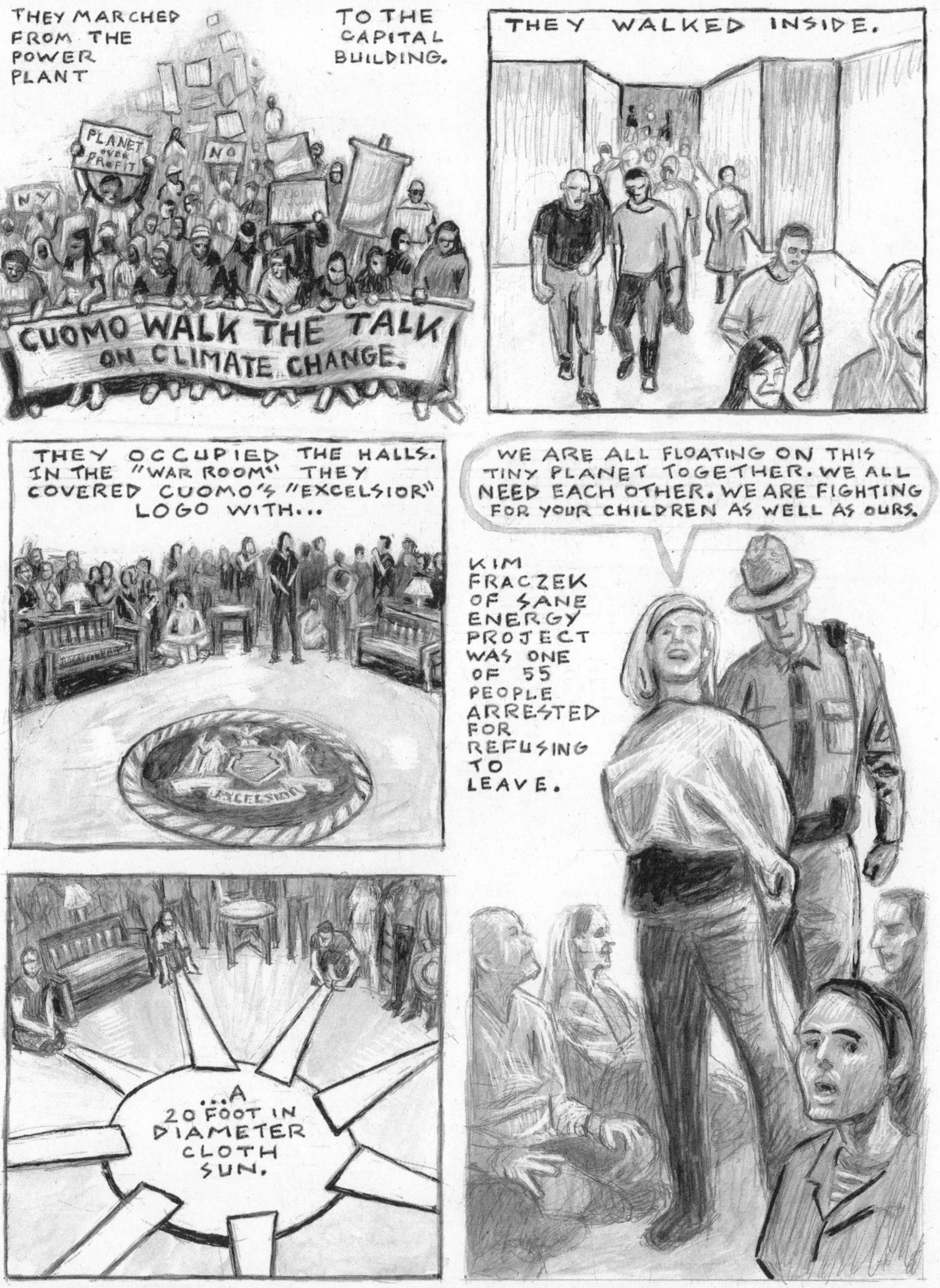
THEY MARCHED FROM THE POWER PLANT
TO THE CAPITAL BUILDING.
PLANET over PROFIT
CUOMO WALK THE TALK ON CLIMATE CHANGE.
THEY WALKED INSIDE.
THEY OCCUPIED THE HALLS. IN THE "WAR ROOM" THEY COVERED CUOMO'S "EXCELSIOR" LOGO WITH...
EXCELSIOR
...A 20 FOOT IN DIAMETER CLOTH SUN.
WE ARE ALL FLOATING ON THIS TINY PLANET TOGETHER. WE ALL NEED EACH OTHER. WE ARE FIGHTING FOR YOUR CHILDREN AS WELL AS OURS.
KIM FRACZEK OF SANE ENERGY PROJECT WAS ONE OF 55 PEOPLE ARRESTED FOR REFUSING TO LEAVE.

AMONG THOSE MARCHING WAS CYNTHIA NIXON, A CANDIDATE FOR GOVERNOR.

AN ACTIVIST I KNEW PUT ME IN TOUCH WITH HER. THAT TURNED INTO SOME NICE CONVERSATIONS. I GAVE CYNTHIA NIXON A GAS-101. SHE ASKED HARD QUESTIONS. LITTLE NERDY DETAILS I TEND TO LEAVE OFF. SHE DEEPLY PAID ATTENTION. I SAW HER FACE.

SHE GETS COOL SUPER STREET CRED FOR ANNOUNCING HER CLIMATE PLATFORM IN THE ROCKAWAYS, A COMMUNITY HARD HIT BY HURRICANE SANDY.

I AM HONORED TO STAND WITH YOU.

THANK YOU FOR THE WORK YOU DO EVERY DAY TO PERSEVERE.

DURING HER SPEECH, CUOMO CHOSE THAT VERY MOMENT TO DENY A PERMIT TO A GAS PIPELINE. PEOPLE HAD BEEN PRESSURING HIM TO STOP THAT PIPELINE FOR A YEAR. WHETHER OR NOT SHE GETS ELECTED, CYNTHIA HAS DONE AN AMAZING JOB ALREADY!

WITH CYNTHIA NIXON HOT ON HIS TRAIL, CUOMO STARTED TO TALK A GREAT FIGHT ON THE ENVIRONMENT.

I WILL BAN FRACKED GAS POWER PLANTS.

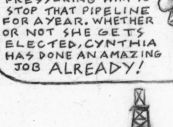

I WILL LEAD A DUNKIRK STYLE FLOATILLA TO BLOCKADE ANY TRUMP PLANS FOR OFFSHORE OIL DRILLING IN NEW YORK WATERS!

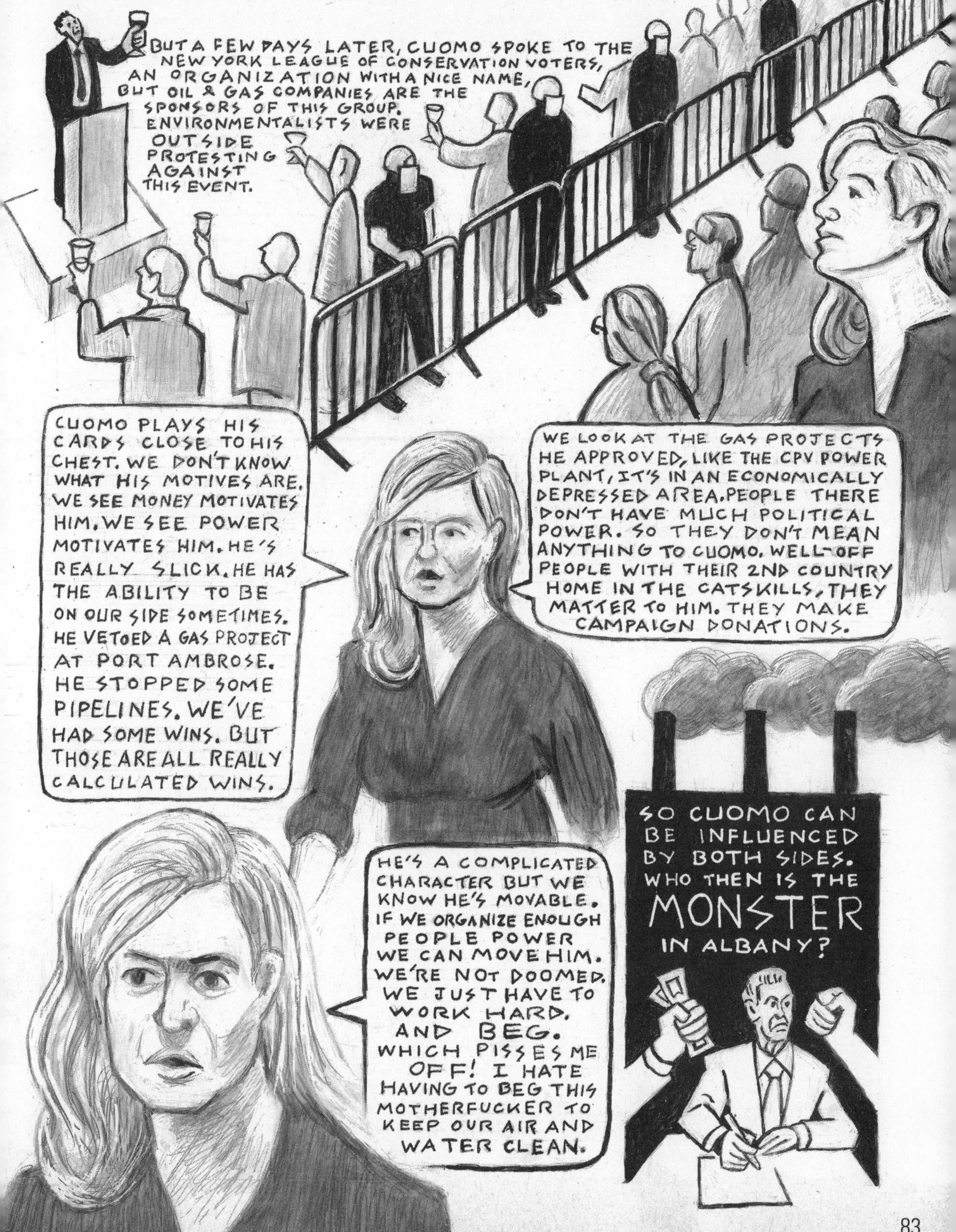

BUT A FEW DAYS LATER, CUOMO SPOKE TO THE NEW YORK LEAGUE OF CONSERVATION VOTERS, AN ORGANIZATION WITH A NICE NAME, BUT OIL & GAS COMPANIES ARE THE SPONSORS OF THIS GROUP. ENVIRONMENTALISTS WERE OUTSIDE PROTESTING AGAINST THIS EVENT.
CUOMO PLAYS HIS CARDS CLOSE TO HIS CHEST. WE DON'T KNOW WHAT HIS MOTIVES ARE. WE SEE MONEY MOTIVATES HIM. WE SEE POWER MOTIVATES HIM. HE'S REALLY SLICK. HE HAS THE ABILITY TO BE ON OUR SIDE SOMETIMES. HE VETOED A GAS PROJECT AT PORT AMBROSE. HE STOPPED SOME PIPELINES. WE'VE HAD SOME WINS. BUT THOSE ARE ALL REALLY CALCULATED WINS.
WE LOOK AT THE GAS PROJECTS HE APPROVED, LIKE THE CPV POWER PLANT, IT'S IN AN ECONOMICALLY DEPRESSED AREA. PEOPLE THERE DON'T HAVE MUCH POLITICAL POWER. SO THEY DON'T MEAN ANYTHING TO CUOMO. WELL-OFF PEOPLE WITH THEIR 2ND COUNTRY HOME IN THE CATSKILLS, THEY MATTER TO HIM. THEY MAKE CAMPAIGN DONATIONS.
HE'S A COMPLICATED CHARACTER BUT WE KNOW HE'S MOVABLE. IF WE ORGANIZE ENOUGH PEOPLE POWER WE CAN MOVE HIM. WE'RE NOT DOOMED. WE JUST HAVE TO WORK HARD. AND BEG. WHICH PISSES ME OFF! I HATE HAVING TO BEG THIS MOTHERFUCKER TO KEEP OUR AIR AND WATER CLEAN.
SO CUOMO CAN BE INFLUENCED BY BOTH SIDES. WHO THEN IS THE MONSTER IN ALBANY?

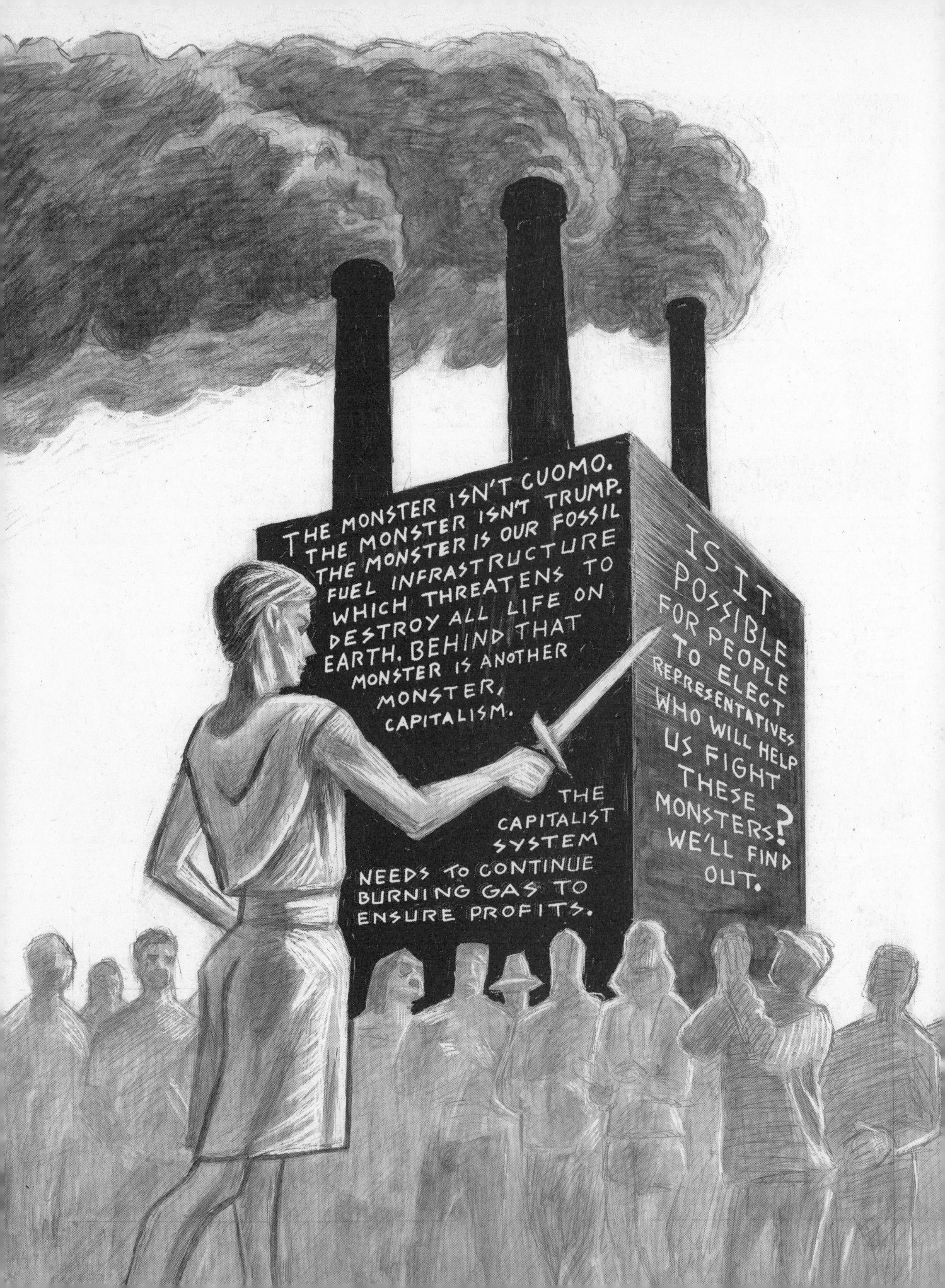
THE MONSTER ISN'T CUOMO. THE MONSTER ISN'T TRUMP. THE MONSTER IS OUR FOSSIL FUEL INFRASTRUCTURE WHICH THREATENS TO DESTROY ALL LIFE ON EARTH. BEHIND THAT MONSTER IS ANOTHER MONSTER, CAPITALISM.
THE CAPITALIST SYSTEM NEEDS TO CONTINUE BURNING GAS TO ENSURE PROFITS.
IS IT POSSIBLE FOR PEOPLE TO ELECT REPRESENTATIVES WHO WILL HELP US FIGHT THESE MONSTERS? WE'LL FIND OUT.

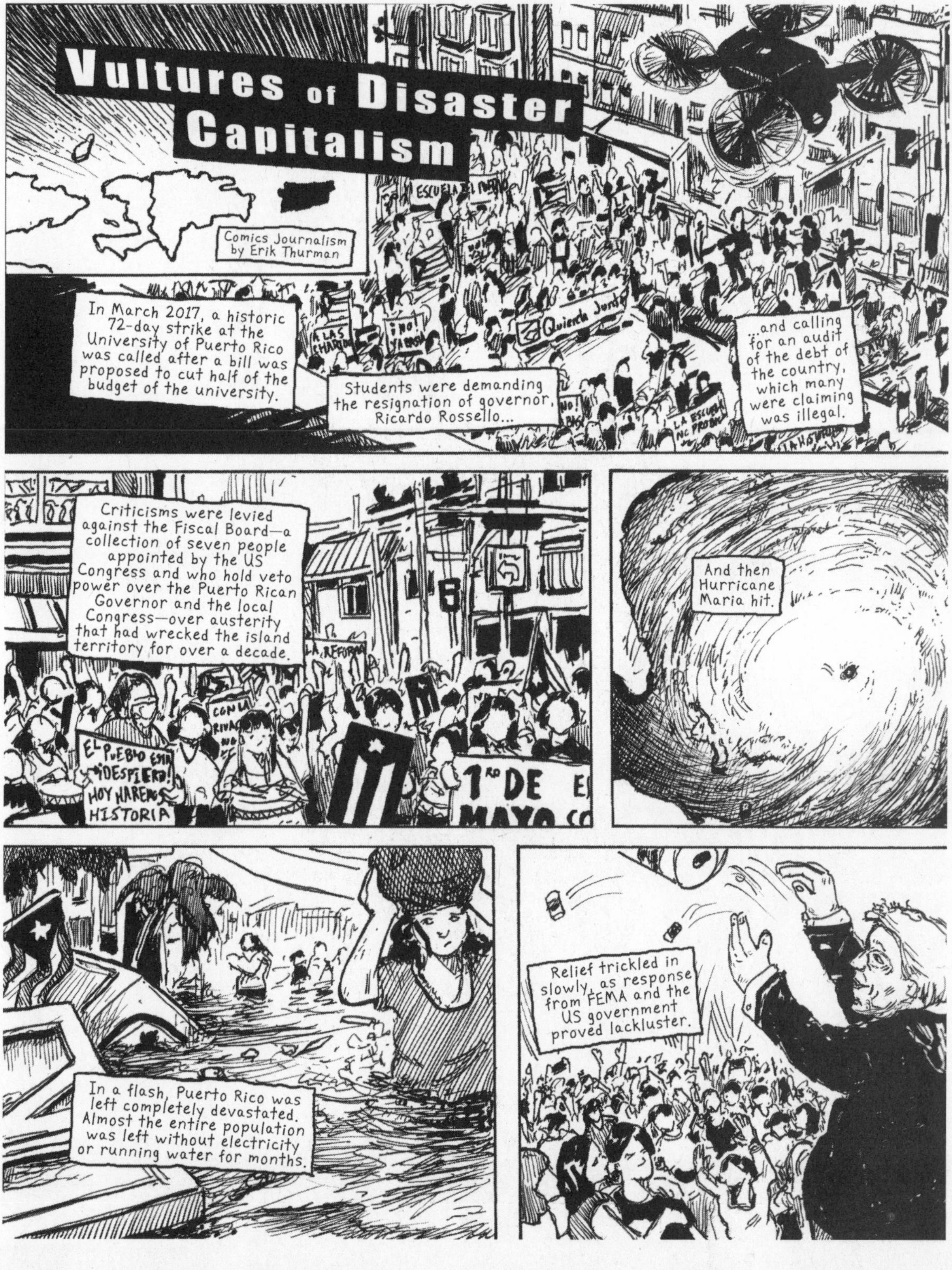
Vultures of Disaster Capitalism
Comics Journalism by Erik Thurman
In March 2017, a historic 72-day strike at the University of Puerto Rico was called after a bill was proposed to cut half of the budget of the university.
Students were demanding the resignation of governor, Ricardo Rossello...
...and calling for an audit of the debt of the country, which many were claiming was illegal.
Criticisms were levied against the Fiscal Board—a collection of seven people appointed by the US Congress and who hold veto power over the Puerto Rican Governor and the local Congress—over austerity that had wrecked the island territory for over a decade.
And then Hurricane Maria hit.
In a flash, Puerto Rico was left completely devastated. Almost the entire population was left without electricity or running water for months.
Relief trickled in slowly, as response from FEMA and the US government proved lackluster.

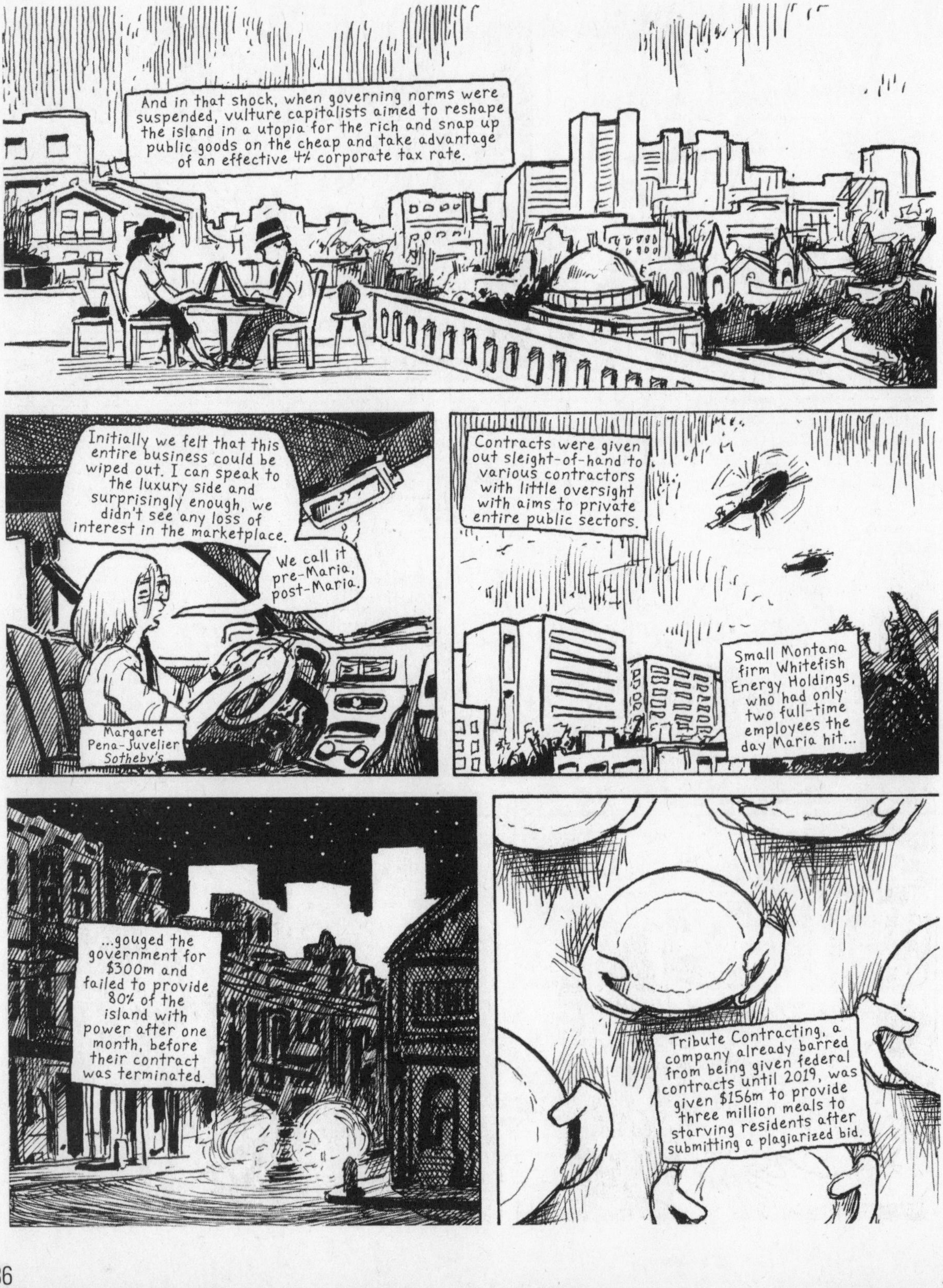
And in that shock, when governing norms were suspended, vulture capitalists aimed to reshape the island in a utopia for the rich and snap up public goods on the cheap and take advantage of an effective 4% corporate tax rate.
Initially we felt that this entire business could be wiped out. I can speak to the luxury side and surprisingly enough, we didn't see any loss of interest in the marketplace.
We call it pre-Maria, post-Maria.
Margaret Pena-Juvelier Sotheby's.
Contracts were given out sleight-of-hand to various contractors with little oversight with aims to private entire public sectors.
Small Montana firm Whitefish Energy Holdings, who had only two full-time employees the day Maria hit...
...gouged the government for $300m and failed to provide 80% of the island with power after one month, before their contract was terminated.
Tribute Contracting, a company already barred from being given federal contracts until 2019, was given $156m to provide three million meals to starving residents after submitting a plagiarized bid.

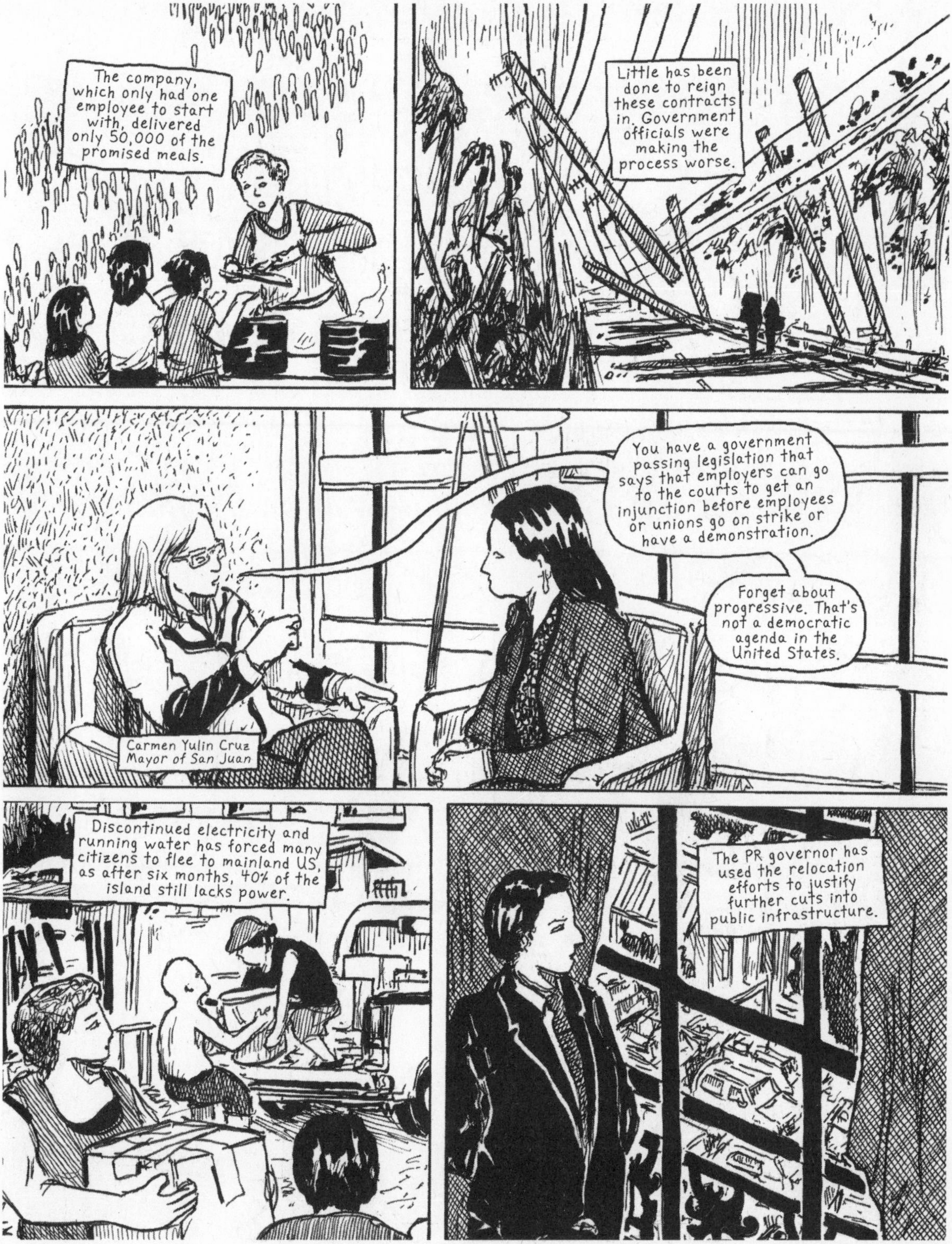

The company, which only had one employee to start with, delivered only 50,000 of the promised meals.
Little has been done to reign these contracts in. Government officials were making the process worse.
You have a government passing legislation that says that employers can go to the courts to get an injunction before employees or unions go on strike or have a demonstration.
Forget about progressive. That's not a democratic agenda in the United States.
Carmen Yulin Cruz
Mayor of San Juan
Discontinued electricity and running water has forced many citizens to flee to mainland US, as after six months, 40% of the island still lacks power.
The PR governor has used the relocation efforts to justify further cuts into public infrastructure.

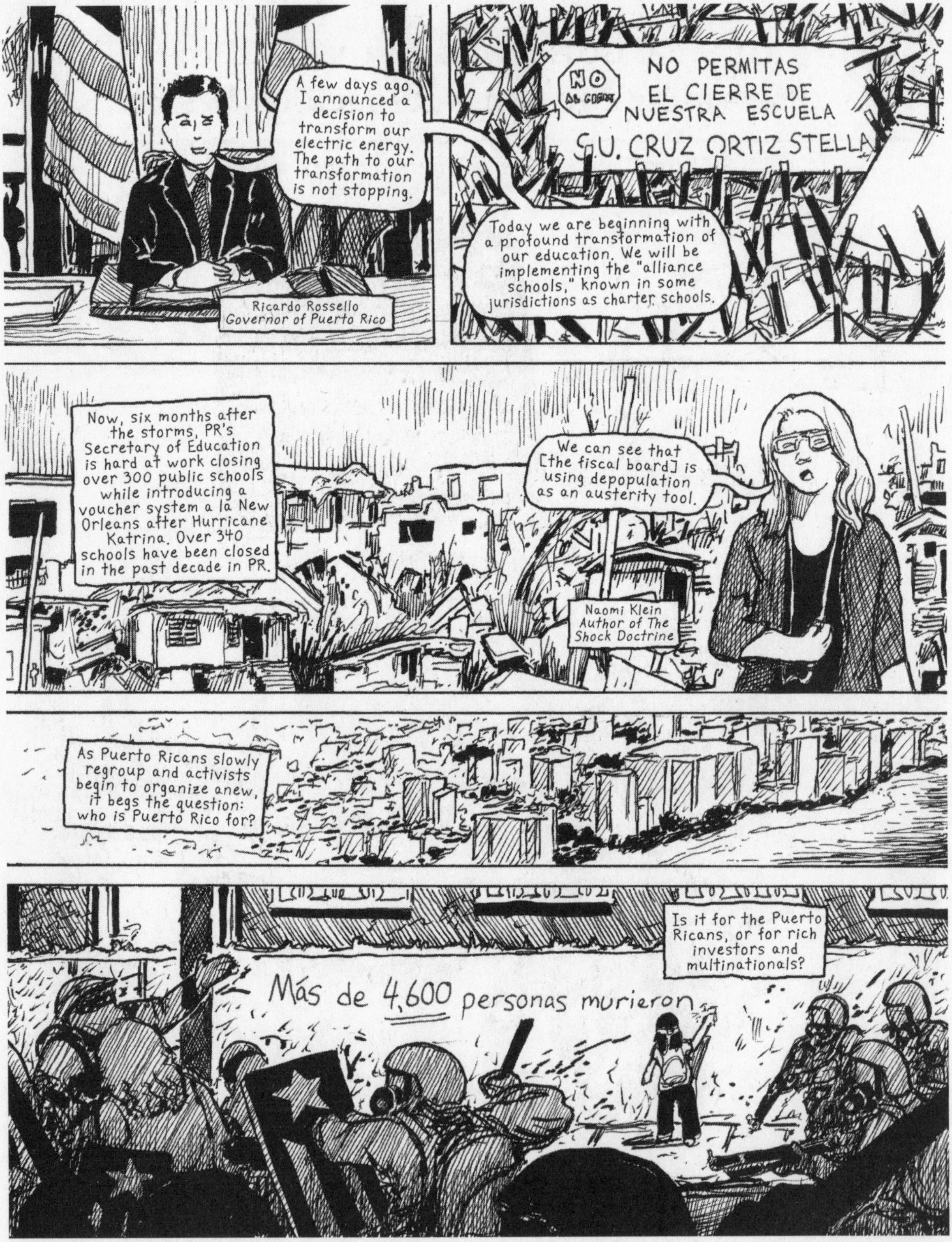
A few days ago, I announced a decision to transform our electric energy. The path to our transformation is not stopping.
Ricardo Rossello
Governor of Puerto Rico
NO
NO PERMITAS
EL CIERRE DE
NUESTRA ESCUELA
S.U. CRUZ ORTIZ STELLA
Today we are beginning with a profound transformation of our education. We will be implementing the "alliance schools," known in some jurisdictions as charter schools.
Now, six months after the storms, PR's Secretary of Education is hard at work closing over 300 public schools while introducing a voucher system a la New Orleans after Hurricane Katrina. Over 340 schools have been closed in the past decade in PR.
We can see that [the fiscal board] is using depopulation as an austerity tool.
Naomi Klein
Author of The Shock Doctrine
As Puerto Ricans slowly regroup and activists begin to organize anew, it begs the question: who is Puerto Rico for?
Is it for the Puerto Ricans, or for rich investors and multinationals?
Más de 4,600 personas murieron

Civil Forfeiture; or, How the Monster Takes on a Multitude of Guises and Shapes, All the While Retaining the Same Rapacious Desire.

A Short Tale in Three Parts by Erik Jacobson

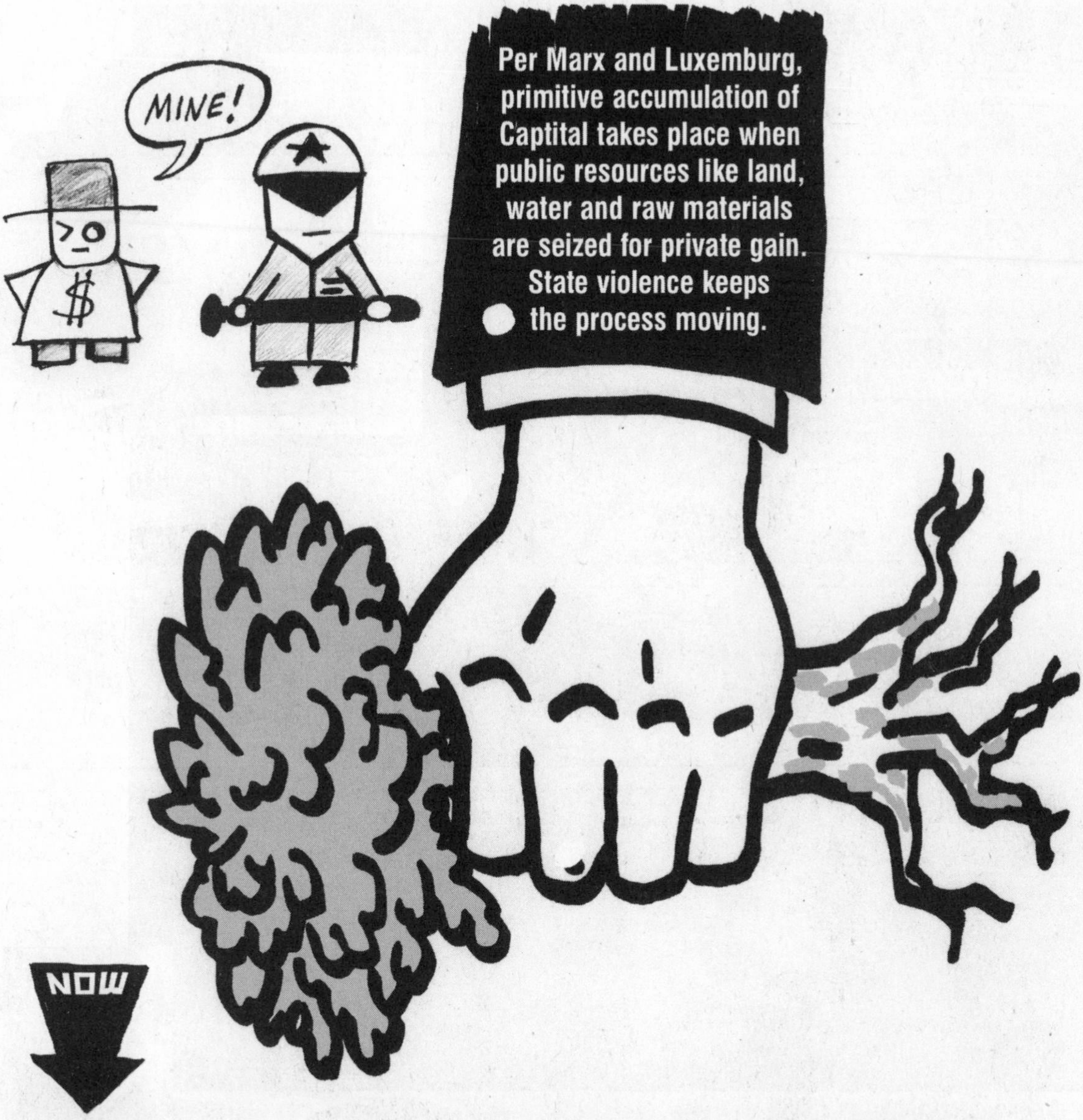
MINE!
Per Marx and Luxemburg, primitive accumulation of Captital takes place when public resources like land, water and raw materials are seized for private gain. State violence keeps the process moving.
NOW

Nestle makes massive profits from water it gets on the cheap from the state of Michigan while people in Flint (amongst other places) don't have clean drinking water.

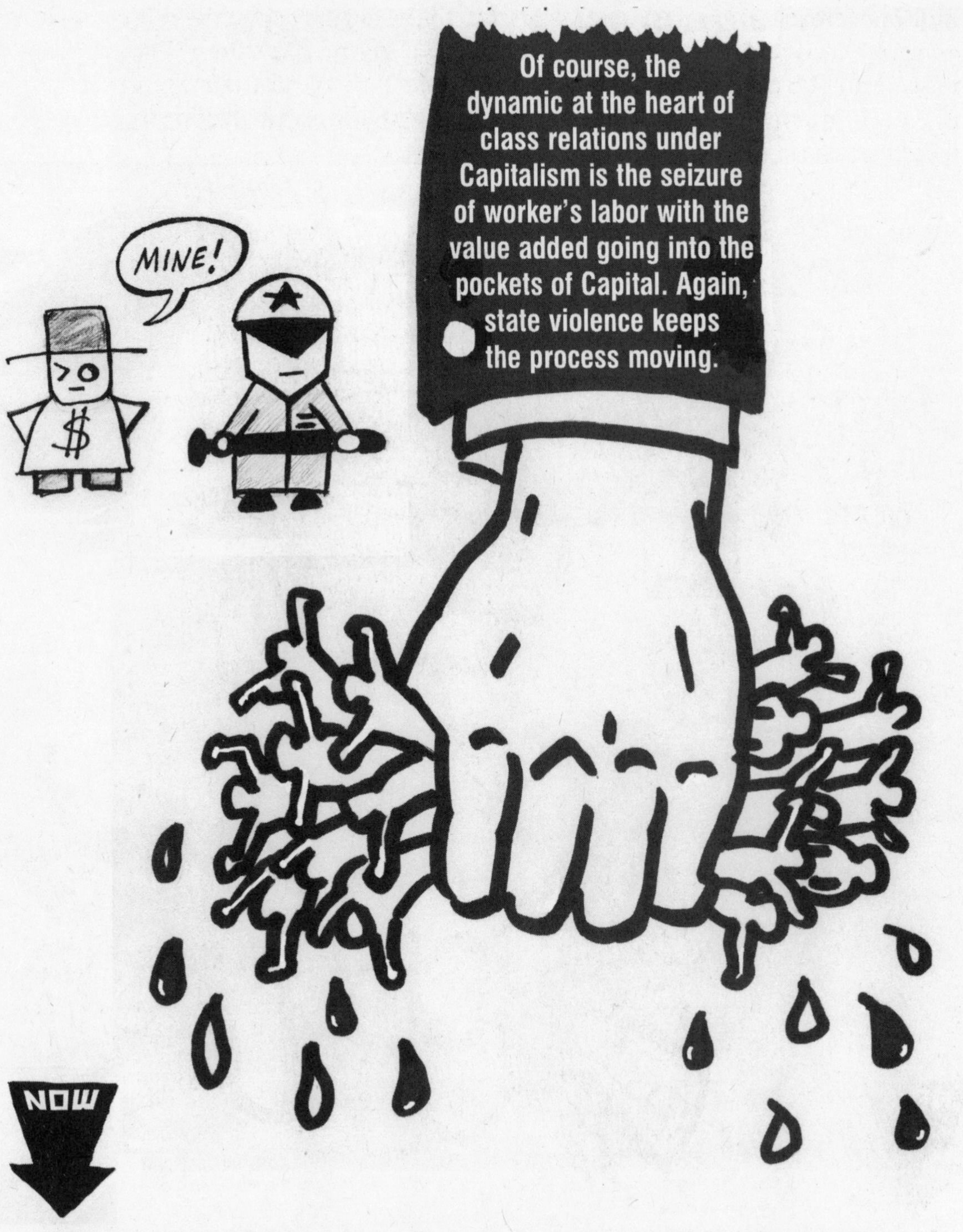
Of course, the dynamic at the heart of class relations under Capitalism is the seizure of worker's labor with the value added going into the pockets of Capital. Again, state violence keeps the process moving.
MINE!
NOW

Disneyworld, Walmart, Amazon and the like make billions of dollars in profits while their workers sleep in cars, have to skip meals and lack adequate health insurance.

Civil Forfeiture allows the State to seize the assets of individuals without a criminal conviction, or even evidence that a crime has taken place. Local police and ICE take cars, boat, houses and cash to fund their activities and buy equipment. It can take years, if ever, for innocent people to get their property back.

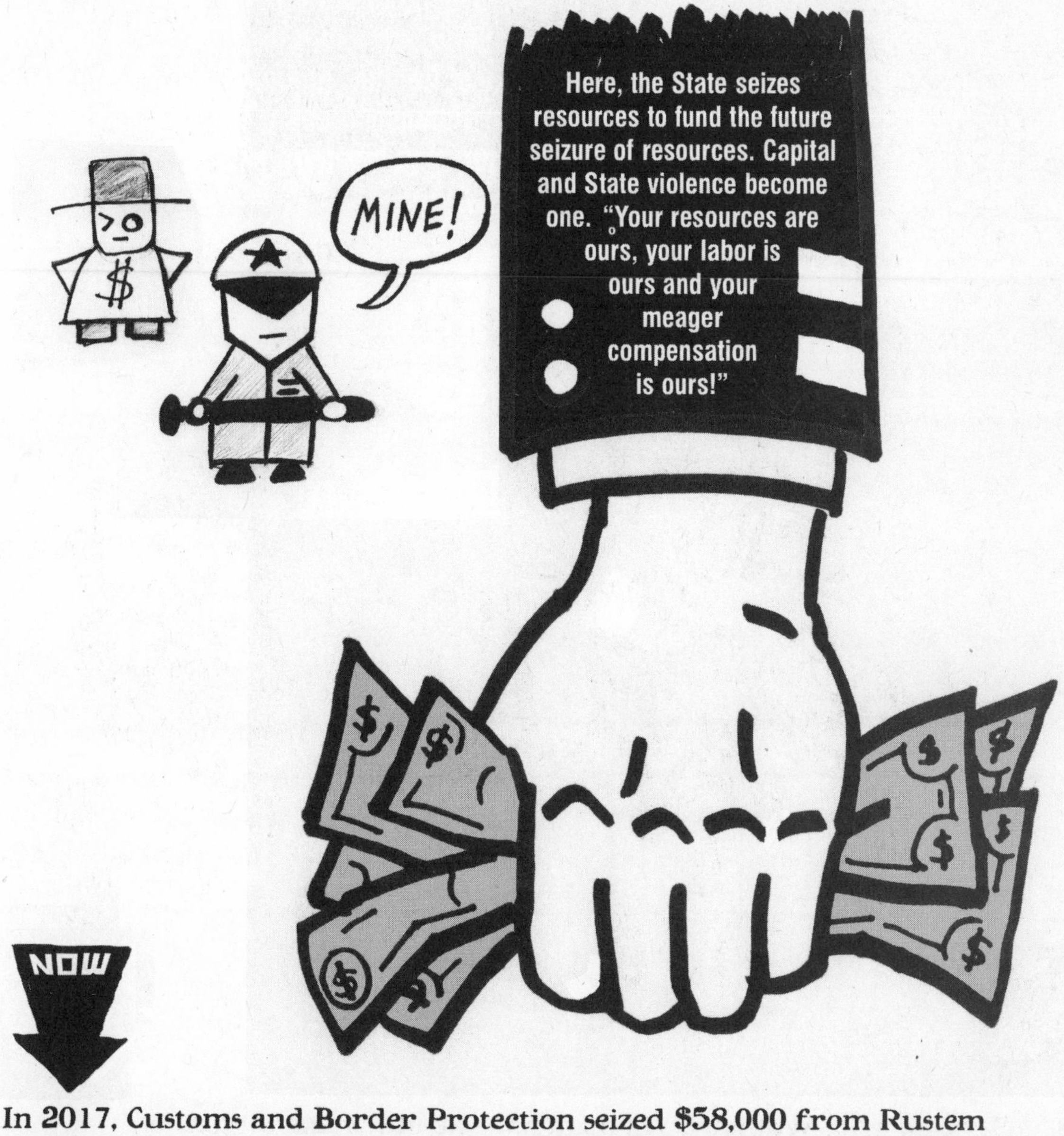
MINE!
Here, the State seizes resources to fund the future seizure of resources. Capital and State violence become one. "Your resources are ours, your labor is ours and your meager compensation is ours!"
NOW

In 2017, Customs and Border Protection seized $58,000 from Rustem Kazazi without charging him of a crime. It seizes millions more each year.

And so, the monster continues to feed...

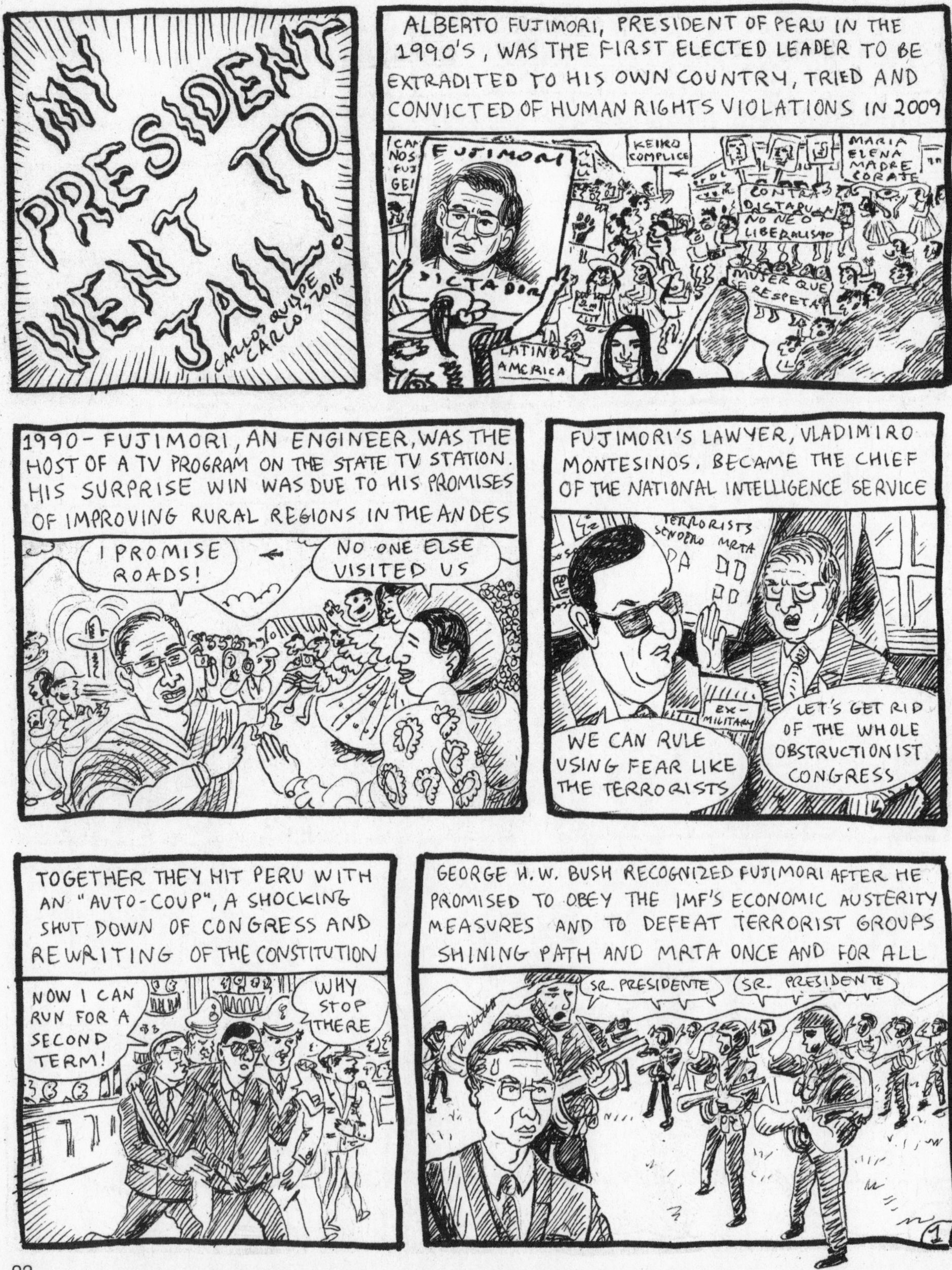
MY PRESIDENT WENT TO JAIL!
CARLOS QUISPE
CARLOS 2018
ALBERTO FUJIMORI, PRESIDENT OF PERU IN THE 1990'S, WAS THE FIRST ELECTED LEADER TO BE EXTRADITED TO HIS OWN COUNTRY, TRIED AND CONVICTED OF HUMAN RIGHTS VIOLATIONS IN 2009
FUJIMORI
DICTADOR
KEIKO COMPLICE
MARIA ELENA MADRE CORAJE
CONTRA DICTADURA
NO NEO LIBERALISMO
MUJER QUE SE RESPETA
LATINO AMERICA
1990 - FUJIMORI, AN ENGINEER, WAS THE HOST OF A TV PROGRAM ON THE STATE TV STATION. HIS SURPRISE WIN WAS DUE TO HIS PROMISES OF IMPROVING RURAL REGIONS IN THE ANDES
I PROMISE ROADS!
NO ONE ELSE VISITED US
FUJIMORI'S LAWYER, VLADIMIRO MONTESINOS, BECAME THE CHIEF OF THE NATIONAL INTELLIGENCE SERVICE
TERRORISTS SENDERO MRTA
EX-MILITARY
WE CAN RULE USING FEAR LIKE THE TERRORISTS
LET'S GET RID OF THE WHOLE OBSTRUCTIONIST CONGRESS
TOGETHER THEY HIT PERU WITH AN "AUTO-COUP", A SHOCKING SHUT DOWN OF CONGRESS AND REWRITING OF THE CONSTITUTION
NOW I CAN RUN FOR A SECOND TERM!
WHY STOP THERE
GEORGE H.W. BUSH RECOGNIZED FUJIMORI AFTER HE PROMISED TO OBEY THE IMF'S ECONOMIC AUSTERITY MEASURES AND TO DEFEAT TERRORIST GROUPS SHINING PATH AND MRTA ONCE AND FOR ALL
SR. PRESIDENTE
SR. PRESIDENTE
1

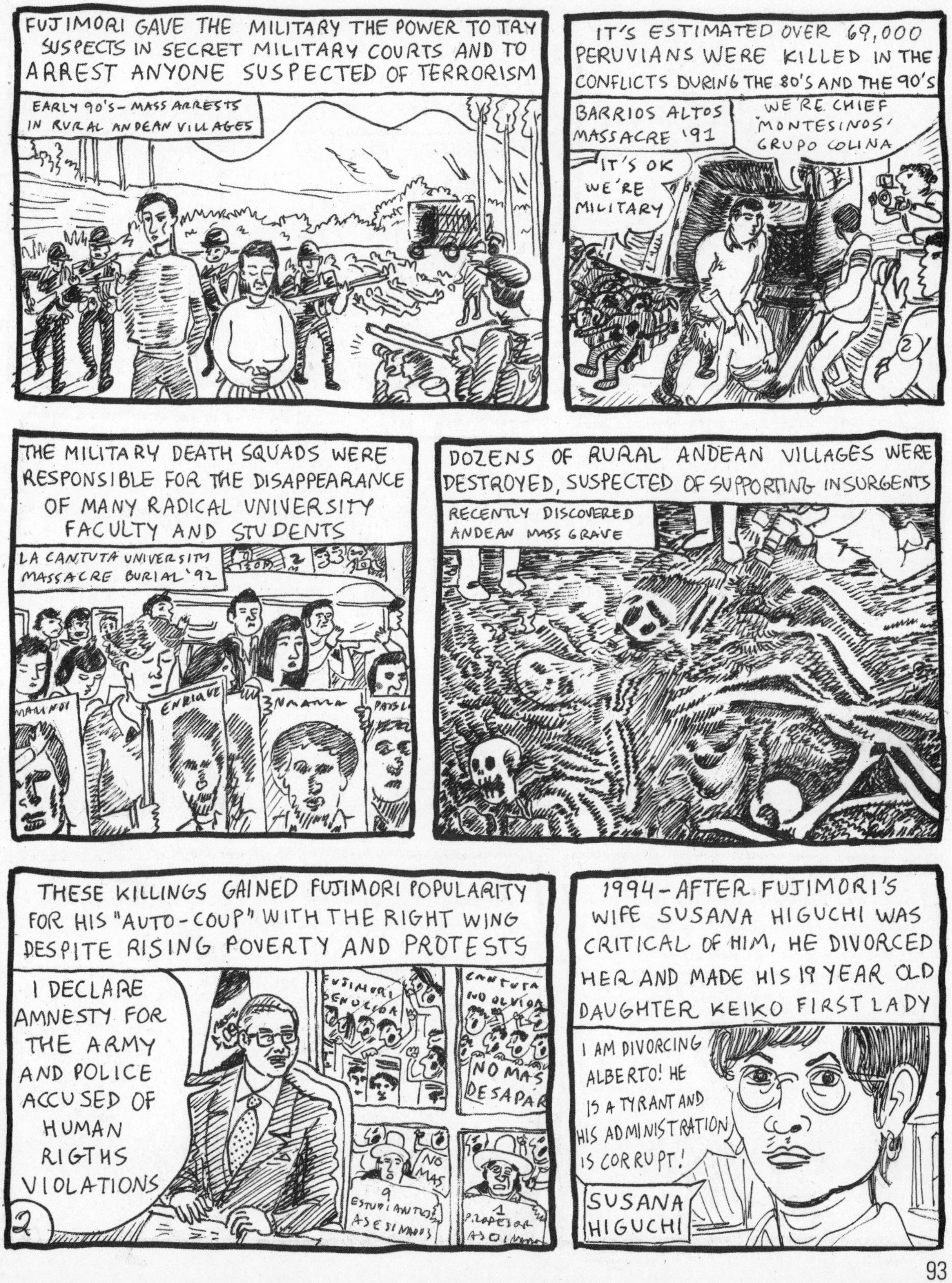
FUJIMORI GAVE THE MILITARY THE POWER TO TRY SUSPECTS IN SECRET MILITARY COURTS AND TO ARREST ANYONE SUSPECTED OF TERRORISM
EARLY 90'S—MASS ARRESTS IN RURAL ANDEAN VILLAGES
IT'S ESTIMATED OVER 69,000 PERUVIANS WERE KILLED IN THE CONFLICTS DURING THE 80'S AND THE 90'S
BARRIOS ALTOS MASSACRE '91
WE'RE CHIEF 'MONTESINOS' GRUPO COLINA
IT'S OK WE'RE MILITARY
THE MILITARY DEATH SQUADS WERE RESPONSIBLE FOR THE DISAPPEARANCE OF MANY RADICAL UNIVERSITY FACULTY AND STUDENTS
LA CANTUTA UNIVERSITY MASSACRE BURIAL '92
ENRIQUE
DOZENS OF RURAL ANDEAN VILLAGES WERE DESTROYED, SUSPECTED OF SUPPORTING INSURGENTS
RECENTLY DISCOVERED ANDEAN MASS GRAVE
THESE KILLINGS GAINED FUJIMORI POPULARITY FOR HIS "AUTO-COUP" WITH THE RIGHT WING DESPITE RISING POVERTY AND PROTESTS
I DECLARE AMNESTY FOR THE ARMY AND POLICE ACCUSED OF HUMAN RIGTHS VIOLATIONS
CANTUTA NO OLVIDA
NO MAS DESAPAR
NO MAS
1994—AFTER FUJIMORI'S WIFE SUSANA HIGUCHI WAS CRITICAL OF HIM, HE DIVORCED HER AND MADE HIS 19 YEAR OLD DAUGHTER KEIKO FIRST LADY
I AM DIVORCING ALBERTO! HE IS A TYRANT AND HIS ADMINISTRATION IS CORRUPT!
SUSANA HIGUCHI

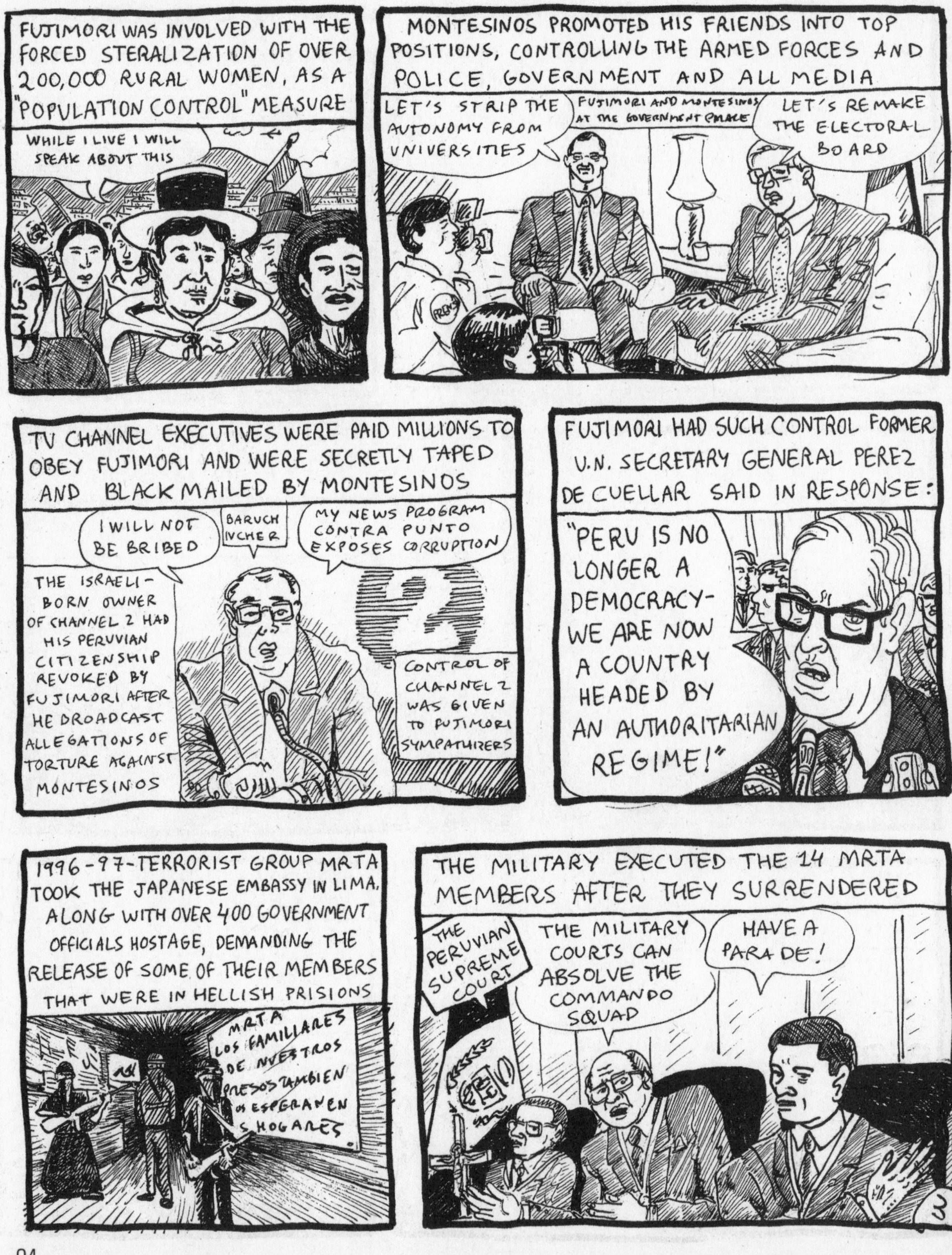
FUJIMORI WAS INVOLVED WITH THE FORCED STERALIZATION OF OVER 200,000 RURAL WOMEN, AS A "POPULATION CONTROL" MEASURE
WHILE I LIVE I WILL SPEAK ABOUT THIS
MONTESINOS PROMOTED HIS FRIENDS INTO TOP POSITIONS, CONTROLLING THE ARMED FORCES AND POLICE, GOVERNMENT AND ALL MEDIA
LET'S STRIP THE AUTONOMY FROM UNIVERSITIES
FUJIMORI AND MONTESINOS AT THE GOVERNMENT PALACE
LET'S REMAKE THE ELECTORAL BOARD
PRENSA
TV CHANNEL EXECUTIVES WERE PAID MILLIONS TO OBEY FUJIMORI AND WERE SECRETLY TAPED AND BLACKMAILED BY MONTESINOS
I WILL NOT BE BRIBED
BARUCH IVCHER
MY NEWS PROGRAM CONTRA PUNTO EXPOSES CORRUPTION
THE ISRAELI-BORN OWNER OF CHANNEL 2 HAD HIS PERUVIAN CITIZENSHIP REVOKED BY FUJIMORI AFTER HE BROADCAST ALLEGATIONS OF TORTURE AGAINST MONTESINOS
CONTROL OF CHANNEL 2 WAS GIVEN TO FUJIMORI SYMPATHIZERS
FUJIMORI HAD SUCH CONTROL FORMER U.N. SECRETARY GENERAL PEREZ DE CUELLAR SAID IN RESPONSE:
"PERU IS NO LONGER A DEMOCRACY- WE ARE NOW A COUNTRY HEADED BY AN AUTHORITARIAN REGIME!"
1996-97-TERRORIST GROUP MRTA TOOK THE JAPANESE EMBASSY IN LIMA, ALONG WITH OVER 400 GOVERNMENT OFFICIALS HOSTAGE, DEMANDING THE RELEASE OF SOME OF THEIR MEMBERS THAT WERE IN HELLISH PRISIONS
MRTA LOS FAMILIARES DE NUESTROS PRESOS TAMBIEN LOS ESPERAN EN SUS HOGARES
THE MILITARY EXECUTED THE 14 MRTA MEMBERS AFTER THEY SURRENDERED
THE PERUVIAN SUPREME COURT
THE MILITARY COURTS CAN ABSOLVE THE COMMANDO SQUAD
HAVE A PARADE!

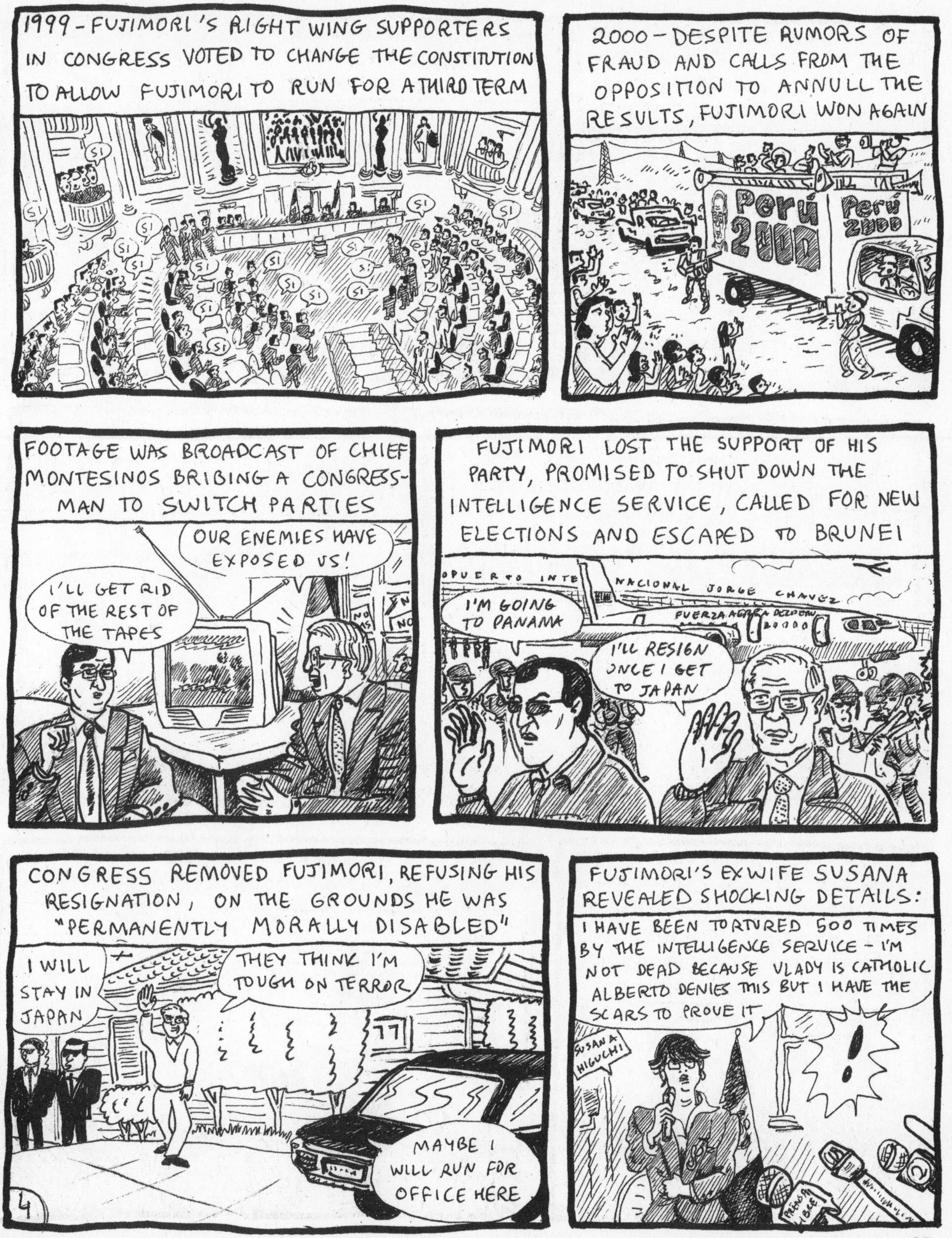
1999 - FUJIMORI'S RIGHT WING SUPPORTERS IN CONGRESS VOTED TO CHANGE THE CONSTITUTION TO ALLOW FUJIMORI TO RUN FOR A THIRD TERM
SÍ
2000 - DESPITE RUMORS OF FRAUD AND CALLS FROM THE OPPOSITION TO ANNULL THE RESULTS, FUJIMORI WON AGAIN
Perú 2000
Perú 2000
FOOTAGE WAS BROADCAST OF CHIEF MONTESINOS BRIBING A CONGRESSMAN TO SWITCH PARTIES
OUR ENEMIES HAVE EXPOSED US!
I'LL GET RID OF THE REST OF THE TAPES
FUJIMORI LOST THE SUPPORT OF HIS PARTY, PROMISED TO SHUT DOWN THE INTELLIGENCE SERVICE, CALLED FOR NEW ELECTIONS AND ESCAPED TO BRUNEI
I'M GOING TO PANAMA
I'LL RESIGN ONCE I GET TO JAPAN
CONGRESS REMOVED FUJIMORI, REFUSING HIS RESIGNATION, ON THE GROUNDS HE WAS "PERMANENTLY MORALLY DISABLED"
I WILL STAY IN JAPAN
THEY THINK I'M TOUGH ON TERROR
MAYBE I WILL RUN FOR OFFICE HERE
FUJIMORI'S EX WIFE SUSANA REVEALED SHOCKING DETAILS:
I HAVE BEEN TORTURED 500 TIMES BY THE INTELLIGENCE SERVICE - I'M NOT DEAD BECAUSE VLADY IS CATHOLIC ALBERTO DENIES THIS BUT I HAVE THE SCARS TO PROVE IT
SUSANA HIGUCHI
!

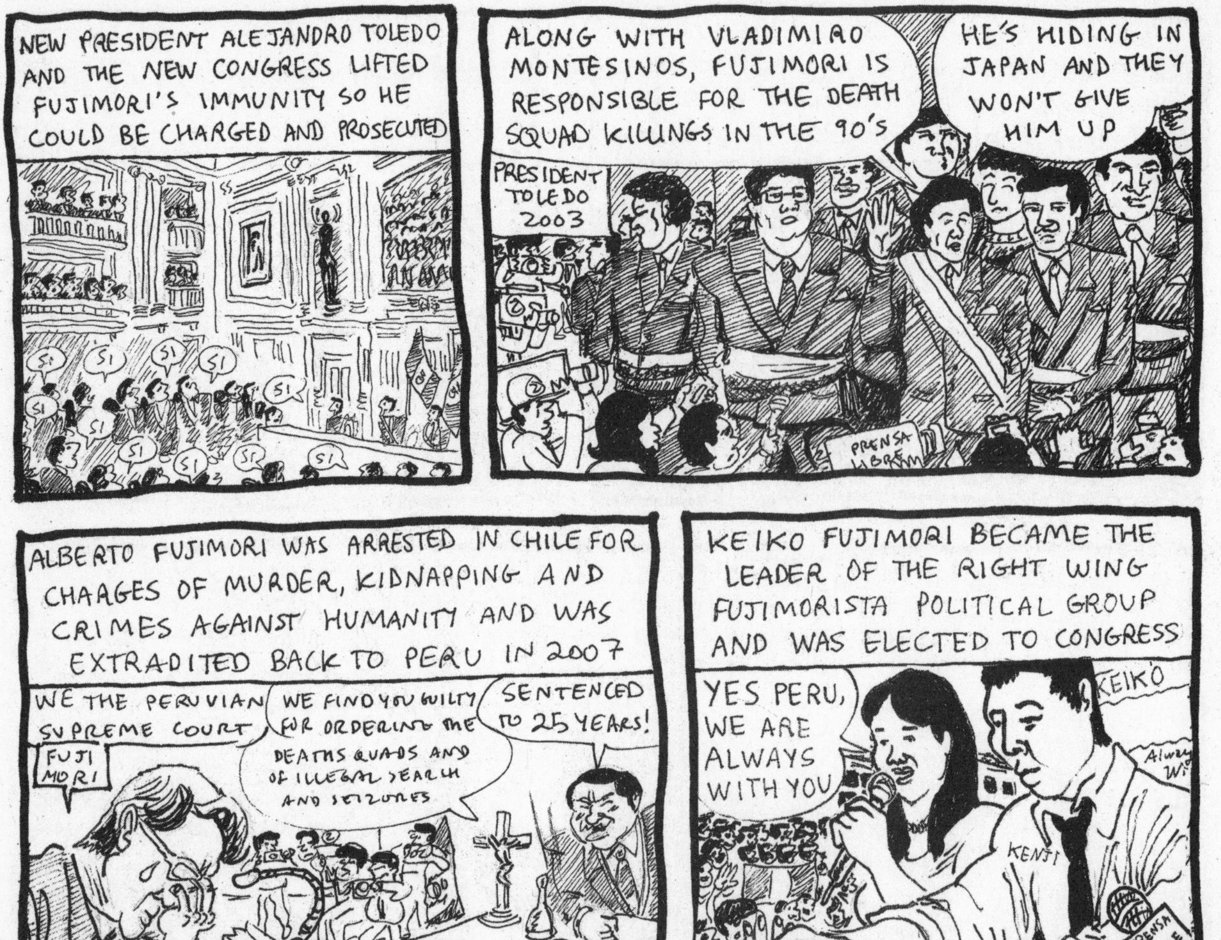
NEW PRESIDENT ALEJANDRO TOLEDO AND THE NEW CONGRESS LIFTED FUJIMORI'S IMMUNITY SO HE COULD BE CHARGED AND PROSECUTED
SI
SI
SI
SI
SI
SI
SI
SI
SI
SI
ALONG WITH VLADIMIRO MONTESINOS, FUJIMORI IS RESPONSIBLE FOR THE DEATH SQUAD KILLINGS IN THE 90'S
HE'S HIDING IN JAPAN AND THEY WON'T GIVE HIM UP
PRESIDENT TOLEDO 2003
PRENSA LIBRE
ALBERTO FUJIMORI WAS ARRESTED IN CHILE FOR CHARGES OF MURDER, KIDNAPPING AND CRIMES AGAINST HUMANITY AND WAS EXTRADITED BACK TO PERU IN 2007
WE THE PERUVIAN SUPREME COURT
WE FIND YOU GUILTY FOR ORDERING THE DEATH SQUADS AND OF ILLEGAL SEARCH AND SEIZURES
SENTENCED TO 25 YEARS!
FUJI MORI
KEIKO FUJIMORI BECAME THE LEADER OF THE RIGHT WING FUJIMORISTA POLITICAL GROUP AND WAS ELECTED TO CONGRESS
YES PERU, WE ARE ALWAYS WITH YOU
KEIKO
KENJI
PRENSA LIBRE
AFTER MANY MORE TRIALS FUJI-MORI PLEADED GUILTY TO MORE CRIMES HE DID WITH MONTESINOS
THESE TRIALS ARE POLITICALLY MOTIVATED!
THEY JUST WANT TO HURT MY DAUGHTER'S CAREER!
5
VLADIMIRO MONTESINOS WAS EVENTUALLY CAPTURED AND IS CURRENTLY IN PRISION. HE WAS ON TRIAL FOR ORDERING THE KILLINGS OF THE MRTA MEMBERS THAT TOOK THE JAPANESE EMBASSY HOSTAGE
MAKE WAY
PRENSA LIBRE
POLICE

Panel 1:

KEIKO AND HER BROTHER KENJI ARE CURRENTLY IN PERUVIAN POLITICS, DEFENDING THEIR FATHER'S RECORD, POPULAR WITH THE RIGHT WING

FUJI MORI

FUERZA KEIKO

K

ALWAYS WITH YOU

Panel 2:

KEIKO FUJIMORI FORMED HER OWN RIGHT WING POLITICAL PARTY AND IN 2010 WAS ELECTED TO CONGRESS

RUDOLPH GIULIANI FUJIMORI POLITICAL CONSULTANT

"*MANSPLAINING*"

KEIKO K K

HMM

Panel 3:

KEIKO ALMOST BECAME PRESIDENT IN 2016 BUT LOST TO KUCZYNSKI, KENJI BECAME A CONGRESSMAN

KEIKO K K

KEIKO 2016

NOW I CAN RUN FOR PRESIDENT!

KEIKO 2016

I'M NOT LIKE MY FATHER

BUT I'LL BE TOUGH ON CRIME!

Panel 4:

IN 2017 ALBERTO FUJIMORI WAS PARDONED BY NEW PRESIDENT KUCZYNSKI AND WAS LET OUT OF JAIL AS A SICK OLD MAN

RECENT PROTESTS- FUJIMORY WAS PARDONED FOR "HEALTH REASON"

CRIMINAL

NO MAS!

NO FUJIMORI LA MORI NO!

KEIKO COMPLICE ASESINA LADRONA

FUJIMORI NO MAS

NO MAS ESTERILIZACIONES NO A LOS FUJIMORI

¡NUNCA MAS!

¡NUNCA MAS!

¡NUNCA MAS!

ASESINO

Panel 5:

2018- FOOTAGE WAS RELEASED OF PRESIDENT KUCZYNSKI AND KENJI FUJIMORI CONSPIRING TO PARDON HIS FATHER FOR A VOTE

WE WERE ADVISED TO BE NON-COMMITAL ABOUT FATHER'S PARDON

I WAS BEING SECRETLY TAPED BY MY ENEMIES!

NOW WE CAN'T BE ON THE SAME SIDE

Panel 6:

AFTER THE TAPE WAS RELEASED PRESIDENT KUCZYNSKI RESIGNED AND KENJI FUJIMORI WAS SUSPENDED FROM CONGRESS

MY FATHER'S GOING BACK TO JAIL FOR MORE CRIMES

KEIKO 2021

NOW CAN I BE PRESIDENT

AND MY BROTHER'S EXPOSED AS A CRIMINAL

PERU

Carlos N. Carlos

6

The FLOWER in the RUBBLE

Rojava & the Kurdish Resistance in Turkey

by Rebecca Migdal

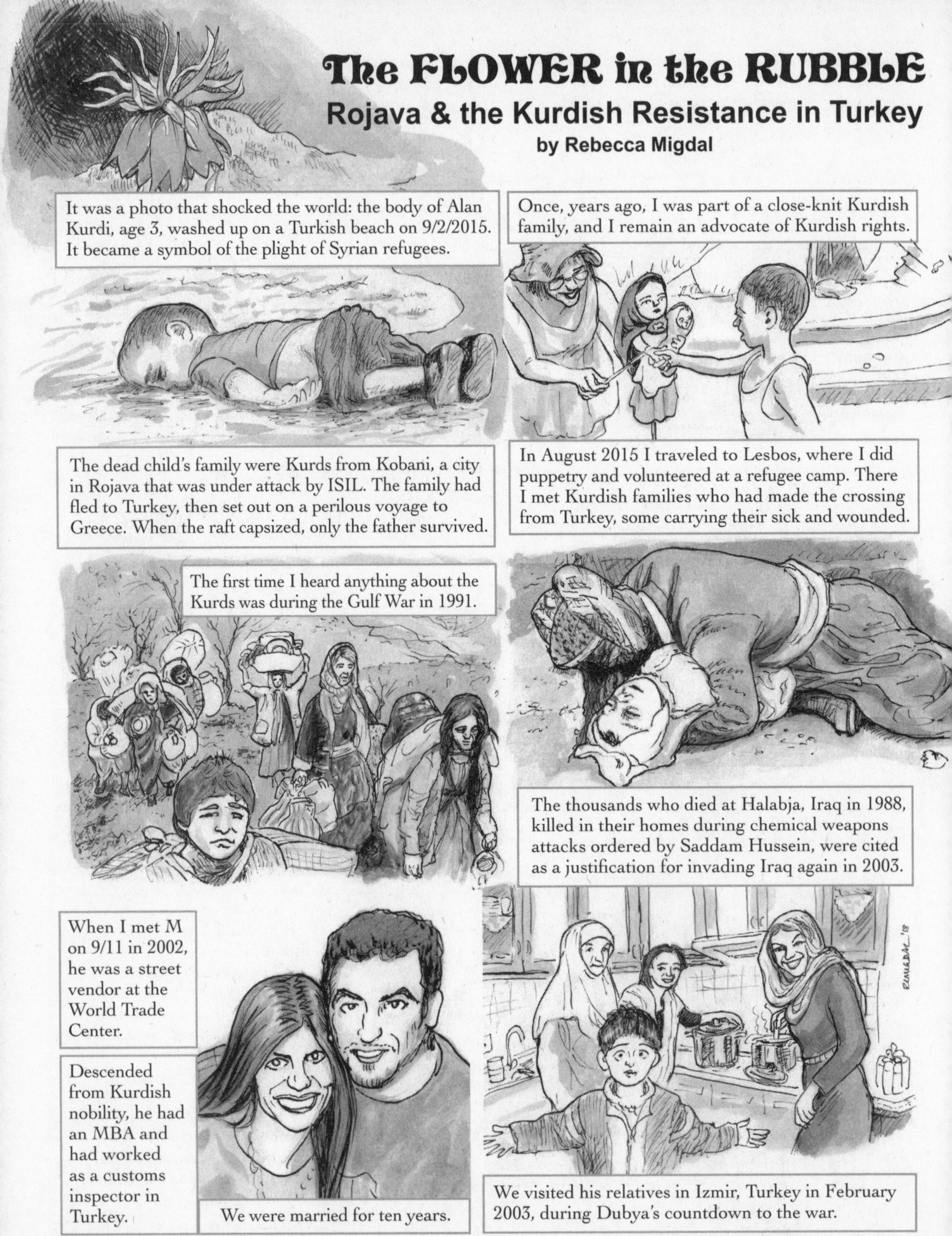

It was a photo that shocked the world: the body of Alan Kurdi, age 3, washed up on a Turkish beach on 9/2/2015. It became a symbol of the plight of Syrian refugees.
The dead child's family were Kurds from Kobani, a city in Rojava that was under attack by ISIL. The family had fled to Turkey, then set out on a perilous voyage to Greece. When the raft capsized, only the father survived.
Once, years ago, I was part of a close-knit Kurdish family, and I remain an advocate of Kurdish rights.
In August 2015 I traveled to Lesbos, where I did puppetry and volunteered at a refugee camp. There I met Kurdish families who had made the crossing from Turkey, some carrying their sick and wounded.
The first time I heard anything about the Kurds was during the Gulf War in 1991.
The thousands who died at Halabja, Iraq in 1988, killed in their homes during chemical weapons attacks ordered by Saddam Hussein, were cited as a justification for invading Iraq again in 2003.
When I met M on 9/11 in 2002, he was a street vendor at the World Trade Center.
Descended from Kurdish nobility, he had an MBA and had worked as a customs inspector in Turkey.
We were married for ten years.
We visited his relatives in Izmir, Turkey in February 2003, during Dubya's countdown to the war.

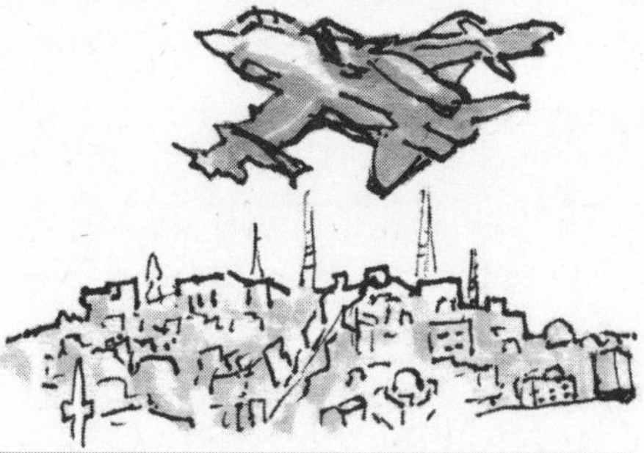

Every few minutes, we could hear a military jet launched from the nearby airport, and I imagined bombing raids roaring toward Iraq–the heart of Kurdistan.

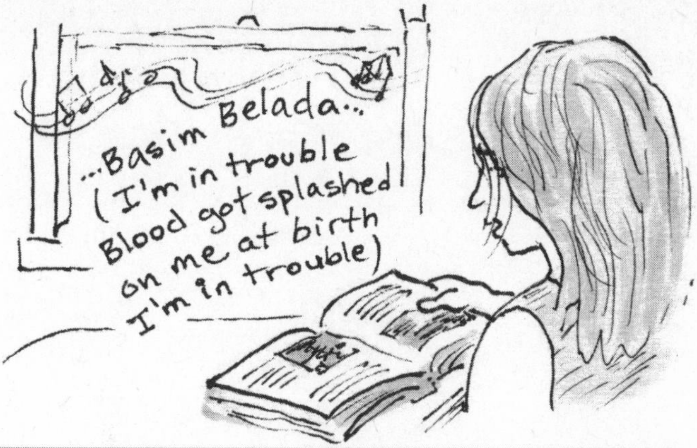

...Basim Belada...
(I'm in trouble
Blood got splashed
on me at birth
I'm in trouble)

I was fascinated by the history, music and politics of the Kurds.

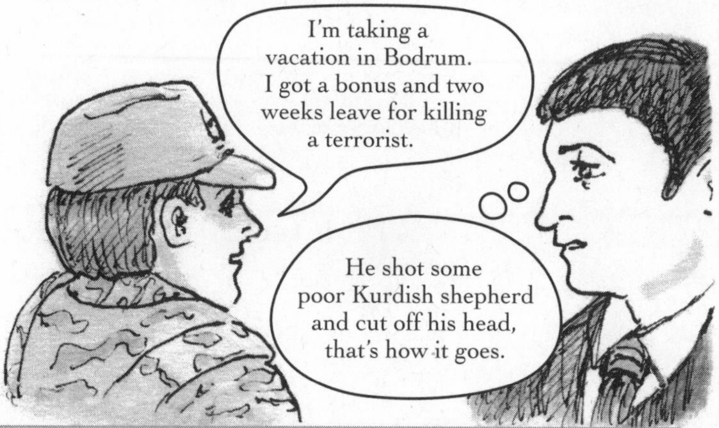

I'm taking a vacation in Bodrum. I got a bonus and two weeks leave for killing a terrorist.
He shot some poor Kurdish shepherd and cut off his head, that's how it goes.

When I showed my books on Kurdish history to M, he wept. His own story was foreign to him. He could not speak the tongue of his mother, for he had grown up where it was illegal to speak it. The musicians who made the music he loved were murdered or imprisoned for their work. His was a story of cultural erasure.

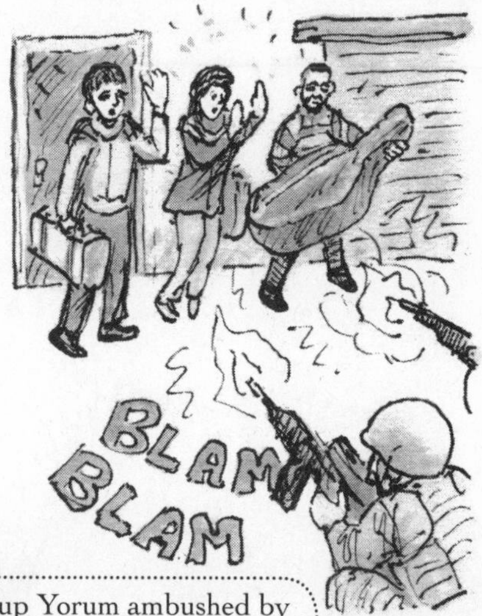

BLAM
BLAM

Grup Yorum ambushed by military police outside their recording studio

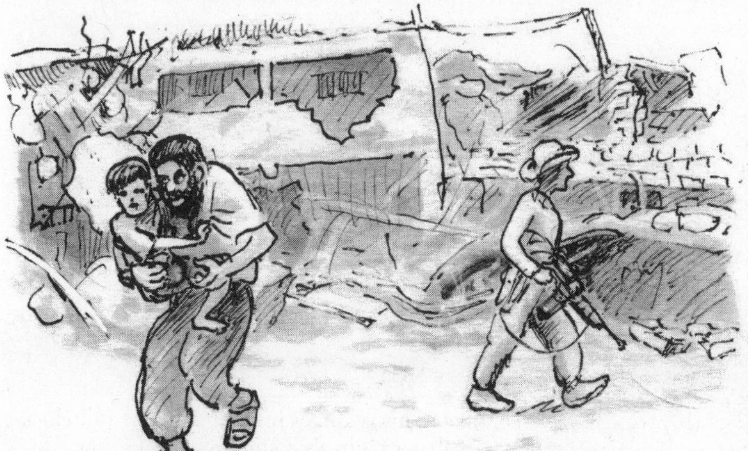

In a country where racism is enshrined in law, there are limited routes of legal remedy for victims of injustice, state sponsored destruction and slaughter. In Turkey, Kurdish politicians who speak out are quickly silenced, outlawed and imprisoned. Resistance both within and outside the law has been put down with appalling brutality. Though the violence has been perpetuated on both sides, the blame is laid entirely upon Kurdish terror.

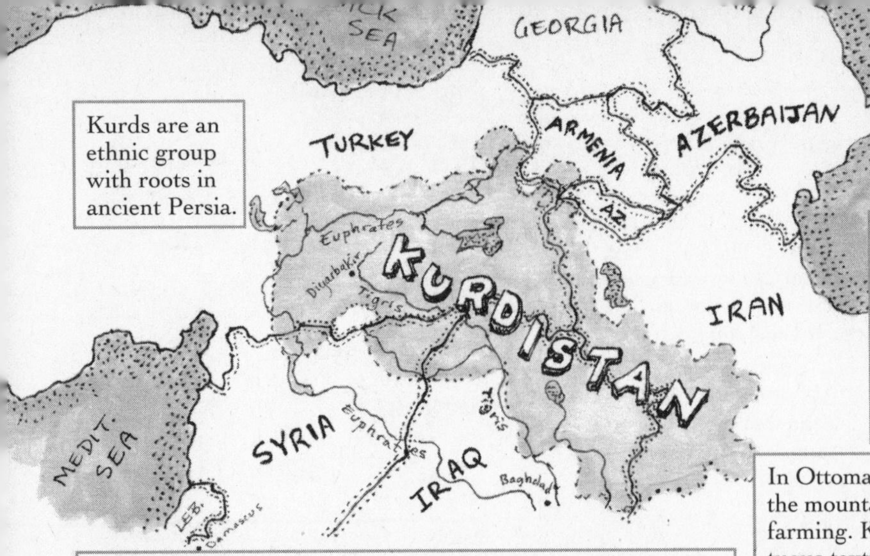

SEA
GEORGIA
TURKEY
ARMENIA
AZERBAIJAN
AZ.
Euphrates
Diyarbakir
KURDISTAN
Tigris
IRAN
SYRIA
Euphrates
Tigris
IRAQ
Baghdad
MEDIT. SEA
LEB.
Damascus

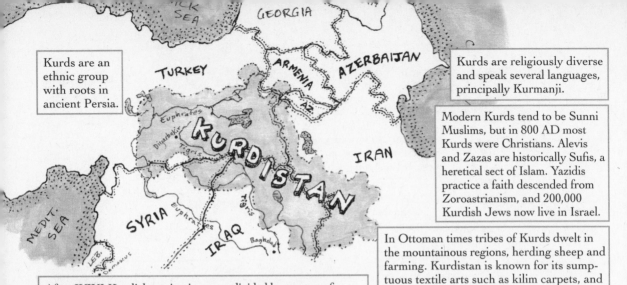

Kurds are an ethnic group with roots in ancient Persia.

Kurds are religiously diverse and speak several languages, principally Kurmanji.

Modern Kurds tend to be Sunni Muslims, but in 800 AD most Kurds were Christians. Alevis and Zazas are historically Sufis, a heretical sect of Islam. Yazidis practice a faith descended from Zoroastrianism, and 200,000 Kurdish Jews now live in Israel.

In Ottoman times tribes of Kurds dwelt in the mountainous regions, herding sheep and farming. Kurdistan is known for its sumptuous textile arts such as kilim carpets, and for its poets, bandits and revolutionaries.

After WWI Kurdish territories were divided by treaty to form the boundaries we know today. In the era of Middle Eastern nation-states, the stateless Kurds lack official political agency.

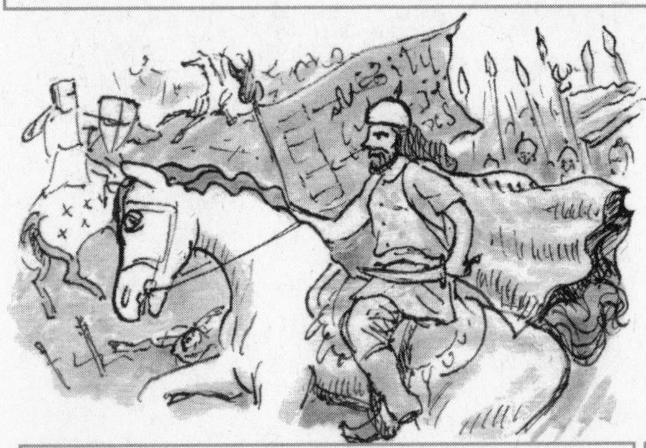

The most famous Kurd in history was Saladin, who defeated the Crusaders in 1187 at the Battle of Hattin.

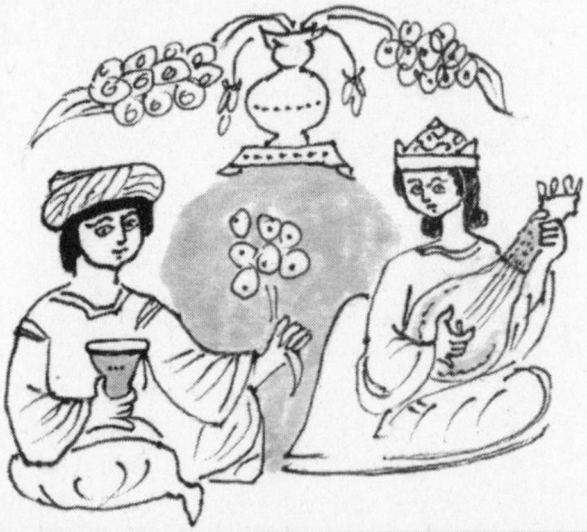

The revered defender of Islam was not just a brilliant general. Saladin was a scholar and a lover of poetry.

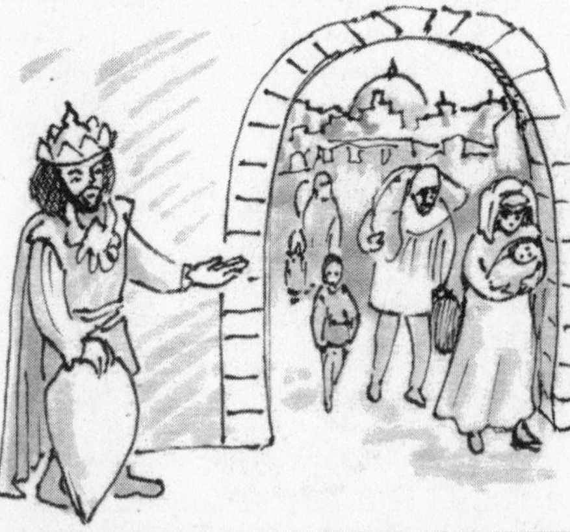

He is remembered for his magnanimous treatment of the defeated Crusaders at Jerusalem.

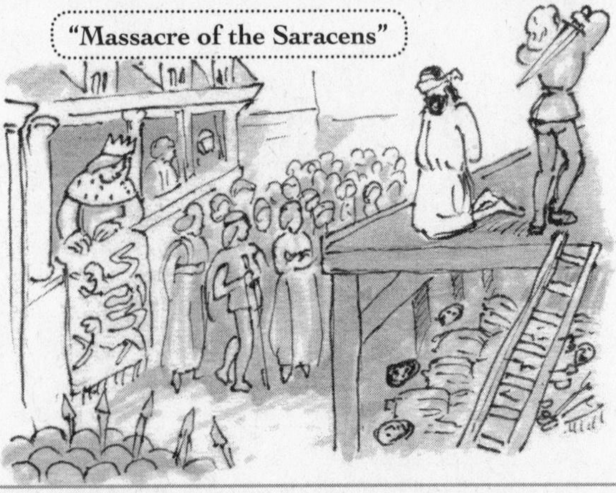

"Massacre of the Saracens"

His foe King Richard the Lionheart responded with a more ruthless policy when he conquered nearby Acre.

World War I
the Birth of Fascism

Blue eyes

Mustafa Kemal Ataturk
"Father Turk"
President 1923-1938

Headline, daily Cumhuriyet dated July 13, 1930:

Cleaning Started

Those at Zeylân valley were totally annihilated

Not one of them survived
Operations at Ağrı continue

The genocide and plunder of Armenian, Greek and Assyrian Christians by the Ottomans during WWI was a profitable enterprise. Ataturk, like Hitler, was inspired. His fascist idea was *Turkification*, a campaign of cultural assimilation aimed at the Kurdish minority.

These "rebels" were executed immediately after this photo was taken. ⇩

It was a policy of forced relocation and ethnic cleansing. Those who objected to the new laws were simply eliminated.

MASSACRES:
Zeylan, 1930: 5000? 15,000? 50,000? **Dersim,** 1937-8: 13,000? 50,000? 80,000?

Sheik Said
Kurdish Sufi leader hanged in 1925

Dersim, Dec. 31, 1937

Leyla Zana, first female member of Parliament

In office 1991-1994, 2011-2018

In prison 1995-2005

Kurdish Activists
of modern Turkey

Ataturk-style fascism remains a central force in mainstream Turkish politics and culture.

Kurdish intellectuals adopted Marxist ideas in the 1970's and guerrilla tactics in the 1980's.

"Sara" Sakine Cansiz,
PKK leader, Imprisoned and tortured, 1980-1991

Deniz Gezmiş, militant, executed in 1972, age 25

Ahmet Kaya,
musician

"Apo" Abdullah Ocalan,
PKK leader, imprisoned 1998-present

In 1999, beloved Kurdish folk singer Ahmet Kaya accepted Turkey's top music award at an industry dinner.

When Kaya revealed that he was recording a song in Kurdish, he was attacked by fellow attendees with forks and knives.

Kaya was forced to flee the country, dying of heart failure in Paris in 2000, age 43.

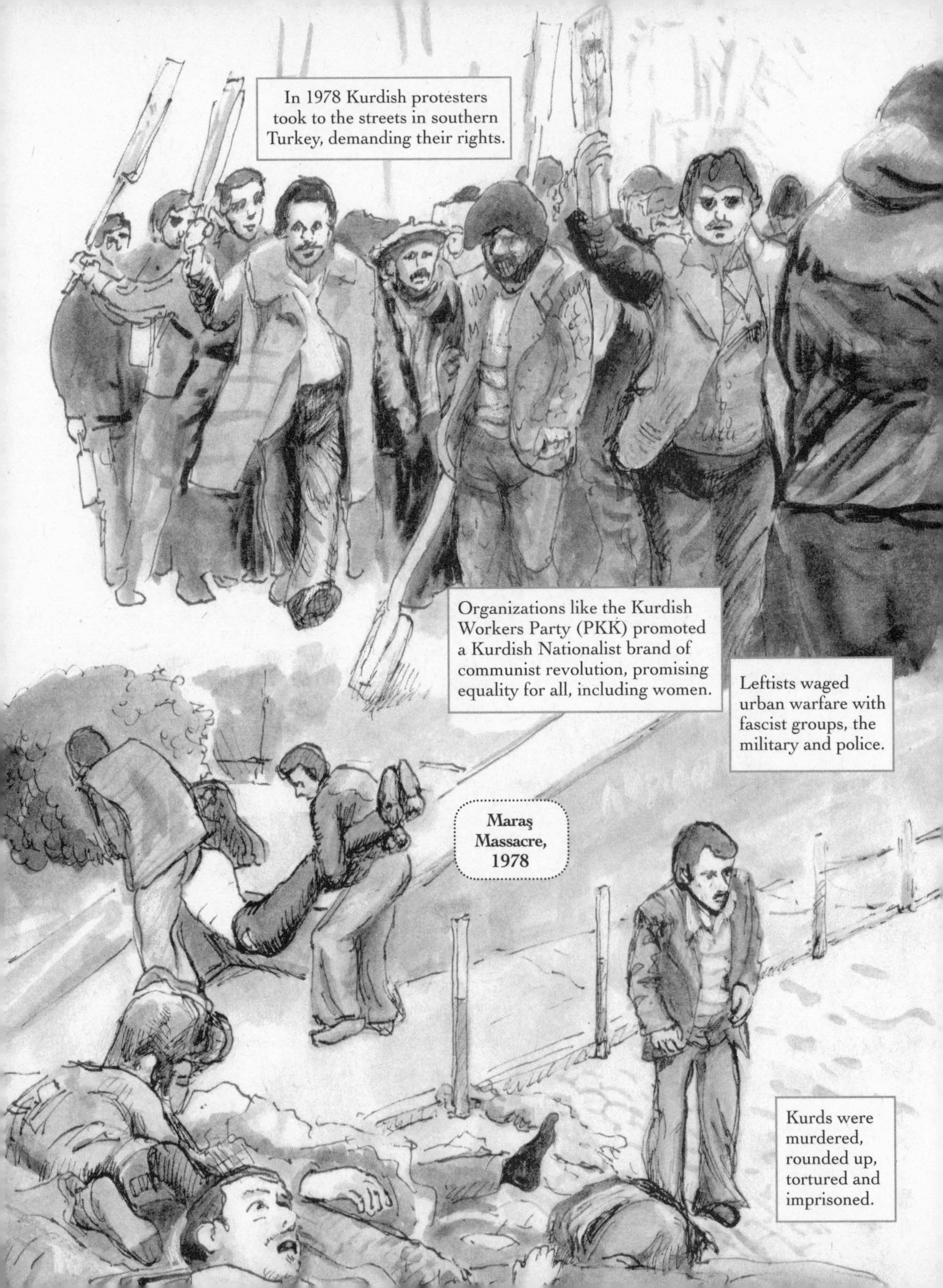

In 1978 Kurdish protesters took to the streets in southern Turkey, demanding their rights.
Organizations like the Kurdish Workers Party (PKK) promoted a Kurdish Nationalist brand of communist revolution, promising equality for all, including women.
Leftists waged urban warfare with fascist groups, the military and police.
Maraş Massacre, 1978
Kurds were murdered, rounded up, tortured and imprisoned.

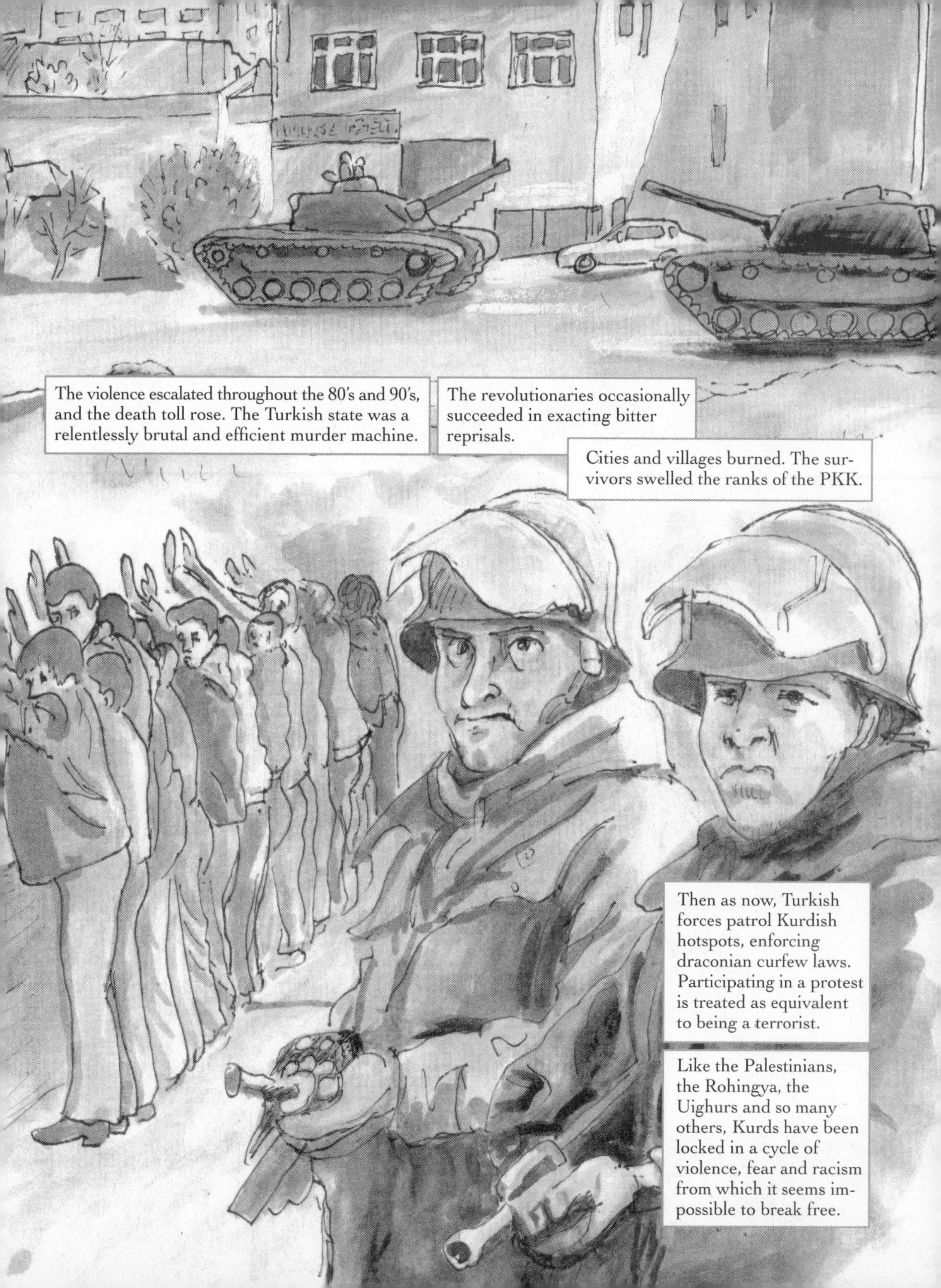
The violence escalated throughout the 80's and 90's, and the death toll rose. The Turkish state was a relentlessly brutal and efficient murder machine.
The revolutionaries occasionally succeeded in exacting bitter reprisals.
Cities and villages burned. The survivors swelled the ranks of the PKK.
Then as now, Turkish forces patrol Kurdish hotspots, enforcing draconian curfew laws. Participating in a protest is treated as equivalent to being a terrorist.
Like the Palestinians, the Rohingya, the Uighurs and so many others, Kurds have been locked in a cycle of violence, fear and racism from which it seems impossible to break free.

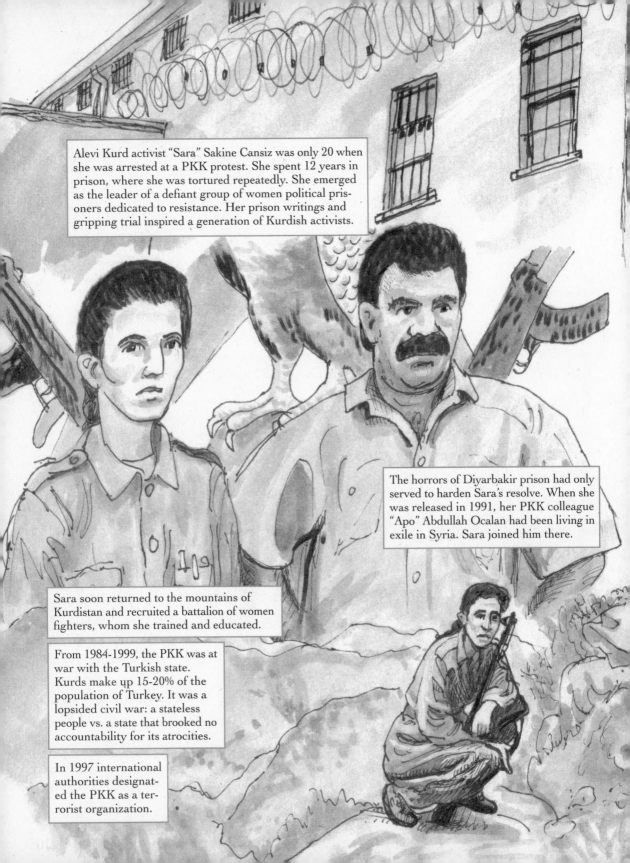

Alevi Kurd activist "Sara" Sakine Cansiz was only 20 when she was arrested at a PKK protest. She spent 12 years in prison, where she was tortured repeatedly. She emerged as the leader of a defiant group of women political prisoners dedicated to resistance. Her prison writings and gripping trial inspired a generation of Kurdish activists.

The horrors of Diyarbakir prison had only served to harden Sara's resolve. When she was released in 1991, her PKK colleague "Apo" Abdullah Ocalan had been living in exile in Syria. Sara joined him there.

Sara soon returned to the mountains of Kurdistan and recruited a battalion of women fighters, whom she trained and educated.

From 1984-1999, the PKK was at war with the Turkish state. Kurds make up 15-20% of the population of Turkey. It was a lopsided civil war: a stateless people vs. a state that brooked no accountability for its atrocities.

In 1997 international authorities designated the PKK as a terrorist organization.

Estimated casualties and catastrophes of the Kurdish-Turkish conflict since 1978
(compiled from official online sources)

4,000 villages destroyed
1,000,000 villagers forcibly evacuated
3,000,000 people displaced
40,000 Kurdish militants killed
17,000 Kurds "disappeared"
119,000 Kurds imprisoned
20,000 Kurds executed
7,000 civilians killed
14,000 civilians wounded
8,000 Turkish soldiers killed
21,000 Turkish soldiers wounded

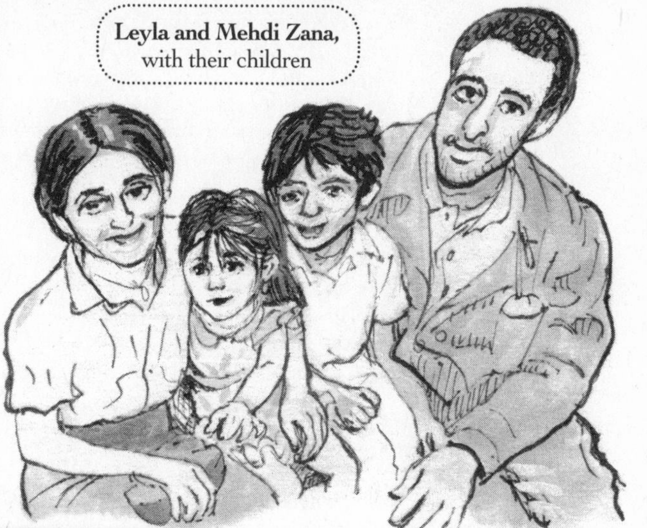

Leyla and Mehdi Zana, with their children

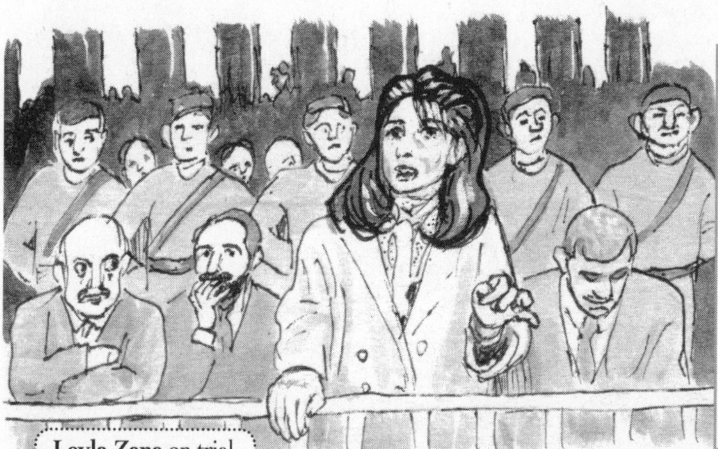

Leyla Zana on trial

Toward Peaceful Change

1988- Mehdi Zana, elected the first socialist mayor of the Kurdish city of Diyarbakir, is imprisoned for 16 years for his politics.

1991- Zana's wife **Leyla Zana** is elected to parliament, then imprisoned from 1994-2004 for speaking Kurdish in Parliament, and for wearing a hair ribbon in the colors of the flag of Kurdistan.

1998 - Abdullah Ocalan (social theorist, co-founder and leader of the PKK,) calls for a unilateral ceasefire and the PKK begins trying to establish peace talks. Ocalan is hunted down, arrested and sentenced to death for treason.

His sentence is suspended when Turkey abolishes the death penalty while seeking to qualify for EU membership. Ocalan is imprisoned on Imrali Island, where he remains to this day the only inmate. There are rumored to be 2000 guards.

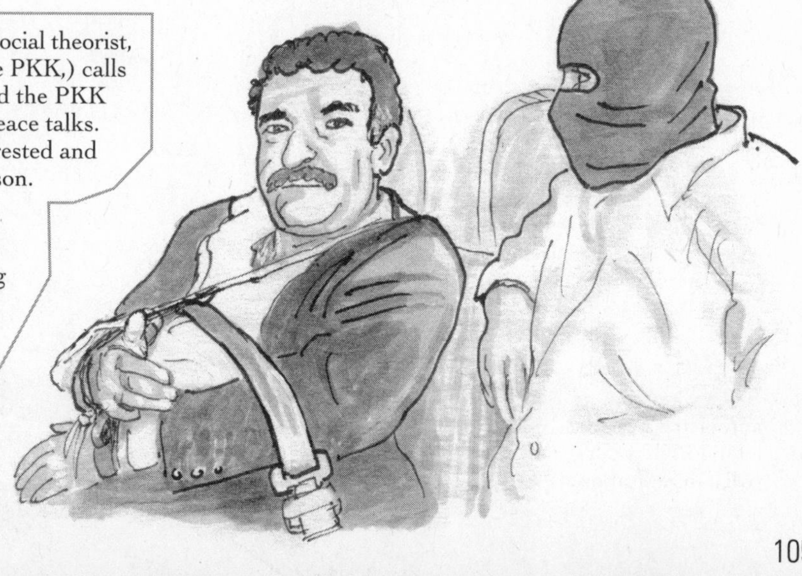

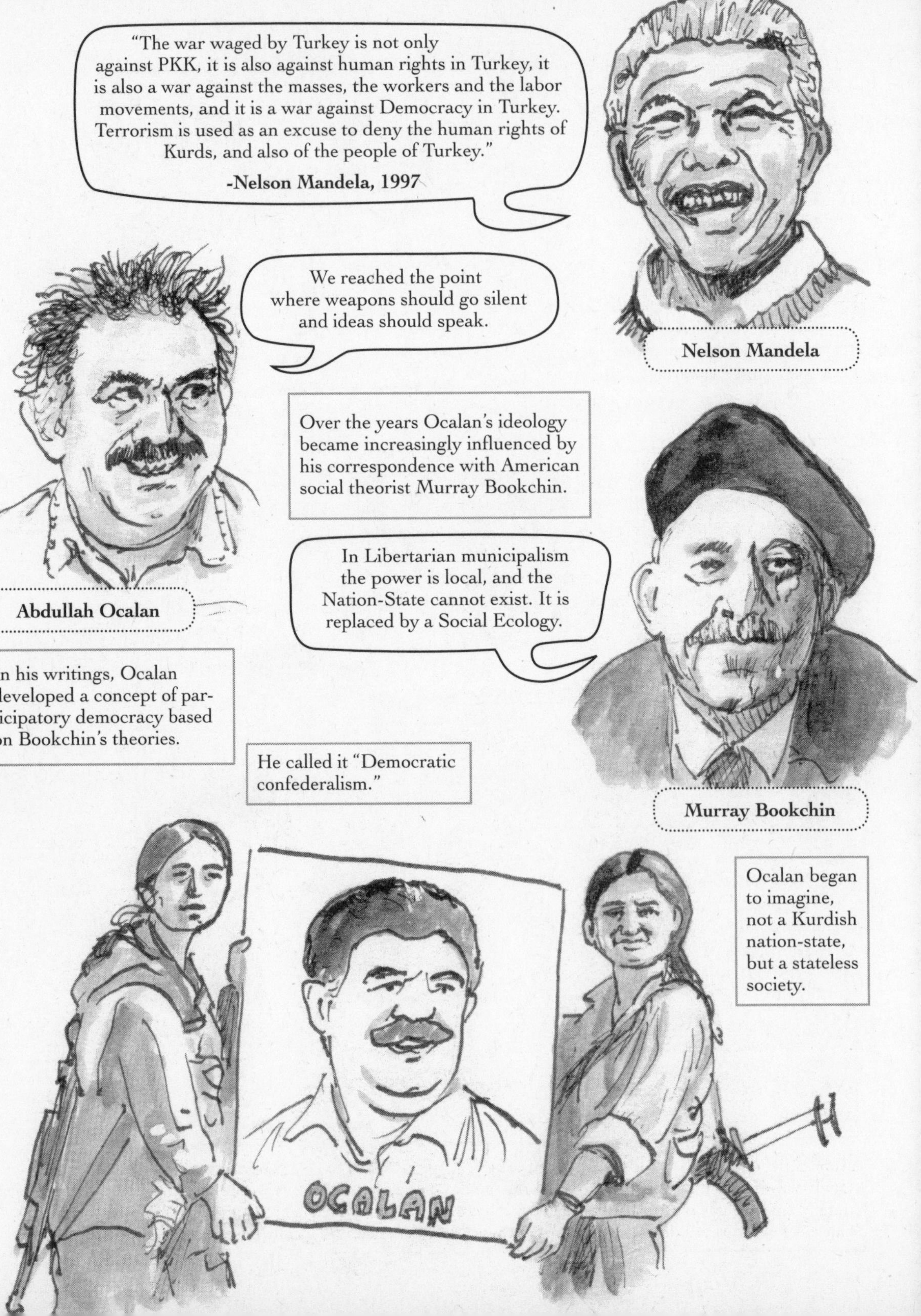
"The war waged by Turkey is not only against PKK, it is also against human rights in Turkey, it is also a war against the masses, the workers and the labor movements, and it is a war against Democracy in Turkey. Terrorism is used as an excuse to deny the human rights of Kurds, and also of the people of Turkey."
-Nelson Mandela, 1997
Nelson Mandela
We reached the point where weapons should go silent and ideas should speak.
Abdullah Ocalan
Over the years Ocalan's ideology became increasingly influenced by his correspondence with American social theorist Murray Bookchin.
In Libertarian municipalism the power is local, and the Nation-State cannot exist. It is replaced by a Social Ecology.
Murray Bookchin
In his writings, Ocalan developed a concept of participatory democracy based on Bookchin's theories.
He called it "Democratic confederalism."
Ocalan began to imagine, not a Kurdish nation-state, but a stateless society.
OCALAN

Freedom is not possible without the liberation of women.

-Abdullah Ocalan

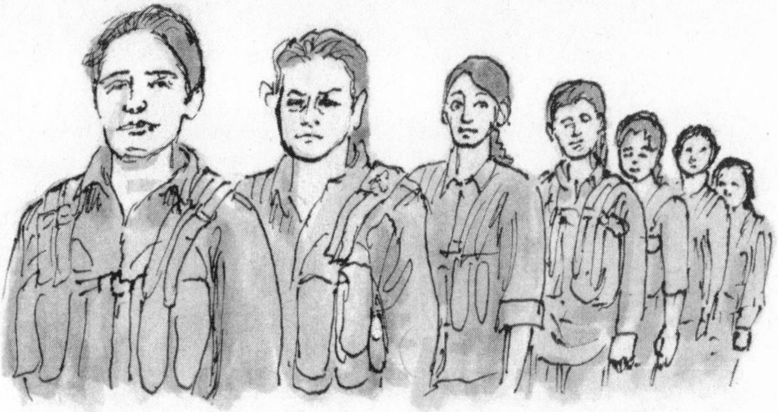

Ocalan envisions a utopian, communalist future, one where environmental justice is built into the community process, and where no-one can be oppressed on the basis of class, race, religion, gender or sexual orientation.

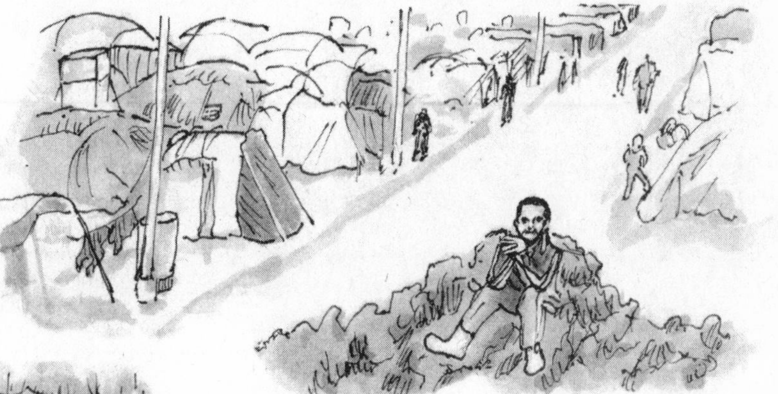

Kurdish leaders first put Ocalan's system for direct democracy into practice to organize people in refugee camps in Northern Iraq. In Rojava they began applying these methods in the self-governing zone. Founded in 2012, it is now called the ***Democratic Federation of Northern Syria.***

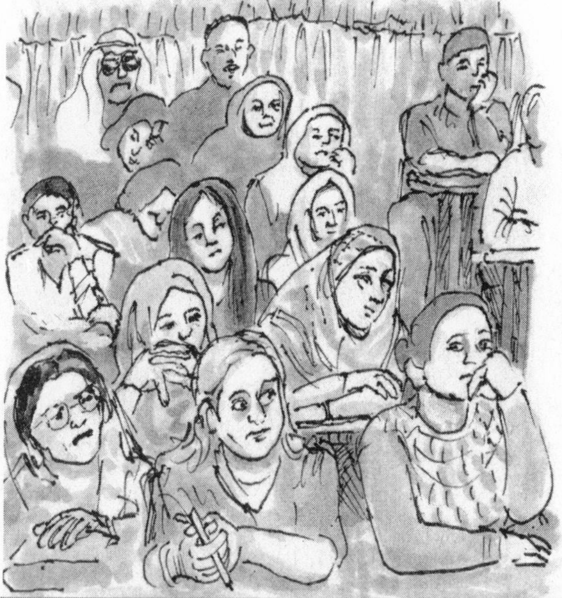

Amidst the chaos and bloodshed of the Syrian Civil War, Kurdish special forces called the YPG defend small local communes where every citizen can meet and discuss decisions that affect them.

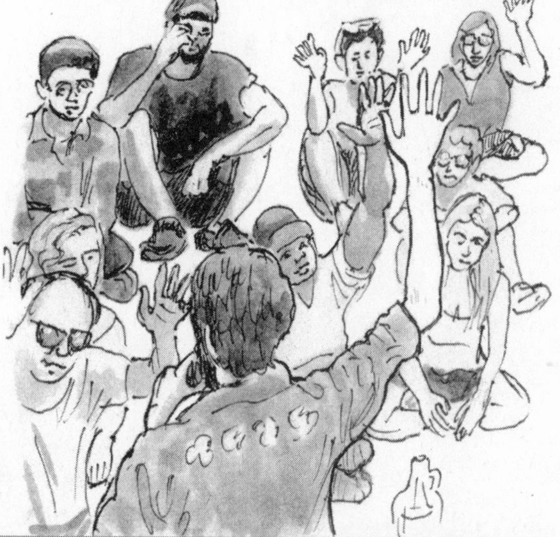

Rojava, the Arab Spring and the Occupy movement are interconnected. The three pillars of Democratic Confederalism are women's liberation, ecological justice, and locally based direct democracy.

If you mention the Kurds today, people think of the all-woman battalion who famously beat ISIL at Kobani.

This is the YPJ, a part of the YPG, Rojava's People's Defense Forces, and military victory is just one part of their story.

What is happening in Rojava is at the grassroots level. It starts with electing representative bodies composed of at least 40% women. Community workers then set up services for the people, by the people.

Rojava gives the power to woman-run courts

to arbitrate family matters and hold abusers accountable.

They support woman-run businesses,

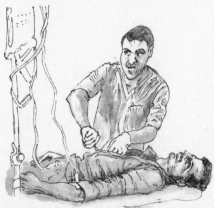

and provide medical services for all: the military, the populace and refugees.

Community Theater in Rojava

Rojava has established public theater, music and art exhibitions, book fairs, and a freedom of speech conference for the Journalists Union. The DFNS is responding to needs and concerns both within their communities and from the international community.

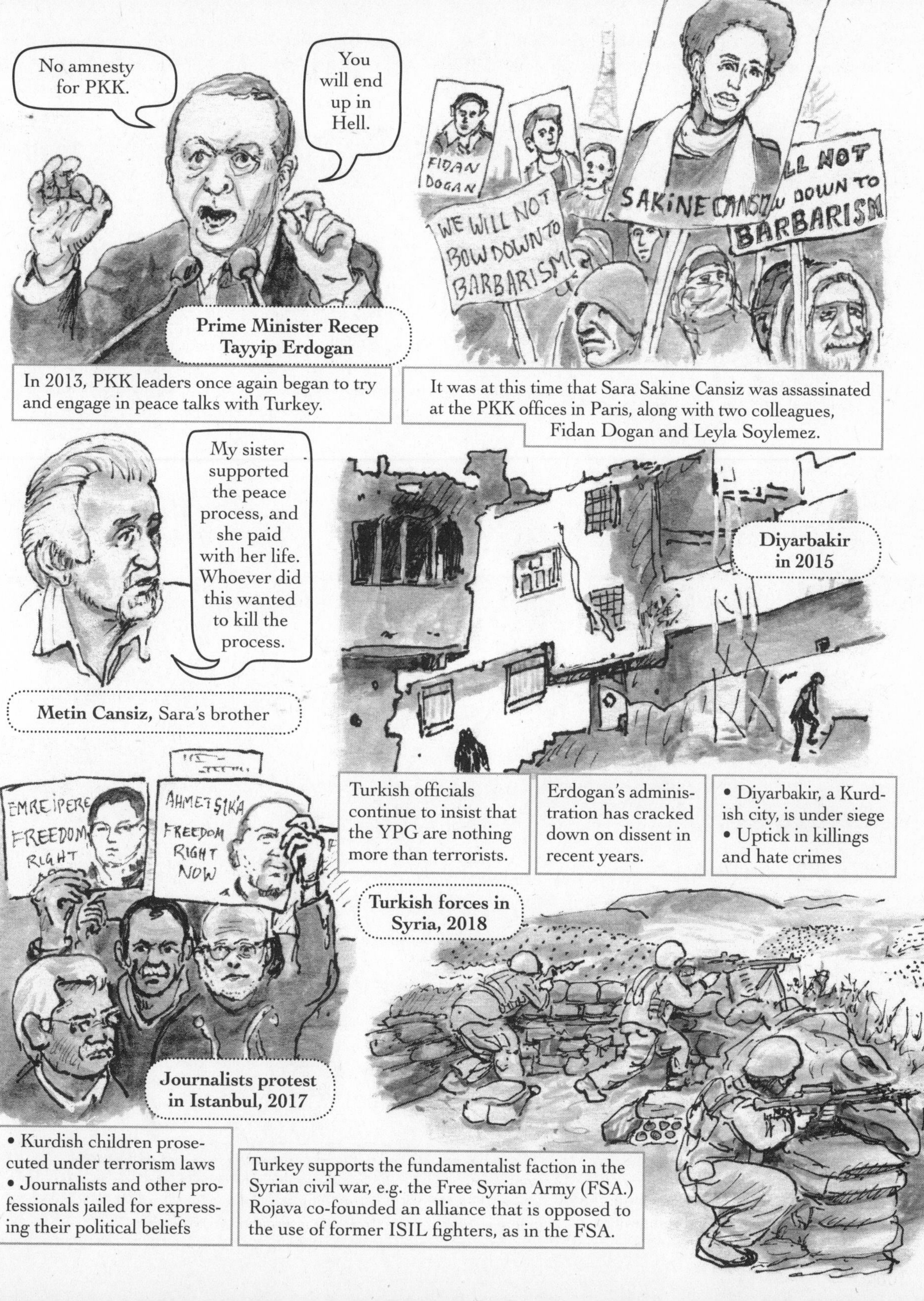
No amnesty for PKK.
You will end up in Hell.
Prime Minister Recep Tayyip Erdogan
FIDAN DOGAN
WE WILL NOT BOW DOWN TO BARBARISM
SAKINE CANSIZ
LL NOT
W DOWN TO BARBARISM
In 2013, PKK leaders once again began to try and engage in peace talks with Turkey.
It was at this time that Sara Sakine Cansiz was assassinated at the PKK offices in Paris, along with two colleagues, Fidan Dogan and Leyla Soylemez.
My sister supported the peace process, and she paid with her life. Whoever did this wanted to kill the process.
Metin Cansiz, Sara's brother
Diyarbakir in 2015
Turkish officials continue to insist that the YPG are nothing more than terrorists.
Erdogan's administration has cracked down on dissent in recent years.
• Diyarbakir, a Kurdish city, is under siege
• Uptick in killings and hate crimes
EMRE iPERE FREEDOM RIGHT
AHMET SIK'A FREEDOM RIGHT NOW
Journalists protest in Istanbul, 2017
Turkish forces in Syria, 2018
• Kurdish children prosecuted under terrorism laws
• Journalists and other professionals jailed for expressing their political beliefs
Turkey supports the fundamentalist faction in the Syrian civil war, e.g. the Free Syrian Army (FSA.) Rojava co-founded an alliance that is opposed to the use of former ISIL fighters, as in the FSA.

Whether you're on the left or the right, there's much about Rojava to admire, and much that is problematic.

Yet the alleged criminal activities of the PKK are known by other names when we speak of "legitimate" governments.

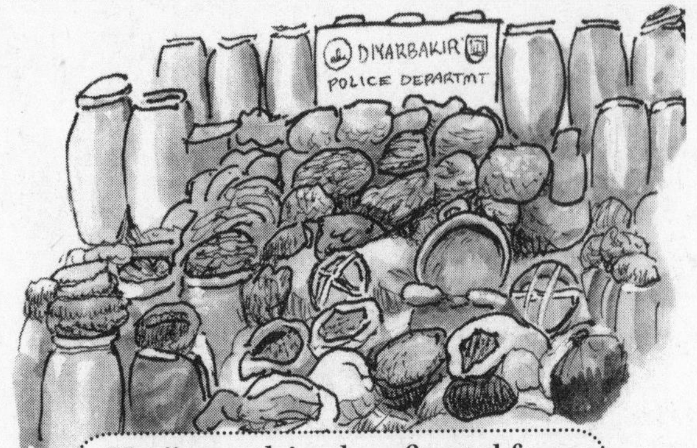
DIYARBAKIR
POLICE DEPARTMT

Marijuana claimed confiscated from the PKK in Diyarbakir, Turkey

The Semantics of Statelessness

Stateless group:	**State:**
Extortion racket	Taxation
War crimes	Martial law
Illegally detained	Awaiting trial
Smuggling	Trade

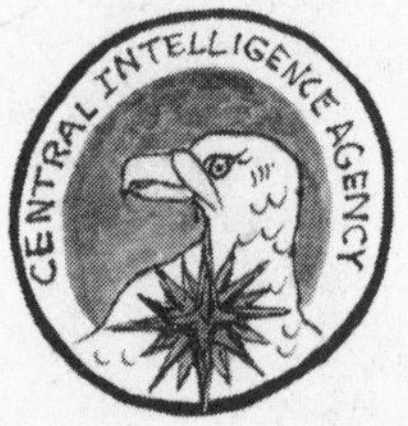
CENTRAL INTELLIGENCE AGENCY

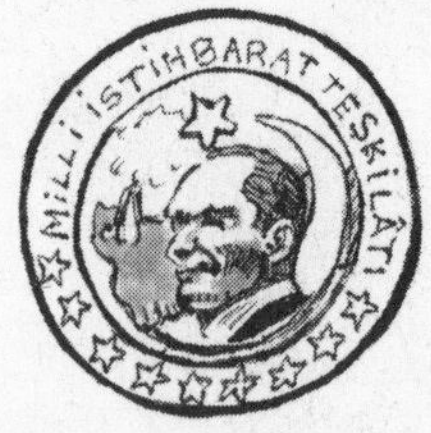
MILLI ISTIHBARAT TESKILATI

Such crimes as these have been carried out in secret by the US and Turkish governments:

- Drug Trafficking
- Ghost Prisoners
- Cover-ups
- Torture
- Atrocities
- Assassinations
- Privacy violations
- Racketeering
- Impunity for personnel
- Secret trials of journalists

The Turkish government has gotten a lot of mileage out of fighting terror.

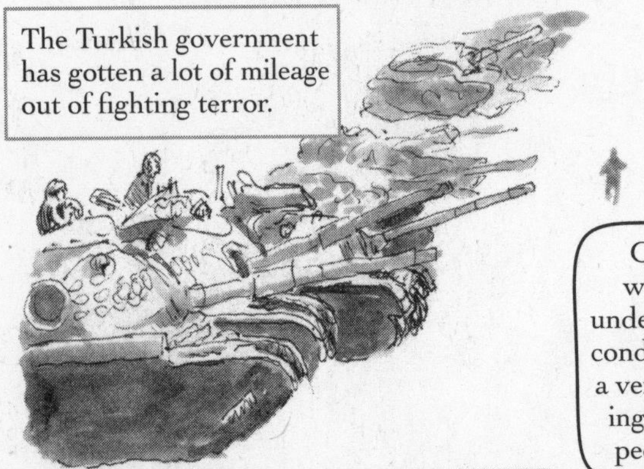

Turkey is complicit in perpetuating right wing terrorism via backroom deals, selective enforcement and direct aid. Plus, a system that criminalizes Kurdishness creates resistance, and thus a pretext to attack Kurdish civilians and now, to invade Syria and Iraq.

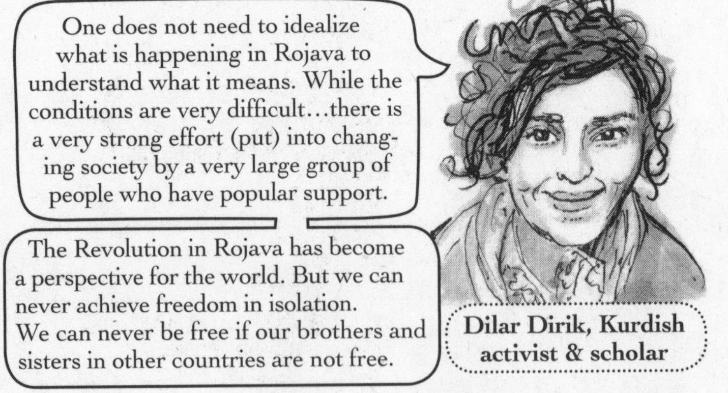
One does not need to idealize what is happening in Rojava to understand what it means. While the conditions are very difficult…there is a very strong effort (put) into changing society by a very large group of people who have popular support.
The Revolution in Rojava has become a perspective for the world. But we can never achieve freedom in isolation. We can never be free if our brothers and sisters in other countries are not free.

Dilar Dirik, Kurdish activist & scholar

As of this writing the Future Syria Party (FSP), a progressive party influenced by the revolution in Rojava, has emerged.

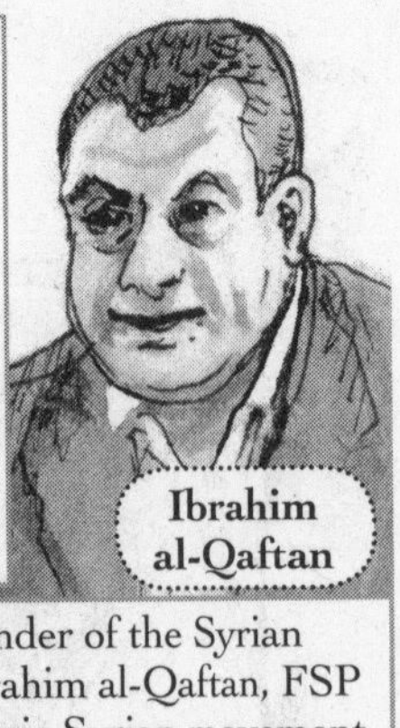

Ibrahim al-Qaftan

Led by a founder of the Syrian rebellion, Ibrahim al-Qaftan, FSP is a multi-ethnic Syrian movement.

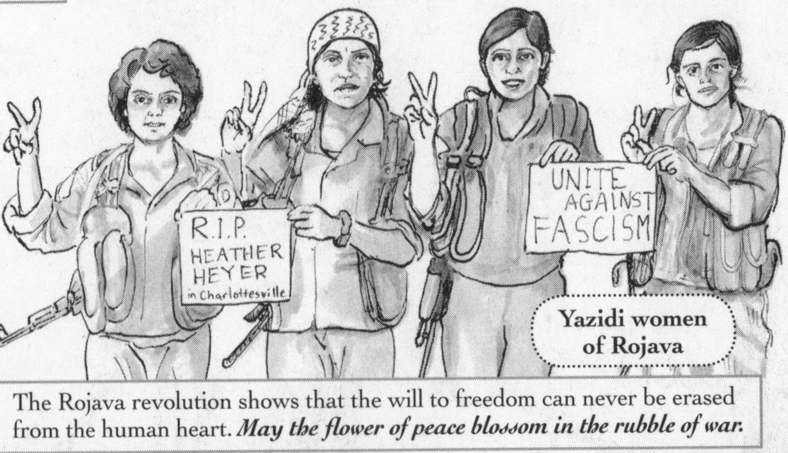
R.I.P.
HEATHER HEYER
in Charlottesville
UNITE AGAINST FASCISM

Yazidi women of Rojava

The Rojava revolution shows that the will to freedom can never be erased from the human heart. ***May the flower of peace blossom in the rubble of war.***

End

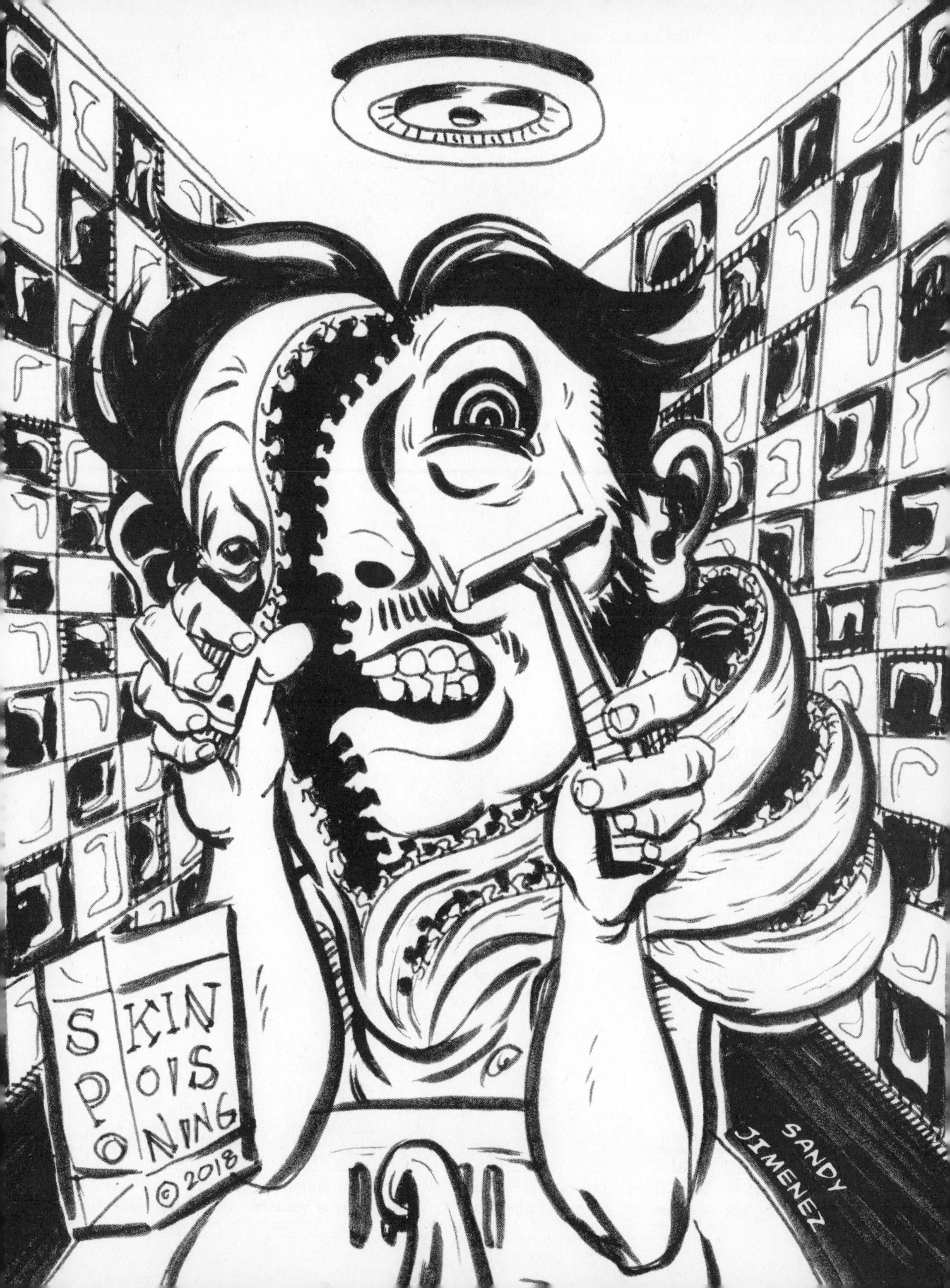
SKIN
POISONING
© 2018
SANDY
JIMENEZ

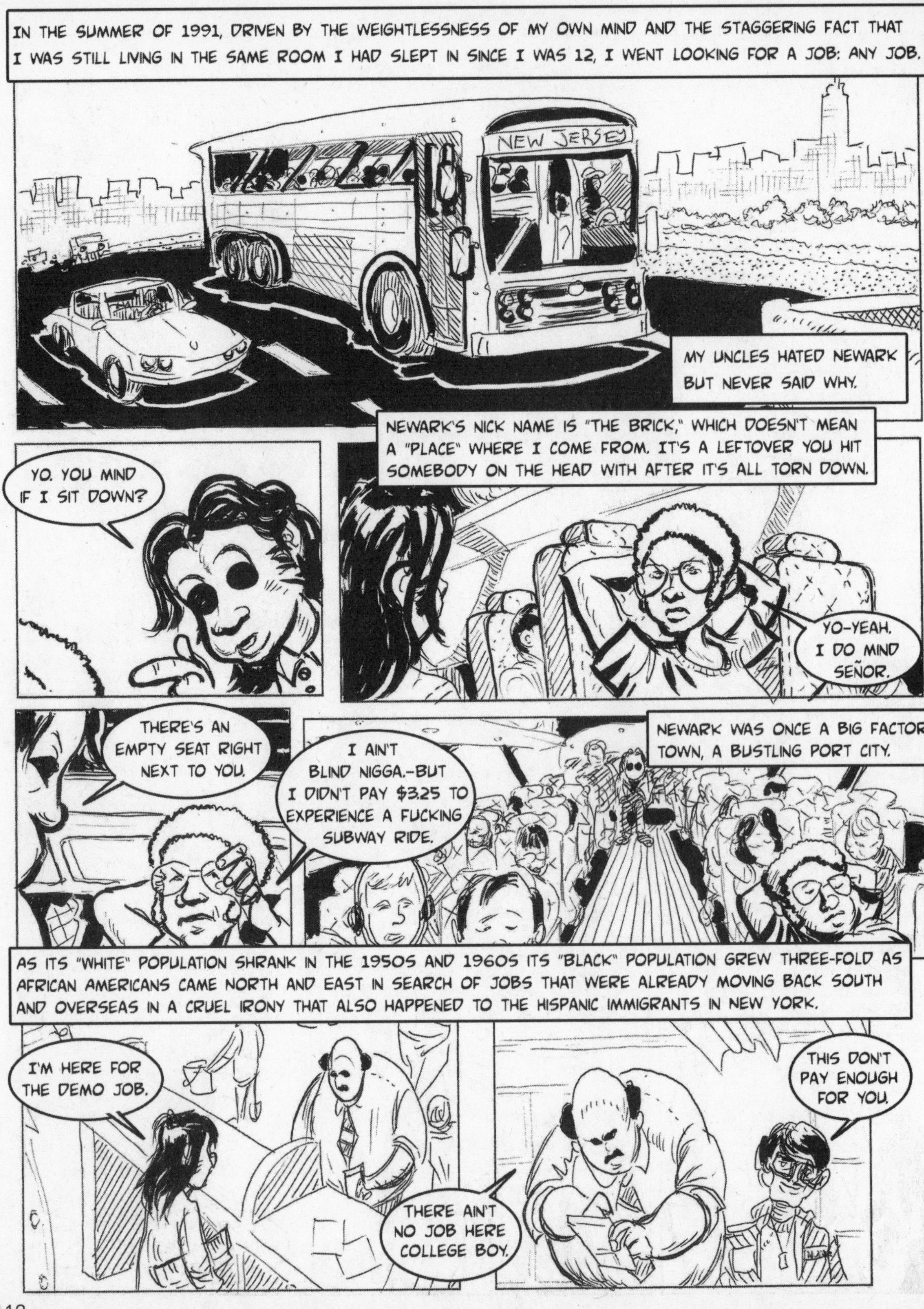
IN THE SUMMER OF 1991, DRIVEN BY THE WEIGHTLESSNESS OF MY OWN MIND AND THE STAGGERING FACT THAT I WAS STILL LIVING IN THE SAME ROOM I HAD SLEPT IN SINCE I WAS 12, I WENT LOOKING FOR A JOB: ANY JOB.
NEW JERSEY
MY UNCLES HATED NEWARK BUT NEVER SAID WHY.
NEWARK'S NICK NAME IS "THE BRICK," WHICH DOESN'T MEAN A "PLACE" WHERE I COME FROM. IT'S A LEFTOVER YOU HIT SOMEBODY ON THE HEAD WITH AFTER IT'S ALL TORN DOWN.
YO. YOU MIND IF I SIT DOWN?
YO-YEAH. I DO MIND SEÑOR.
THERE'S AN EMPTY SEAT RIGHT NEXT TO YOU.
I AIN'T BLIND NIGGA.-BUT I DIDN'T PAY $3.25 TO EXPERIENCE A FUCKING SUBWAY RIDE.
NEWARK WAS ONCE A BIG FACTORY TOWN, A BUSTLING PORT CITY.
AS ITS "WHITE" POPULATION SHRANK IN THE 1950S AND 1960S ITS "BLACK" POPULATION GREW THREE-FOLD AS AFRICAN AMERICANS CAME NORTH AND EAST IN SEARCH OF JOBS THAT WERE ALREADY MOVING BACK SOUTH AND OVERSEAS IN A CRUEL IRONY THAT ALSO HAPPENED TO THE HISPANIC IMMIGRANTS IN NEW YORK.
I'M HERE FOR THE DEMO JOB.
THERE AIN'T NO JOB HERE COLLEGE BOY.
THIS DON'T PAY ENOUGH FOR YOU.

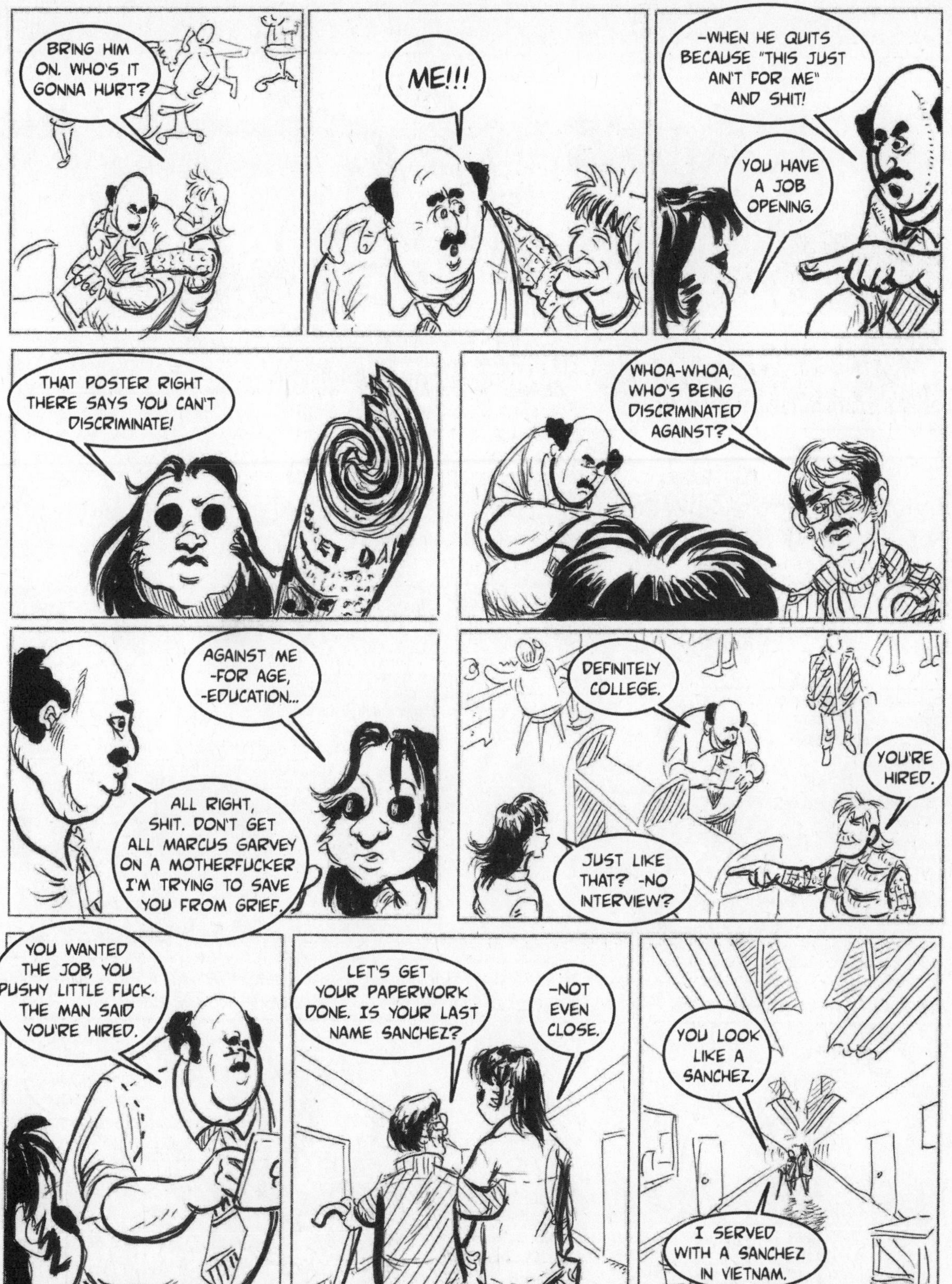

BRING HIM ON. WHO'S IT GONNA HURT?
ME!!!
-WHEN HE QUITS BECAUSE "THIS JUST AIN'T FOR ME" AND SHIT!
YOU HAVE A JOB OPENING.
THAT POSTER RIGHT THERE SAYS YOU CAN'T DISCRIMINATE!
WHOA-WHOA, WHO'S BEING DISCRIMINATED AGAINST?
AGAINST ME -FOR AGE, -EDUCATION...
ALL RIGHT, SHIT. DON'T GET ALL MARCUS GARVEY ON A MOTHERFUCKER I'M TRYING TO SAVE YOU FROM GRIEF.
DEFINITELY COLLEGE.
YOU'RE HIRED.
JUST LIKE THAT? -NO INTERVIEW?
YOU WANTED THE JOB, YOU PUSHY LITTLE FUCK. THE MAN SAID YOU'RE HIRED.
LET'S GET YOUR PAPERWORK DONE. IS YOUR LAST NAME SANCHEZ?
-NOT EVEN CLOSE.
YOU LOOK LIKE A SANCHEZ.
I SERVED WITH A SANCHEZ IN VIETNAM.

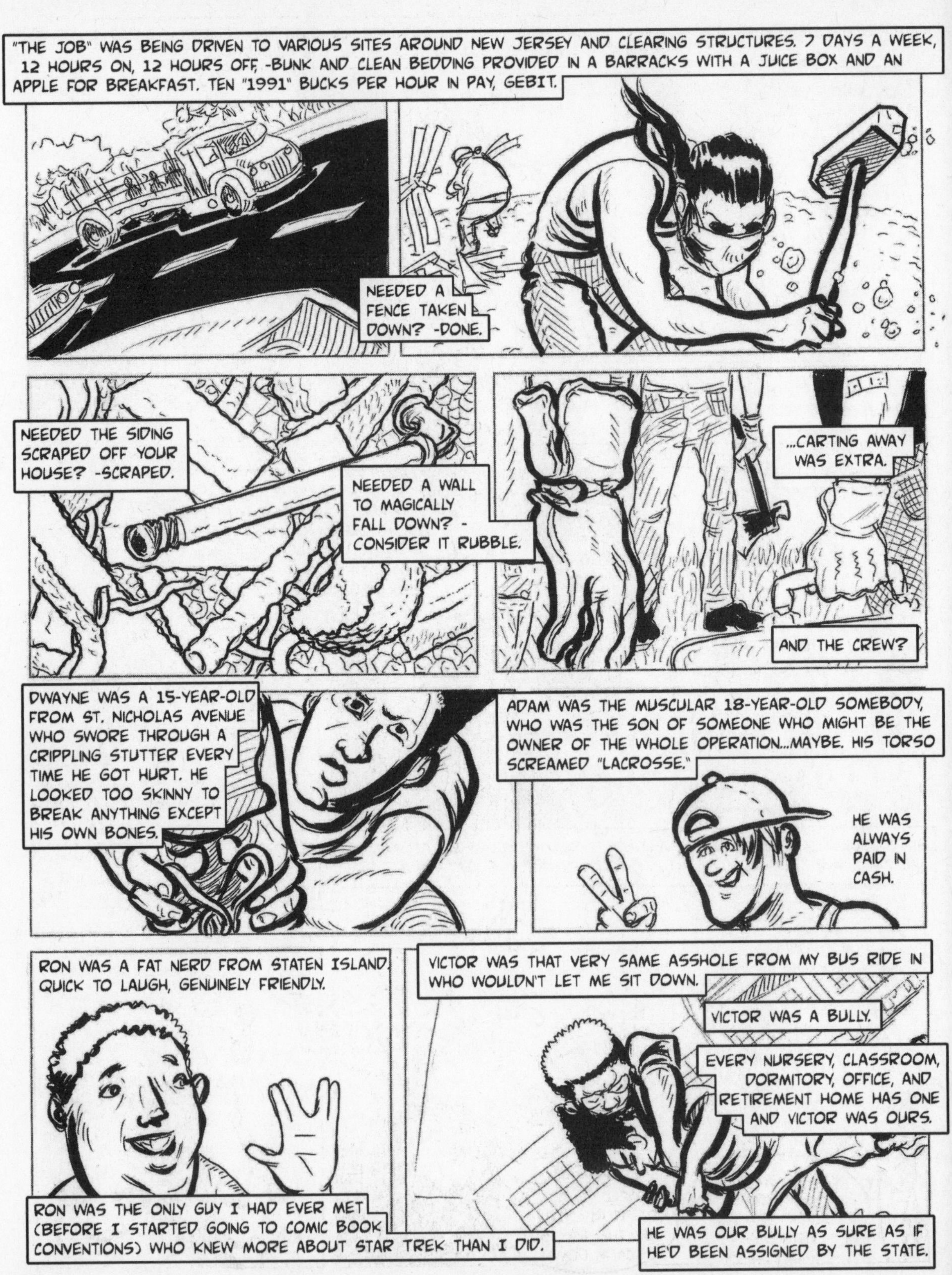
"THE JOB" WAS BEING DRIVEN TO VARIOUS SITES AROUND NEW JERSEY AND CLEARING STRUCTURES. 7 DAYS A WEEK, 12 HOURS ON, 12 HOURS OFF, -BUNK AND CLEAN BEDDING PROVIDED IN A BARRACKS WITH A JUICE BOX AND AN APPLE FOR BREAKFAST. TEN "1991" BUCKS PER HOUR IN PAY, GEBIT.
NEEDED A FENCE TAKEN DOWN? -DONE.
NEEDED THE SIDING SCRAPED OFF YOUR HOUSE? -SCRAPED.
NEEDED A WALL TO MAGICALLY FALL DOWN? -CONSIDER IT RUBBLE.
...CARTING AWAY WAS EXTRA.
AND THE CREW?
DWAYNE WAS A 15-YEAR-OLD FROM ST. NICHOLAS AVENUE WHO SWORE THROUGH A CRIPPLING STUTTER EVERY TIME HE GOT HURT. HE LOOKED TOO SKINNY TO BREAK ANYTHING EXCEPT HIS OWN BONES.
ADAM WAS THE MUSCULAR 18-YEAR-OLD SOMEBODY, WHO WAS THE SON OF SOMEONE WHO MIGHT BE THE OWNER OF THE WHOLE OPERATION...MAYBE. HIS TORSO SCREAMED "LACROSSE."
HE WAS ALWAYS PAID IN CASH.
RON WAS A FAT NERD FROM STATEN ISLAND. QUICK TO LAUGH, GENUINELY FRIENDLY.
RON WAS THE ONLY GUY I HAD EVER MET (BEFORE I STARTED GOING TO COMIC BOOK CONVENTIONS) WHO KNEW MORE ABOUT STAR TREK THAN I DID.
VICTOR WAS THAT VERY SAME ASSHOLE FROM MY BUS RIDE IN WHO WOULDN'T LET ME SIT DOWN.
VICTOR WAS A BULLY.
EVERY NURSERY, CLASSROOM, DORMITORY, OFFICE, AND RETIREMENT HOME HAS ONE AND VICTOR WAS OURS.
HE WAS OUR BULLY AS SURE AS IF HE'D BEEN ASSIGNED BY THE STATE.

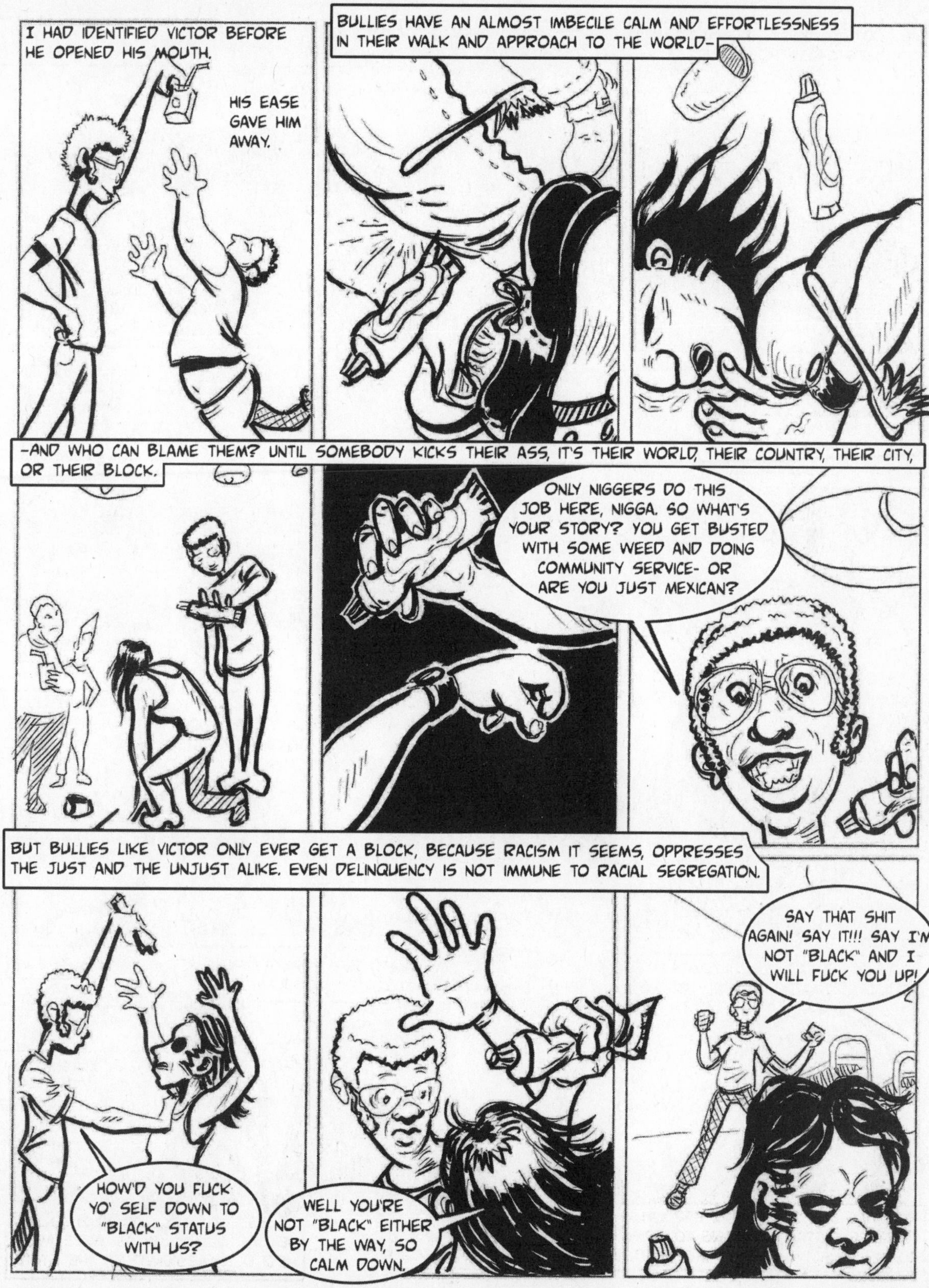
I HAD IDENTIFIED VICTOR BEFORE HE OPENED HIS MOUTH.
HIS EASE GAVE HIM AWAY.
BULLIES HAVE AN ALMOST IMBECILE CALM AND EFFORTLESSNESS IN THEIR WALK AND APPROACH TO THE WORLD-
-AND WHO CAN BLAME THEM? UNTIL SOMEBODY KICKS THEIR ASS, IT'S THEIR WORLD, THEIR COUNTRY, THEIR CITY, OR THEIR BLOCK.
ONLY NIGGERS DO THIS JOB HERE, NIGGA. SO WHAT'S YOUR STORY? YOU GET BUSTED WITH SOME WEED AND DOING COMMUNITY SERVICE- OR ARE YOU JUST MEXICAN?
BUT BULLIES LIKE VICTOR ONLY EVER GET A BLOCK, BECAUSE RACISM IT SEEMS, OPPRESSES THE JUST AND THE UNJUST ALIKE. EVEN DELINQUENCY IS NOT IMMUNE TO RACIAL SEGREGATION.
HOW'D YOU FUCK YO' SELF DOWN TO "BLACK" STATUS WITH US?
WELL YOU'RE NOT "BLACK" EITHER BY THE WAY, SO CALM DOWN.
SAY THAT SHIT AGAIN! SAY IT!!! SAY I'M NOT "BLACK" AND I WILL FUCK YOU UP!

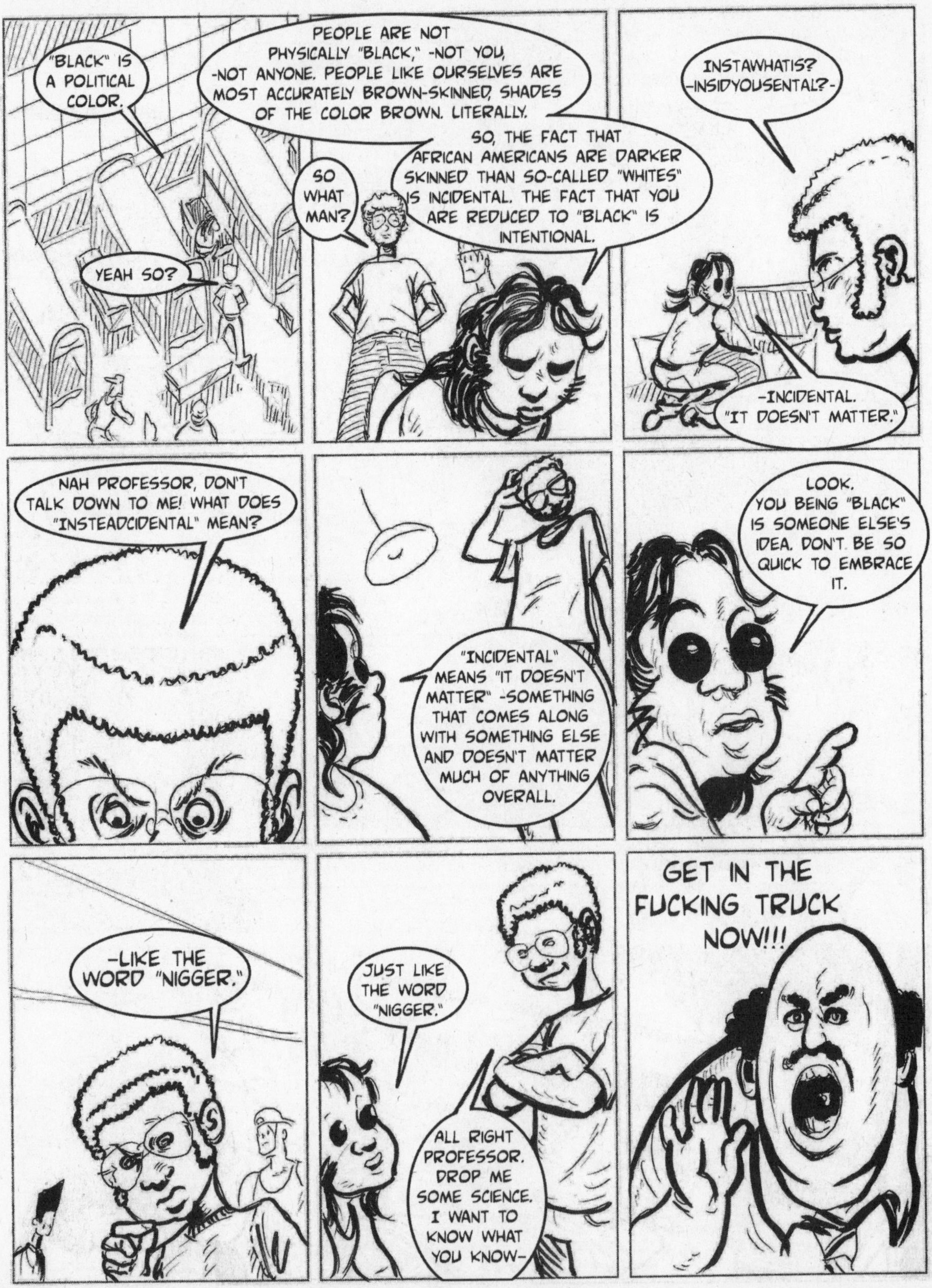
"BLACK" IS A POLITICAL COLOR.
YEAH SO?
PEOPLE ARE NOT PHYSICALLY "BLACK," -NOT YOU, -NOT ANYONE. PEOPLE LIKE OURSELVES ARE MOST ACCURATELY BROWN-SKINNED, SHADES OF THE COLOR BROWN. LITERALLY.
SO WHAT MAN?
SO, THE FACT THAT AFRICAN AMERICANS ARE DARKER SKINNED THAN SO-CALLED "WHITES" IS INCIDENTAL. THE FACT THAT YOU ARE REDUCED TO "BLACK" IS INTENTIONAL.
INSTAWHATIS? -INSIDYOUSENTAL?-
-INCIDENTAL. "IT DOESN'T MATTER."
NAH PROFESSOR, DON'T TALK DOWN TO ME! WHAT DOES "INSTEADCIDENTAL" MEAN?
"INCIDENTAL" MEANS "IT DOESN'T MATTER" -SOMETHING THAT COMES ALONG WITH SOMETHING ELSE AND DOESN'T MATTER MUCH OF ANYTHING OVERALL.
LOOK. YOU BEING "BLACK" IS SOMEONE ELSE'S IDEA. DON'T BE SO QUICK TO EMBRACE IT.
-LIKE THE WORD "NIGGER."
JUST LIKE THE WORD "NIGGER."
ALL RIGHT PROFESSOR. DROP ME SOME SCIENCE. I WANT TO KNOW WHAT YOU KNOW-
GET IN THE FUCKING TRUCK NOW!!!

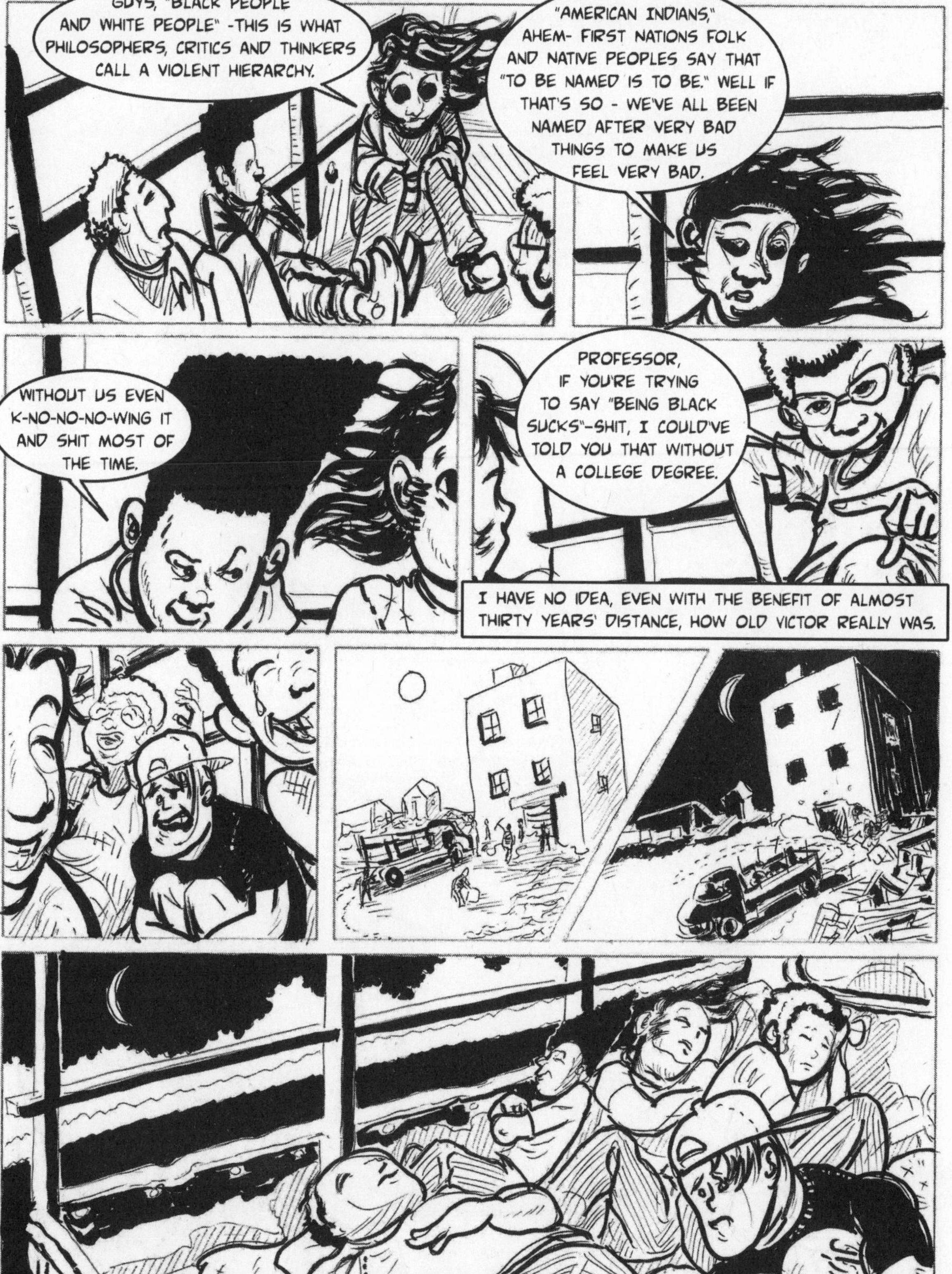
GUYS, "BLACK PEOPLE AND WHITE PEOPLE" -THIS IS WHAT PHILOSOPHERS, CRITICS AND THINKERS CALL A VIOLENT HIERARCHY.
"AMERICAN INDIANS," AHEM- FIRST NATIONS FOLK AND NATIVE PEOPLES SAY THAT "TO BE NAMED IS TO BE." WELL IF THAT'S SO - WE'VE ALL BEEN NAMED AFTER VERY BAD THINGS TO MAKE US FEEL VERY BAD.
WITHOUT US EVEN K-NO-NO-NO-WING IT AND SHIT MOST OF THE TIME.
PROFESSOR, IF YOU'RE TRYING TO SAY "BEING BLACK SUCKS"-SHIT, I COULD'VE TOLD YOU THAT WITHOUT A COLLEGE DEGREE.
I HAVE NO IDEA, EVEN WITH THE BENEFIT OF ALMOST THIRTY YEARS' DISTANCE, HOW OLD VICTOR REALLY WAS.

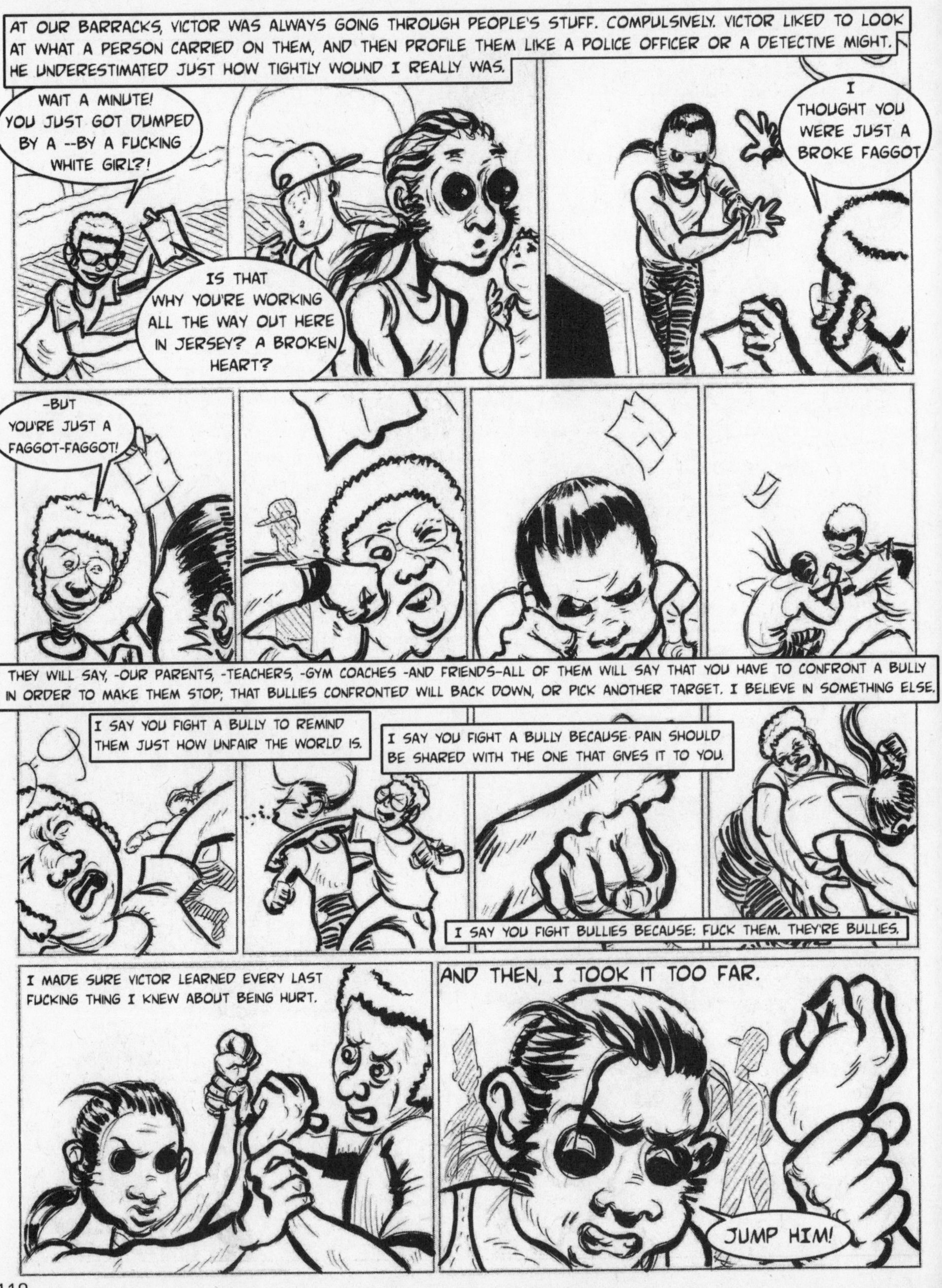

AT OUR BARRACKS, VICTOR WAS ALWAYS GOING THROUGH PEOPLE'S STUFF. COMPULSIVELY. VICTOR LIKED TO LOOK AT WHAT A PERSON CARRIED ON THEM, AND THEN PROFILE THEM LIKE A POLICE OFFICER OR A DETECTIVE MIGHT. HE UNDERESTIMATED JUST HOW TIGHTLY WOUND I REALLY WAS.
WAIT A MINUTE! YOU JUST GOT DUMPED BY A --BY A FUCKING WHITE GIRL?!
IS THAT WHY YOU'RE WORKING ALL THE WAY OUT HERE IN JERSEY? A BROKEN HEART?
I THOUGHT YOU WERE JUST A BROKE FAGGOT
-BUT YOU'RE JUST A FAGGOT-FAGGOT!
THEY WILL SAY, -OUR PARENTS, -TEACHERS, -GYM COACHES -AND FRIENDS-ALL OF THEM WILL SAY THAT YOU HAVE TO CONFRONT A BULLY IN ORDER TO MAKE THEM STOP; THAT BULLIES CONFRONTED WILL BACK DOWN, OR PICK ANOTHER TARGET. I BELIEVE IN SOMETHING ELSE.
I SAY YOU FIGHT A BULLY TO REMIND THEM JUST HOW UNFAIR THE WORLD IS.
I SAY YOU FIGHT A BULLY BECAUSE PAIN SHOULD BE SHARED WITH THE ONE THAT GIVES IT TO YOU.
I SAY YOU FIGHT BULLIES BECAUSE: FUCK THEM. THEY'RE BULLIES.
I MADE SURE VICTOR LEARNED EVERY LAST FUCKING THING I KNEW ABOUT BEING HURT.
AND THEN, I TOOK IT TOO FAR.
JUMP HIM!

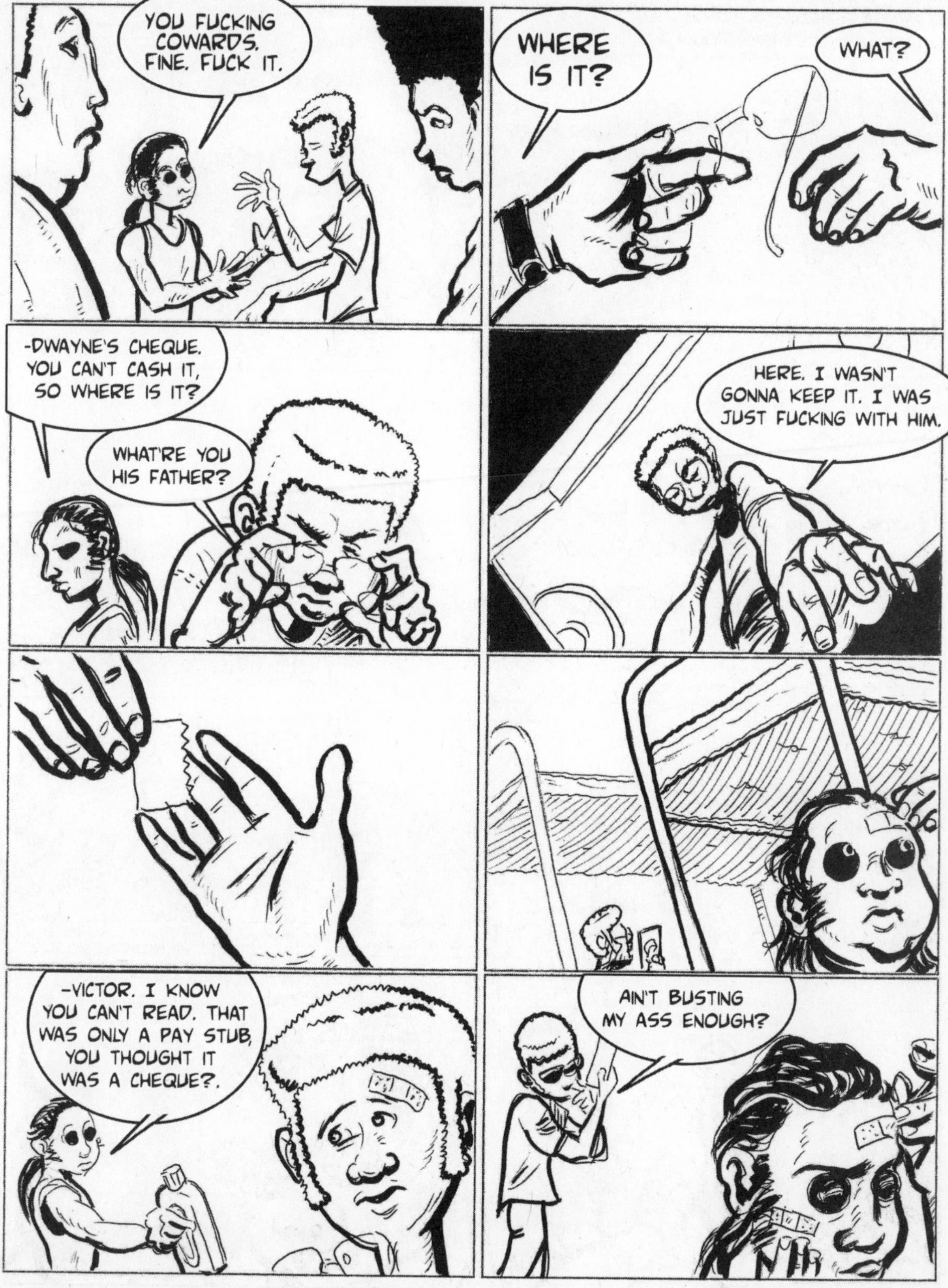
YOU FUCKING COWARDS. FINE. FUCK IT.
WHERE IS IT?
WHAT?
-DWAYNE'S CHEQUE. YOU CAN'T CASH IT, SO WHERE IS IT?
WHAT'RE YOU HIS FATHER?
HERE. I WASN'T GONNA KEEP IT. I WAS JUST FUCKING WITH HIM.
-VICTOR. I KNOW YOU CAN'T READ. THAT WAS ONLY A PAY STUB, YOU THOUGHT IT WAS A CHEQUE?.
AIN'T BUSTING MY ASS ENOUGH?

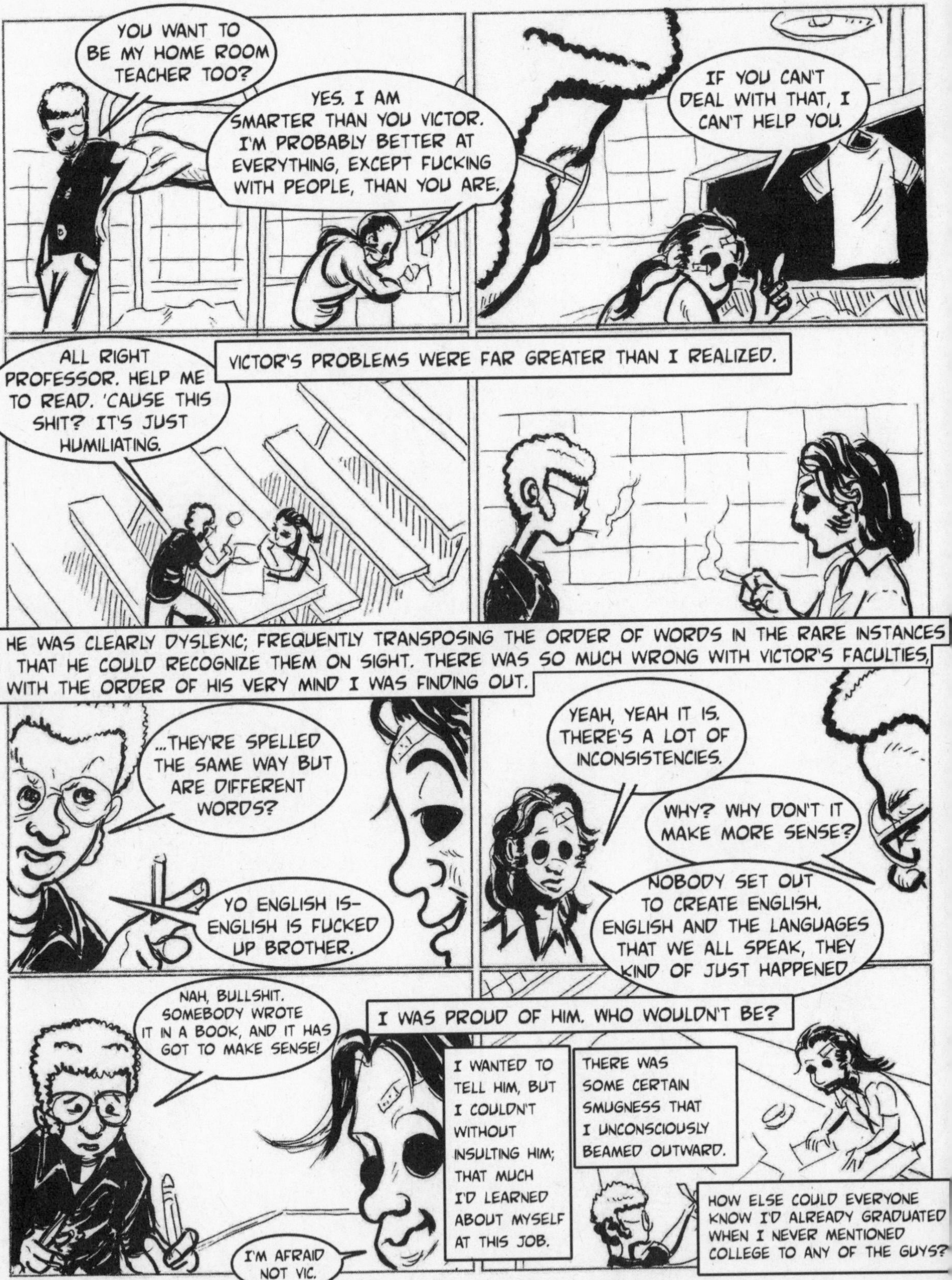
YOU WANT TO BE MY HOME ROOM TEACHER TOO?
YES. I AM SMARTER THAN YOU VICTOR. I'M PROBABLY BETTER AT EVERYTHING, EXCEPT FUCKING WITH PEOPLE, THAN YOU ARE.
IF YOU CAN'T DEAL WITH THAT, I CAN'T HELP YOU.
ALL RIGHT PROFESSOR. HELP ME TO READ. 'CAUSE THIS SHIT? IT'S JUST HUMILIATING.
VICTOR'S PROBLEMS WERE FAR GREATER THAN I REALIZED.
HE WAS CLEARLY DYSLEXIC; FREQUENTLY TRANSPOSING THE ORDER OF WORDS IN THE RARE INSTANCES THAT HE COULD RECOGNIZE THEM ON SIGHT. THERE WAS SO MUCH WRONG WITH VICTOR'S FACULTIES, WITH THE ORDER OF HIS VERY MIND I WAS FINDING OUT.
...THEY'RE SPELLED THE SAME WAY BUT ARE DIFFERENT WORDS?
YO ENGLISH IS– ENGLISH IS FUCKED UP BROTHER.
YEAH, YEAH IT IS. THERE'S A LOT OF INCONSISTENCIES.
WHY? WHY DON'T IT MAKE MORE SENSE?
NOBODY SET OUT TO CREATE ENGLISH. ENGLISH AND THE LANGUAGES THAT WE ALL SPEAK, THEY KIND OF JUST HAPPENED.
NAH, BULLSHIT. SOMEBODY WROTE IT IN A BOOK, AND IT HAS GOT TO MAKE SENSE!
I'M AFRAID NOT VIC.
I WAS PROUD OF HIM. WHO WOULDN'T BE?
I WANTED TO TELL HIM, BUT I COULDN'T WITHOUT INSULTING HIM; THAT MUCH I'D LEARNED ABOUT MYSELF AT THIS JOB.
THERE WAS SOME CERTAIN SMUGNESS THAT I UNCONSCIOUSLY BEAMED OUTWARD.
HOW ELSE COULD EVERYONE KNOW I'D ALREADY GRADUATED WHEN I NEVER MENTIONED COLLEGE TO ANY OF THE GUYS?

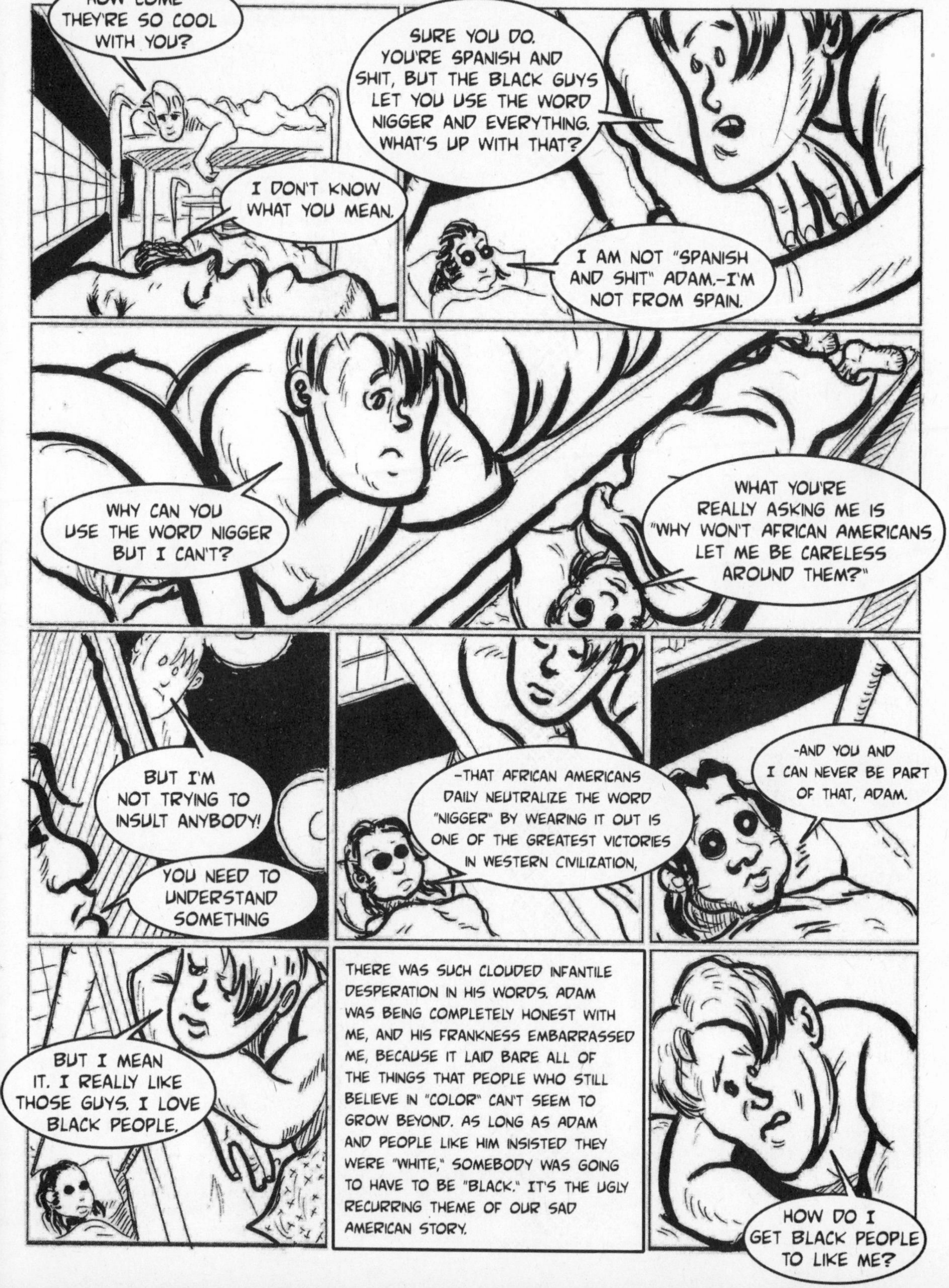
HOW COME THEY'RE SO COOL WITH YOU?
I DON'T KNOW WHAT YOU MEAN.
SURE YOU DO. YOU'RE SPANISH AND SHIT, BUT THE BLACK GUYS LET YOU USE THE WORD NIGGER AND EVERYTHING. WHAT'S UP WITH THAT?
I AM NOT "SPANISH AND SHIT" ADAM.–I'M NOT FROM SPAIN.
WHY CAN YOU USE THE WORD NIGGER BUT I CAN'T?
WHAT YOU'RE REALLY ASKING ME IS "WHY WON'T AFRICAN AMERICANS LET ME BE CARELESS AROUND THEM?"
BUT I'M NOT TRYING TO INSULT ANYBODY!
YOU NEED TO UNDERSTAND SOMETHING
–THAT AFRICAN AMERICANS DAILY NEUTRALIZE THE WORD "NIGGER" BY WEARING IT OUT IS ONE OF THE GREATEST VICTORIES IN WESTERN CIVILIZATION,
-AND YOU AND I CAN NEVER BE PART OF THAT, ADAM.
BUT I MEAN IT. I REALLY LIKE THOSE GUYS. I LOVE BLACK PEOPLE.
THERE WAS SUCH CLOUDED INFANTILE DESPERATION IN HIS WORDS. ADAM WAS BEING COMPLETELY HONEST WITH ME, AND HIS FRANKNESS EMBARRASSED ME, BECAUSE IT LAID BARE ALL OF THE THINGS THAT PEOPLE WHO STILL BELIEVE IN "COLOR" CAN'T SEEM TO GROW BEYOND. AS LONG AS ADAM AND PEOPLE LIKE HIM INSISTED THEY WERE "WHITE," SOMEBODY WAS GOING TO HAVE TO BE "BLACK." IT'S THE UGLY RECURRING THEME OF OUR SAD AMERICAN STORY.
HOW DO I GET BLACK PEOPLE TO LIKE ME?

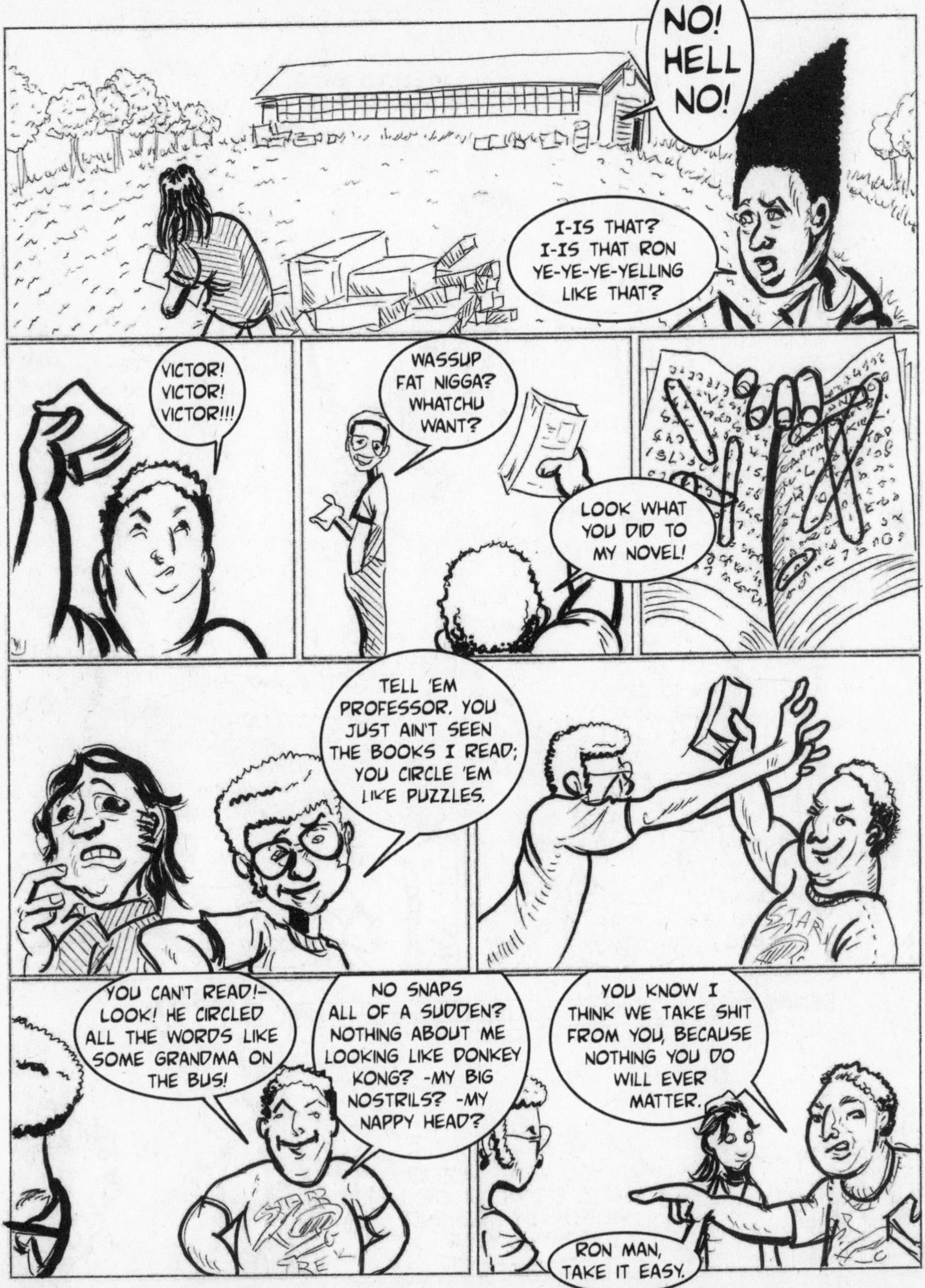

NO! HELL NO!
I-IS THAT? I-IS THAT RON YE-YE-YE-YELLING LIKE THAT?
VICTOR! VICTOR! VICTOR!!!
WASSUP FAT NIGGA? WHATCHU WANT?
LOOK WHAT YOU DID TO MY NOVEL!
TELL 'EM PROFESSOR. YOU JUST AIN'T SEEN THE BOOKS I READ; YOU CIRCLE 'EM LIKE PUZZLES.
YOU CAN'T READ!- LOOK! HE CIRCLED ALL THE WORDS LIKE SOME GRANDMA ON THE BUS!
NO SNAPS ALL OF A SUDDEN? NOTHING ABOUT ME LOOKING LIKE DONKEY KONG? -MY BIG NOSTRILS? -MY NAPPY HEAD?
YOU KNOW I THINK WE TAKE SHIT FROM YOU, BECAUSE NOTHING YOU DO WILL EVER MATTER.
RON MAN, TAKE IT EASY.

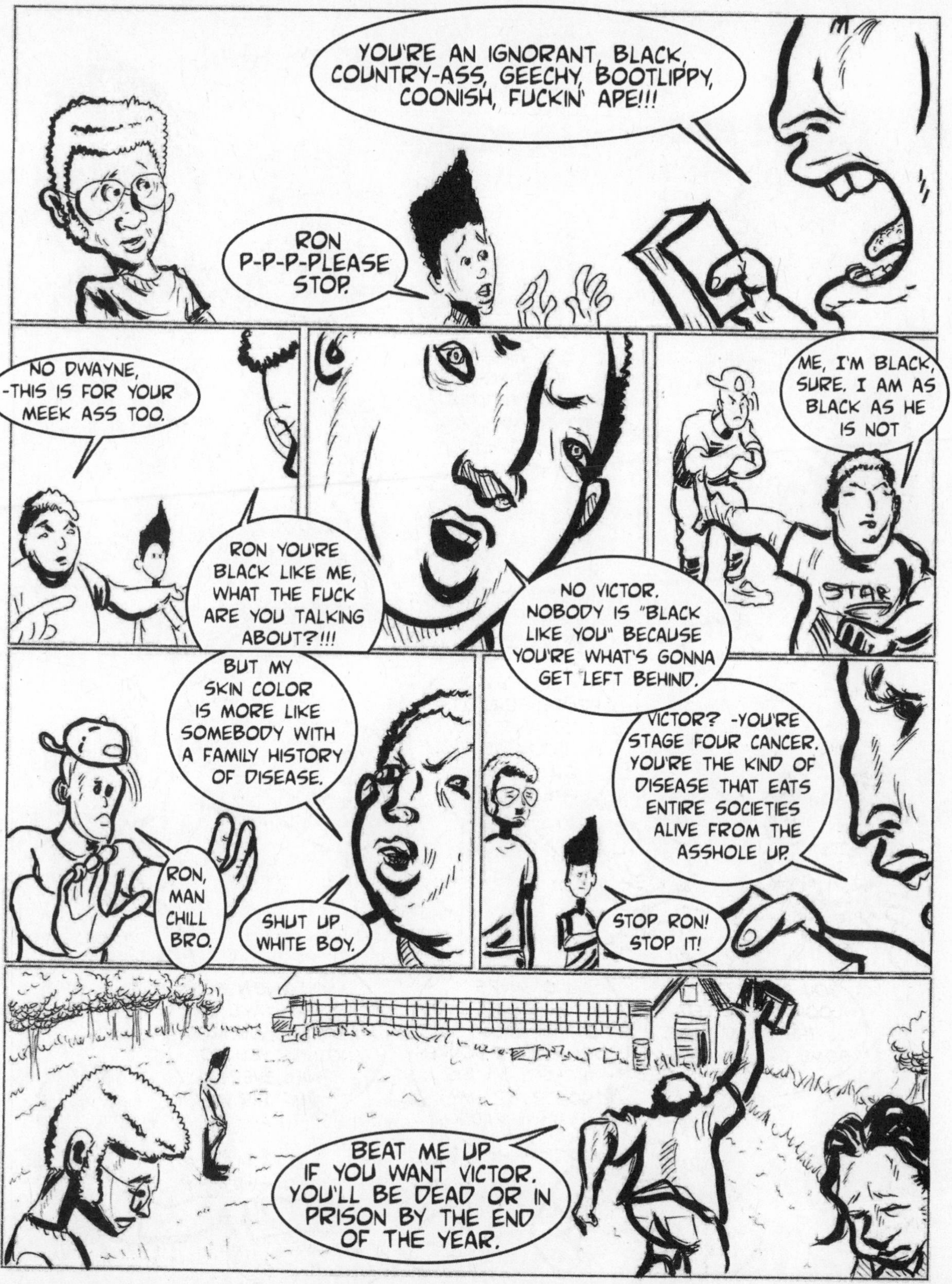
YOU'RE AN IGNORANT, BLACK, COUNTRY-ASS, GEECHY, BOOTLIPPY, COONISH, FUCKIN' APE!!!
RON P-P-P-PLEASE STOP.
NO DWAYNE, -THIS IS FOR YOUR MEEK ASS TOO.
RON YOU'RE BLACK LIKE ME, WHAT THE FUCK ARE YOU TALKING ABOUT?!!!
ME, I'M BLACK, SURE. I AM AS BLACK AS HE IS NOT
NO VICTOR. NOBODY IS "BLACK LIKE YOU" BECAUSE YOU'RE WHAT'S GONNA GET LEFT BEHIND.
STAR
BUT MY SKIN COLOR IS MORE LIKE SOMEBODY WITH A FAMILY HISTORY OF DISEASE.
RON, MAN CHILL BRO.
SHUT UP WHITE BOY.
VICTOR? -YOU'RE STAGE FOUR CANCER. YOU'RE THE KIND OF DISEASE THAT EATS ENTIRE SOCIETIES ALIVE FROM THE ASSHOLE UP.
STOP RON! STOP IT!
BEAT ME UP IF YOU WANT VICTOR. YOU'LL BE DEAD OR IN PRISON BY THE END OF THE YEAR.

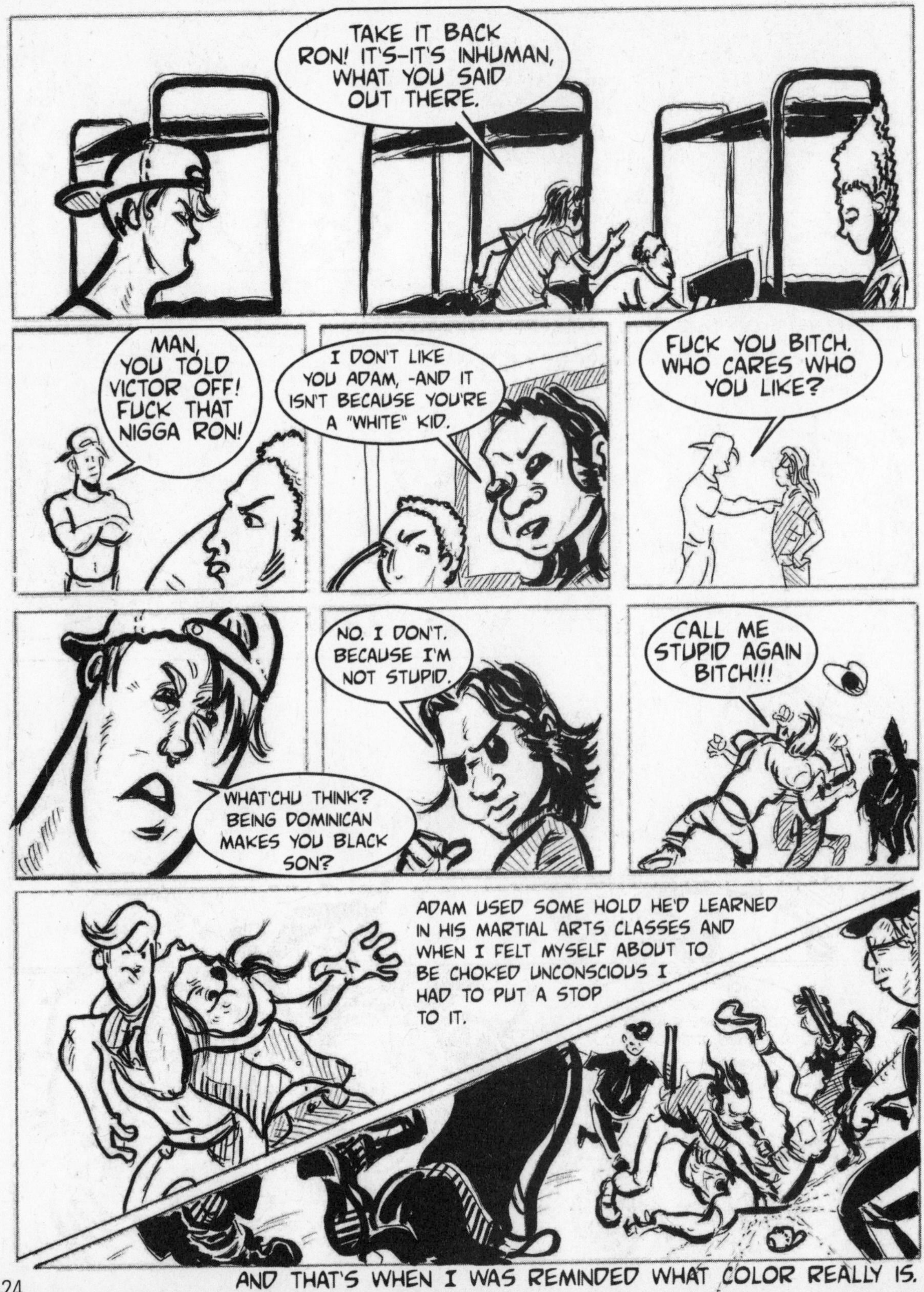

TAKE IT BACK RON! IT'S-IT'S INHUMAN, WHAT YOU SAID OUT THERE.
MAN, YOU TOLD VICTOR OFF! FUCK THAT NIGGA RON!
I DON'T LIKE YOU ADAM, -AND IT ISN'T BECAUSE YOU'RE A "WHITE" KID.
FUCK YOU BITCH. WHO CARES WHO YOU LIKE?
WHAT'CHU THINK? BEING DOMINICAN MAKES YOU BLACK SON?
NO. I DON'T. BECAUSE I'M NOT STUPID.
CALL ME STUPID AGAIN BITCH!!!
ADAM USED SOME HOLD HE'D LEARNED IN HIS MARTIAL ARTS CLASSES AND WHEN I FELT MYSELF ABOUT TO BE CHOKED UNCONSCIOUS I HAD TO PUT A STOP TO IT.
AND THAT'S WHEN I WAS REMINDED WHAT COLOR REALLY IS.

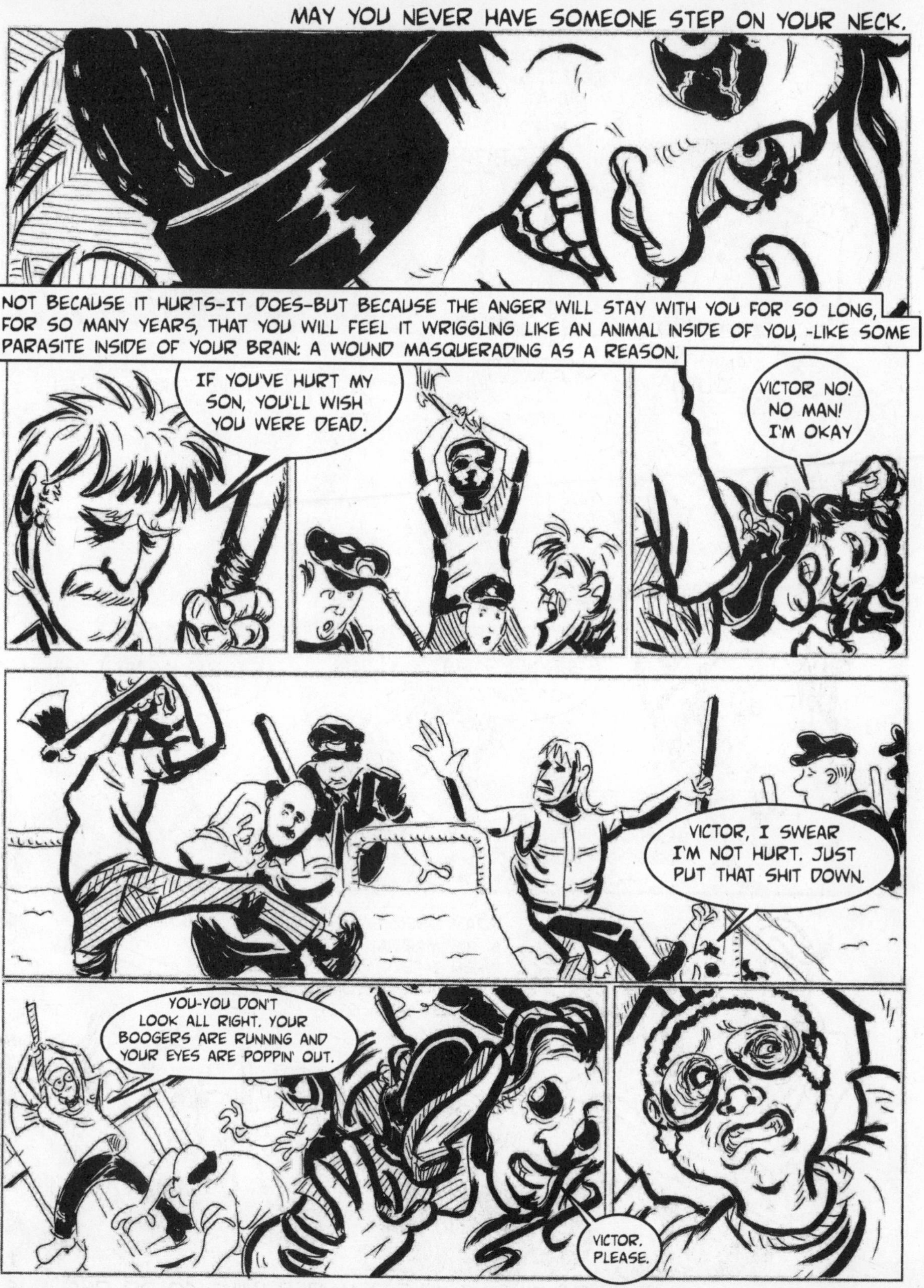
MAY YOU NEVER HAVE SOMEONE STEP ON YOUR NECK.
NOT BECAUSE IT HURTS–IT DOES–BUT BECAUSE THE ANGER WILL STAY WITH YOU FOR SO LONG, FOR SO MANY YEARS, THAT YOU WILL FEEL IT WRIGGLING LIKE AN ANIMAL INSIDE OF YOU, -LIKE SOME PARASITE INSIDE OF YOUR BRAIN: A WOUND MASQUERADING AS A REASON.
IF YOU'VE HURT MY SON, YOU'LL WISH YOU WERE DEAD.
VICTOR NO! NO MAN! I'M OKAY
VICTOR, I SWEAR I'M NOT HURT. JUST PUT THAT SHIT DOWN.
YOU-YOU DON'T LOOK ALL RIGHT. YOUR BOOGERS ARE RUNNING AND YOUR EYES ARE POPPIN' OUT.
VICTOR. PLEASE.

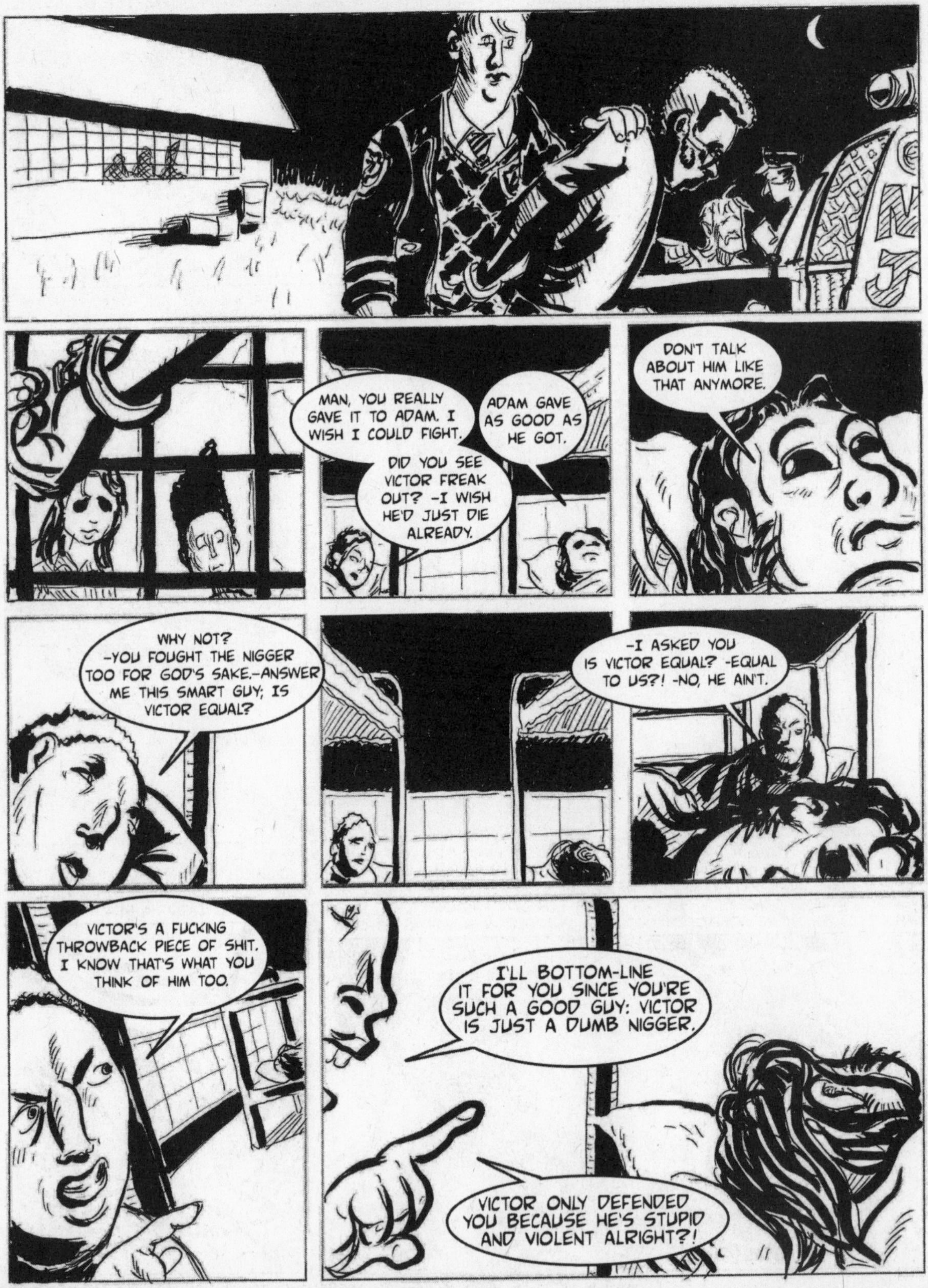
MAN, YOU REALLY GAVE IT TO ADAM. I WISH I COULD FIGHT.
ADAM GAVE AS GOOD AS HE GOT.
DID YOU SEE VICTOR FREAK OUT? -I WISH HE'D JUST DIE ALREADY.
DON'T TALK ABOUT HIM LIKE THAT ANYMORE.
WHY NOT? -YOU FOUGHT THE NIGGER TOO FOR GOD'S SAKE.-ANSWER ME THIS SMART GUY; IS VICTOR EQUAL?
-I ASKED YOU IS VICTOR EQUAL? -EQUAL TO US?! -NO, HE AIN'T.
VICTOR'S A FUCKING THROWBACK PIECE OF SHIT. I KNOW THAT'S WHAT YOU THINK OF HIM TOO.
I'LL BOTTOM-LINE IT FOR YOU SINCE YOU'RE SUCH A GOOD GUY: VICTOR IS JUST A DUMB NIGGER.
VICTOR ONLY DEFENDED YOU BECAUSE HE'S STUPID AND VIOLENT ALRIGHT?!

ME AND RON?—WE ARE THE "GOOD" PEOPLE, WE ARE THE PEOPLE WHO FOR ONE REASON OR ANOTHER HAVE NO PROBLEM FITTING INTO MOST OF WESTERN SOCIETY'S ROUND HOLES. WE ARE THE LAW ABIDERS, THE TAX PAYERS, AND WE ARE THE FUEL OF THE DAYTIME WORLD OF HANDSHAKES BEHIND CLENCHED TEETH. WE BELONG TO THE WORLD OF UNANSWERED INSULTS, AND SLAPS ACROSS THE FACE ENDURED WITH CHRISTIAN DIGNITY.

RON AND I ARE REASONABLE MEN. WE ARE MEN WHO UNDERSTAND WHY THERE IS A LINE, AND WE WILL STAND IN IT AND WAIT UNTIL WE ARE TOLD NOT TO. REASONABLE MEN DO NOT START RIOTS AND BREAK POLICE CORDONS. REASONABLE MEN DO NOT MAKE A SCENE AT THE BANK. REASONABLE MEN DO NOT START SHITSTORMS... AND REASONABLE MEN CANNOT BE COUNTED UPON TO START THE REVOLUTION.

REASONABLE MEN ARE MEANINGLESS TO HISTORY'S CHANGES: FULLY AWARE OF THE FORCES OF EVIL, GREED AND OPPRESSION, AND MAKING DUE FROM RINGSIDE SEATS.

PERHAPS THIS STORY IS A GUIDE TO RECOGNIZING YOUR BROTHERS AND YOUR SAINTS BEFORE THE WORLD SWEEPS THEM AWAY IN MURDER AND VIOLENCE. MAYBE IT'S A FAILED INSTRUCTION MANUAL ON HOW TO SHIELD THE SCAPEGOAT FROM THE CHOPPING BLOCK, OR A REMINDER TO KEEP YOUR EYES PEELED WHEN YOUR PROXY, OR YOUR BROTHER IS BEING PULLED OVER FOR A TRAFFIC VIOLATION; SO THAT A SUMMONS OR PARKING TICKET DOESN'T NECESSARILY CARRY A DEATH SENTENCE SIMPLY BECAUSE THERE ARE FOOLS AMONG US CHARGED WITH MAKING US OBEY.

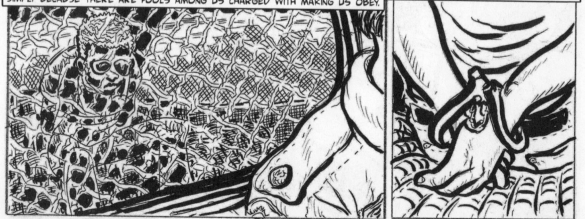

IT WAS IN VICTOR'S VERY BONES TO MISBEHAVE, TO RESIST, TO NOT COOPERATE.

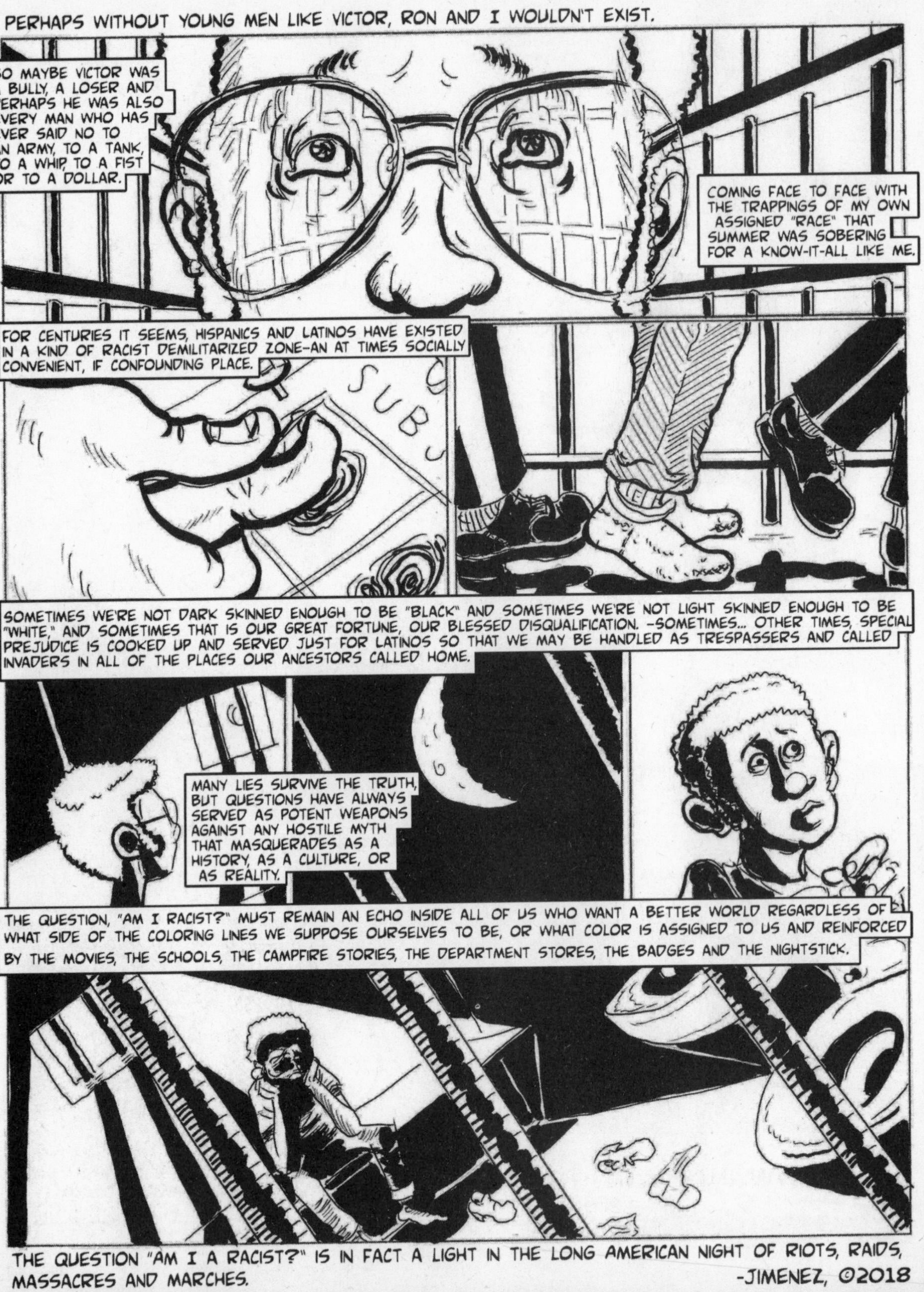
PERHAPS WITHOUT YOUNG MEN LIKE VICTOR, RON AND I WOULDN'T EXIST.
SO MAYBE VICTOR WAS A BULLY, A LOSER AND PERHAPS HE WAS ALSO EVERY MAN WHO HAS EVER SAID NO TO AN ARMY, TO A TANK, TO A WHIP, TO A FIST OR TO A DOLLAR.
COMING FACE TO FACE WITH THE TRAPPINGS OF MY OWN ASSIGNED "RACE" THAT SUMMER WAS SOBERING FOR A KNOW-IT-ALL LIKE ME.
FOR CENTURIES IT SEEMS, HISPANICS AND LATINOS HAVE EXISTED IN A KIND OF RACIST DEMILITARIZED ZONE–AN AT TIMES SOCIALLY CONVENIENT, IF CONFOUNDING PLACE.
SUBS
SOMETIMES WE'RE NOT DARK SKINNED ENOUGH TO BE "BLACK" AND SOMETIMES WE'RE NOT LIGHT SKINNED ENOUGH TO BE "WHITE," AND SOMETIMES THAT IS OUR GREAT FORTUNE, OUR BLESSED DISQUALIFICATION. –SOMETIMES... OTHER TIMES, SPECIAL PREJUDICE IS COOKED UP AND SERVED JUST FOR LATINOS SO THAT WE MAY BE HANDLED AS TRESPASSERS AND CALLED INVADERS IN ALL OF THE PLACES OUR ANCESTORS CALLED HOME.
MANY LIES SURVIVE THE TRUTH, BUT QUESTIONS HAVE ALWAYS SERVED AS POTENT WEAPONS AGAINST ANY HOSTILE MYTH THAT MASQUERADES AS A HISTORY, AS A CULTURE, OR AS REALITY.
THE QUESTION, "AM I RACIST?" MUST REMAIN AN ECHO INSIDE ALL OF US WHO WANT A BETTER WORLD REGARDLESS OF WHAT SIDE OF THE COLORING LINES WE SUPPOSE OURSELVES TO BE, OR WHAT COLOR IS ASSIGNED TO US AND REINFORCED BY THE MOVIES, THE SCHOOLS, THE CAMPFIRE STORIES, THE DEPARTMENT STORES, THE BADGES AND THE NIGHTSTICK.
THE QUESTION "AM I A RACIST?" IS IN FACT A LIGHT IN THE LONG AMERICAN NIGHT OF RIOTS, RAIDS, MASSACRES AND MARCHES.
-JIMENEZ, ©2018

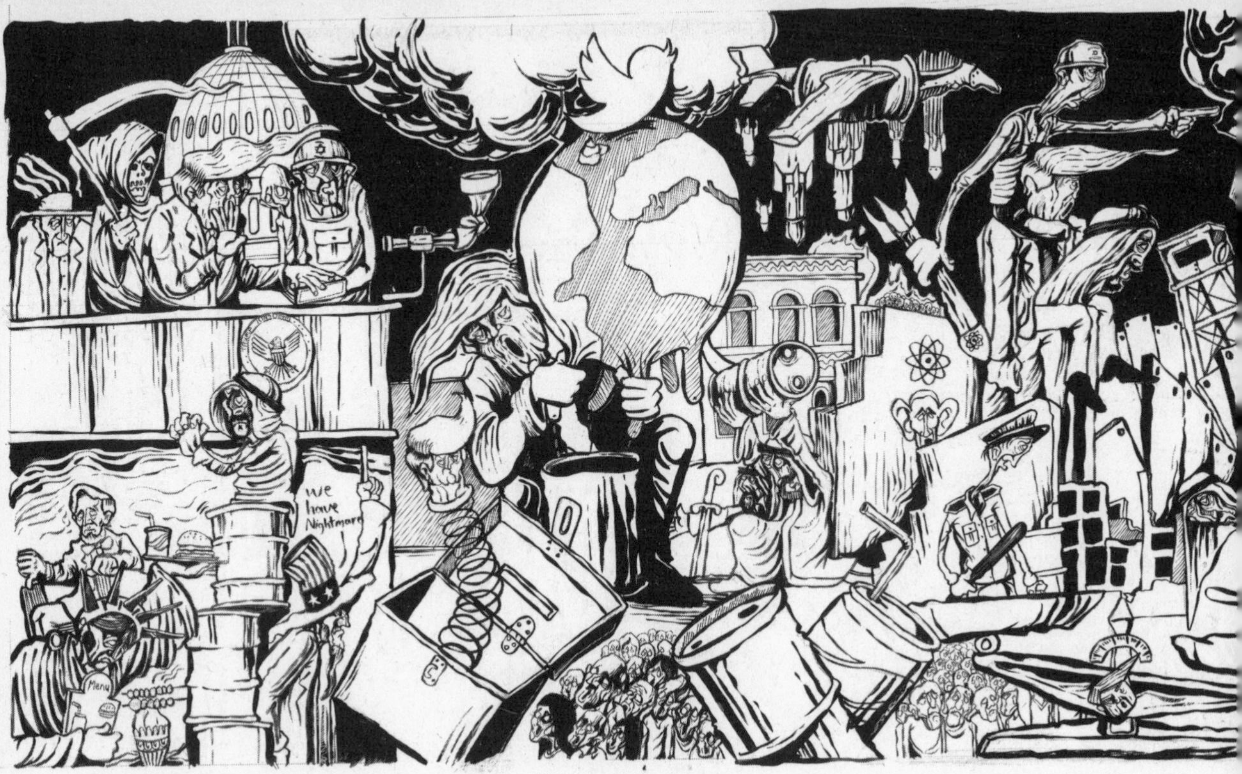
We have
Menu

An interview with Palestinian cartoonist

Mohammad Sabaaneh

What do people in the U.S. need to know about the Palestinian situation?

If we want to talk about Palestine, we should talk in two tracks:

First, the historical track. 1948 is the crucial point in Palestinian history. In 1948, 750,000 Palestinians were expelled from their homes and land by Israeli soldiers and guns, what we call "al-Nakba," which means "the Catastrophe." A new nation was created on the ruins of another nation's stolen land, homes, identity and history. The Palestinians were ethnically cleansed by the Israelis. And this displacement and suffering continues to this day. This settler colonialism goes on until this moment by denying the rights of the indigenous peoples to return to their land.

In 1967, Israel occupied the rest of the Palestinian land in the West Bank and Gaza under the guise of security and expanded the land of the state of Israel and created a new system for 3 million Palestinians. An open-air prison. This land, which is considered to be the Palestinian state according to international law and UN resolutions, has been occupied by Israel since 1967. Israeli governments confiscated the land to build Jewish settlements, and cut up Palestinian cities with checkpoints and a segregation wall. The world claimed that they created a peace process, but the fact is Israel wants the process more than peace. They want to confiscate more land under this ongoing process without peace.

Second track: the daily conditions of Palestinians that result from this history: 2 million in Gaza living under siege; 4 million Palestinians in the West Bank living in the same conditions but with some freedom inside Palestinian

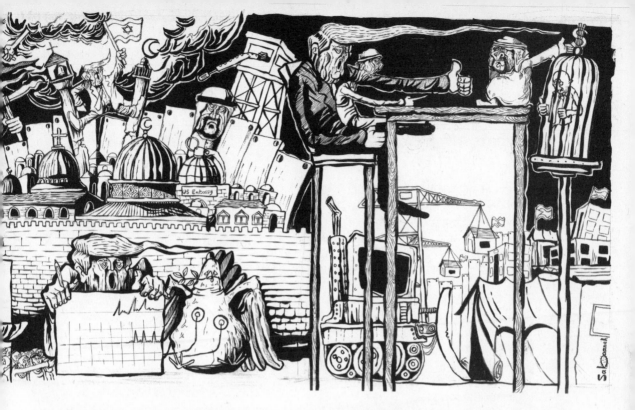

cities (Palestinian islands surrounded by walls, checkpoints and settlements); around 2 million Palestinians in Israel living in an apartheid state. And 4 million refugees around the world who do not have the right to come home.

Why have you chosen cartooning as your form of resistance?

First, because I love to do this kind of art, and I want to be a cartoonist far away from the clichés. But also it is important to prove to the people around the world that what the Israelis claim, that they came to an empty land without a population, without civilization, this is not true. They destroyed a country full of people who had their own identity and culture. And you can see how often the Israeli media attacks Palestinian cartoonists! Because of that I chose to be a cartoonist.

What kinds of cartoons did you see growing up? And what influences you today?

I started with Naji al-Ali, because I grew up in

Kuwait, where Naji was publishing his cartoons. My mother found his cartoons to be a good tool to teach us about Palestine. When I started doing my cartoons while at university, I couldn't find any other cartoonist to learn from, But now I follow a lot of cartoonists like Kevin Kallaugher, Steve Brodner, Seth, Marilena Nardi, Angel Boligán, Ann Telnaes.

Tell us about Naji al-Ali.

Palestinian cartoonist Naji al-Ali was born in 1938. His cartoons were sharply critical of Palestinian and Arab politics and political leaders. He is best known as creator of the character Handala, pictured in his cartoons as a young witness of the satirized policy or event depicted. Handala has since become an icon of Palestinian defiance. On July 22, 1987, while outside the London offices of Al-Qabas, a Kuwaiti newspaper for which he drew political caricatures, al-Ali was shot in the face, and he died five weeks later in Charing Cross Hospital. The shooter was never caught. Naji al-Ali is a hero for all Arab cartoonists because he faced a lot and bravely stood up to Arab leaders, the PLO and Israel.

You were in prison?

*L*ike most Palestinians I have been to prison, for 6 months. I did not do anything against the occupation except my cartoons, so I know the cartoon is an important reason to be attacked by Israel,

You will be surprised to hear that the only time I have been able to spend exclusively on my artwork is my time in prison, because there was nothing else to do there.

In the year 2013, I was coming back from Jordan after having a number of meetings concerning my work with the Arab American University. I was accompanied by my colleague, whom I had invited to meet for breakfast when we got home. Unfortunately, while crossing the border, which is managed by the occupation, I was investigated for several hours. After many hours, the officer came and told me that I was in detention. Thus my journey to prison had begun. I drew this journey, and drew several people who were in a similar situation. For a moment, while drawing, I felt like I was surrounded by human beings.

After moving me out of the border, they left me at the door of an Israeli camp with my hands and feet handcuffed, sitting in a plastic chair. I knew it was a gate due to its sound when it was opening and closing for military vehicles. That sound was familiar to me as a Palestinian. I heard barking dogs for around 7 hours. The only thing that made this situation easier for me was that I had my bucket of cigarettes.

When it was dark, I was led by the soldiers to a container where there were two more soldiers. They asked me to take off my clothes to search me for the second time. I was shuddering at that moment. The first soldiers tried to calm me, but the second ones were just scoffing at me. I don't know if I was shuddering because of fear or because of cold, since this was in February. They searched my bags and they put all my property in plastic bags, including my clothes, gifts to my wife and brother, and my drawing pens. This was the moment when I realized that it was going be a long journey.

After that, they transported me in a special dark car with shackled hands and feet for 3 hours until we reached the place. I did not know where we were going. After this long journey, which I spent sleeping, I heard the soldiers shouting and the car started to slow dawn. I heard the sound of the big gate. They dropped me into a large building where the windows were covered with iron. Iron gates, lights and soldiers all around.

I wished that every soldier who took me to a place would be the last one, without ever having to be transferred to another soldier. The tough words I heard upon meeting each one of them made me feel unsafe. I was afraid of an unknown future. I remember that I asked one of the soldiers where I was, he answered, "Later you will know that."

They put me in a small bathroom for long hours, and then they let me out to search me again. They asked me to get my clothes off and wear brown clothes, very depressing clothes. After this, they locked me in a cell. At that time I thought it was late, but I did not have a watch since they had taken it from me. There was another prisoner in the cell, so I asked him where I was, and he told me that I was in Al Jalameh detention center. I asked him what was going to happen to us, to which he replied, "Sleep and tomorrow you will see." I slept until I heard a soldier shouting, "Adad Adad."

I woke up and saw him looking in through a small metallic window in the heavy metallic door. Then he closed it. A few minutes later, another soldier opened another small metallic window and left two dishes with a small quantity of food. My partner told me to eat, and it was at that moment when I realized that I had not eaten for more than 24 hours, But I could not. This situation made me remember my friend whom I had invited to breakfast.

After hours, the investigation phase started. The investigator asked me about everything in my life, including my work, study and exhibitions. During another investigation session, he also took out a number of my caricatures and asked me about them.

Moreover, do you know what? That investigator was the first Israeli I had ever talked with. Can you imagine that this was my introduction to the Israeli people? How? Shouting at my face when he got an unexpected answer.

They put me back in the cell, which was very small (2x1.5m), with rough walls where you cannot even lie down, with dim light that stays on day and night. I had a hard toothbrush lying on the floor, which the soldiers used to be afraid of, as they thought we could use it to strike the prison warden.

I spent long hours alone inside the cell. I imagined myself as a journalist in marginalized places or war areas. A journalist who is reporting the suffering of people to the rest of the world. I tried to fight the loneliness with these thoughts. I used what I had been taught in the children's camps. I started

using my art. I decided to draw the suffering of the prisoners, starting from the detention until prison and other details.

To pass the time, I started using my imagination. I started thinking of having an exhibition. Who would be invited to this exhibition? Where would I conduct it? What would be the message of this exhibition? These thoughts were the only tool that I had to fight loneliness.

In one of the investigation sessions, I stole a paper and small pencil from the investigator. This theft was a big victory over the occupation in my opinion. I started documenting my drawing ideas in order not to forget them. I used each inch of that paper. Sometimes, I used to draw on it, then clean it in order to have another drawing on the same paper. This paper was all I had at that time. I was struggling to have this paper with me during my movement from one cell to the other; it was a treasure for me. I had it during my stay in the prison. In addition, its photo appears in my book. In the prison, I started drawing the ideas that I had documented on that paper. I used other papers and pens that they allowed me to have. At the beginning, I was drawing caricatures without captions or any dialogue that could give any indication that they were about life inside the prison. This was in order to make the prison

administration allow me to take them out when I would be released. I used to send my drawings out with prisoners when they were being released. My wife was the person who was picking them up to publish some of them at Al Hayat al-Jadidah newsletter while I was in the prison.

When I was released, I had an exhibition. I called it Cell 2, the cell where I spent more than two weeks alone thinking about my drawings. I remember that, in that cell also, I made a small ball from a small towel, as I had to spend my time playing alone.

You will be able to see those drawings in the last section of my book. These drawings are so important to me. These drawings do not incite resistance, they are resistance. Resistance against the jailer, against his investigation tools, against loneliness and fear.

Prison is a very important and tough experience that I do not wish anyone to have. I was not the only one who drew inside the prison. There were others, such as Fadi Khalil, to whom I gifted a sketchbook. He told me that he had not held a sketchbook for 12 years. It was a worthy gift for him. The perfume that had passed with me into the prison in my bag, more than 120 prisoners used this perfume. They used to sit around

and ask me about life outside the prison. They enjoyed hearing about my first visit to the US and UK, my work and studies.

Prison is another world. The period of my detention was a very important period for me: a number of cartoonists and institutions stood beside me all over the world. As a cartoonist you cannot find enough time to work in regular life, but during detention I could be totally dedicated to my art. I was forced to use pens and traditional tools for producing these drawings, not computers.

And what work do you do as an artist now?

I work with a daily newspaper. I'm working on new murals and trying to do some comics.

You work for a newspaper allied with the Palestinian Authority. To what degree are you free to express your own opinion?

It is a hard equation. I had a deal with the newspaper. I told them, "I am drawing what I believe, and you can publish what you want from that." This deal works sometimes, and sometimes it does not. They suspended me a number of times, and tried to kick me off the newspaper many times. But I think international retaliations

I achieved protect me and give me a good power.

What difficulties do you and other political cartoonists in Palestine face today?

The Israeli policy is the first one. Not just arresting us. There is another thing. The accusation of anti-Semitism is something very dangerous for cartoonists. Internationally, cartoonists are besieged with this accusation. Even if you are only criticizing Netanyahu, they will say you that you are anti-Semitic. In European countries the accusation of anti-Semitism has made most European cartoonists stop criticizing Israel.

The second danger is from political parties which use religion as a strategy and a title, like Hamas and al-Jihad. I faced a big campaign of threatening phone calls because I did a cartoon criticizing one of these parties. I think this political party converts the audience into a censorship tool in the name of religion. They become a holy political party, and the people deal with them as a representative of God.

The cartoon you have sent us is about Donald Trump. Americans see him as very different than previous US presidents. In what ways is Trump's policy toward Palestine different from the previous administration's? In what ways is it the same?

There is no peace process. We had a process, and under this process we had the Israeli annexation of Palestinian land, the expansion of settlements and stolen identity going on. And they claim we will reach peace one day. I am living in the West Bank, which is considered part of a Palestinian state. Palestinian cities are islands surrounded by settlements, checkpoints and a wall. How can we believe that we can establish our state and Israel believes in peace? The Zionist mentality doesn't believe in 2 states. They believe they have the right to take the West Bank, not just the land they took in 1948.

I do not think we will find any U.S. President as willing to defy all the international law and resolutions toward Palestine as he is. Most U.S. presidents supported Israel, but not like him.

First, Jerusalem was occupied in 1967. That means, under international law, it's part of a Palestinian state. Second, in Jerusalem you will find holy places for Muslims and Christians. When Trump recognizes it as capital of the state of Israel, he denies the right of Muslims and Christians to pray in their holy places. For me it is important because by our rights under international law, this is Palestinian land. For me it is dangerous to use religion in political conflicts.

Trump seems to be close to the Saudis and very hostile to Iran. What is the role of these countries in the Palestinian situation?

It is clear that abandoning Palestine is the price the Saudis pay for the U.S. supporting Saudi Arabia against Iran. Now the Saudis want the Palestinians to accept any deal from Trump, whatever that deal entails.

Would it be correct to say that the "peace process," and with it the whole idea of a "2-state solution," is a thing of the past? If so, how does this change things?

There have been nonviolent protests in Palestine for years. So are the recent Gaza protests something new? Are these protests led by Hamas or are others involved?

Yes, what is happening in Gaza is new. Hamas has started to believe in nonviolent resistance as an alternative, but I think Hamas does not, and will not, declare that. But they allowed the people to go to the Gaza-Israel border, and I think Hamas found this form of resistance to be a good way to expose Israel. And the people in Gaza created a lot of new things in this protest, such as using balloons and kites, and they will create more and more.

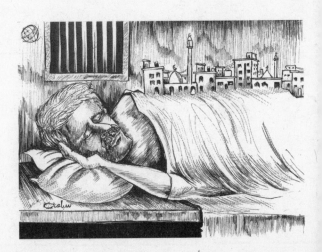

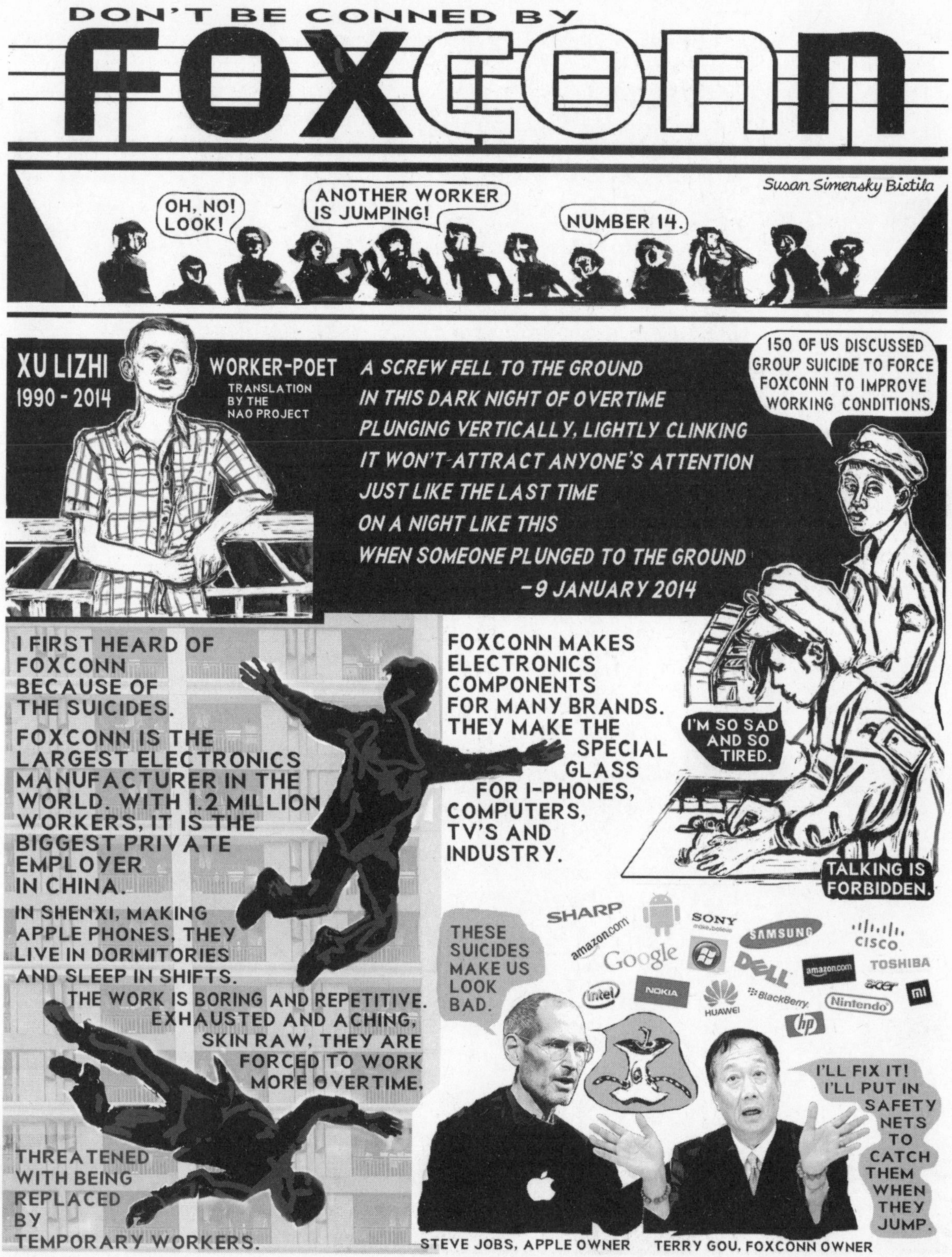
DON'T BE CONNED BY
FOXCONN
Susan Simensky Bietila
OH, NO! LOOK!
ANOTHER WORKER IS JUMPING!
NUMBER 14.
XU LIZHI
1990 - 2014
WORKER-POET
TRANSLATION BY THE NAO PROJECT
A SCREW FELL TO THE GROUND
IN THIS DARK NIGHT OF OVERTIME
PLUNGING VERTICALLY, LIGHTLY CLINKING
IT WON'T ATTRACT ANYONE'S ATTENTION
JUST LIKE THE LAST TIME
ON A NIGHT LIKE THIS
WHEN SOMEONE PLUNGED TO THE GROUND
-9 JANUARY 2014
150 OF US DISCUSSED GROUP SUICIDE TO FORCE FOXCONN TO IMPROVE WORKING CONDITIONS.
I FIRST HEARD OF FOXCONN BECAUSE OF THE SUICIDES.
FOXCONN IS THE LARGEST ELECTRONICS MANUFACTURER IN THE WORLD. WITH 1.2 MILLION WORKERS, IT IS THE BIGGEST PRIVATE EMPLOYER IN CHINA.
IN SHENXI, MAKING APPLE PHONES, THEY LIVE IN DORMITORIES AND SLEEP IN SHIFTS.
THE WORK IS BORING AND REPETITIVE. EXHAUSTED AND ACHING, SKIN RAW, THEY ARE FORCED TO WORK MORE OVERTIME.
THREATENED WITH BEING REPLACED BY TEMPORARY WORKERS.
FOXCONN MAKES ELECTRONICS COMPONENTS FOR MANY BRANDS. THEY MAKE THE SPECIAL GLASS FOR I-PHONES, COMPUTERS, TV'S AND INDUSTRY.
I'M SO SAD AND SO TIRED.
TALKING IS FORBIDDEN.
THESE SUICIDES MAKE US LOOK BAD.
SHARP
amazon.com
SONY
SAMSUNG
CISCO
Google
DELL
amazon.com
TOSHIBA
acer
intel
NOKIA
HUAWEI
BlackBerry
Nintendo
hp
I'LL FIX IT! I'LL PUT IN SAFETY NETS TO CATCH THEM WHEN THEY JUMP.
STEVE JOBS, APPLE OWNER
TERRY GOU, FOXCONN OWNER

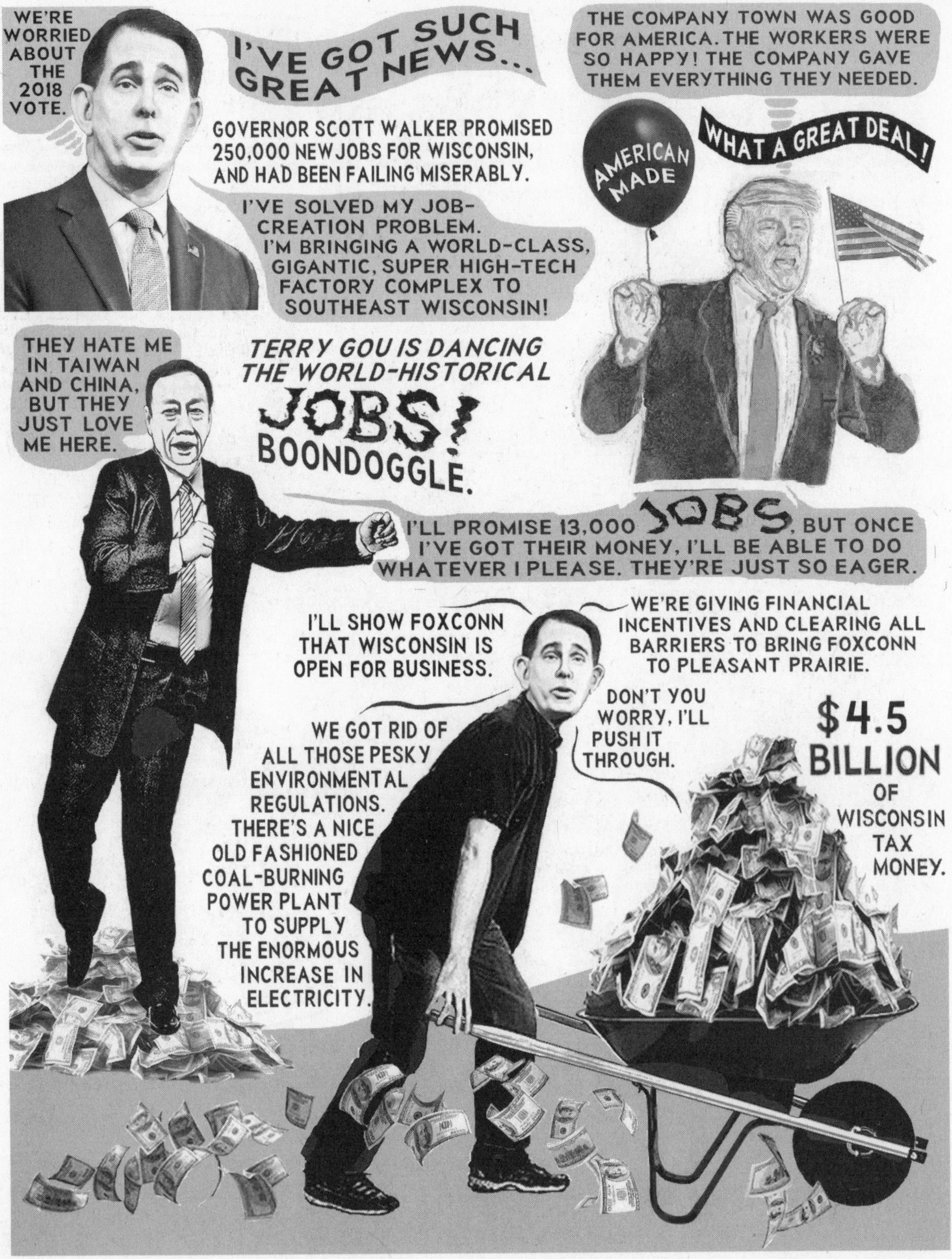

WE'RE WORRIED ABOUT THE 2018 VOTE.
I'VE GOT SUCH GREAT NEWS...
GOVERNOR SCOTT WALKER PROMISED 250,000 NEW JOBS FOR WISCONSIN, AND HAD BEEN FAILING MISERABLY.
I'VE SOLVED MY JOB-CREATION PROBLEM. I'M BRINGING A WORLD-CLASS, GIGANTIC, SUPER HIGH-TECH FACTORY COMPLEX TO SOUTHEAST WISCONSIN!
THE COMPANY TOWN WAS GOOD FOR AMERICA. THE WORKERS WERE SO HAPPY! THE COMPANY GAVE THEM EVERYTHING THEY NEEDED.
AMERICAN MADE
WHAT A GREAT DEAL!
THEY HATE ME IN TAIWAN AND CHINA, BUT THEY JUST LOVE ME HERE.
TERRY GOU IS DANCING THE WORLD-HISTORICAL
JOBS! BOONDOGGLE.
I'LL PROMISE 13,000 JOBS, BUT ONCE I'VE GOT THEIR MONEY, I'LL BE ABLE TO DO WHATEVER I PLEASE. THEY'RE JUST SO EAGER.
I'LL SHOW FOXCONN THAT WISCONSIN IS OPEN FOR BUSINESS.
WE'RE GIVING FINANCIAL INCENTIVES AND CLEARING ALL BARRIERS TO BRING FOXCONN TO PLEASANT PRAIRIE.
WE GOT RID OF ALL THOSE PESKY ENVIRONMENTAL REGULATIONS. THERE'S A NICE OLD FASHIONED COAL-BURNING POWER PLANT TO SUPPLY THE ENORMOUS INCREASE IN ELECTRICITY.
DON'T YOU WORRY, I'LL PUSH IT THROUGH.
$4.5 BILLION OF WISCONSIN TAX MONEY.

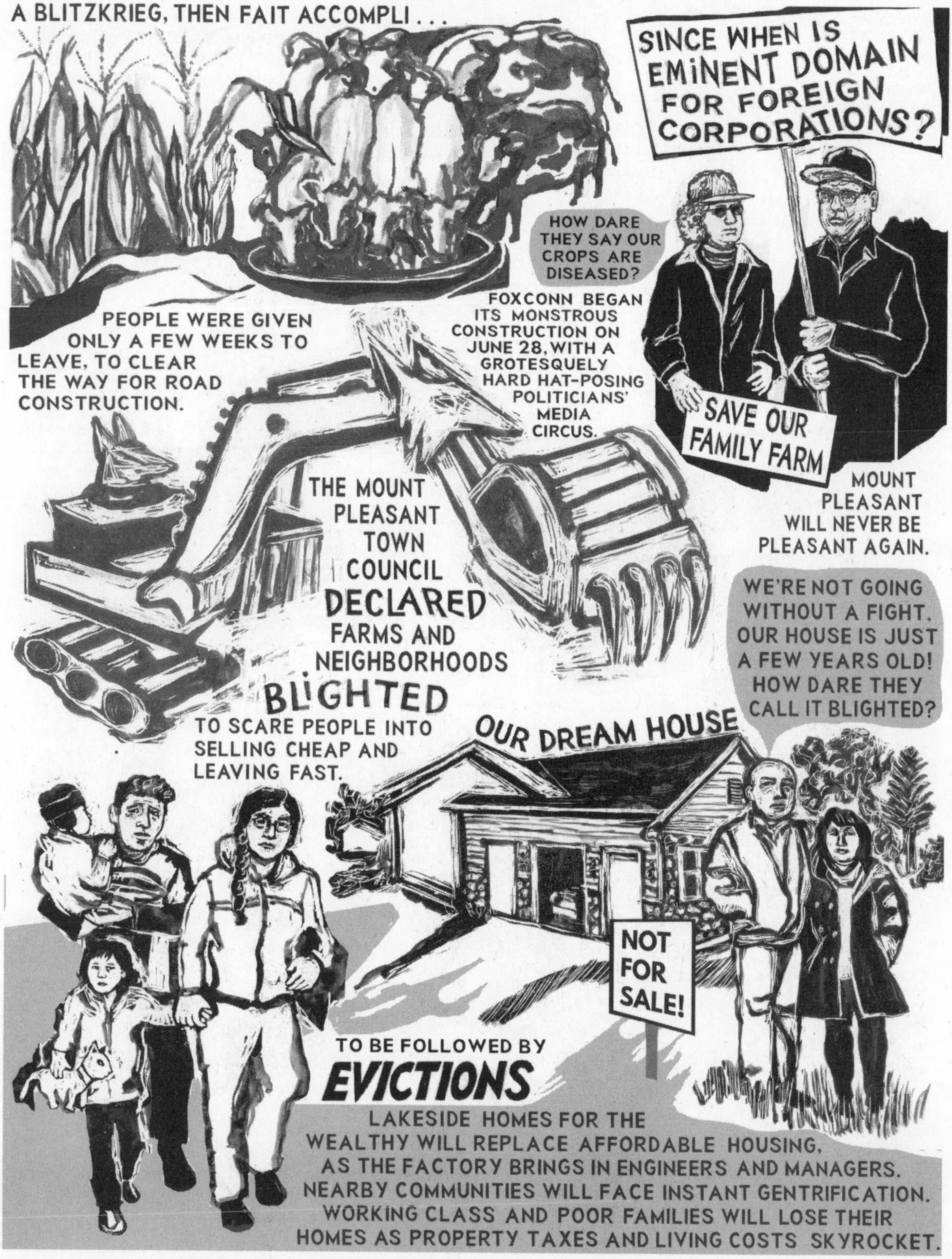
A BLITZKRIEG, THEN FAIT ACCOMPLI . . .
SINCE WHEN IS EMINENT DOMAIN FOR FOREIGN CORPORATIONS?
HOW DARE THEY SAY OUR CROPS ARE DISEASED?
PEOPLE WERE GIVEN ONLY A FEW WEEKS TO LEAVE, TO CLEAR THE WAY FOR ROAD CONSTRUCTION.
FOXCONN BEGAN ITS MONSTROUS CONSTRUCTION ON JUNE 28, WITH A GROTESQUELY HARD HAT-POSING POLITICIANS' MEDIA CIRCUS.
SAVE OUR FAMILY FARM
MOUNT PLEASANT WILL NEVER BE PLEASANT AGAIN.
THE MOUNT PLEASANT TOWN COUNCIL DECLARED FARMS AND NEIGHBORHOODS BLIGHTED TO SCARE PEOPLE INTO SELLING CHEAP AND LEAVING FAST.
WE'RE NOT GOING WITHOUT A FIGHT. OUR HOUSE IS JUST A FEW YEARS OLD! HOW DARE THEY CALL IT BLIGHTED?
OUR DREAM HOUSE
NOT FOR SALE!
TO BE FOLLOWED BY EVICTIONS
LAKESIDE HOMES FOR THE WEALTHY WILL REPLACE AFFORDABLE HOUSING, AS THE FACTORY BRINGS IN ENGINEERS AND MANAGERS. NEARBY COMMUNITIES WILL FACE INSTANT GENTRIFICATION. WORKING CLASS AND POOR FAMILIES WILL LOSE THEIR HOMES AS PROPERTY TAXES AND LIVING COSTS SKYROCKET.

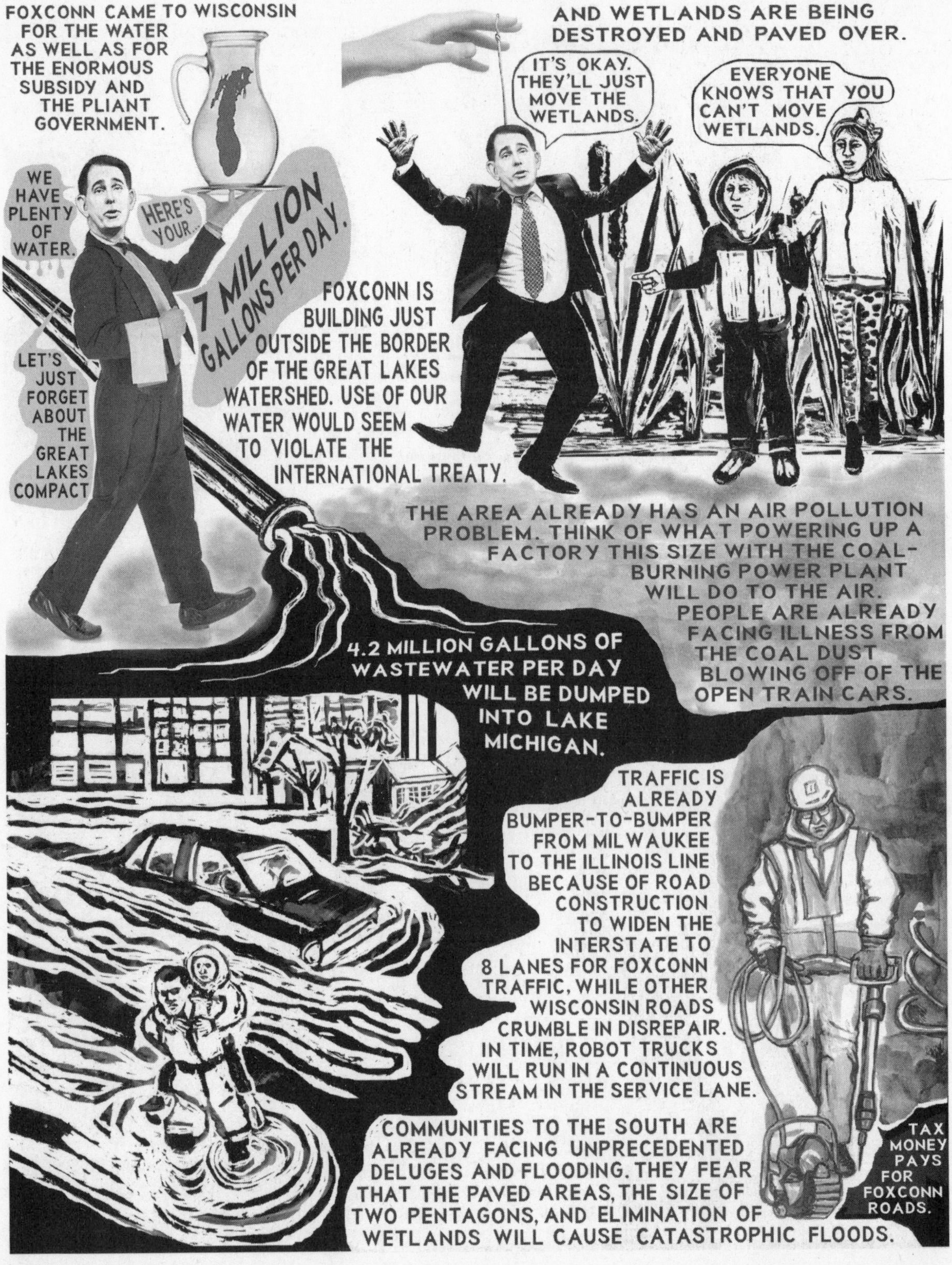

FOXCONN CAME TO WISCONSIN FOR THE WATER AS WELL AS FOR THE ENORMOUS SUBSIDY AND THE PLIANT GOVERNMENT.
WE HAVE PLENTY OF WATER.
HERE'S YOUR...
7 MILLION GALLONS PER DAY.
LET'S JUST FORGET ABOUT THE GREAT LAKES COMPACT
FOXCONN IS BUILDING JUST OUTSIDE THE BORDER OF THE GREAT LAKES WATERSHED. USE OF OUR WATER WOULD SEEM TO VIOLATE THE INTERNATIONAL TREATY.
AND WETLANDS ARE BEING DESTROYED AND PAVED OVER.
IT'S OKAY. THEY'LL JUST MOVE THE WETLANDS.
EVERYONE KNOWS THAT YOU CAN'T MOVE WETLANDS.
THE AREA ALREADY HAS AN AIR POLLUTION PROBLEM. THINK OF WHAT POWERING UP A FACTORY THIS SIZE WITH THE COAL-BURNING POWER PLANT WILL DO TO THE AIR. PEOPLE ARE ALREADY FACING ILLNESS FROM THE COAL DUST BLOWING OFF OF THE OPEN TRAIN CARS.
4.2 MILLION GALLONS OF WASTEWATER PER DAY WILL BE DUMPED INTO LAKE MICHIGAN.
TRAFFIC IS ALREADY BUMPER-TO-BUMPER FROM MILWAUKEE TO THE ILLINOIS LINE BECAUSE OF ROAD CONSTRUCTION TO WIDEN THE INTERSTATE TO 8 LANES FOR FOXCONN TRAFFIC, WHILE OTHER WISCONSIN ROADS CRUMBLE IN DISREPAIR. IN TIME, ROBOT TRUCKS WILL RUN IN A CONTINUOUS STREAM IN THE SERVICE LANE.
COMMUNITIES TO THE SOUTH ARE ALREADY FACING UNPRECEDENTED DELUGES AND FLOODING. THEY FEAR THAT THE PAVED AREAS, THE SIZE OF TWO PENTAGONS, AND ELIMINATION OF WETLANDS WILL CAUSE CATASTROPHIC FLOODS.
TAX MONEY PAYS FOR FOXCONN ROADS.

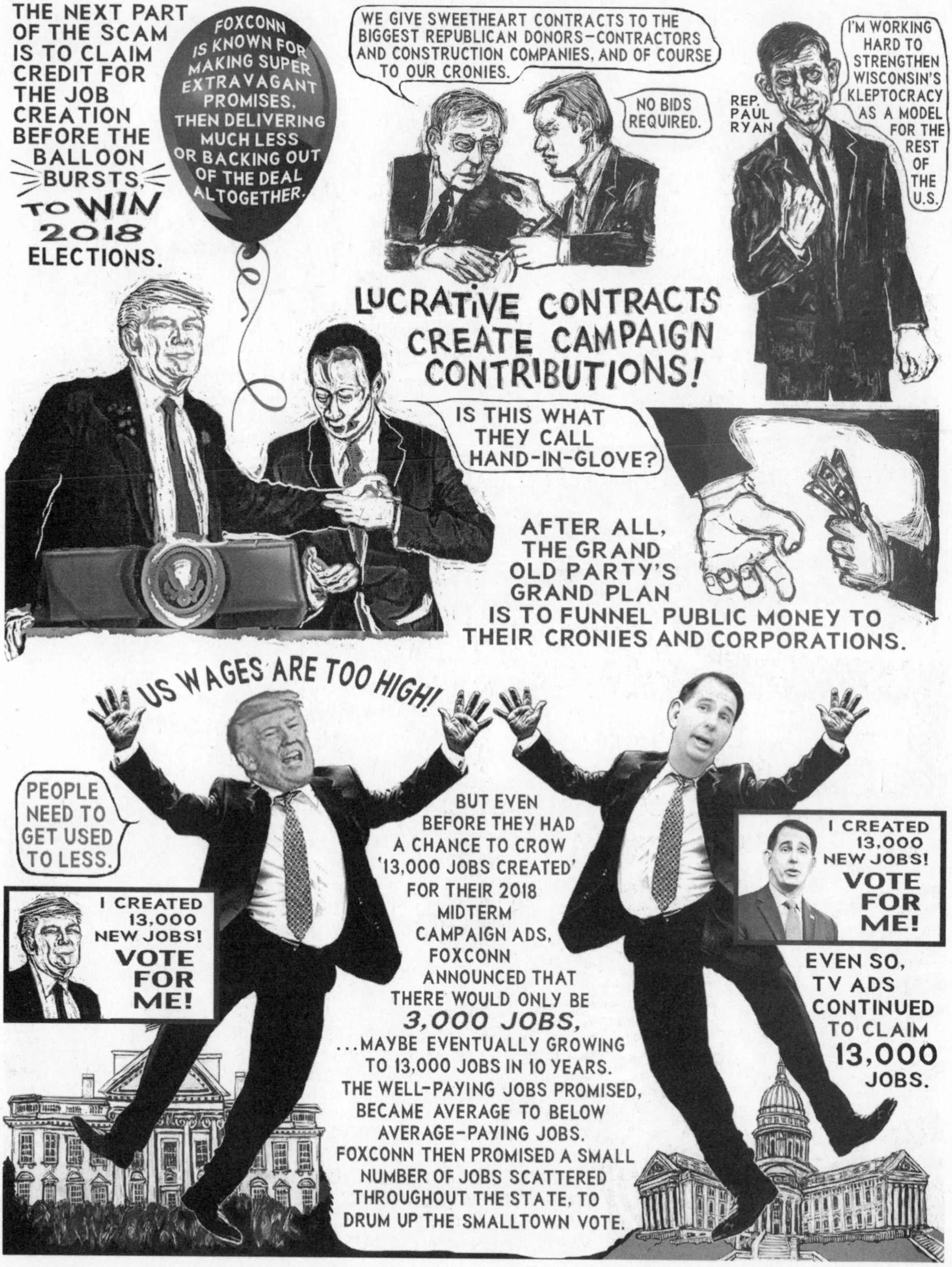

THE NEXT PART OF THE SCAM IS TO CLAIM CREDIT FOR THE JOB CREATION BEFORE THE BALLOON BURSTS, TO WIN 2018 ELECTIONS.
FOXCONN IS KNOWN FOR MAKING SUPER EXTRAVAGANT PROMISES, THEN DELIVERING MUCH LESS OR BACKING OUT OF THE DEAL ALTOGETHER.
WE GIVE SWEETHEART CONTRACTS TO THE BIGGEST REPUBLICAN DONORS—CONTRACTORS AND CONSTRUCTION COMPANIES, AND OF COURSE TO OUR CRONIES.
NO BIDS REQUIRED.
REP. PAUL RYAN
I'M WORKING HARD TO STRENGTHEN WISCONSIN'S KLEPTOCRACY AS A MODEL FOR THE REST OF THE U.S.
LUCRATIVE CONTRACTS CREATE CAMPAIGN CONTRIBUTIONS!
IS THIS WHAT THEY CALL HAND-IN-GLOVE?
AFTER ALL, THE GRAND OLD PARTY'S GRAND PLAN IS TO FUNNEL PUBLIC MONEY TO THEIR CRONIES AND CORPORATIONS.
US WAGES ARE TOO HIGH!
PEOPLE NEED TO GET USED TO LESS.
I CREATED 13,000 NEW JOBS! VOTE FOR ME!
BUT EVEN BEFORE THEY HAD A CHANCE TO CROW '13,000 JOBS CREATED' FOR THEIR 2018 MIDTERM CAMPAIGN ADS, FOXCONN ANNOUNCED THAT THERE WOULD ONLY BE 3,000 JOBS, ...MAYBE EVENTUALLY GROWING TO 13,000 JOBS IN 10 YEARS. THE WELL-PAYING JOBS PROMISED, BECAME AVERAGE TO BELOW AVERAGE-PAYING JOBS. FOXCONN THEN PROMISED A SMALL NUMBER OF JOBS SCATTERED THROUGHOUT THE STATE, TO DRUM UP THE SMALLTOWN VOTE.
I CREATED 13,000 NEW JOBS! VOTE FOR ME!
EVEN SO, TV ADS CONTINUED TO CLAIM 13,000 JOBS.

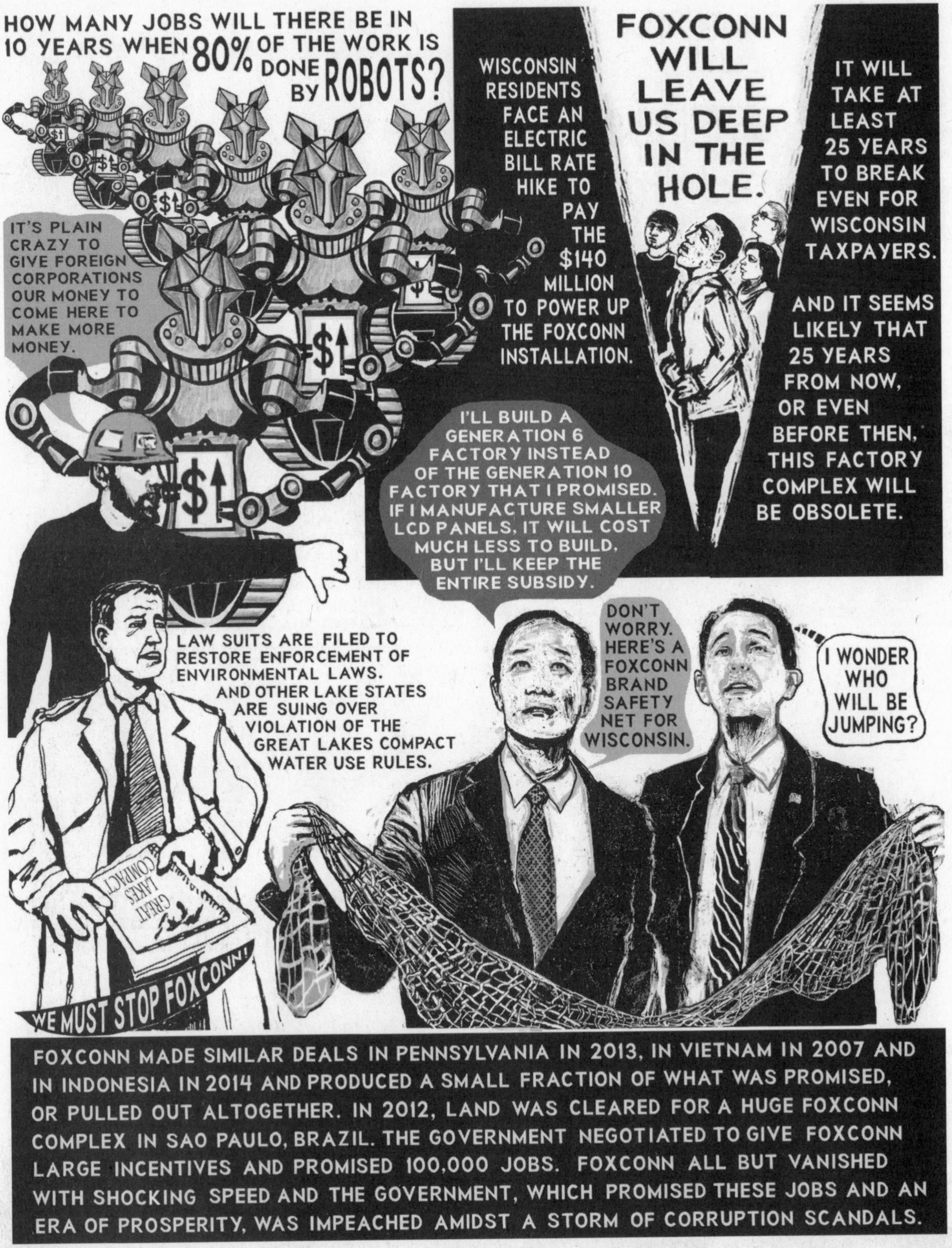
HOW MANY JOBS WILL THERE BE IN 10 YEARS WHEN 80% OF THE WORK IS DONE BY ROBOTS?
IT'S PLAIN CRAZY TO GIVE FOREIGN CORPORATIONS OUR MONEY TO COME HERE TO MAKE MORE MONEY.
WISCONSIN RESIDENTS FACE AN ELECTRIC BILL RATE HIKE TO PAY THE $140 MILLION TO POWER UP THE FOXCONN INSTALLATION.
FOXCONN WILL LEAVE US DEEP IN THE HOLE.
IT WILL TAKE AT LEAST 25 YEARS TO BREAK EVEN FOR WISCONSIN TAXPAYERS.
AND IT SEEMS LIKELY THAT 25 YEARS FROM NOW, OR EVEN BEFORE THEN, THIS FACTORY COMPLEX WILL BE OBSOLETE.
I'LL BUILD A GENERATION 6 FACTORY INSTEAD OF THE GENERATION 10 FACTORY THAT I PROMISED. IF I MANUFACTURE SMALLER LCD PANELS, IT WILL COST MUCH LESS TO BUILD, BUT I'LL KEEP THE ENTIRE SUBSIDY.
LAW SUITS ARE FILED TO RESTORE ENFORCEMENT OF ENVIRONMENTAL LAWS. AND OTHER LAKE STATES ARE SUING OVER VIOLATION OF THE GREAT LAKES COMPACT WATER USE RULES.
DON'T WORRY. HERE'S A FOXCONN BRAND SAFETY NET FOR WISCONSIN.
I WONDER WHO WILL BE JUMPING?
GREAT LAKES COMPACT
WE MUST STOP FOXCONN!

FOXCONN MADE SIMILAR DEALS IN PENNSYLVANIA IN 2013, IN VIETNAM IN 2007 AND IN INDONESIA IN 2014 AND PRODUCED A SMALL FRACTION OF WHAT WAS PROMISED, OR PULLED OUT ALTOGETHER. IN 2012, LAND WAS CLEARED FOR A HUGE FOXCONN COMPLEX IN SAO PAULO, BRAZIL. THE GOVERNMENT NEGOTIATED TO GIVE FOXCONN LARGE INCENTIVES AND PROMISED 100,000 JOBS. FOXCONN ALL BUT VANISHED WITH SHOCKING SPEED AND THE GOVERNMENT, WHICH PROMISED THESE JOBS AND AN ERA OF PROSPERITY, WAS IMPEACHED AMIDST A STORM OF CORRUPTION SCANDALS.

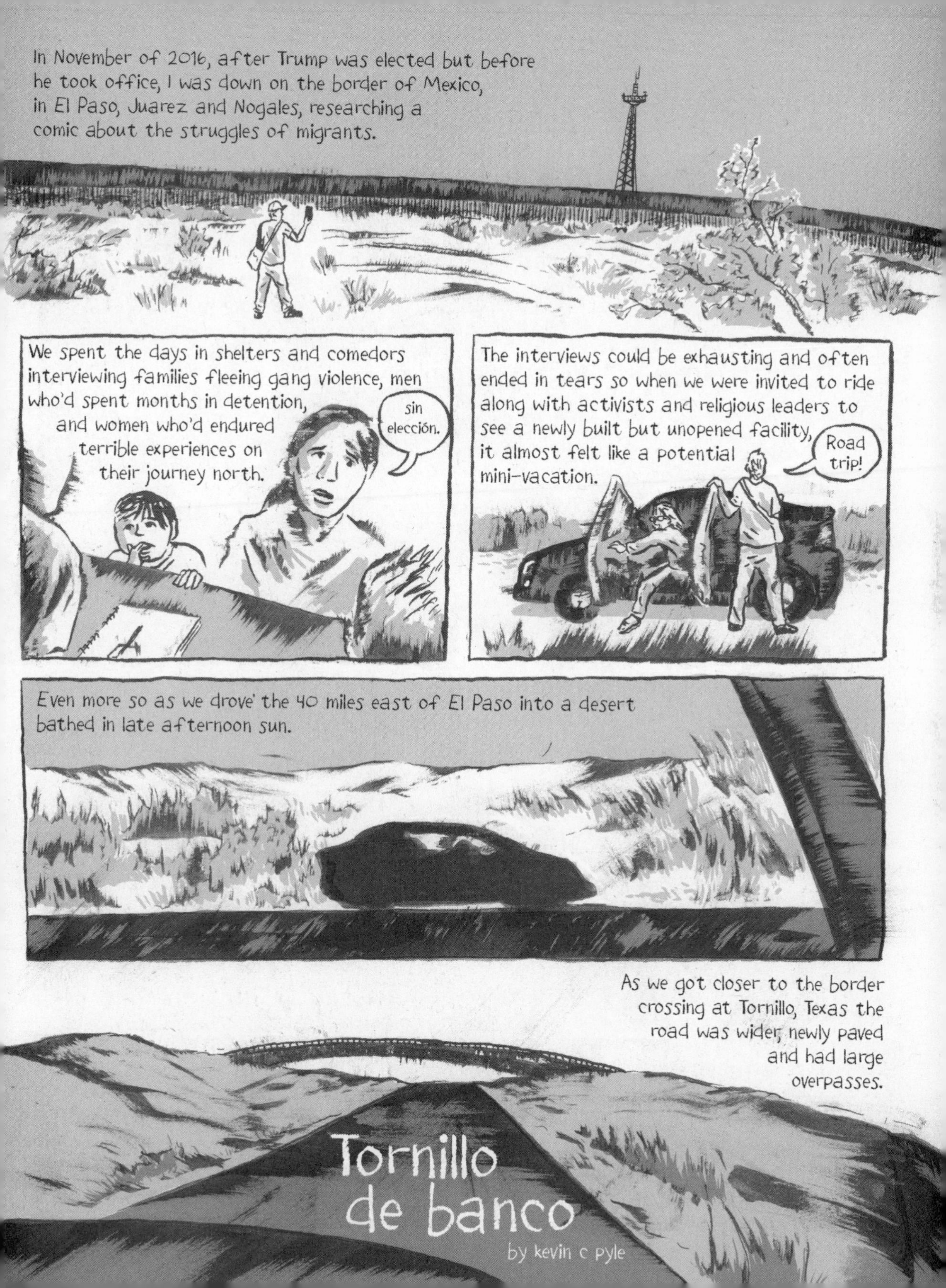
In November of 2016, after Trump was elected but before he took office, I was down on the border of Mexico, in El Paso, Juarez and Nogales, researching a comic about the struggles of migrants.
We spent the days in shelters and comedors interviewing families fleeing gang violence, men who'd spent months in detention,
and women who'd endured terrible experiences on their journey north.
sin elección.
The interviews could be exhausting and often ended in tears so when we were invited to ride along with activists and religious leaders to see a newly built but unopened facility, it almost felt like a potential mini-vacation.
Road trip!
Even more so as we drove the 40 miles east of El Paso into a desert bathed in late afternoon sun.
As we got closer to the border crossing at Tornillo, Texas the road was wider, newly paved and had large overpasses.
Tornillo de banco
by kevin c pyle

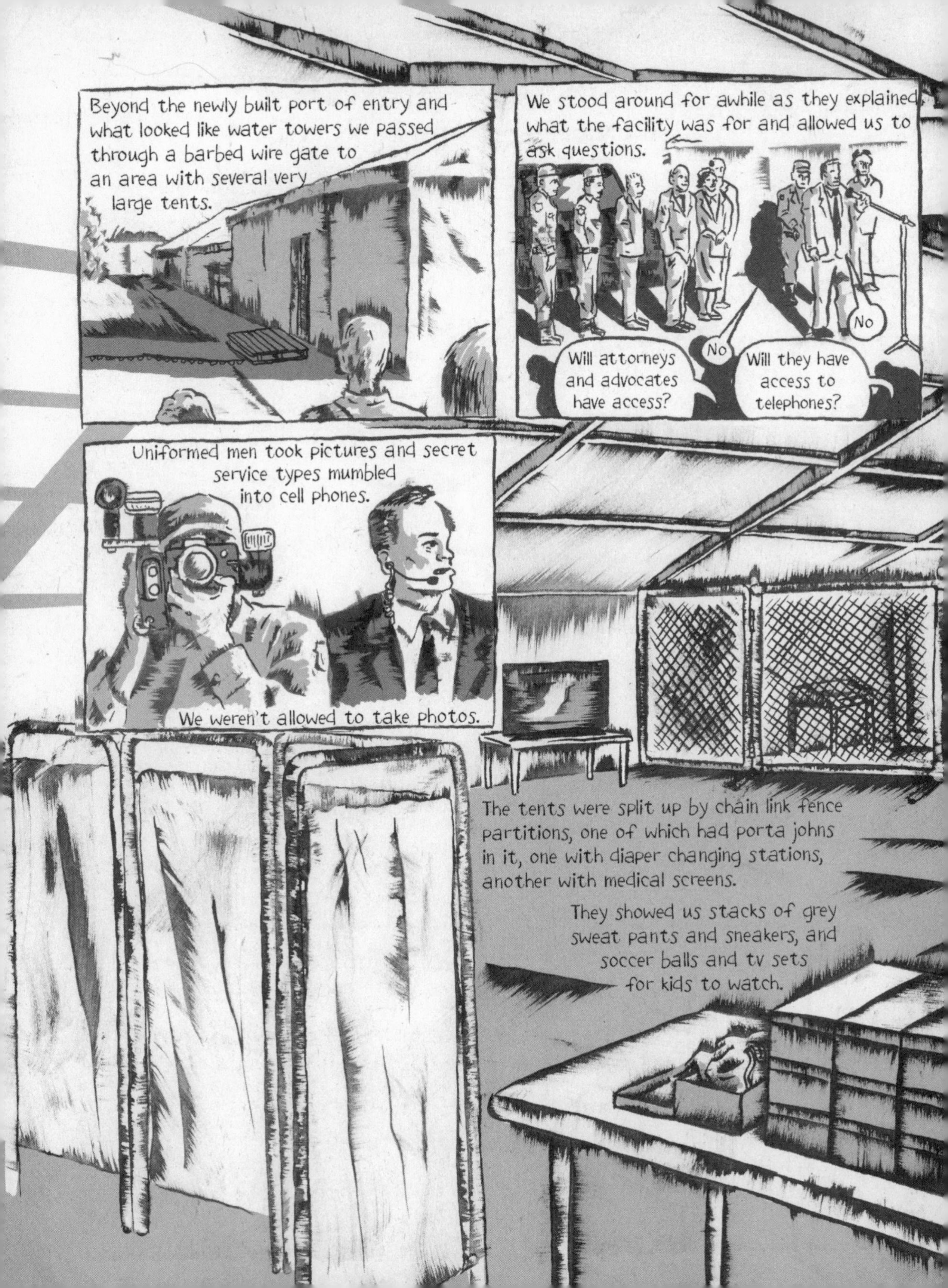

Beyond the newly built port of entry and what looked like water towers we passed through a barbed wire gate to an area with several very large tents.
We stood around for awhile as they explained what the facility was for and allowed us to ask questions.
Will attorneys and advocates have access?
No
Will they have access to telephones?
No
Uniformed men took pictures and secret service types mumbled into cell phones.
We weren't allowed to take photos.
The tents were split up by chain link fence partitions, one of which had porta johns in it, one with diaper changing stations, another with medical screens.
They showed us stacks of grey sweat pants and sneakers, and soccer balls and tv sets for kids to watch.

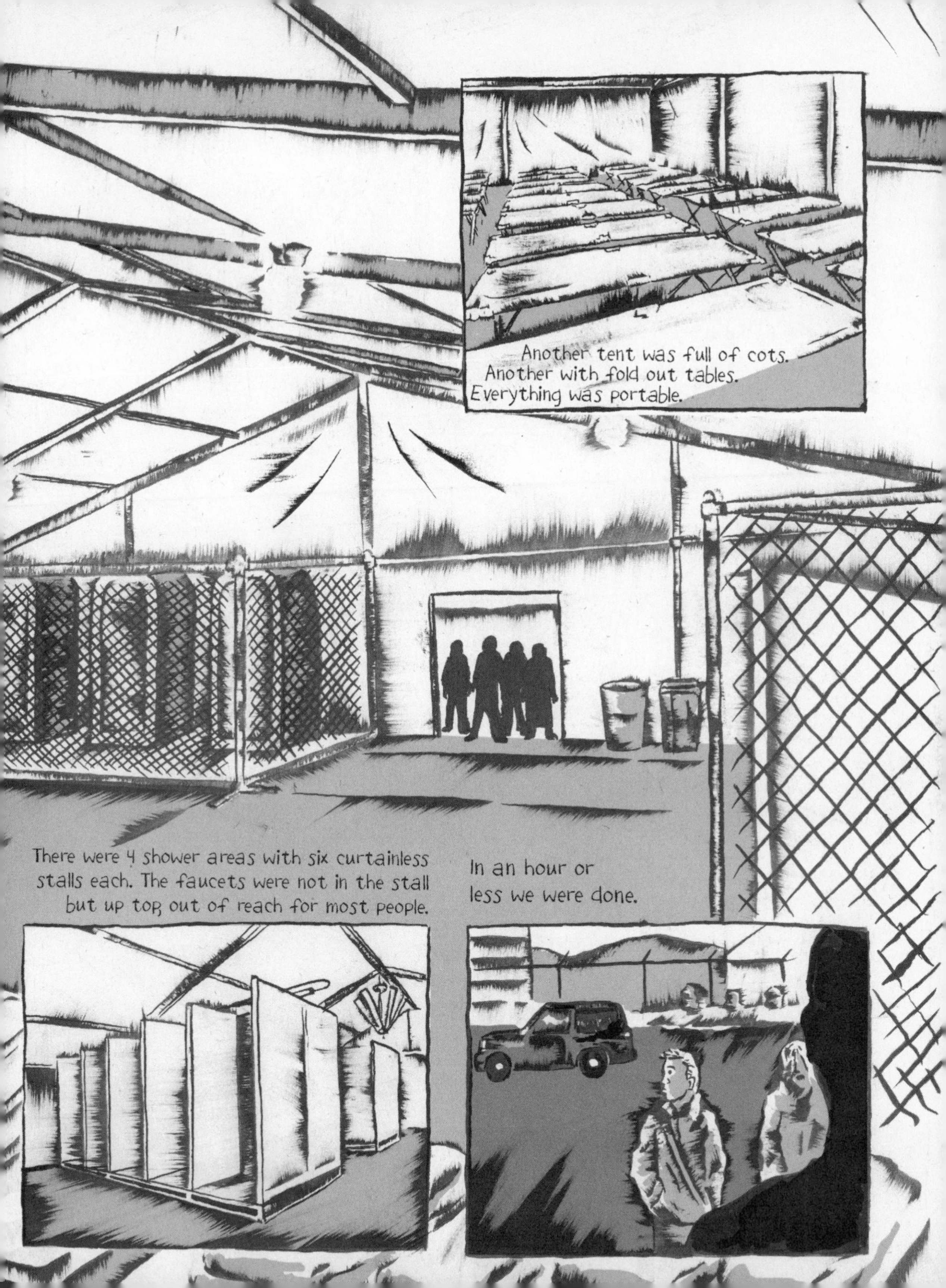
Another tent was full of cots.
Another with fold out tables.
Everything was portable.
There were 4 shower areas with six curtainless stalls each. The faucets were not in the stall but up top, out of reach for most people.
In an hour or less we were done.

The sun set as we stood in the parking lot, processing what we'd seen.

Why would they even want to drive them all the way out here?

I think the woman in the pants suit is DHS— I'll check the website.

And disappeared as we drove back to El Paso.

That was really kind of eerie— like a scene from the X-files or something.

The showers creeped me out. What's with the faucets up on top?

Did you see the black SUVs that kept circling around?

I thought back to the wide roads and over-passes.

Seems like they are preparing for something big.

In the following months, when I would tell the story, I emphasized the eerie details and the mystery of the place.

The big tents were here.

We were told it would be a facility for processing families seeking asy-lum— something the local jails and shel-ters weren't designed to do. Given the tvs, soccer balls, clothing etc. it seemed the intention was that families would be kept together.

For awhile you couldn't find much information. There were only a couple of articles about the place, one which came out the day after I visited.

census-designated place and border town in El
, Texas, United States. The population was 1,568
census. It is part of the El Paso Metropolitan
rea. Wikipedia

Which made sense because back then when you heard stories about family separation, it meant something different.

There were stories like Rosita's, who tried to cross multiple times to be with her daughter Emily, a US citizen getting medical treatment for Cushings syndrome in Chicago.

She doesn't understand...

As opposed to now, when children who can't deal with separation are being forcibly drugged with psycho pharmaceuticals at facilities in Texas and Virginia.

It was stories like Soccorro's, whose teenage son was pulled off a school bus and deported while on his way to a soccer game.

As opposed to children as young as 2 years old, dubbed tender care cases, pulled from the arms of their mothers and fathers, not yet having the language to understand or express their trauma.

It was stories of families who had loved ones disappear into the desert, never knowing what became of them. Victims of a policy designed to use nature as a deterrent.

As opposed to children forcibly taken and disappeared into a system that made little or no effort to keep track of them and was designed to use separation itself as a deterrent.

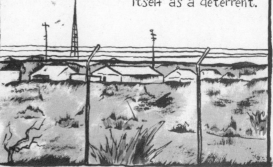

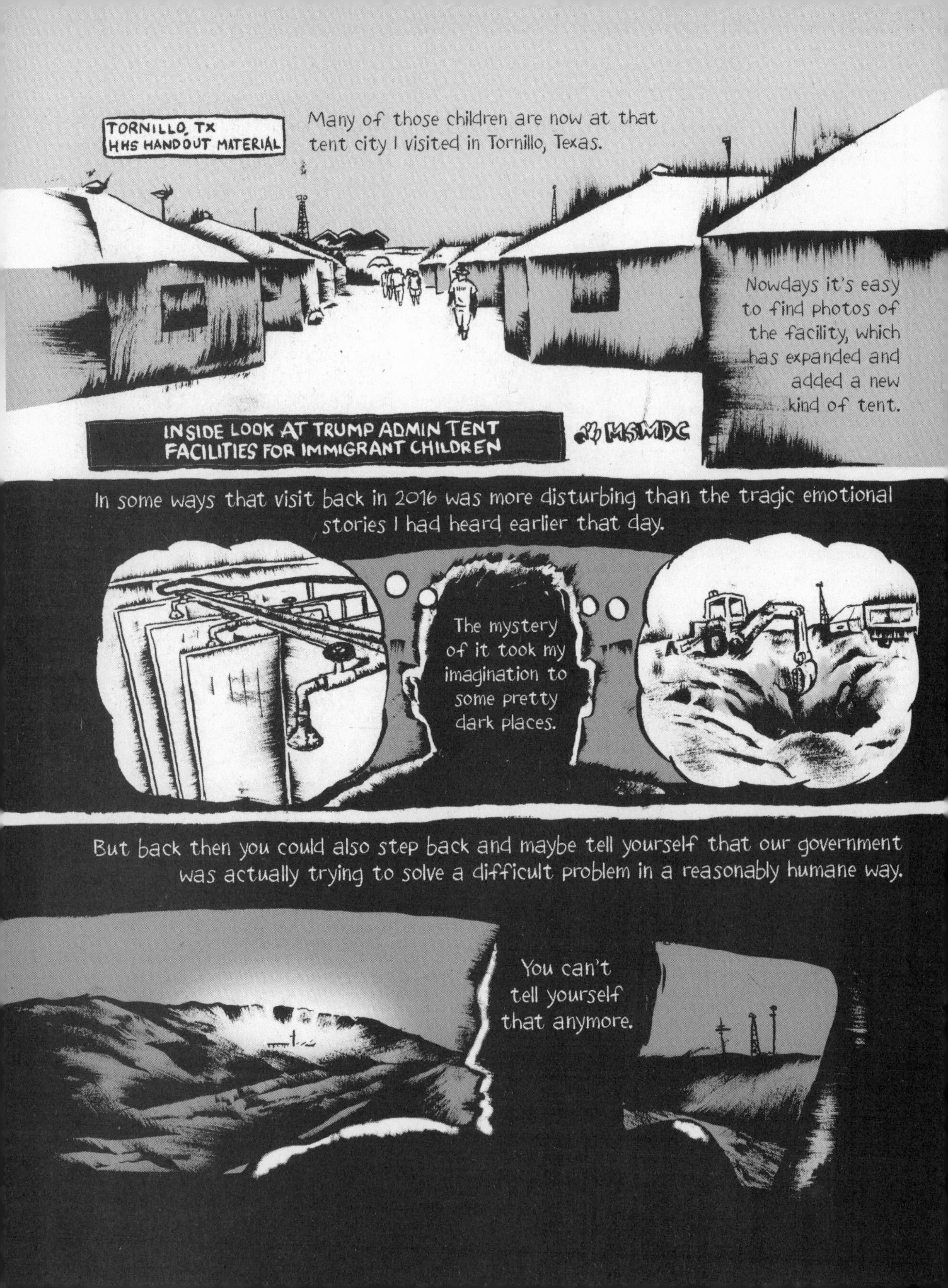
TORNILLO, TX
HHS HANDOUT MATERIAL
Many of those children are now at that tent city I visited in Tornillo, Texas.
Nowdays it's easy to find photos of the facility, which has expanded and added a new kind of tent.
INSIDE LOOK AT TRUMP ADMIN TENT FACILITIES FOR IMMIGRANT CHILDREN
MSMDC
In some ways that visit back in 2016 was more disturbing than the tragic emotional stories I had heard earlier that day.
The mystery of it took my imagination to some pretty dark places.
But back then you could also step back and maybe tell yourself that our government was actually trying to solve a difficult problem in a reasonably humane way.
You can't tell yourself that anymore.

APPENDIX: FINANCIAL STATEMENT

Back in 2016, one of the persistent mysteries of the site was its size and scope, given what the activists had told me.
In August DOJ announced they were ending the Federal Bureau of Prisons use of private prisons and DHS was starting a review to do the same with immigration detention.
So maybe it's a government built site?
Yeah- but still with private contracts.
It seemed like the private prison industry was on the ropes. Correction Corporation of America (CCA) and Geo Group saw their stock drop 40%.
016
But they had enough money left over to give a combined $725,000 to the Trump campaign and inauguration. Geo also held a leadership conference at a Trump resort and gave another $225,000 to a pro-Trump super pac.
A month into Trump's presidency Jeff Sessions reversed the DoJ's policy on private prisons and has requested $2.8 billion dollars to expand the detention effort.
There is a place for the private prison industry...
$
Both CCA (now renamed CoreCivic) and Geo Group saw an immediate spike in their stock values.
2017
This is probably the most robust kind of sales environment we've seen in probably 10 years.
Core Civic's CEO, Damon Hininger
Core Civic and Geo Group have also found a way to increase profits by saving on labor costs. Detainees in their facilities are cleaning bathrooms, preparing meals, waxing floors and doing laundry for as little as $1.00 a day.
Lord please protect my daughter.

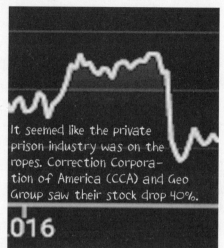

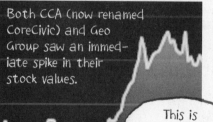

WHILE THE CURRENT IMMIGRATION CRISIS SEPARATING CHILDREN FROM THEIR FAMILIES IS HORRIFYING, IT IS NOT NEW. IN THE SUMMER OF 2017, THE TRUMP ADMINISTRATION SOUGHT TO DEPORT CHALDEAN IRAQIS BASED IN METRO DETROIT. THIS GROUP WAS TARGETED DESPITE THEIR VOCAL SUPPORT FOR TRUMP. WHAT FOLLOWS IS ONE ACTIVIST'S ACCOUNT OF TRYING TO STOP THE DEPORTATIONS AND SEPARATION OF FAMILIES.

WE GOT THE MESSAGE AFTER DINNER ABOUT THE PROTEST—"PEOPLE NEEDED AT ICE ON JEFFERSON AVE. DEPORTING CHALDEANS. HELP!"

ROSA PARKS FEDERAL BUILDING

U.S. Department of Homeland Security

WE HEADED OUT AS FAST AS WE COULD.

WHEN WE GOT UP THERE THE BUS WAS RUNNING. PEOPLE WERE MESSAGING FRIENDS AND FAMILY TO COME OUT. IT WAS REALLY INTENSE. THERE WERE OLDER PEOPLE AND FAMILIES.

MANY WERE REALLY SCARED THAT IF THEIR FAMILY MEMBERS WERE SENT BACK TO IRAQ THEY WOULD BE KILLED. SOME OF THESE PEOPLE HAD BEEN IN THE US FOR LIKE 30-40 YEARS AT THIS POINT.

ICE: Deportations in Detroit
Written by Jeffrey Wilson
Illustrated by Armin Ozdic

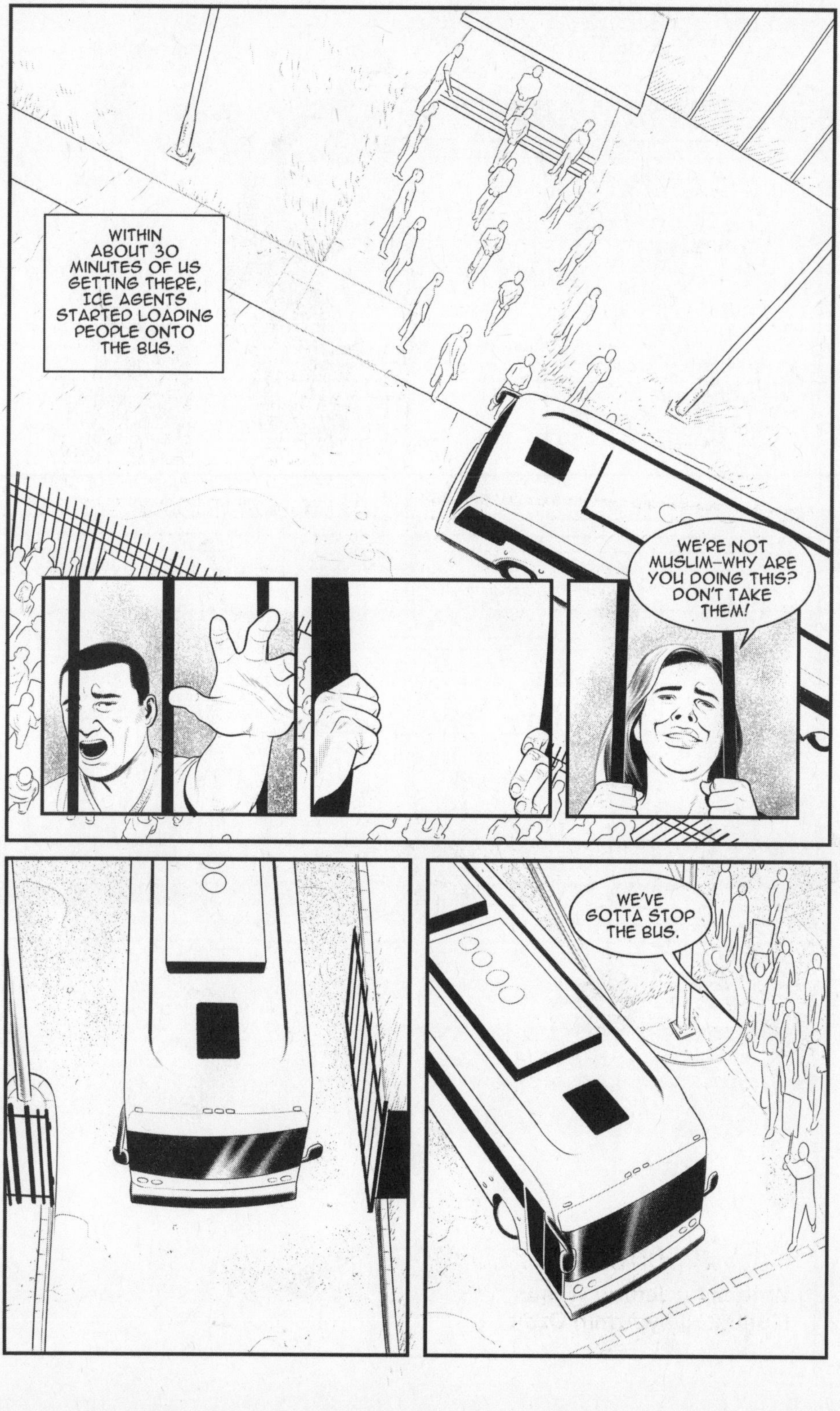
WITHIN ABOUT 30 MINUTES OF US GETTING THERE, ICE AGENTS STARTED LOADING PEOPLE ONTO THE BUS.
WE'RE NOT MUSLIM–WHY ARE YOU DOING THIS? DON'T TAKE THEM!
WE'VE GOTTA STOP THE BUS.

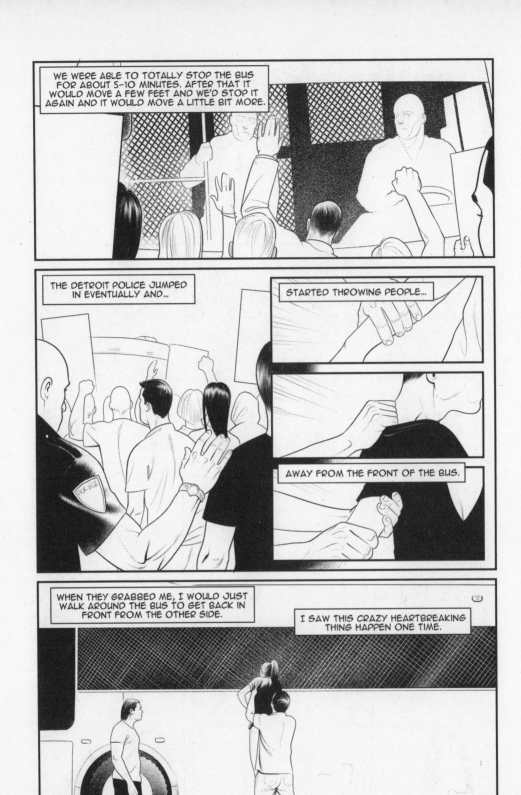

WE WERE ABLE TO TOTALLY STOP THE BUS FOR ABOUT 5-10 MINUTES. AFTER THAT IT WOULD MOVE A FEW FEET AND WE'D STOP IT AGAIN AND IT WOULD MOVE A LITTLE BIT MORE.

THE DETROIT POLICE JUMPED IN EVENTUALLY AND...

STARTED THROWING PEOPLE...

AWAY FROM THE FRONT OF THE BUS.

WHEN THEY GRABBED ME, I WOULD JUST WALK AROUND THE BUS TO GET BACK IN FRONT FROM THE OTHER SIDE.

I SAW THIS CRAZY HEARTBREAKING THING HAPPEN ONE TIME.

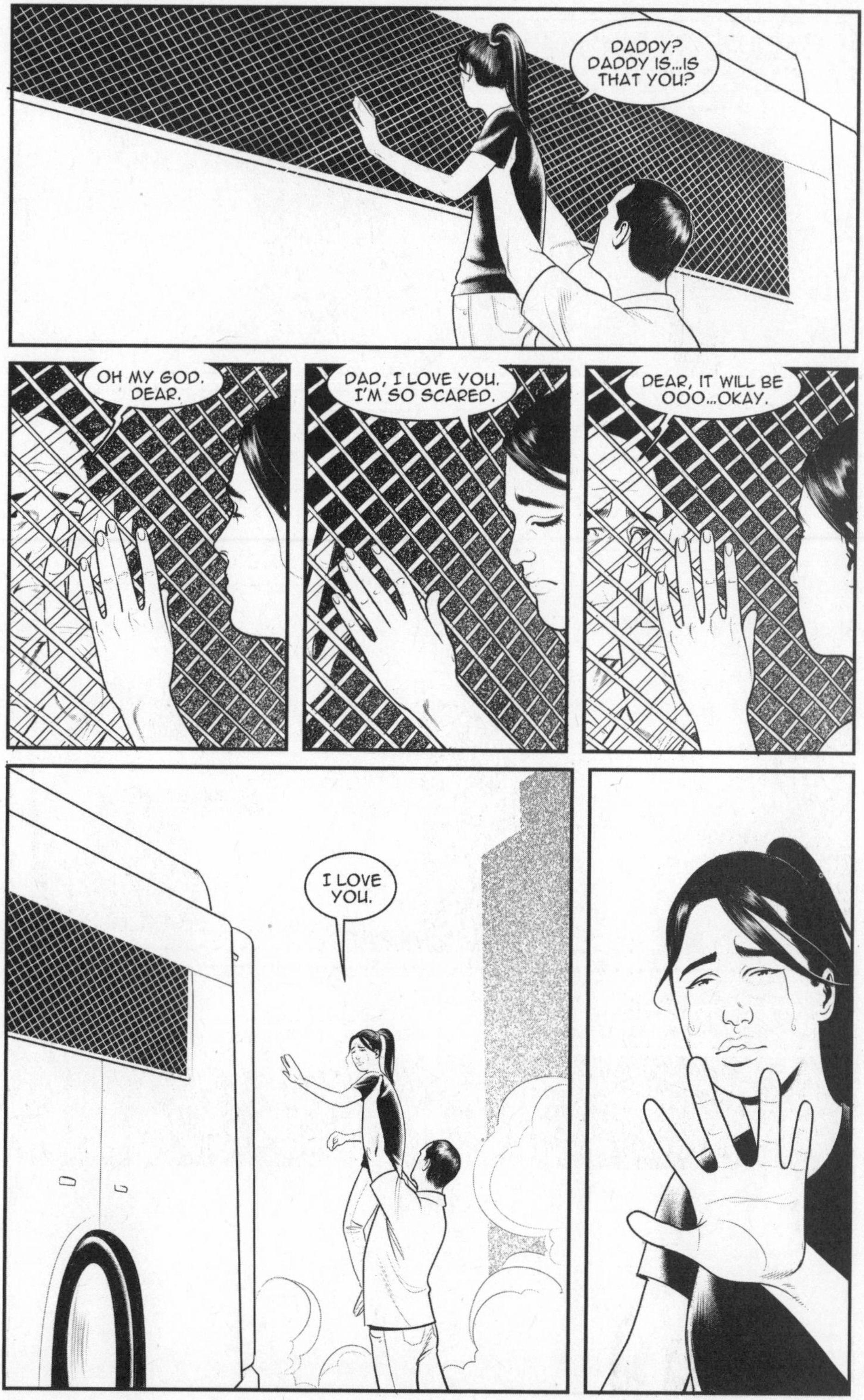
DADDY? DADDY IS...IS THAT YOU?
OH MY GOD. DEAR.
DAD, I LOVE YOU. I'M SO SCARED.
DEAR, IT WILL BE OOO...OKAY.
I LOVE YOU.

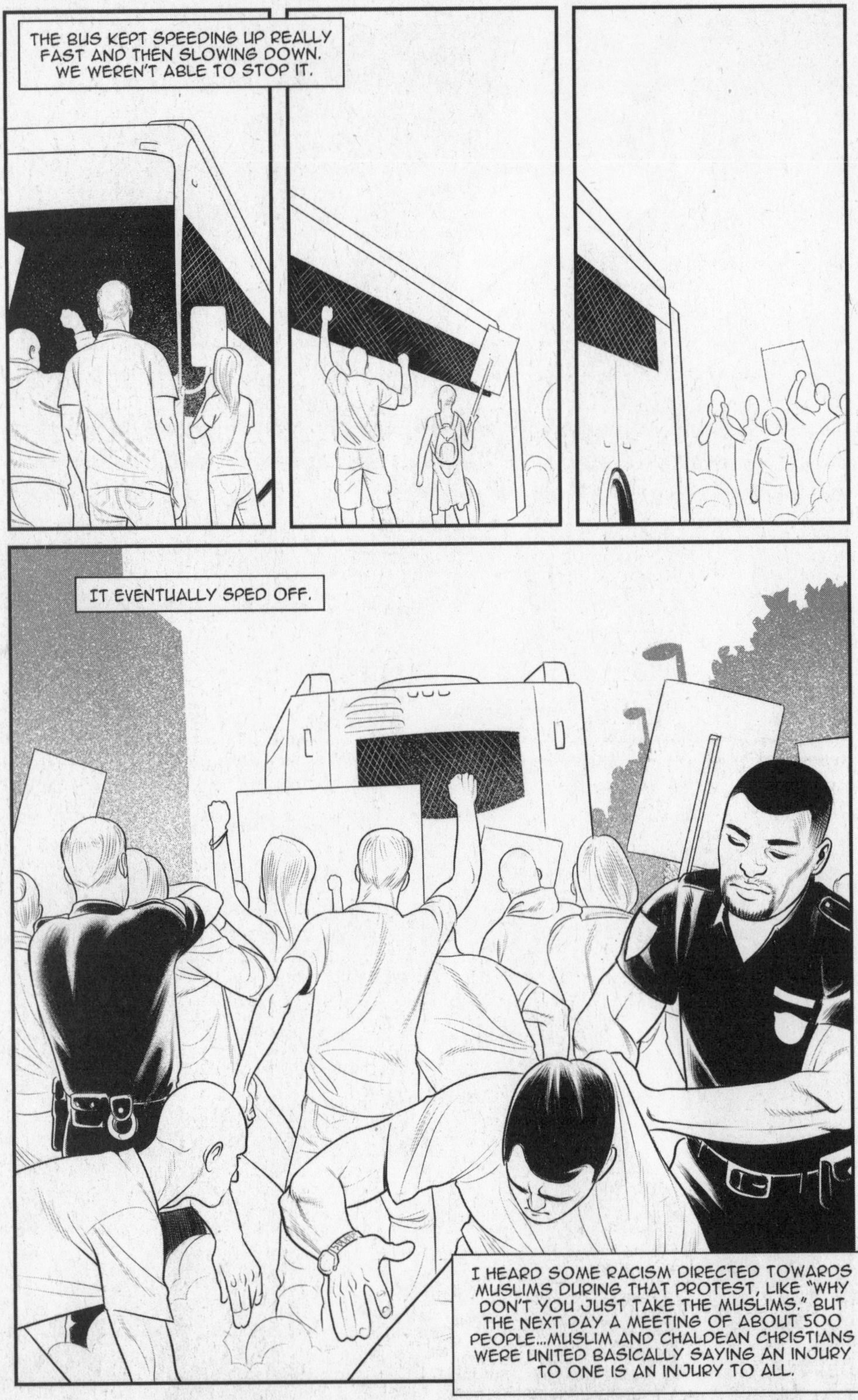
THE BUS KEPT SPEEDING UP REALLY FAST AND THEN SLOWING DOWN. WE WEREN'T ABLE TO STOP IT.
IT EVENTUALLY SPED OFF.
I HEARD SOME RACISM DIRECTED TOWARDS MUSLIMS DURING THAT PROTEST, LIKE "WHY DON'T YOU JUST TAKE THE MUSLIMS." BUT THE NEXT DAY A MEETING OF ABOUT 500 PEOPLE...MUSLIM AND CHALDEAN CHRISTIANS WERE UNITED BASICALLY SAYING AN INJURY TO ONE IS AN INJURY TO ALL.

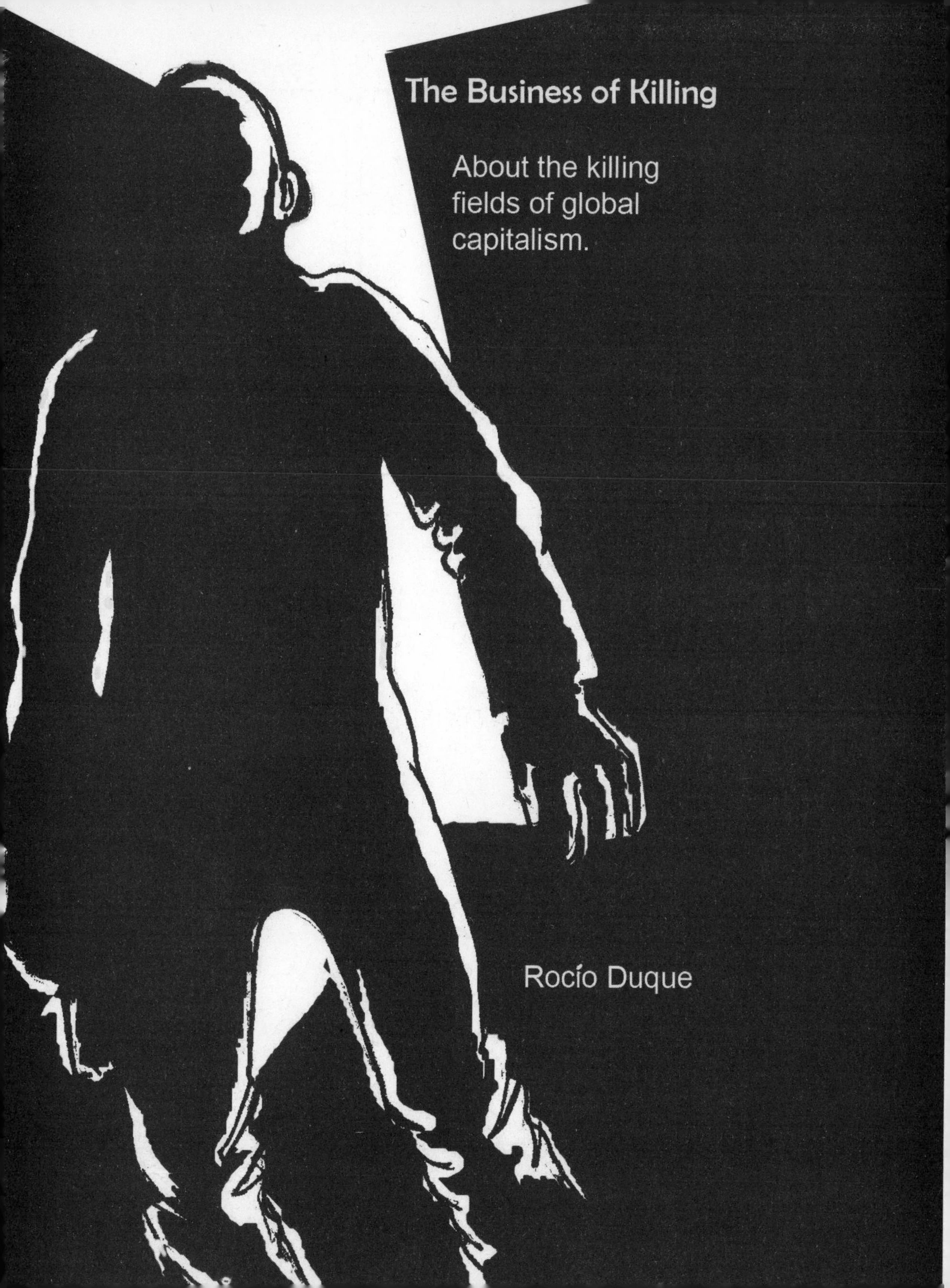
The Business of Killing
About the killing fields of global capitalism.
Rocío Duque

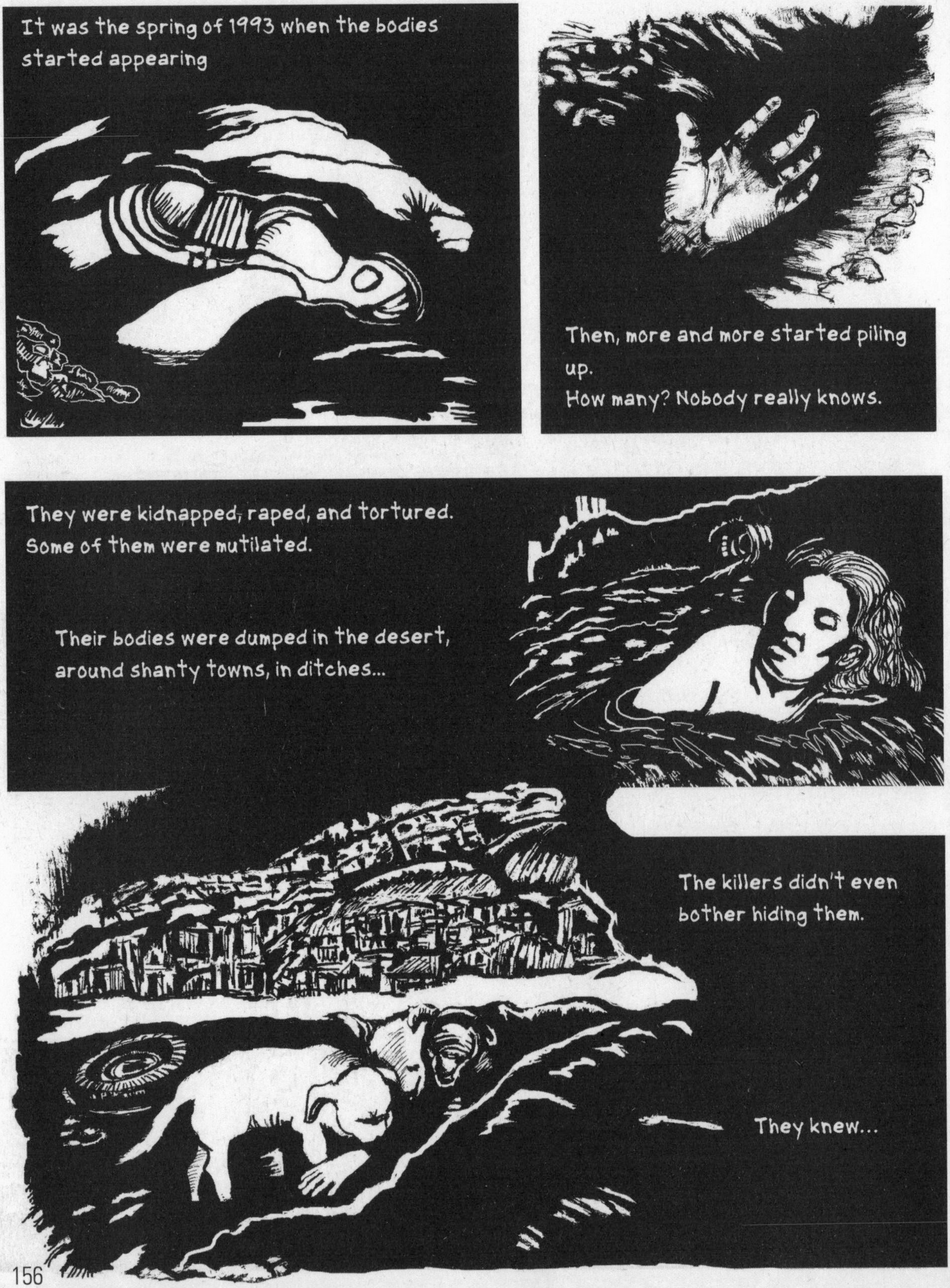
It was the spring of 1993 when the bodies started appearing
Then, more and more started piling up.
How many? Nobody really knows.
They were kidnapped, raped, and tortured. Some of them were mutilated.
Their bodies were dumped in the desert, around shanty towns, in ditches...
The killers didn't even bother hiding them.
They knew...

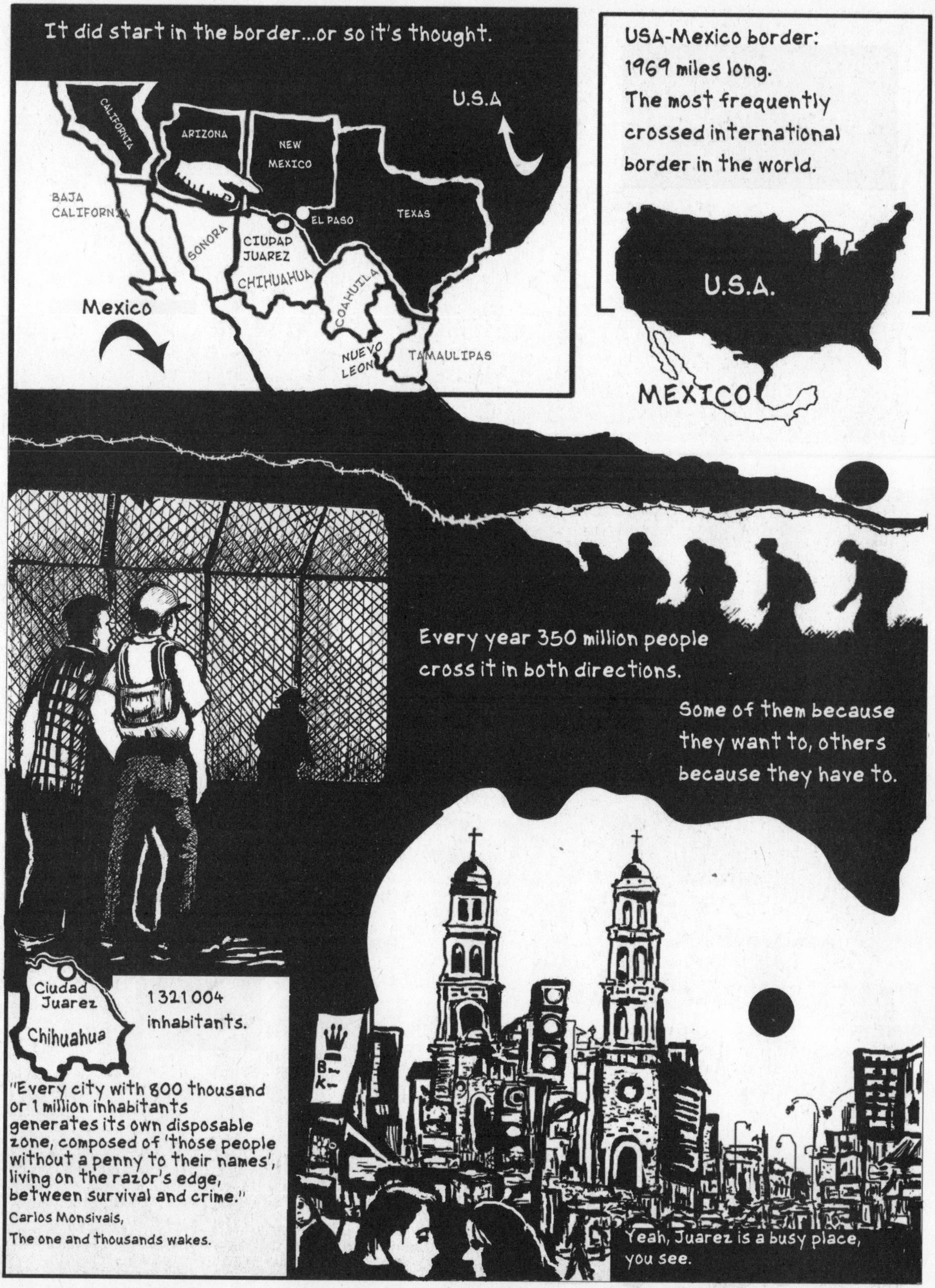

It did start in the border...or so it's thought.
CALIFORNIA
ARIZONA
NEW MEXICO
U.S.A
BAJA CALIFORNIA
SONORA
EL PASO
TEXAS
CIUDAD JUAREZ
CHIHUAHUA
COAHUILA
Mexico
NUEVO LEON
TAMAULIPAS
USA-Mexico border:
1969 miles long.
The most frequently crossed international border in the world.
U.S.A.
MEXICO
Every year 350 million people cross it in both directions.
Some of them because they want to, others because they have to.
Ciudad Juarez
Chihuahua
1321004 inhabitants.
"Every city with 800 thousand or 1 million inhabitants generates its own disposable zone, composed of 'those people without a penny to their names', living on the razor's edge, between survival and crime."
Carlos Monsivais,
The one and thousands wakes.
Yeah, Juarez is a busy place, you see.

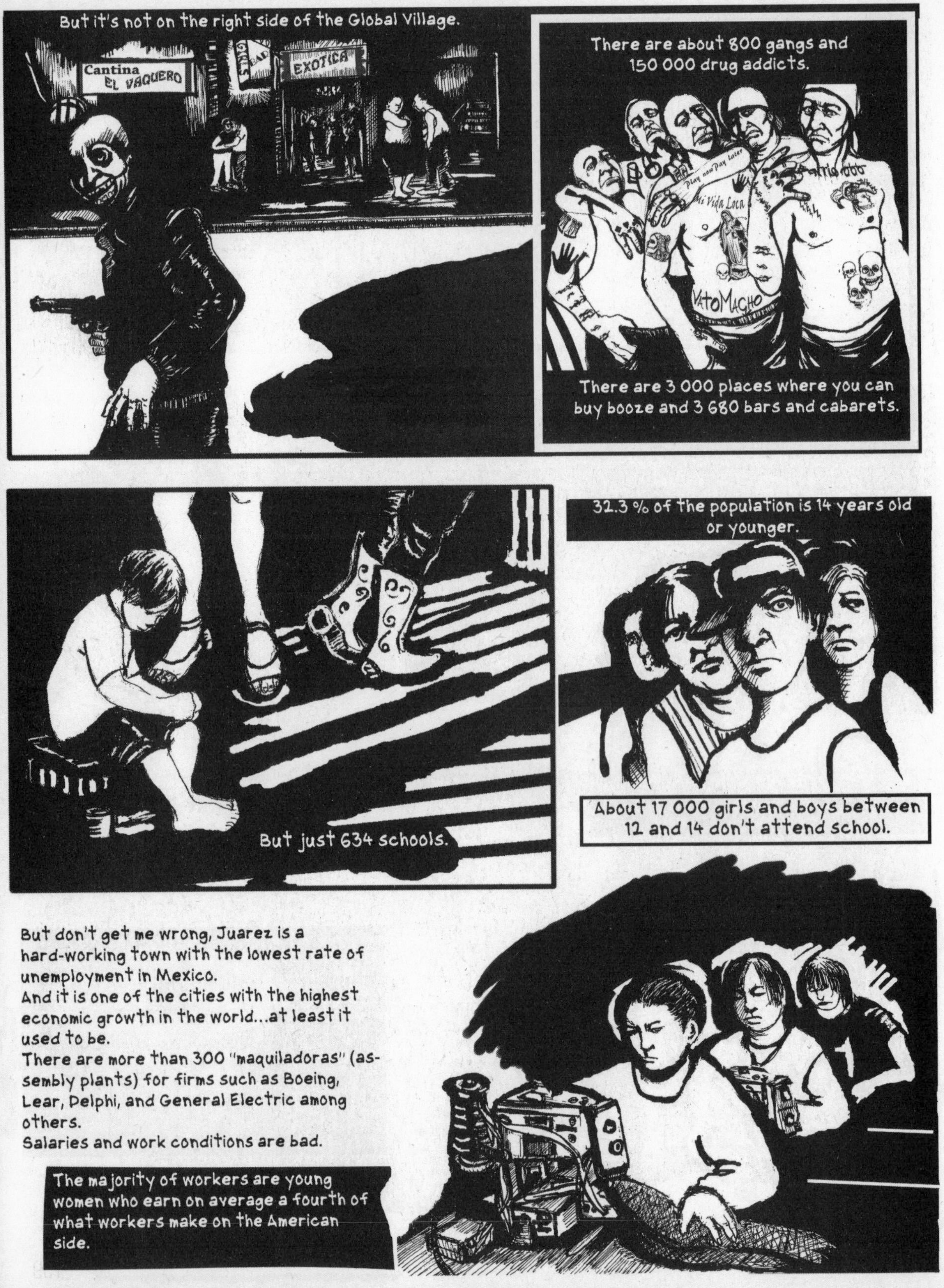
But it's not on the right side of the Global Village.
Cantina EL VAQUERO
EXOTICA
There are about 800 gangs and 150 000 drug addicts.
Play now Pay later
Mi Vida Loca
VATOMACHO
There are 3 000 places where you can buy booze and 3 680 bars and cabarets.
But just 634 schools.
32.3 % of the population is 14 years old or younger.
About 17 000 girls and boys between 12 and 14 don't attend school.
But don't get me wrong, Juarez is a hard-working town with the lowest rate of unemployment in Mexico.
And it is one of the cities with the highest economic growth in the world...at least it used to be.
There are more than 300 "maquiladoras" (assembly plants) for firms such as Boeing, Lear, Delphi, and General Electric among others.
Salaries and work conditions are bad.
The majority of workers are young women who earn on average a fourth of what workers make on the American side.

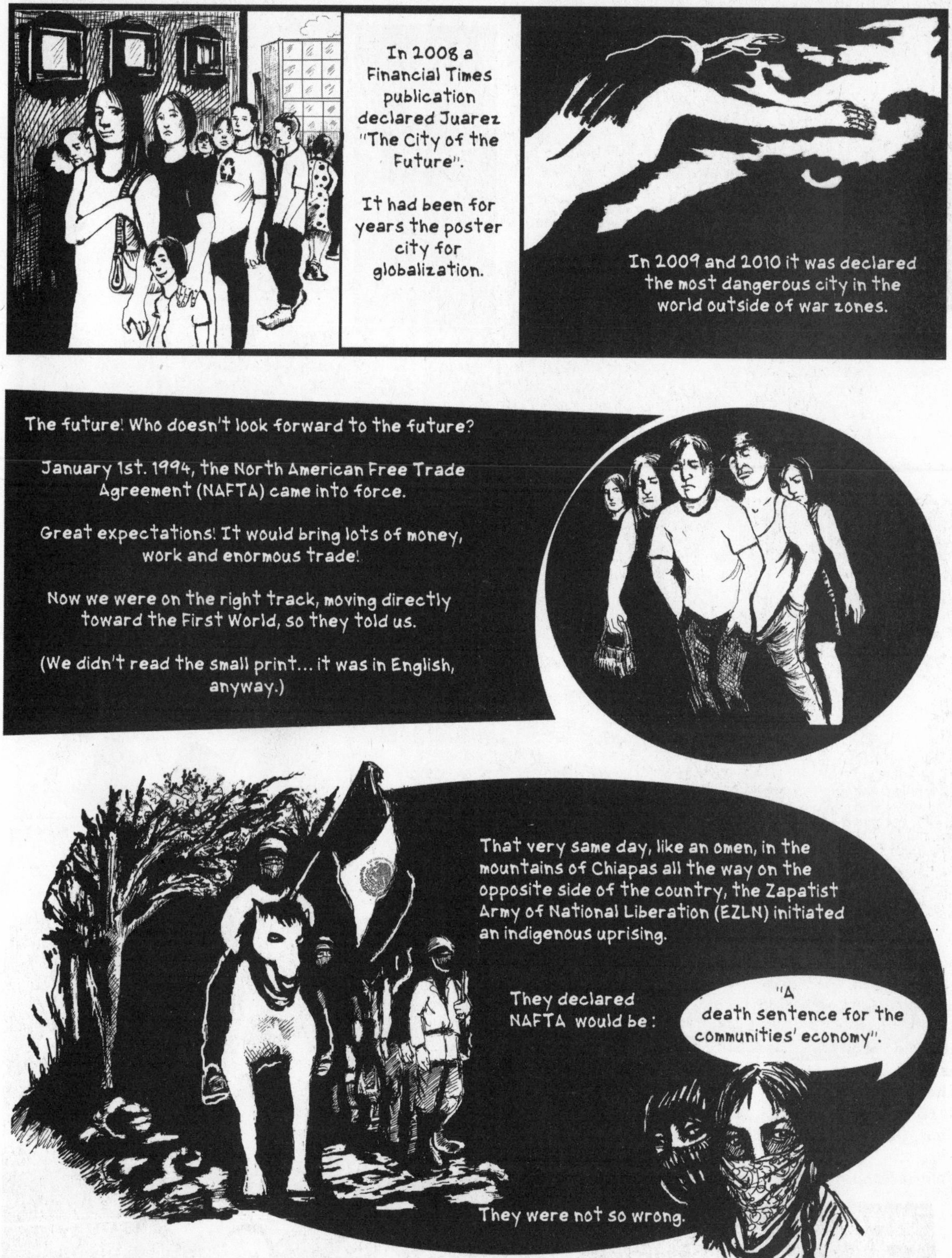
In 2008 a Financial Times publication declared Juarez "The City of the Future".
It had been for years the poster city for globalization.
In 2009 and 2010 it was declared the most dangerous city in the world outside of war zones.
The future! Who doesn't look forward to the future?
January 1st. 1994, the North American Free Trade Agreement (NAFTA) came into force.
Great expectations! It would bring lots of money, work and enormous trade!
Now we were on the right track, moving directly toward the First World, so they told us.
(We didn't read the small print... it was in English, anyway.)
That very same day, like an omen, in the mountains of Chiapas all the way on the opposite side of the country, the Zapatist Army of National Liberation (EZLN) initiated an indigenous uprising.
They declared NAFTA would be:
"A death sentence for the communities' economy".
They were not so wrong.

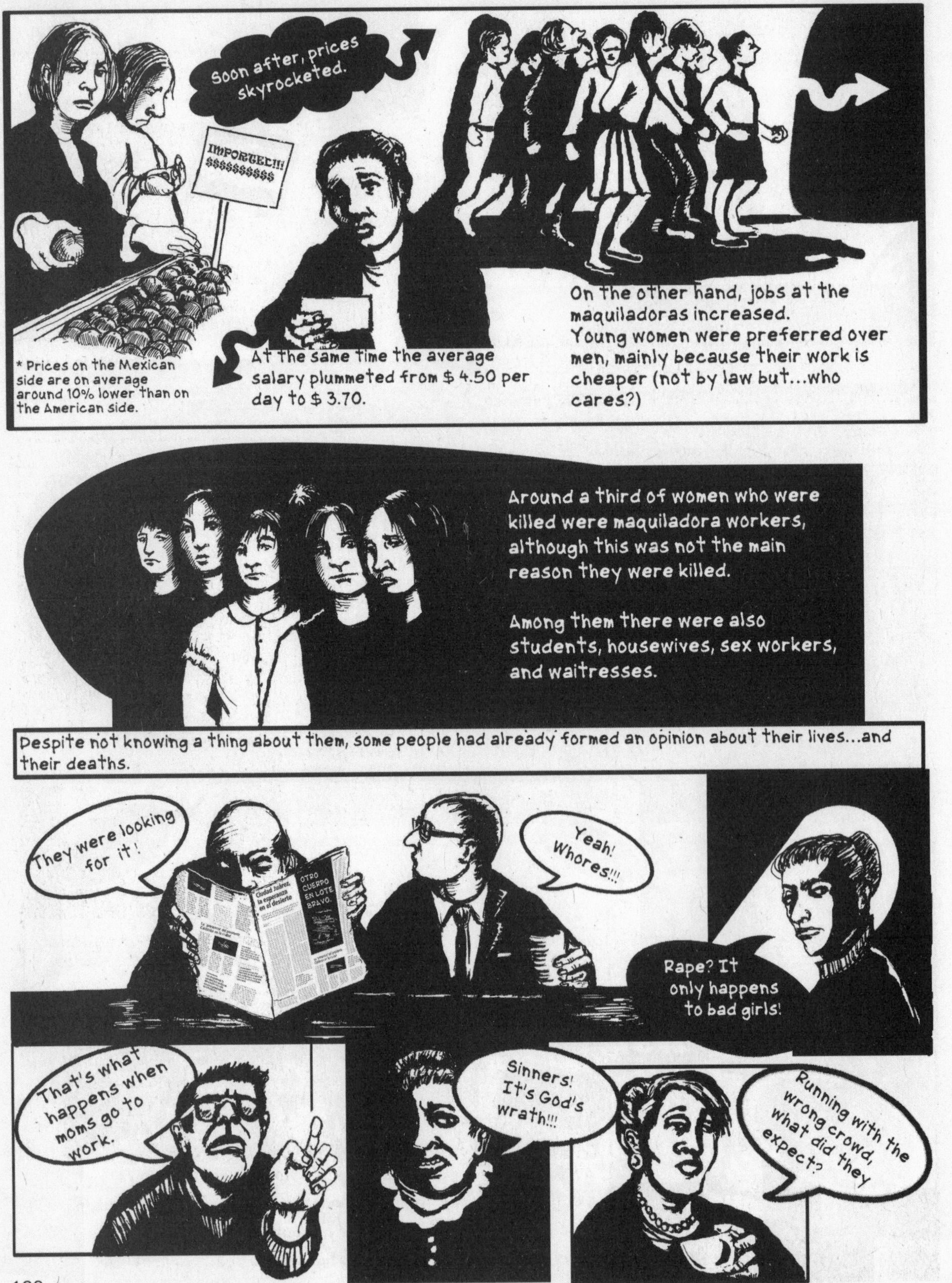
IMPORTED!!!
$$$$$$$$$$
Soon after, prices skyrocketed.
* Prices on the Mexican side are on average around 10% lower than on the American side.
At the same time the average salary plummeted from $ 4.50 per day to $ 3.70.
On the other hand, jobs at the maquiladoras increased.
Young women were preferred over men, mainly because their work is cheaper (not by law but...who cares?)
Around a third of women who were killed were maquiladora workers, although this was not the main reason they were killed.
Among them there were also students, housewives, sex workers, and waitresses.
Despite not knowing a thing about them, some people had already formed an opinion about their lives...and their deaths.
They were looking for it!
Ciudad Juárez, la esperanza en el desierto
OTRO CUERPO EN LOTE BRAVO.
Yeah! Whores!!!
Rape? It only happens to bad girls!
That's what happens when moms go to work.
Sinners! It's God's wrath!!!
Running with the wrong crowd, what did they expect?

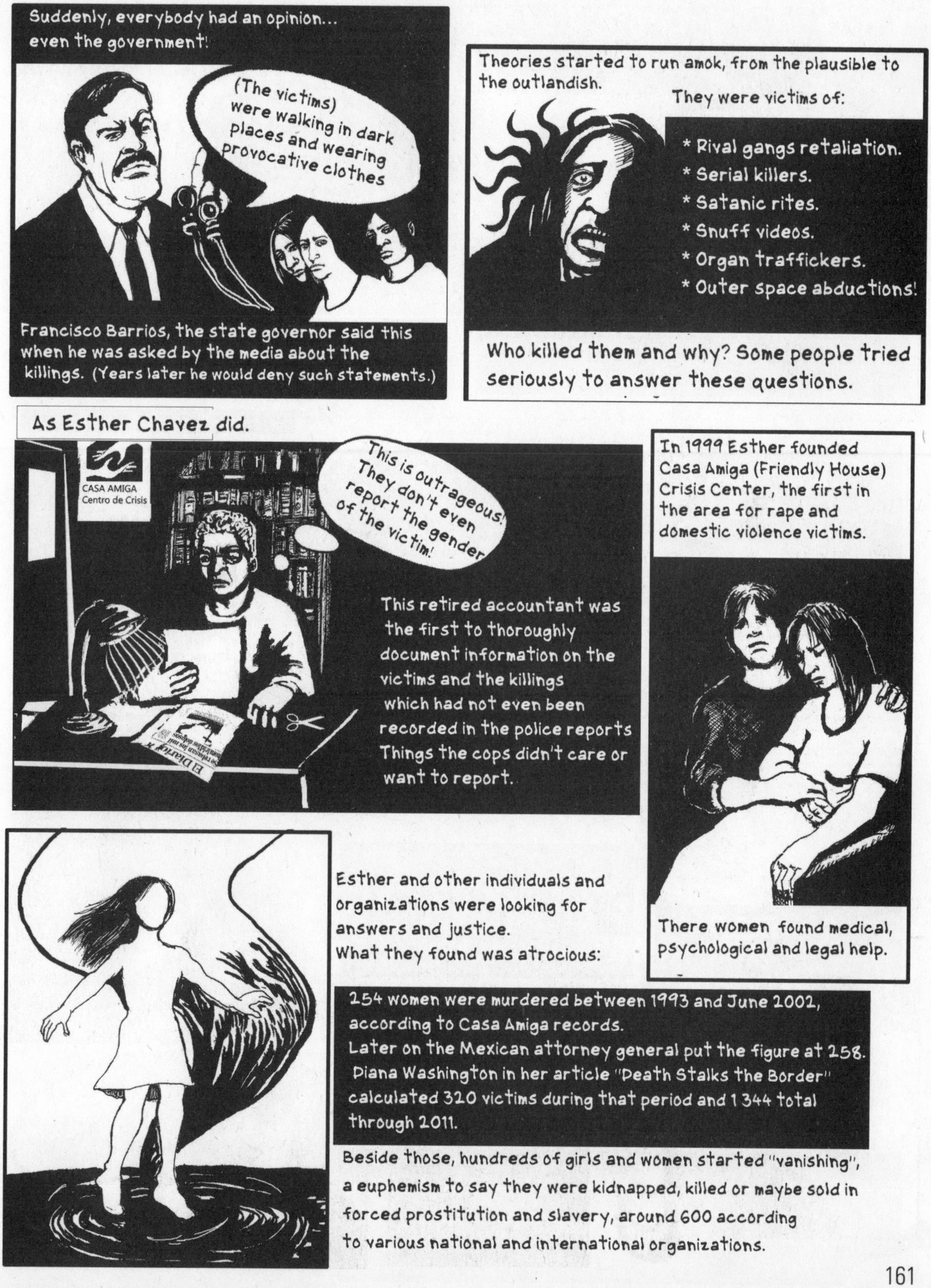
Suddenly, everybody had an opinion...
even the government!
(The victims) were walking in dark places and wearing provocative clothes
Francisco Barrios, the state governor said this when he was asked by the media about the killings. (Years later he would deny such statements.)
Theories started to run amok, from the plausible to the outlandish.
They were victims of:
* Rival gangs retaliation.
* Serial killers.
* Satanic rites.
* Snuff videos.
* Organ traffickers.
* Outer space abductions!
Who killed them and why? Some people tried seriously to answer these questions.
As Esther Chavez did.
CASA AMIGA
Centro de Crisis
This is outrageous! They don't even report the gender of the victim!
This retired accountant was the first to thoroughly document information on the victims and the killings which had not even been recorded in the police reports Things the cops didn't care or want to report.
In 1999 Esther founded Casa Amiga (Friendly House) Crisis Center, the first in the area for rape and domestic violence victims.
There women found medical, psychological and legal help.
Esther and other individuals and organizations were looking for answers and justice.
What they found was atrocious:
254 women were murdered between 1993 and June 2002, according to Casa Amiga records.
Later on the Mexican attorney general put the figure at 258.
Diana Washington in her article "Death Stalks the Border" calculated 320 victims during that period and 1 344 total through 2011.
Beside those, hundreds of girls and women started "vanishing", a euphemism to say they were kidnapped, killed or maybe sold in forced prostitution and slavery, around 600 according to various national and international organizations.

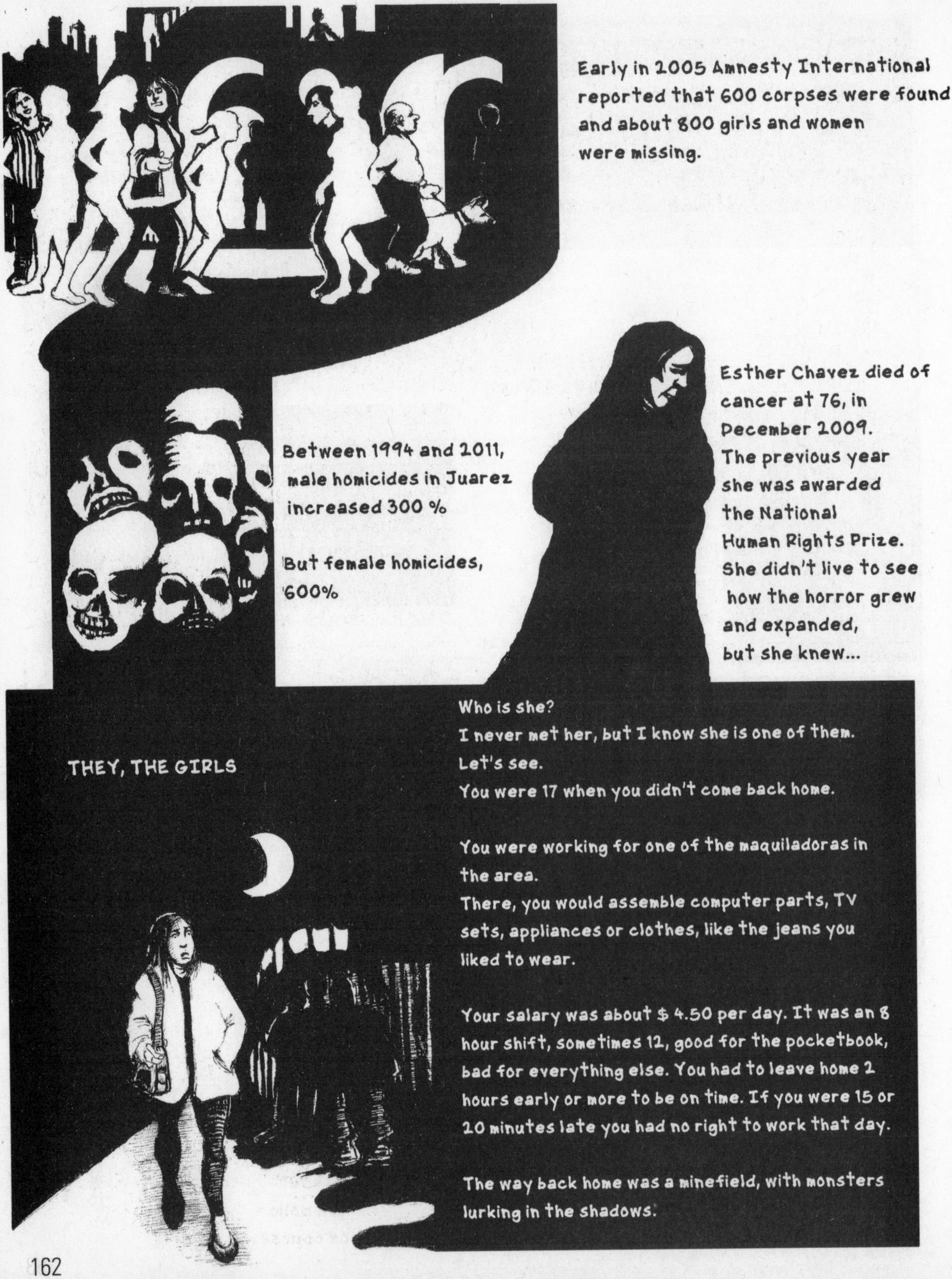
Early in 2005 Amnesty International reported that 600 corpses were found and about 800 girls and women were missing.
Between 1994 and 2011, male homicides in Juarez increased 300 %
But female homicides, 600%
Esther Chavez died of cancer at 76, in December 2009. The previous year she was awarded the National Human Rights Prize. She didn't live to see how the horror grew and expanded, but she knew...
THEY, THE GIRLS
Who is she?
I never met her, but I know she is one of them.
Let's see.
You were 17 when you didn't come back home.
You were working for one of the maquiladoras in the area.
There, you would assemble computer parts, TV sets, appliances or clothes, like the jeans you liked to wear.
Your salary was about $ 4.50 per day. It was an 8 hour shift, sometimes 12, good for the pocketbook, bad for everything else. You had to leave home 2 hours early or more to be on time. If you were 15 or 20 minutes late you had no right to work that day.
The way back home was a minefield, with monsters lurking in the shadows.

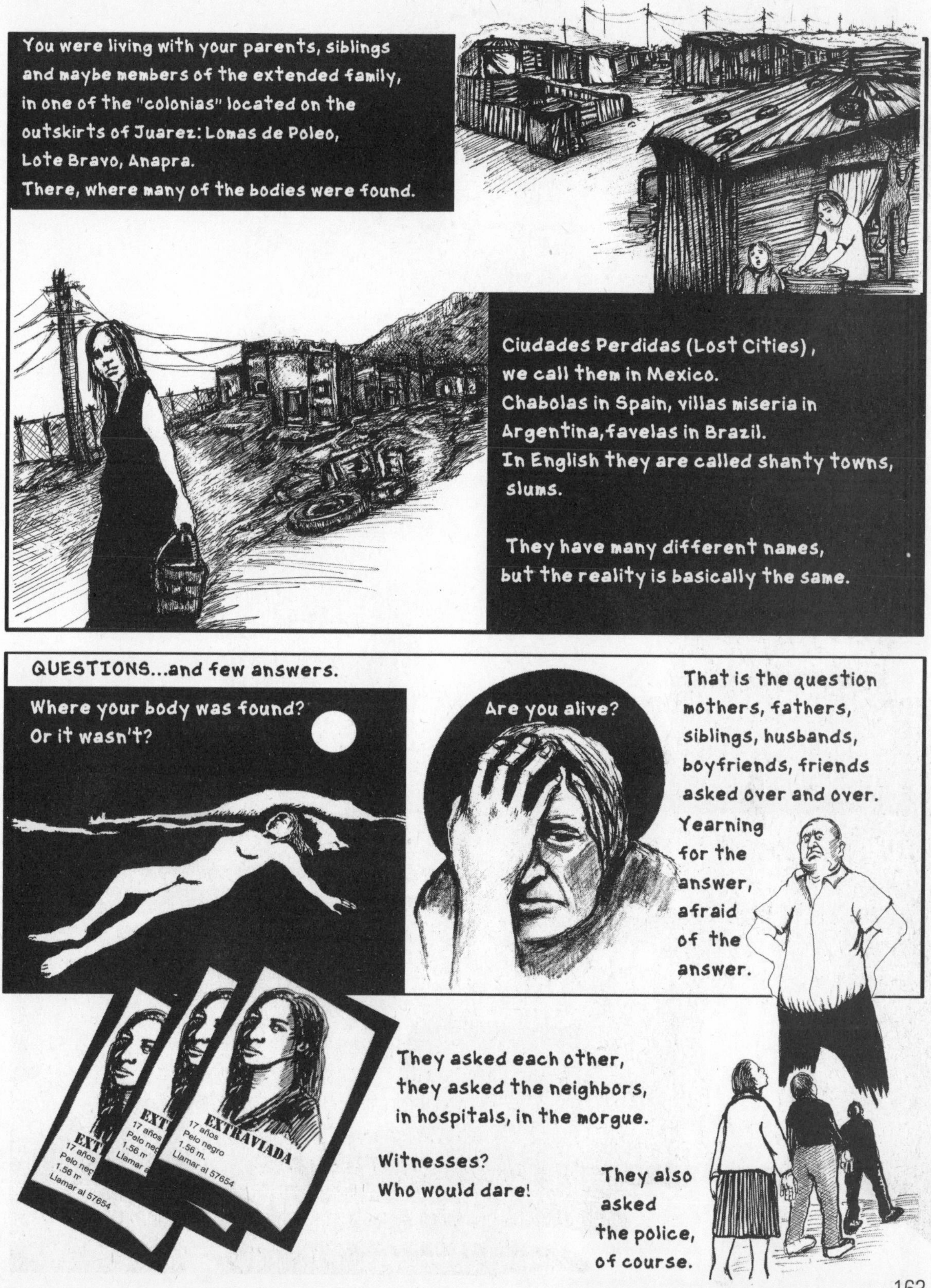

You were living with your parents, siblings and maybe members of the extended family, in one of the "colonias" located on the outskirts of Juarez: Lomas de Poleo, Lote Bravo, Anapra.
There, where many of the bodies were found.
Ciudades Perdidas (Lost Cities), we call them in Mexico.
Chabolas in Spain, villas miseria in Argentina, favelas in Brazil.
In English they are called shanty towns, slums.
They have many different names, but the reality is basically the same.
QUESTIONS...and few answers.
Where your body was found? Or it wasn't?
Are you alive?
That is the question mothers, fathers, siblings, husbands, boyfriends, friends asked over and over.
Yearning for the answer, afraid of the answer.
EXTRAVIADA
17 años
Pelo negro
1.56 m.
Llamar al 57654
They asked each other, they asked the neighbors, in hospitals, in the morgue.
Witnesses? Who would dare!
They also asked the police, of course.

The cops always had answers ready:

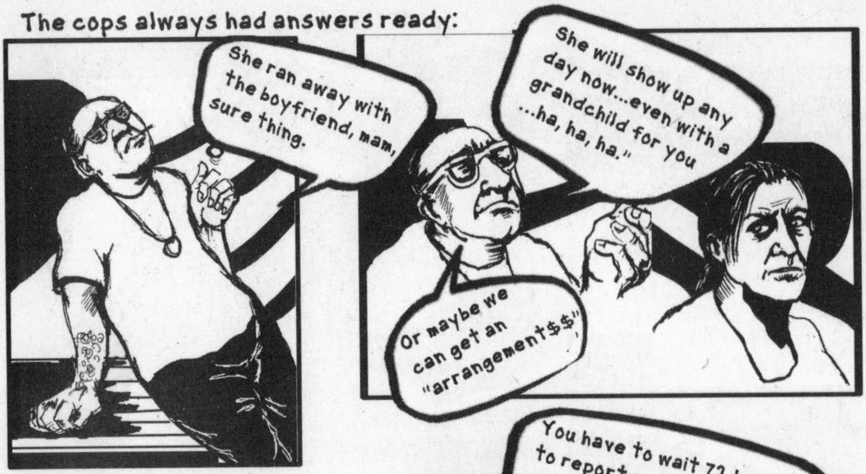
She ran away with the boyfriend, mam, sure thing.
She will show up any day now...even with a grandchild for you ...ha, ha, ha."
Or maybe we can get an "arrangement$$"

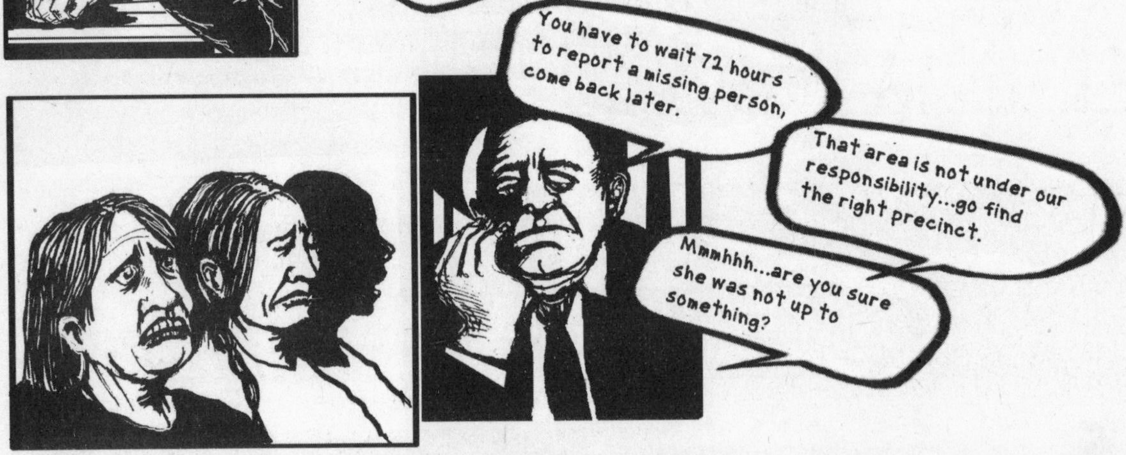
You have to wait 72 hours to report a missing person, come back later.
That area is not under our responsibility...go find the right precinct.
Mmmhhh...are you sure she was not up to something?

If the report of a missing girl was finally accepted, the file would sleep inside a drawer for months, years ...or forever. Abandon hope all ye who enter a Mexican justice office.

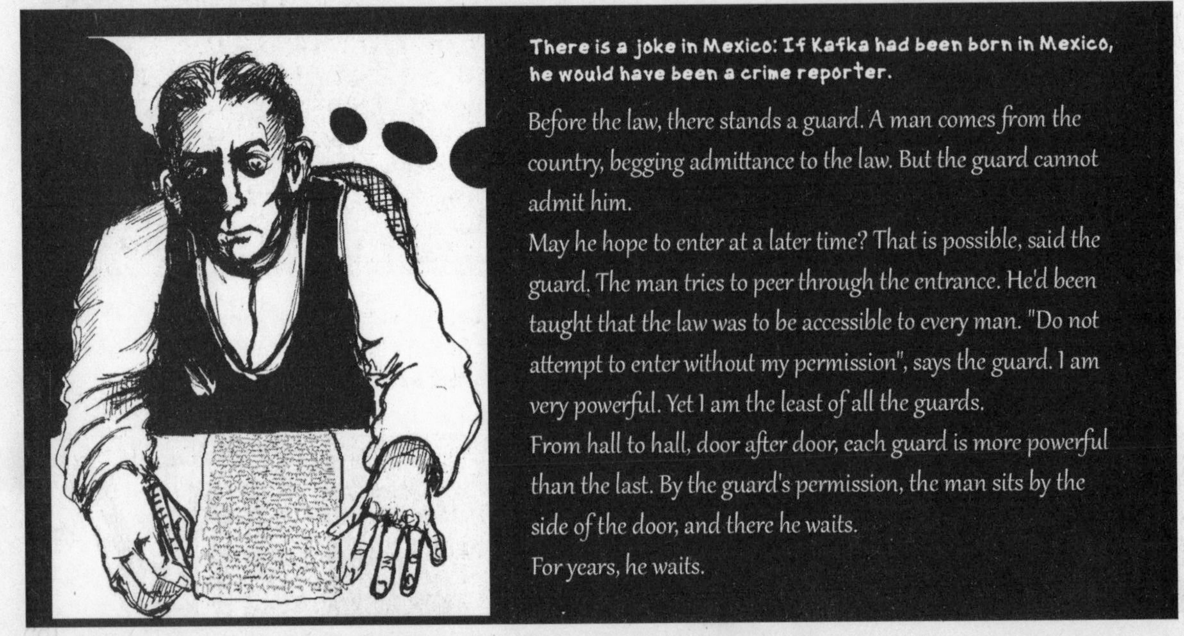

There is a joke in Mexico: If Kafka had been born in Mexico, he would have been a crime reporter.

Before the law, there stands a guard. A man comes from the country, begging admittance to the law. But the guard cannot admit him.

May he hope to enter at a later time? That is possible, said the guard. The man tries to peer through the entrance. He'd been taught that the law was to be accessible to every man. "Do not attempt to enter without my permission", says the guard. I am very powerful. Yet I am the least of all the guards.

From hall to hall, door after door, each guard is more powerful than the last. By the guard's permission, the man sits by the side of the door, and there he waits.

For years, he waits.

Looking for justice.

At the turn of the XXI century, the assassination of hundreds of girls and women in the area took a turn from a note in the crime section of the newspapers to an international scandal.

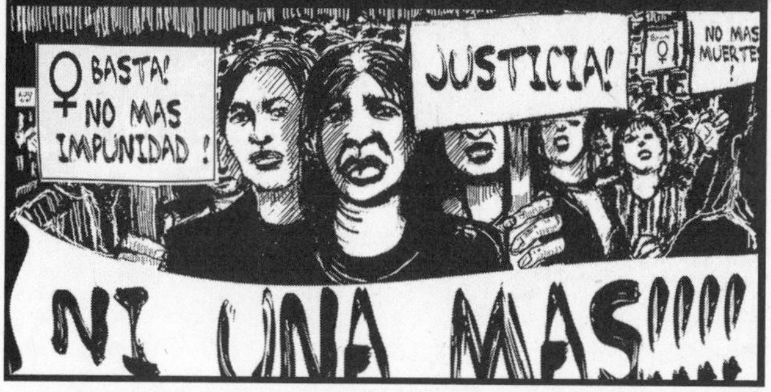
BASTA! NO MAS IMPUNIDAD !
JUSTICIA!
NO MAS MUERTES !
NI UNA MAS!!!!!

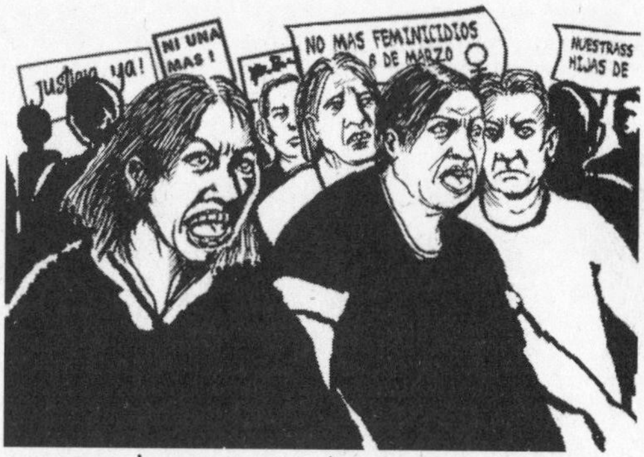
Justicia ya!
NI UNA MAS!
NO MAS FEMINICIDIOS 8 DE MARZO
NUESTRASS HIJAS DE

By then many organizations had arisen, they were looking for the missing girls or their bodies, they wanted to solve the cases, take the killers to justice and demanded accountability to negligent and abusive authorities.

Some of the organizations survived, some others had a short life.
Political, ideological and even financial rivalries would divide them.
The dream of a national and unified front never happened.

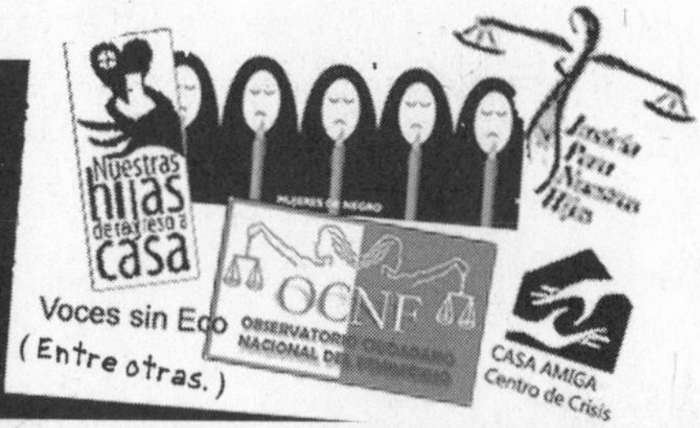
Nuestras hijas de regreso a casa
Justicia Para Nuestras Hijas
MUJERES DE NEGRO
OCNF
OBSERVATORIO CIUDADANO NACIONAL DEL FEMINICIDIO
Voces sin Eco
(Entre otras.)
CASA AMIGA
Centro de Crisis

But above all, they wanted the carnage to stop...
It didn't happen either.

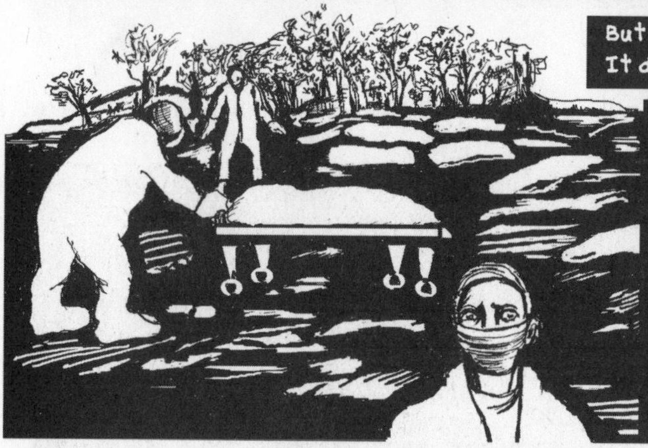

The Cotton Field Case

November 2001: In a cotton field, not far from one of the maquiladoras, the corpses of 8 young women and teen agers, showing the yet familiar signs of sexual violence, were found.
And, as usual, local authorities ignored the cases, insulted and humiliated the families and called it a day...

Sadness and fear made way to anger and firm resolution. This time, the mothers of three of the victims decided to complain to the Inter-American Commission on Human Rights (IACHR).
More than 8 years would pass before they got a little justice, but it was a stepping stone and it established an international precedent.

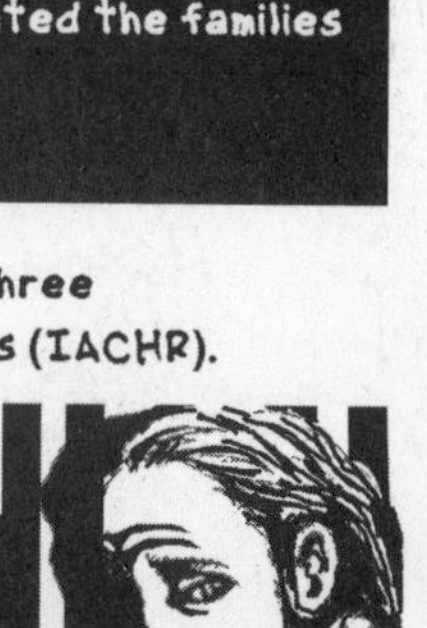

In 2008, 168 complaints were filed against the Mexican government.
IACHR is working on 75 Mexican cases, which include, torture, kidnapping, executions, impunity, threats against human rights defenders, discrimination against women, violations to the due process, and violations to reproductive rights, among others.

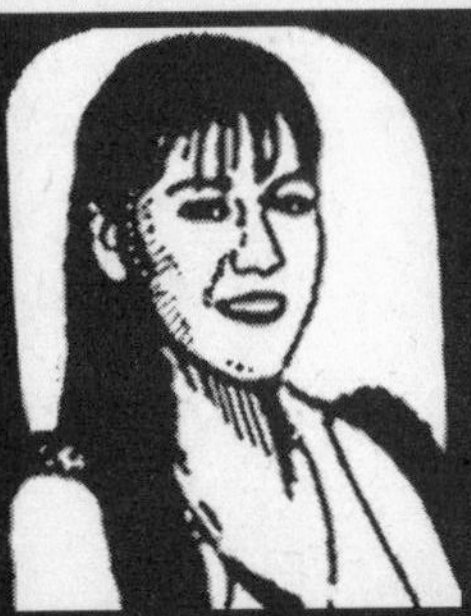

Claudia Ivette González (20)

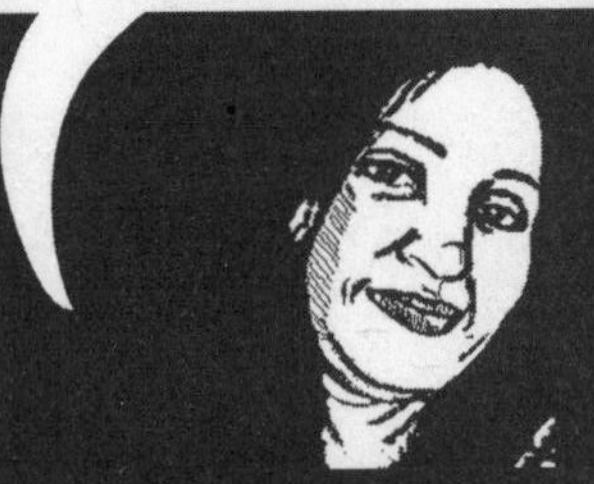

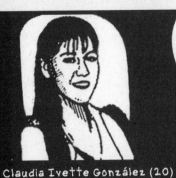

Laura Berenice Ramos Monárrez (17)

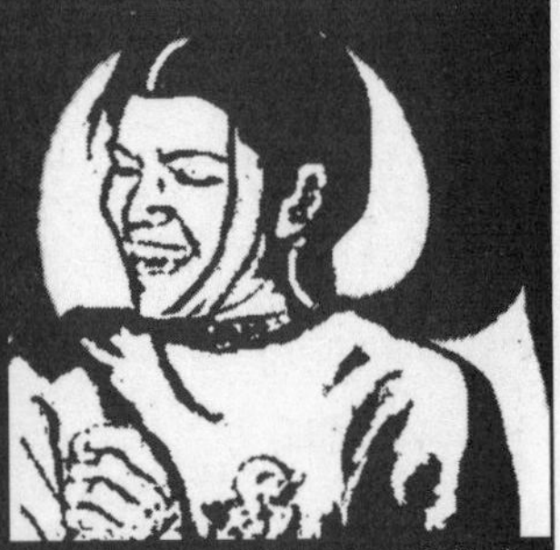

Esmeralda Herrera Monreal (14)

November 2009: the Inter-American Court of Human Rights ruled that Mexico was guilty of longstanding failure to investigate, prosecute, or prevent the crimes in this case and violated Mexico's obligations under the American Convention, the Convention Belem do Para, and international human rights norms.

The Court ordered Mexico to conduct a new investigation of the murders (5 of the 8 victims in the Cotton Field Case had not been identified), create a national memorial for the victims to dignify the memory of all the killed victims, pay reparations to the families of the victims, and to improve measures which prevent the murder of women and girls. Also, the Court urged the Mexican government to investigate the threats and intimidation against the victim's families.

It was the first time in history where the concept of "femicide" was used in an international trial.

What is FEMICIDE?

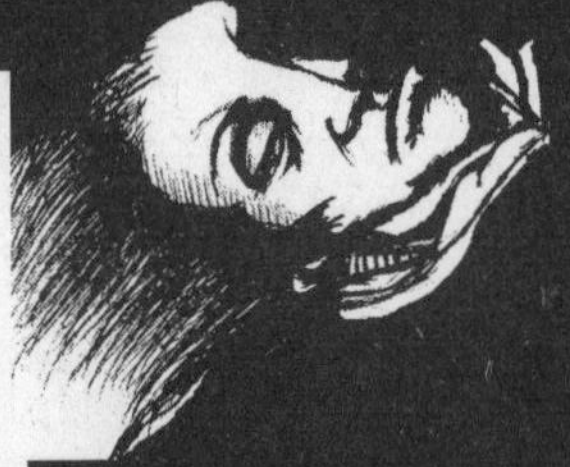

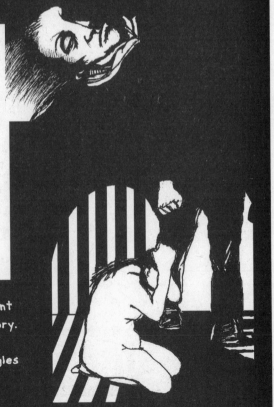

Femicide or feminicide was first used in England in 1801 meaning "the killing of a woman."
In 1848, this word was published in Wharton's Law Lexicon, which suggests that it had become a prosecutable offense. On 1976, Dianna Russell re defined the term as: "The killing of females by males because they are female", like other "hate crimes", such as those motivated by race, ethnicity, sexual identity or religious preference.
Femicide includes physical, psychological and sexual violence. Femicides usually are tolerated and even encouraged by the State and its institutions.
Femicide is a mechanism of domination, control, oppression, and power over women.

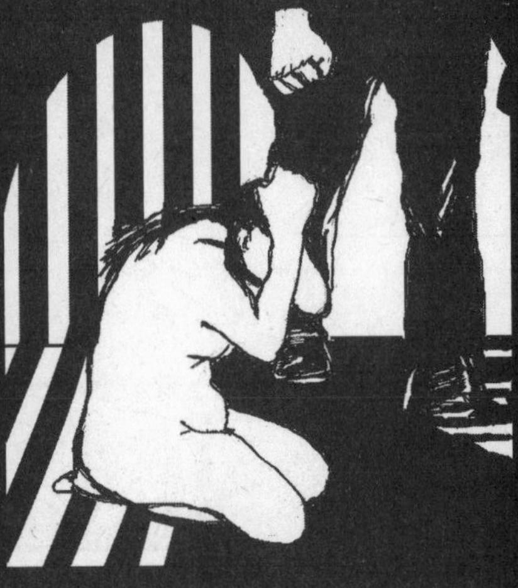

The sentence on the Cotton Field Case was an important legal victory but not at all the end of an atrocious story. We just start realizing that, as Antonio Gramsci said: "The old world is dying away, and the new world struggles to come forth: now is the time of monsters."

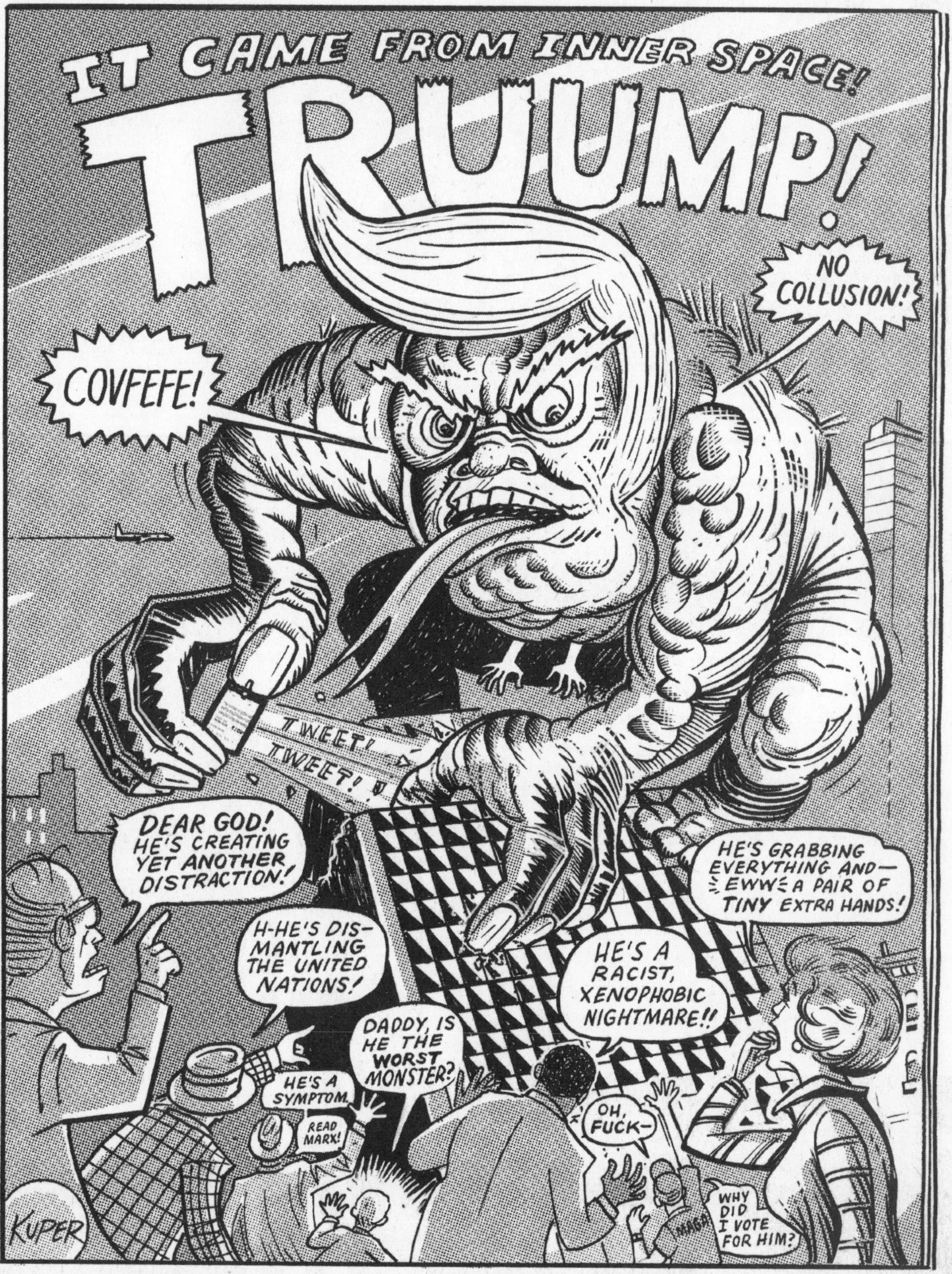
IT CAME FROM INNER SPACE!
TRUUMP!
COVFEFE!
NO COLLUSION!
TWEET!
TWEET!
DEAR GOD! HE'S CREATING YET ANOTHER DISTRACTION!
HE'S GRABBING EVERYTHING AND— EWW— A PAIR OF TINY EXTRA HANDS!
H-HE'S DIS-MANTLING THE UNITED NATIONS!
HE'S A RACIST, XENOPHOBIC NIGHTMARE!!
DADDY, IS HE THE WORST MONSTER?
HE'S A SYMPTOM.
READ MARX!
OH, FUCK—
MAGA
WHY DID I VOTE FOR HIM?
KUPER

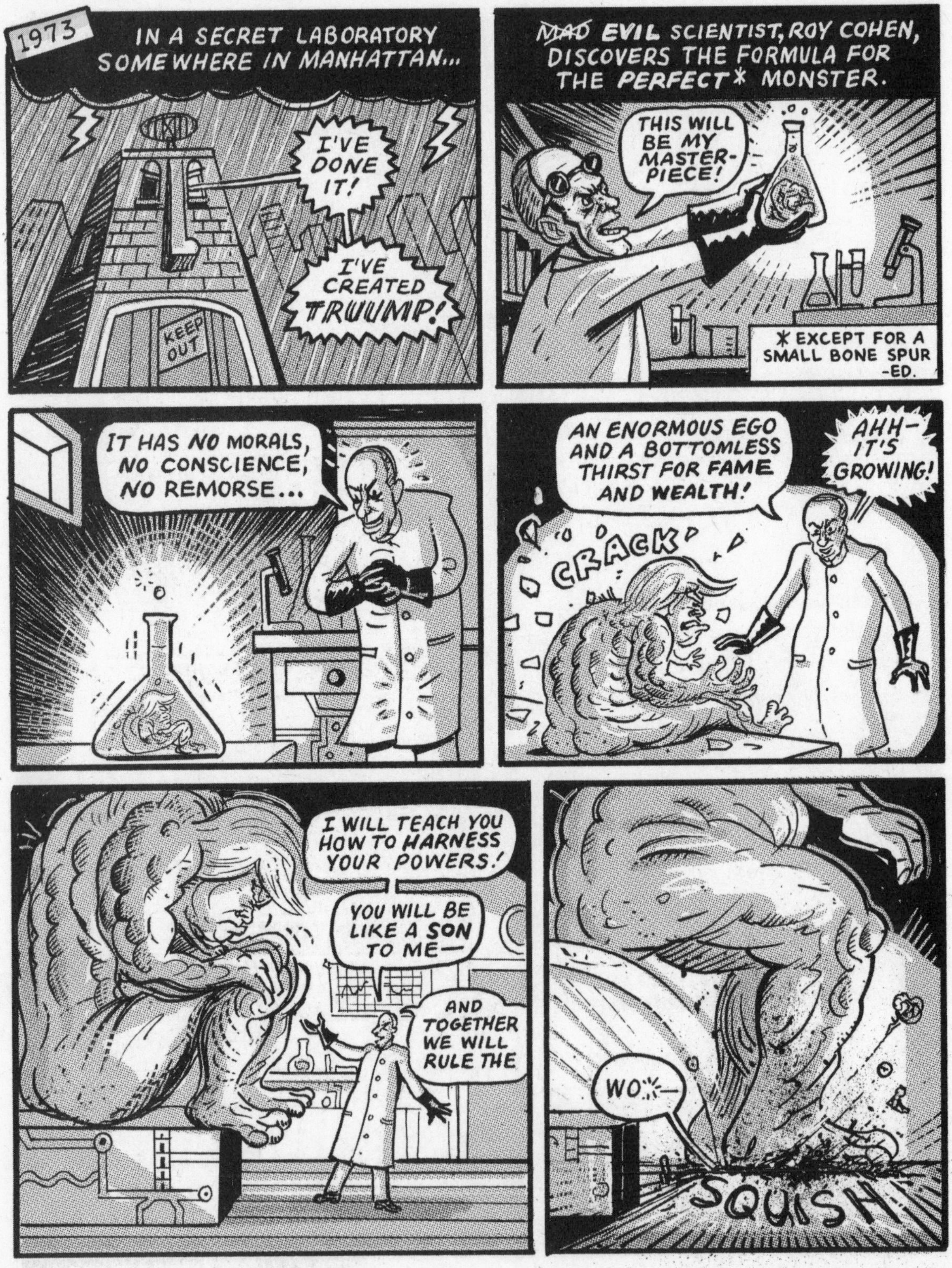
1973
IN A SECRET LABORATORY SOMEWHERE IN MANHATTAN...
I'VE DONE IT!
I'VE CREATED TRUUMP!
KEEP OUT
~~MAD~~ EVIL SCIENTIST, ROY COHEN, DISCOVERS THE FORMULA FOR THE PERFECT* MONSTER.
THIS WILL BE MY MASTER-PIECE!
* EXCEPT FOR A SMALL BONE SPUR -ED.
IT HAS NO MORALS, NO CONSCIENCE, NO REMORSE...
AN ENORMOUS EGO AND A BOTTOMLESS THIRST FOR FAME AND WEALTH!
AHH— IT'S GROWING!
CRACK
I WILL TEACH YOU HOW TO HARNESS YOUR POWERS!
YOU WILL BE LIKE A SON TO ME—
AND TOGETHER WE WILL RULE THE
WO—
SQUISH

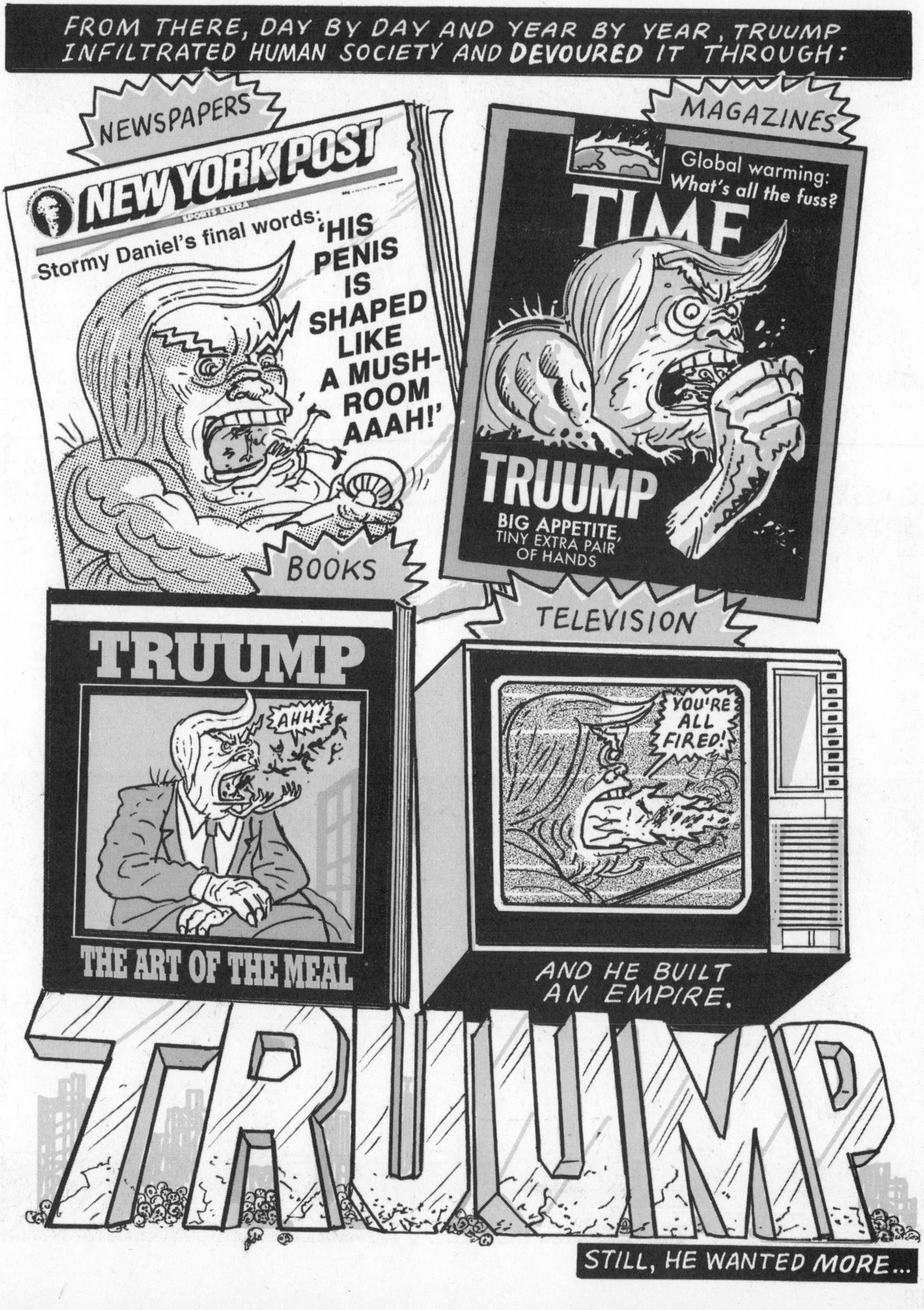
FROM THERE, DAY BY DAY AND YEAR BY YEAR, TRUUMP INFILTRATED HUMAN SOCIETY AND DEVOURED IT THROUGH:
NEWSPAPERS
NEW YORK POST
SPORTS EXTRA
Stormy Daniel's final words: 'HIS PENIS IS SHAPED LIKE A MUSH-ROOM AAAH!'
MAGAZINES
Global warming: What's all the fuss?
TIME
TRUUMP
BIG APPETITE, TINY EXTRA PAIR OF HANDS
BOOKS
TRUUMP
AHH!
THE ART OF THE MEAL
TELEVISION
YOU'RE ALL FIRED!
AND HE BUILT AN EMPIRE.
TRUUMP
STILL, HE WANTED MORE...

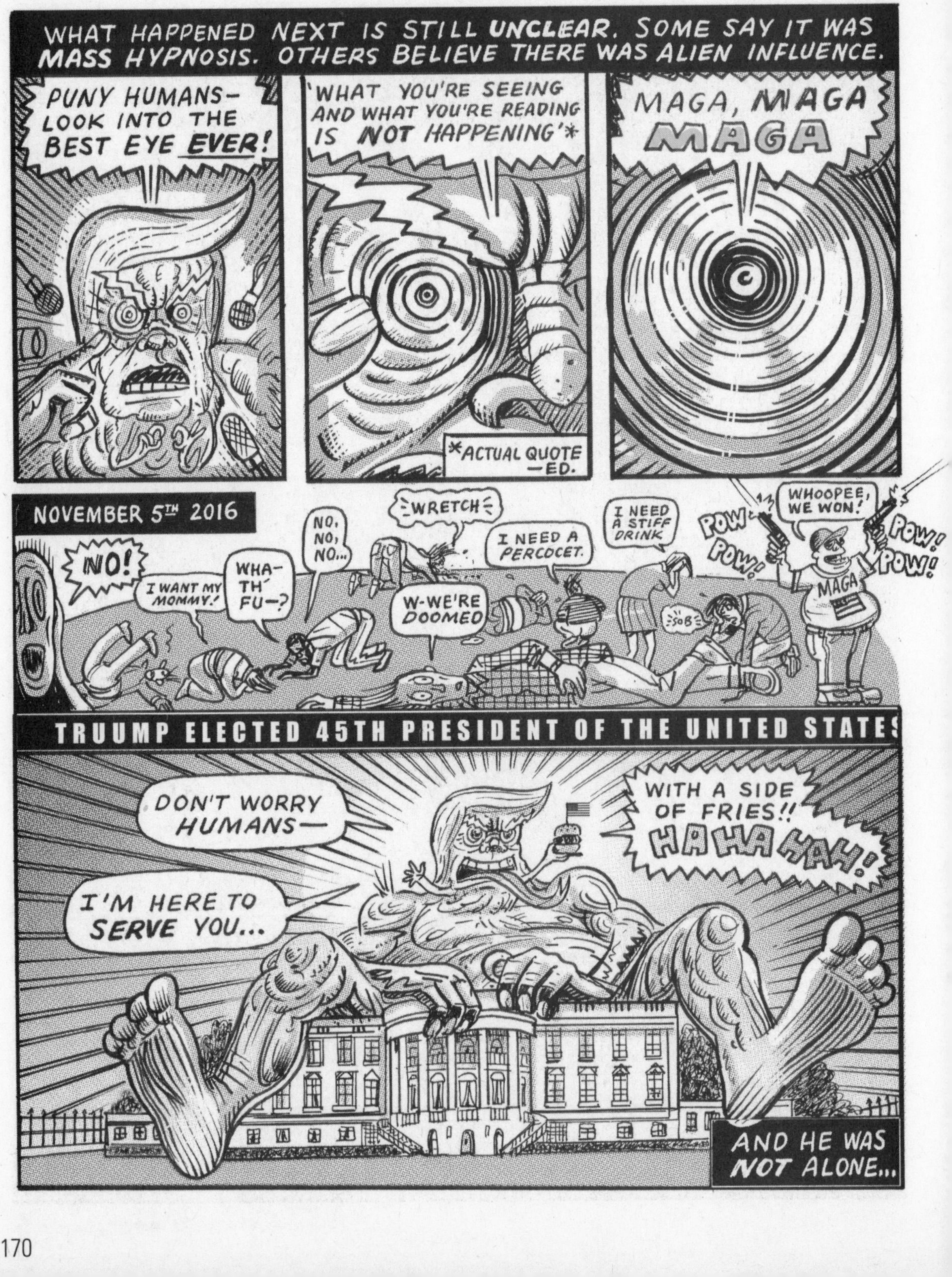

WHAT HAPPENED NEXT IS STILL UNCLEAR. SOME SAY IT WAS MASS HYPNOSIS. OTHERS BELIEVE THERE WAS ALIEN INFLUENCE.
PUNY HUMANS- LOOK INTO THE BEST EYE EVER!
'WHAT YOU'RE SEEING AND WHAT YOU'RE READING IS NOT HAPPENING'*
*ACTUAL QUOTE —ED.
MAGA, MAGA MAGA
NOVEMBER 5TH 2016
NO!
I WANT MY MOMMY!
WHA- TH' FU—?
NO, NO, NO...
WRETCH
W-WE'RE DOOMED
I NEED A PERCOCET.
I NEED A STIFF DRINK
SOB
WHOOPEE, WE WON!
POW POW!
POW! POW!
MAGA
TRUUMP ELECTED 45TH PRESIDENT OF THE UNITED STATES
DON'T WORRY HUMANS—
I'M HERE TO SERVE YOU...
WITH A SIDE OF FRIES!! HA HA HAH!
AND HE WAS NOT ALONE...

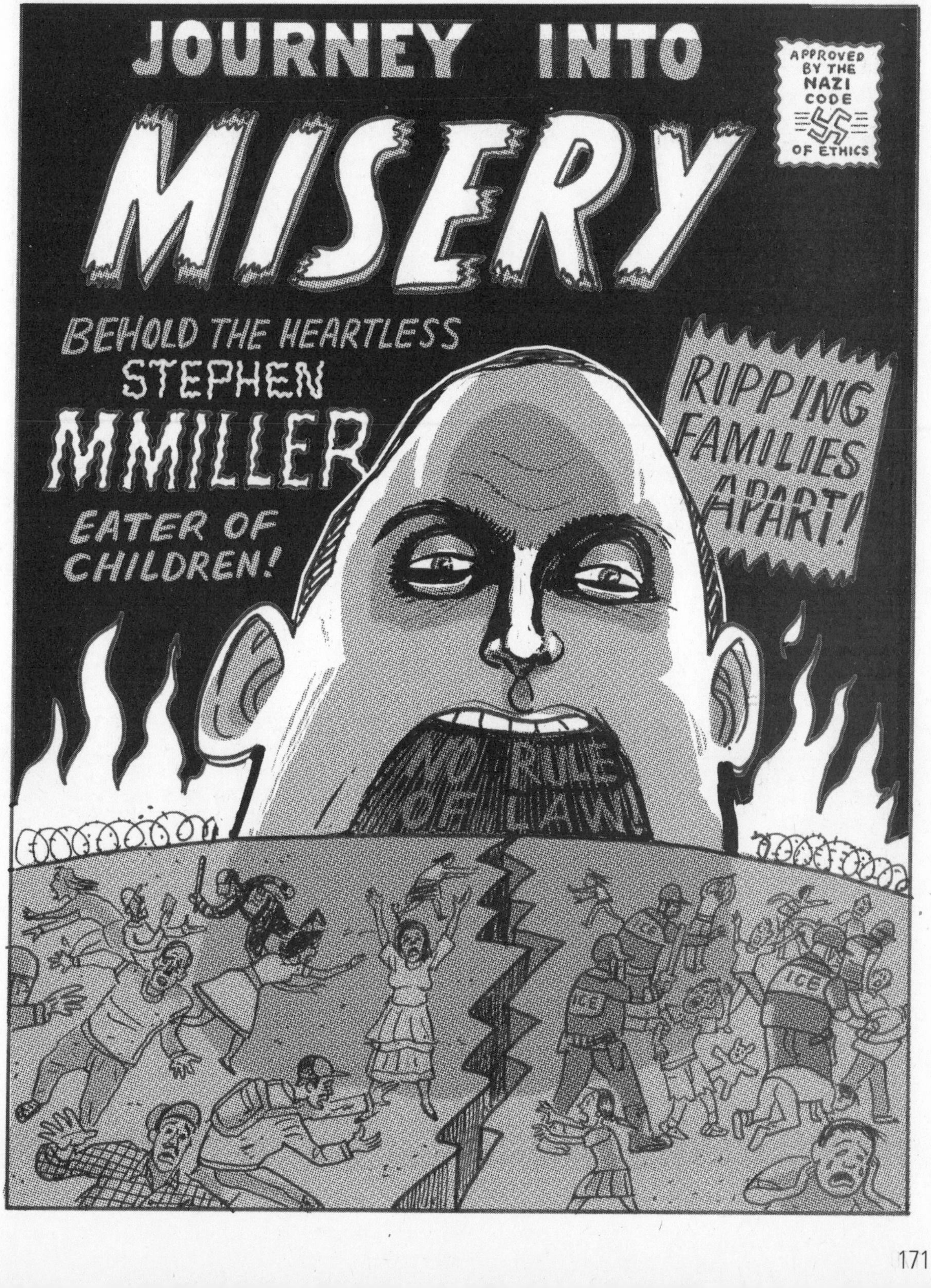
JOURNEY INTO
MISERY
APPROVED BY THE NAZI CODE OF ETHICS
BEHOLD THE HEARTLESS
STEPHEN
MMILLER
EATER OF
CHILDREN!
RIPPING FAMILIES APART!
NO RULE OF LAW

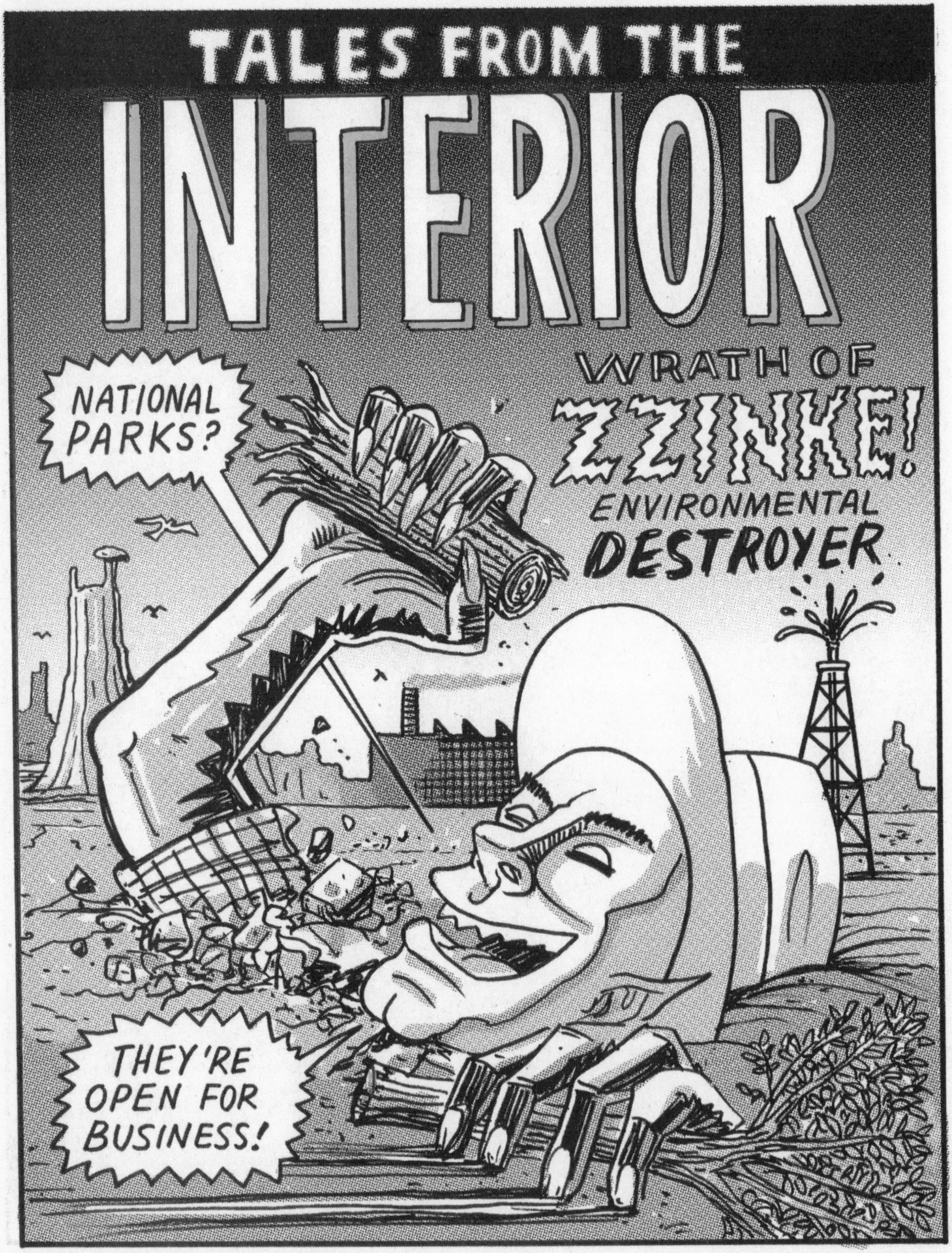
TALES FROM THE
INTERIOR
WRATH OF
ZZINKE!
ENVIRONMENTAL
DESTROYER
NATIONAL PARKS?
THEY'RE OPEN FOR BUSINESS!

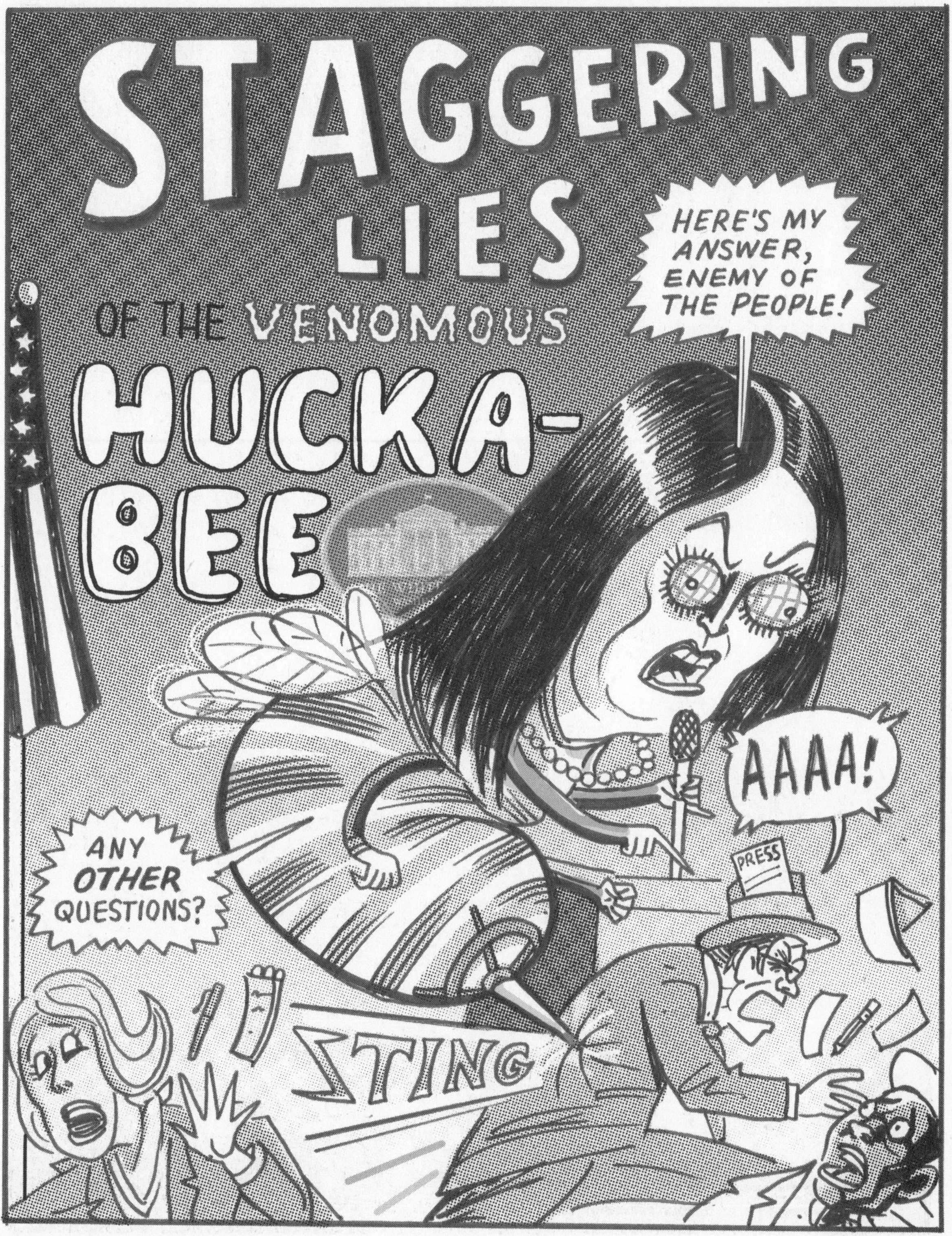
STAGGERING LIES
OF THE VENOMOUS
HUCKA-BEE
HERE'S MY ANSWER, ENEMY OF THE PEOPLE!
AAAA!
PRESS
ANY OTHER QUESTIONS?
STING

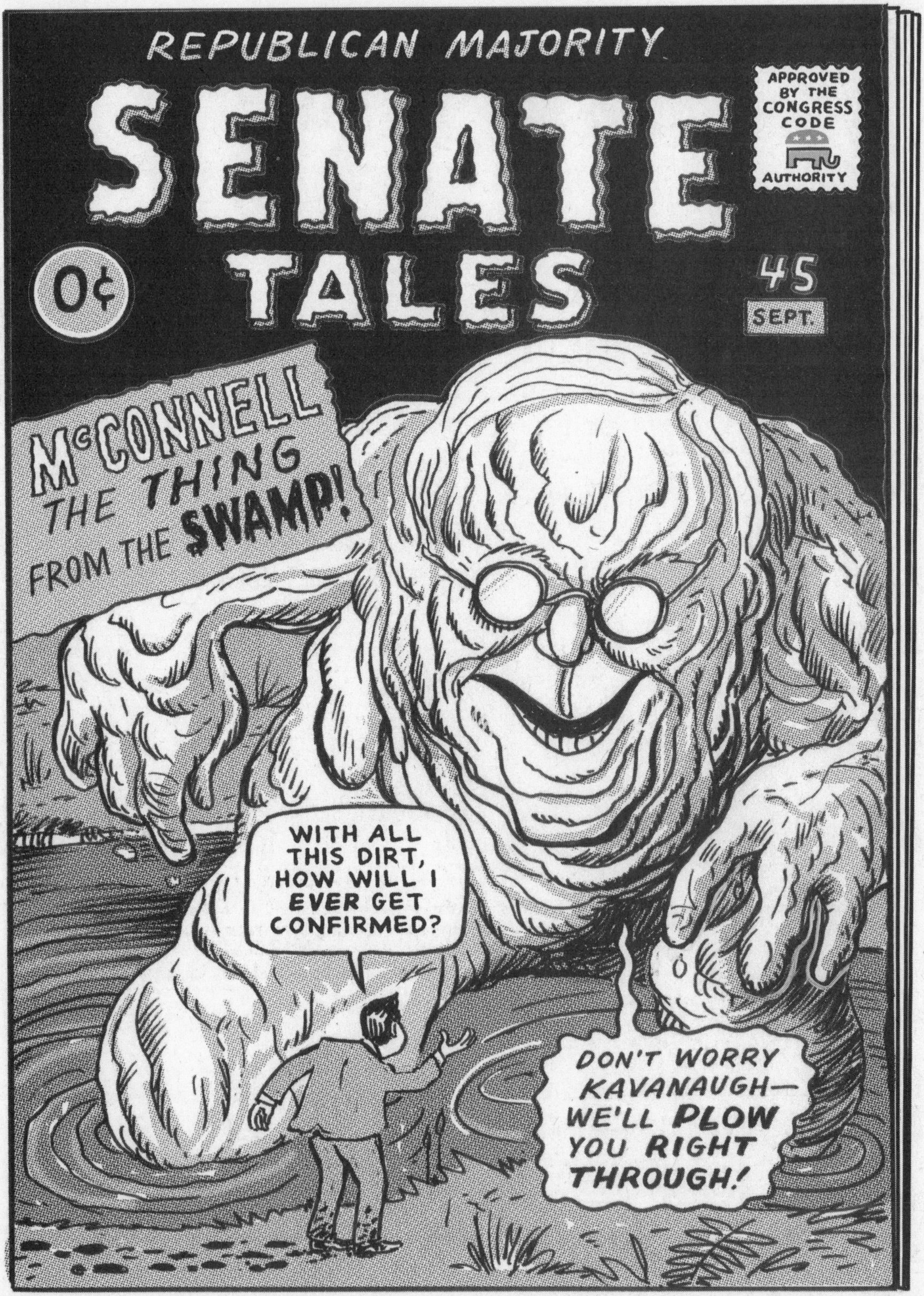
REPUBLICAN MAJORITY
SENATE TALES
APPROVED BY THE CONGRESS CODE AUTHORITY
0¢
45 SEPT.
McCONNELL THE THING FROM THE SWAMP!
WITH ALL THIS DIRT, HOW WILL I EVER GET CONFIRMED?
DON'T WORRY KAVANAUGH— WE'LL PLOW YOU RIGHT THROUGH!

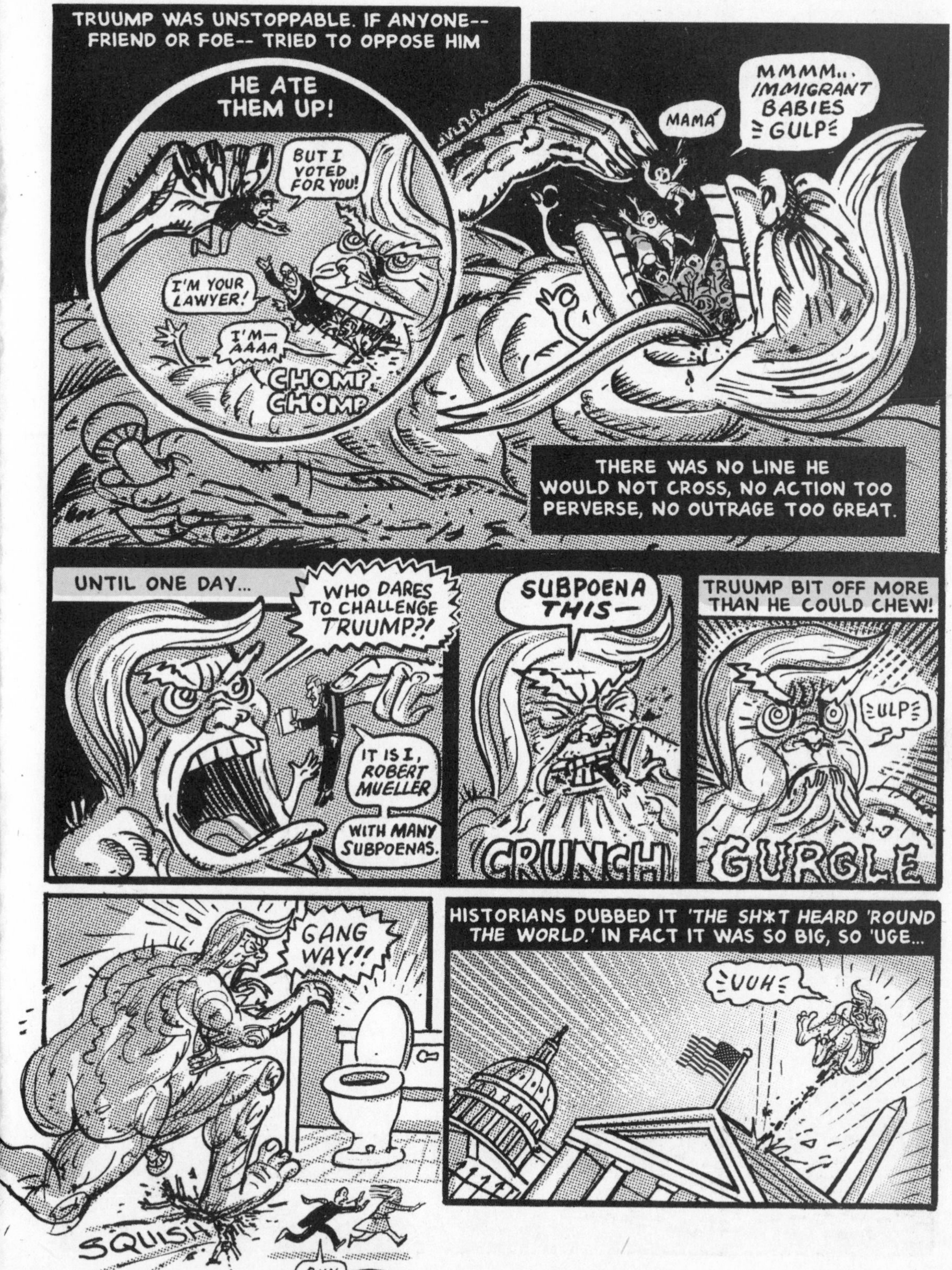
TRUUMP WAS UNSTOPPABLE. IF ANYONE-- FRIEND OR FOE-- TRIED TO OPPOSE HIM
HE ATE THEM UP!
BUT I VOTED FOR YOU!
I'M YOUR LAWYER!
I'M— AAAA
CHOMP CHOMP
MAMA
MMMM... IMMIGRANT BABIES GULP
THERE WAS NO LINE HE WOULD NOT CROSS, NO ACTION TOO PERVERSE, NO OUTRAGE TOO GREAT.
UNTIL ONE DAY...
WHO DARES TO CHALLENGE TRUUMP?!
IT IS I, ROBERT MUELLER
WITH MANY SUBPOENAS.
SUBPOENA THIS—
CRUNCH
TRUUMP BIT OFF MORE THAN HE COULD CHEW!
ULP
GURGLE
GANG WAY!!
SQUISH
RUN KELLYANNE!
HISTORIANS DUBBED IT 'THE SH*T HEARD 'ROUND THE WORLD.' IN FACT IT WAS SO BIG, SO 'UGE...
UUH

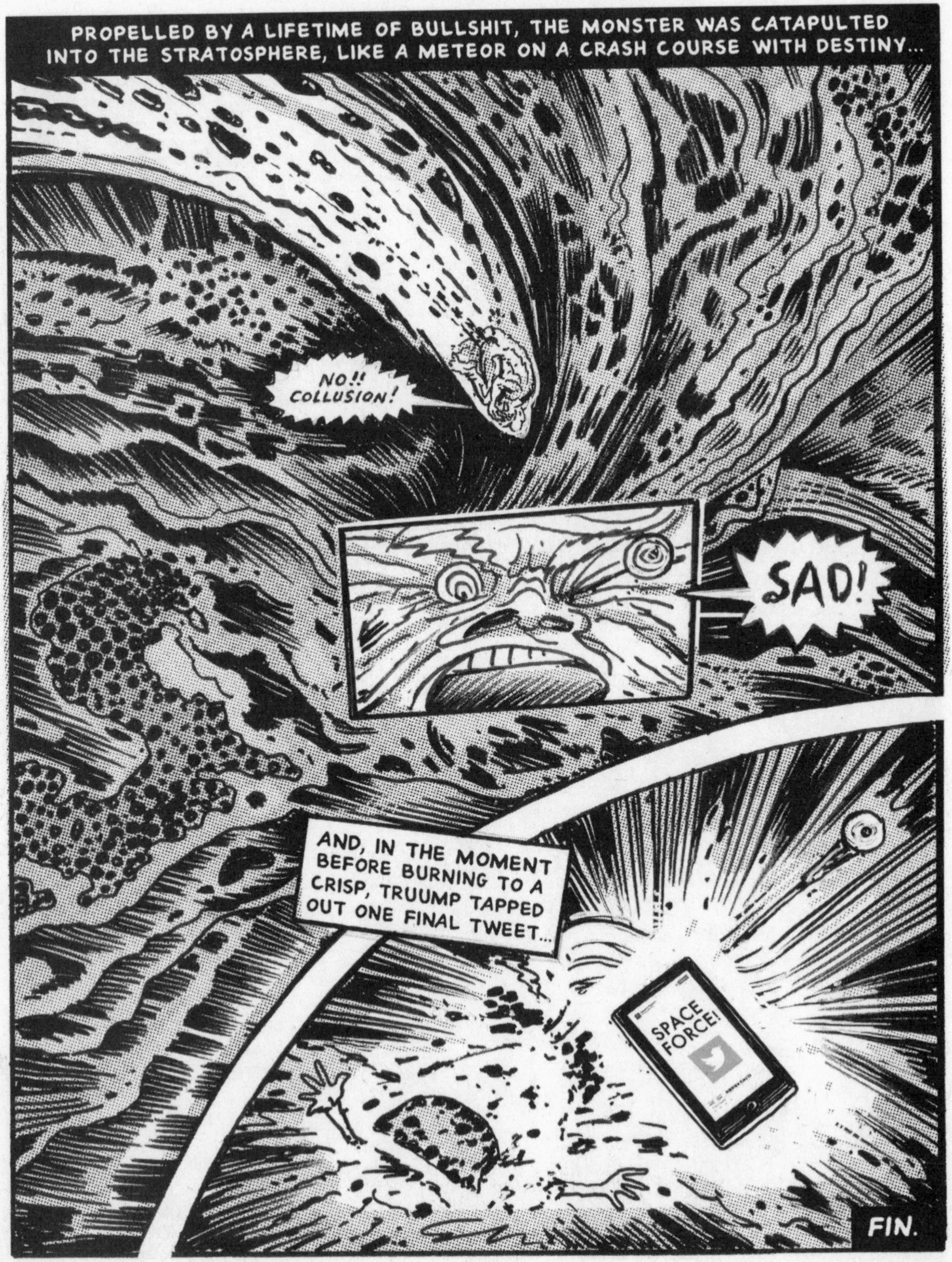
PROPELLED BY A LIFETIME OF BULLSHIT, THE MONSTER WAS CATAPULTED INTO THE STRATOSPHERE, LIKE A METEOR ON A CRASH COURSE WITH DESTINY...
NO!! COLLUSION!
SAD!
AND, IN THE MOMENT BEFORE BURNING TO A CRISP, TRUUMP TAPPED OUT ONE FINAL TWEET...
SPACE FORCE!
FIN.